The Crises of Capitalism

# THE CRISES OF CAPITALISM
## A Different Study of Political Economy

SARAL SARKAR
translated by Graciela Calderón

COUNTERPOINT
Berkeley

Library of Congress Cataloging-in-Publication Data is available.

ISBN: 978-1-61902-187-7

COUNTERPOINT
2560 Ninth Street, Suite 318
Berkeley, CA 94710

www.counterpointpress.com

Interior design by VJBScribe
Cover design by Faceout Studios

Printed in the United States of America

# Contents

## VI

## The Crises in Globalized Neo-Liberal Capitalism    131

## VII

## Can Keynesianism Solve the Problems This Time?    191

## VIII

## Why Globalization Should Be Criticized   221

## IX

## Aspects of the Crisis *of* Capitalism   239

## X

## Where Does the Surplus Come From?   275

# Note on the English Edition

It is a great pleasure for me to see the English translation of the book finally published. When I conceived it, I decided to write it in German. For, firstly, unlike in the case of my previous books, which were originally written in English, no publisher gave an advance assurance that it would publish the book. Secondly, I guessed I stood a better chance of finding a publisher in Germany, where I live and have many political friends. So the book first appeared in Germany with a small print order for a small number of potential readers. But a fundamental-theoretical book like this must be presented to the reading public of the whole world. And that is possible only if it is available in English.

The manuscript of the German original was sent to press in December 2008, when the current financial and economic crisis had just become acute. In 2009 one could not even imagine that Europe would be in such a mess as it is today. One had moreover thought that the crisis would soon be over, that the strong economies of the emerging markets like China, India, Brazil, etc., would pull the world economy out of the morass. But, today, the growth rates of both the Chinese and the Indian economy are falling. Both countries are suffering from high inflation rates, and the Chinese housing bubble is threatening to burst. In the three years that have passed since December 2008, my conviction has deepened that this crisis of capitalism cannot be overcome. Christine Lagarde, the managing director of the International Monetary Fund, is now warning that the world economy may be heading towards another great depression like the one of the 1930s. I had to slightly revise the last chapter because of the developments since December 2008.

I want to take this opportunity to express my gratitude to Doug Tompkins, who helped find a translator and also financed the translation work through his Foundation for Deep Ecology. I also benefited a lot from many discussions with him and from reading the numerous materials he sent to me. I also sincerely thank the translator, Ms. Graciela Calderón, who did a great job in translating this deep theoretical work. I rarely had to correct her translation. In some cases, however, I myself changed the formulations I had used in the German original. Also Ms. Kirsten Janene-Nelson, the copy editor, did an excellent job. Since Ms. Calderón and I are not native speakers of English, it was a great help that she improved our diction and brought it somewhat closer to American English. I very much enjoyed working with her and am grateful to her for her hard work. And, last but not least, I sincerely thank Jack Shoemaker and his colleagues at Counterpoint Press for bringing out the book fairly quickly after accepting it for publication.

Cologne, March 2012

# Preface

In the anti-globalization movement and among those who are generally critical of globalization, there are two very popular slogans: "A different world is possible," and "The world is not a commodity." I have my doubts whether all activists of the movement are really aware of the implications of these slogans. It is the world they talk about, so one may expect that these activists have overcome thinking in terms of national interests. They also talk of another world that they dream about, but what is this other world supposed to look like? Here the second slogan helps us. It criticizes an economic system in which almost everything has become a commodity. Since widespread commoditization is one of the main characteristics of capitalism, one could conclude that these activists dream of a non-capitalist world. I have always been well aware of this potential slant of this very important slogan of this movement I have been part of since 1997 (starting with the anti-MAI campaign[1]). I did not bring up this discussion before, however, out of consideration for my reformist partners in the alliance.

But in the following years it has become apparent — and it has also repeatedly been made clear to me by other activists — that the majority of the participants in the movement, and also the majority of its leaders, do not want to create a non-capitalist world. They only want to make the present one, the global-capitalistic world, a little better, fairer, more social, and more ecological. Moreover, they are not against globalization, but merely critical of globalization. And this applies also to the other social movements associated with the merely critical section of the movement: the trade union movement, the Third World solidarity movement, the unemployed workers' movement, the peace movement, and the ecology movement, which in the meantime has come to a halt.

In all these movements, there is — and there has always been — a minority of activists, myself included, whose vision of a better/different world is that of a non-capitalist one — a socialist one, to be more precise. For a few years after 1989, i.e., after the collapse of the state-socialist regimes in Eastern Europe, they refrained from openly speaking about the necessity of a socialist society — maybe out of fear of being ridiculed. But just ten years later, during the anti-WTO (World Trade Organization) demonstrations in Seattle in 1999, a large number of people expressed the opinion that in capitalism there can be no solution to even a single social problem. After the end of the Cold War there had been a euphoric, festive mood in large parts of the world population and among their opinion leaders. The hope of a great "peace dividend" was in the air. In Europe, there was talk of a "common European house." By 1999, this euphoric-festive mood had totally evaporated. What determined the general picture of the world in the 1990s and ever since was a series of severe economic crises (Eastern Europe, Russia, Mexico, East Asia, etc.); a series of wars and civil wars (for instance, in the Balkans and in Rwanda); and the growing impoverishment and economic insecurity of large parts of the world population, side by side with the growing wealth of a minority, environmental and natural calamities, and large numbers of refugees fleeing from wars, environmental degradations, economic crises, and just sheer poverty. In Seattle protesters cried, "Let us smash capitalism!" Many were convinced that a different world was not only possible but also necessary. In 1989, one could not imagine that the worldwide victory of capitalism as an ideology — though not as a concrete system — would be so short-lived, that already in the year 2000 people would be talking of its failure.

But that, indeed, is now the case. Many people are so convinced of this failure that they are now asking for an alternative. But is there an alternative at all? Should we look for an alternative to capitalism itself or for alternatives to parts within capitalism? As stated above, the majority of the participants in the new social movements are reformists. They are so because in their view there is (unfortunately) no alternative to capitalism. Those who want to overcome capitalism, the radicals, work together with reformists. They think even a mere alleviation of sufferings is in itself a worthwhile objective, especially because these radicals have lost the firm conviction of their Marxist past that the *laws of history* will lead humankind to socialism or communism or to a higher, better form of society, and that they themselves are mere instruments of history.

In 1999, I gave a lecture on the contents of my new book *Eco-Socialism or Eco-Capitalism?* before an audience composed largely of such activists, that is to say, socialists. They did not agree with any of my main theses, which deviated very much from their old and noble positions. On my way home I asked a leading member of a small Trotskyist socialist party how he could expect capitalism would one day get into such a severe crisis that the organized working class — in spite of their disappointing history — would at last do away with it. The great majority of the workers, even of the unemployed, after all live quite well in highly developed capitalism, I argued. This system has so far managed to overcome all crises, at least in the highly industrialized countries, even the Great Depression and the destruction of World War II. The comrade could give no clear answer.

On a different occasion, also in 1999, another socialist friend told me my analyses and my view of the future perspective were right. But, he asked, who would realize the eco-socialist society? Only when the working class has taken over power and socialized the means of production, he thought, would it understand that the present industrial society per se, and certainly a continuously growing industrial economy, would entirely destroy the natural environment. And then, freed from the profit and growth compulsions of capitalism and from the power of the capitalists, it would be possible for society to shape the economy in an ecologically sustainable way. In other words, he argued, capitalism has to be overcome first; only then can there be any hope for change for the better. The logic of these statements is convincing. However, this friend also could not answer the question of what *interest* the working class of the rich industrialized countries could have in trying to eliminate capitalism, given that workers, at least the great majority of them, live very well in this system.

Earlier on I had put the same question to a leading comrade of another small Trotskyist socialist party. And again, I received no clear answer. But he was able to give me a convincing answer to another question, namely, what could save us when the capitalist society finally collapsed, which clearly appeared to be imminent. He asserted it was necessary to build up a revolutionary socialist party, right now. This would be the only force strong enough to build a better world when the capitalist society finally plunged into a big crisis — when, sooner or later, its collapse clearly appeared to be imminent. He also said he expected the collapse of capitalism as a matter of course.

The whole discussion among Marxist socialists on the question regarding the final crisis of capitalism is a sad story. They have been waiting for the final crisis or the collapse of capitalism for over a hundred years. They have written hundreds of books and thousands of essays on this topic. The final crisis, however, has not arrived yet. In the relevant literature that I could read, I found descriptions and analyses of the first, second, third, and most recent stage of the *general crisis of capitalism* (see, e.g., Varga 1962, Kuczynski 1977). In 1962, at a time when Western economists were speaking of a long boom and even of economic miracles, Eugen Varga, the famous Marxist political economist and theoretician of the former Soviet Union, prophesied: "We may ... forecast as a matter of great probability that the twentieth century will be the last century of capitalism. By the end of the century there will either be no capitalism at all, or there will remain insignificant remnants of it" (Varga 1962: 156). And Jürgen Kuczynski, the great Marxist scholar of the former GDR, thought in 1977 that the "international cyclical crisis of overproduction," which at the time afflicted capitalism in the industrialized countries, "is tending to heighten the contradictions working within the general crisis of capitalism" (Kuczynski 1977: 40). He concluded: "We declare that the general crisis of capitalism has advanced so far that if we are able to prevent a major war and the special factors it brings with it, then we can reckon with capitalism undergoing a process of decay interrupted by short bursts of life" (140).

As we know today, both Varga and Kuczynski were totally wrong in their forecast and conclusion. In the thirty years after 1977, there have been many crises in the capitalist world: stock market crashes, financial crises, economic crises, debt crises of the Third World countries. They came and went, like so many crises before them. But neither did the twentieth century turn out to be the last century of capitalism, nor did capitalism undergo a process of decay during this period. Quite the contrary, it was the world of the socialist industrialized countries that fell apart in the last decade of the twentieth century.

During every crisis in the 1980s and 1990s, hope arose in some leftist quarters that capitalism — as prophesied by Kuczynski — was at last undergoing a process of decay. Expressions such as "the party is over" and "Titanic" were used (Garnreiter et al. 1998: 32, 37). But each time, after the subsequent successful crisis management and recovery, hopeful leftists were ridiculed by bourgeois commentators. For the "short bursts of life," which Kuczynski also held possible, were not so short-lived after all. In the United States economic commentators spoke of "the roaring nineties," and how the great East Asian crisis of 1997–1998 could not seriously harm the rest of the capitalist world.

Only at the beginning of the twenty-first century and in the years thereafter could a real atmosphere of crisis be felt. And it did not appear to be fading away; on the contrary, it persisted and was deepening. But not so much because of the aggravation of the inner contradictions of capitalism, which Marxists always talk about and which do indeed exist. And not because of conflicts between national state monopoly capitalisms, between imperialist blocks, between the former colonial powers and the former colonies, half-colonies, and the present-day emerging industrial powers. And not because of the contradiction between the working class and the capitalist class (although a whole capitalist economy, that of Argentina, broke down because of some of such conflicts and contradictions). No, the most important cause of this crisis atmosphere is something very different, something that Marxists and other leftists could never before imagine as a cause of crisis. It is global warming, which is creating climate catastrophes, together with various other destructive ecological crises, over and above the everyday global pollution and degradation of the environment. And, in future, all this will be happening increasingly and most certainly.

At the same time — and this is the second most important cause of the crisis atmosphere — a prognosis made by Donella Meadows and her coauthors in 1972 in their book *The Limits to Growth* is coming true, namely, that the cheap reserves of nonrenewable resources would gradually get exhausted. As we know, since the beginning of the twenty-first century the world market price for oil, the most important energy source of industrial economies, has been rising almost continuously. In knowledgeable circles people are already talking of "peak oil," and many predict a big crisis when oil is no longer affordable for most people. There is even talk of the impending end of the oil era. The world market prices for natural gas, coal, and important industrial metals have also been rising for a number of years now (since the beginning of the recession of 2008–2009 some prices have again fallen). What is even worse, since 2007 food prices have sharply risen worldwide.

This double crisis (I call it the pincer-grip crisis; see chapter X, section 5) is not just the crisis of capitalism, as how most leftists would like to see it. In the long run, it will also inevitably cause the end of industrial society. This will happen whether we like it or not. Even a truly socialist industrial society would perish because of this crisis. In my previous work I contended that the socialist industrial society of the former Soviet Union failed mainly (however, not only) because of ecological and resource-related crises.

But a socialist society need not be an industrial one. There is no compelling reason for that. But, as the friend I quoted above pointed out, the work for the transition to a non-industrial, sustainable society cannot possibly even begin until capitalism is overcome.

The question now is, therefore: Is it possible or likely that capitalism will collapse, due to one or more of its inner contradictions pointed out by Marxists, *before* we are hit by even more severe resource-related crises and greater ecological and climate-related catastrophes than we are already experiencing today? Or, is it possible or likely that the working class will — in the context of a big crisis and *out of self-interest* — revolt in several big, important, powerful countries and sweep away capitalism by means of class struggle, and thus clear the way for a peaceful and orderly transition to a sustainable and just (fairer) society? If the answer is yes, will that happen *before* the present civilization ends in global chaos, various kinds of war, and destruction? On the ruins of the present-day civilization it might not at all be possible to build a sustainable and socialist society. The survivors would probably not have the needed strength to achieve that.

It is not easy to answer these questions today. But we — both reformers and radicals — should intensively ponder them in order to clarify the situation we are in, which is necessary for orienting ourselves in our political work. To state it more precisely, it is important to understand why capitalism has not collapsed yet; why until now all previous attempts to eliminate it by means of class struggle have failed; why the powers that be are scaling down the welfare state and the social part of the social market economy built up in the rich industrialized countries after World War II; why Keynesianism, which was regarded in the 1950s and 1960s almost as a doctrine of salvation, was rejected in the 1980s. It is necessary to find an answer to each of these questions (and to many other relevant ones) in order to be able to form an opinion on whether our particular midterm project stands a chance or not, whether our particular long-term objective is at least to some extent realistic — and not totally utopian in the negative sense.

I have explored these questions extensively, beginning with my previous book *Eco-Socialism or Eco-Capitalism? A Critical Analysis of Humanity's Fundamental Choices.* I maintain now the same basic standpoint I expounded then, namely, that a paradigm shift — from the hitherto-prevailing growth paradigm to what I call the limits-to-growth paradigm — is overdue in all thinking on economic, political, political-economic, and social issues, both theoretical and practical. In this previous work I thoroughly examined the question of whether capitalism can acquire a new legitimacy by transforming itself into eco-capitalism. My conclusion: No. I also showed why the Soviet model of a socialist industrial society could not but fail. In this book I want to demonstrate that a capitalist industrial society will fail for similar reasons. I aim to build on this previous book, as if writing the second volume of the same work. But in addition, in light of the overdue paradigm shift mentioned above, I feel it has become necessary to study political economy differently, to partly rewrite it. This book is a humble effort to do just that in one area, a very important area, of the discipline.

In order to better understand the theories and facts related to the crises of capitalism and the explanations for them, I have studied the relevant parts of economics and political economy. On the basis of the knowledge thus acquired, I gained some insights and reached certain conclusions that I want to share with those who are also trying to create a different and better world.

I am aware that some might question my qualification to do this study, since I am not a trained economist. My justification for thinking I have a contribution to make regarding the crisis/crises of capitalism relies on my observation that the great majority of trained economists have not understood the most important aspect of the crisis of capitalism, or, exactly speaking, the crisis of all industrial economies. My beliefs are shared by a small minority of economists, from whom I have learned a great deal about ecological economics. Kenneth Boulding, who was for some time president of the American Economic Association, wrote: "Anyone who believes exponential growth can go on forever in a finite world is either a madman or an economist" (quoted in Heinberg 2003: 167). It is unfortunately a fact that most economists believe in infinite growth. A second critique comes from Nicholas Georgescu-Roegen, who reported that the famous Paul Samuelson maintained that science can temporarily override the entropy law (Georgescu-Roegen 1987: 17). Any good natural scientist knows this is impossible. Also, very recently, some young and critical economists found it necessary to form a study circle called "Post-Autistic Economics." In their critique of present-day economics (Arbeitskreis 2004) they asserted: "The conception of man behind the term *Homo Oeconomicus* is autistic," and "Economics totally devotes itself to adhering to formal rules. That *diminishes the faculty of judgment* needed for assessing real economic connections" (emphasis added). Many economic journalists too have lost their formerly usual respect for economists. For instance, Markus Sievers, of the *Frankfurter Rundschau*, wrote:

> Economists, especially in Germany, are a bit of a problem. They
> gladly produce, particularly if the remuneration is good,
> scientific economic studies with complicated models. ... In most
> cases, the title is very promising, but the content delivers little.
> Nearly always the gain in knowledge and understanding is far
> below scientific standards and customary fees in the profession.
> The advisory council of the Ministry of Economy is no

> exception. These economists, too, do not let themselves be
> drawn into any danger and led off of the beaten track through
> any curiosity or desire to discover something new and unusual.
> How should Germany react to globalization? Cut wages, make
> the labor market more flexible, relax rules regarding protection
> against unfair dismissal. Oh yes, one should also do something
> about innovations.
>
> Twenty-five professors have worked to produce this knowl-
> edge and recommendation. Forgive me, but John Q. Public
> could also have worked that out. (Sievers 2006)

I am not afraid of any "danger." I think I have presented many new and
unusual insights and thoughts in this book.

There are a few more serious reasons for us not to wholly rely on economists and to form our own opinions. Firstly, most of the issues debated in
connection with the subject of this book are ultimately questions of value.
Scientists can help us with their knowledge, but value decisions cannot be
made by scientists as scientists. Secondly, I, of course, do not doubt that a
purely objective scientific approach is possible. This is possible also in the
social sciences, and social scientists can convey scientific knowledge objectively. But they are *also* human beings; they can make mistakes and, as
human beings, they too have private, group, and class interests, for which
they use, consciously or unconsciously, their status and their power. Especially in political-economic matters they have a lot of power. John Maynard Keynes was convinced that the world was dominated by not much
more than the thoughts of economists and political philosophers. "Practical men ... are usually the slaves of some defunct economist" (quoted in
Koesters 1985: 254). Economists also often get themselves hired by rulers
and interest groups, with a resultant loss of independence and freedom of
opinion. Or they gladly become soldiers of one or the other side in class
struggle or in the competitive business world, and they, then, legitimize
their side's policy by developing suitable theories. This was the case with
Marx's labor theory of value. C. George Caffentzis, an American Marxist
philosophy professor, wrote in the context of defending Marxian theory:

> Marx's theory of machines was deployed in a political struggle;
> it was not the result of some suprahistorical, a-prioristic
> ratiocination. Theoretically, Marx could have taken different
> paths in the understanding of machines and still remained
> anti-capitalist. For example, he could have argued that machines
> create value but that this value was the product of a general

social and scientific labor which ought not be appropriated by the capitalist class. Such an approach was indeed taken up by Veblen and others in the early twentieth century. . . .

Marx's theoretical choice against the value creativity of machines was rooted in the complex political situation he and his faction of the working class movement of Western Europe faced. . . .

In the face of the ideological attack arising from the depths of the system [namely, that machines create value; workers are not so important], Marx needed a direct reply. It was to point out that . . . for all the thunder of its steam hammers, for all the intimidating silence of its chemical plants, capital could not dispense with labor. Labor is not the only source of wealth, but it is the only source of value. Thus capital was mortally tied to the working class, whatever the forces that it unleashed that were driving to a form of labor-less production. This was the political card that Marx played in the political game against the ideological suffocation of the machine = capital [i.e., machine is the same as capital] metaphor. It . . . proved to be a useful one not only in the struggles of the 1860s. (1997: 42–45)

I shall deal with the critique of Marx's labor theory of value in chapters I and X. Here I only want to show that even the great Marx was not motivated only by the pure search for knowledge and understanding.

Thirdly, as Lawrence R. Klein (1947: 31), a trained economist and author of possibly the first book on Keynesian economics, wrote, ". . . practical economics is simply common sense, while theoretical economics is common sense made difficult." But at least political-economic (and political) theories are not so difficult that an average intelligent person could not learn them without going to a university, i.e., by self-study. For that it is not necessary to read all the original works of the great masters. As we know, a physicist does not have to read Newton's and Galileo's original works. Fourthly, apart from the exact natural sciences, there is hardly a science in which consensus prevails on all questions. Even in the exact natural sciences, particularly in their application, there are often great differences of opinion, for instance, when it comes to applying particular chemicals in agriculture and medicine. Another example is the controversy on the economic efficiency and viability of solar energy technologies. In such cases, informed laypersons must form their own opinions, especially if the issues in question have relevance for politics or one's philosophy of life. After all, politics, especially economic policy, concerns everybody. Economic policy is too important to be left to professional economists and politicians. And, last but not least, we should remember the story of the emperor's new clothes. It was a child, not the ministers or the expert dressmakers, who noticed and dared to say aloud that the emperor was naked.

When they begin their work, authors of theoretical or nonfiction books ask themselves what kind of readers they are writing for. In the case of this book, it is clear: I am writing primarily for political activists who are trying to create a different, a better, world, but who, in my opinion, cherish many illusions and adhere to many false theories. It is precisely such people who need theoretical clarity and objective knowledge of the state of the world. I think that also people who are not activists but are generally interested in political-economic issues will find this book interesting and informative. Economists, of course, will find here much that they already know. But they too should read this book if they are interested in a *new* critique of political economy.

In the long years of my participation in social and political movements, in India as well as in Germany, I have found that activists very soon become specialized activists. A peace activist ends up being only a peace activist. She/he knows a lot about war and peace, but, for instance, might know hardly anything about the contradiction between ecology and economy. An environmentalist who knows a lot about water quality in Germany doesn't necessarily know, for instance, much about the real causes of wars, and so on and so forth. This is not good. Were we not told in the 1980s that everything has to do with everything else and that we should think holistically and in connections? Such advice is still sound. And for this reason all political activists should acquire some basic knowledge of political economy — particularly in times like these, when humanity is endangered by climate catastrophes, environmental destruction, resource wars, waves of refugees, mass unemployment, mass poverty. Through this book I want to contribute to this process by discussing some of the most important questions of political economy. This book should also be seen as a kind of critical introduction to the theories on the crisis of capitalism.

For this reason, a large part of the book consists of, so to speak, discursive presentations of selected severe economic crises and crisis trends of the twentieth century and the beginning of the twenty-first. It also presents the most important of the competing bourgeois theories that were constructed to explain the crises — and which have given rise to economic policies aimed at ridding capitalism of serious crises and ensuring constant growth. I have also presented, whenever necessary, my criticism and doubts about these theories and their policy recommendations. Bourgeois economic theories see no possibility of an economic crisis that could lead to the collapse of capitalism, but Marxist economic theories do. So in the beginning, in the first chapter I present both a summary and also critiques of the Marxist crisis theories.

Amongst the bourgeois theories, I have afforded most space to Keynesianism. I have done so because in the years that followed the traumatic experience of the Great Depression of the 1930s, especially after World War II, Keynesianism was received as a doctrine of salvation, which purportedly made the long post-war boom possible. Keynesianism promised to make capitalism socially just and totally crisis-free. So, when Keynesianism foundered in the mid-seventies, the shock was all the greater. The history of the rise and decline of Keynesianism, and of the continuing controversy between monetarists and neo-liberals on the one side and the rest of the Keynesians on the other, is not only fascinating but also very instructive for answering the key questions posed at the beginning of this book.

In chapters IX and X, I abandon the narrow view of the crisis of capitalism — namely, crisis is the same as economic crisis — and discuss other aspects of the crisis of capitalism as well as deeper questions relating to our subject matter. In chapter XI I present some visions of a reformed capitalism and report on some success stories — and I elucidate why they do not convince me. The book ends with chapter XII, where I present my analysis of the current economic and financial crisis that began in 2008. Here I also venture a perspective on the future.

Every author's knowledge base is the result of the continuous search for knowledge and understanding carried out by thousands of scholars and researchers and of the work of many other authors. If an author has something new or unusual to say, it only became possible on the basis of the knowledge thus accumulated. This truth also applies to this book. Therefore, I sincerely thank all the authors — scientists, publicists, and journalists — from whose works I have learned so much. I cannot here mention all of them; they are far too many. Their names and their works are listed in the references. I would also like to thank some critics whose names I do not know, audience members at my lectures who pointed out some lacunae in my knowledge and identified some weak spots in my argumentation. I have benefited from them as well.

I would like to specially thank a few very good friends: Bruno Kern, my activist friend, who has shared with me much political work for an ecological socialist society, who edited the original German text and did the greater part of the work connected with the production of the book in German; Bob Tatam, my British friend and a political sympathizer, who regularly supplied me with articles from the British press relevant to my book; Heide and Hermann Huber, who have helped me in various ways, Heide especially with the design of the book cover of the German original; Amir Mortasawi, who did a lot of editing work and prepared the PDF version of the English translation; and, last but not least, my wife, Maria Mies, without whose moral and material support I could not have even started this work.

The Crises of Capitalism

# Marxist Theories of Crisis

For the great majority of bourgeois economists there can be no crisis *of* capitalism as an economic system, but rather only crises *in* capitalism. Only Marxists expect(ed) a crisis so severe that it would cause capitalism to break down, i.e., a crisis *of* capitalism. The classical economists believed that capitalism — in its pure form of a free-market economy — was the best of all possible *economic worlds*. The profit motive and competition ensured an optimal allocation of scarce resources, optimal production costs, and optimal distribution. Here, there are no excessively high prices. If everyone only tries to increase his/her prosperity, that automatically generates prosperity of the whole society, quasi through an invisible hand. Classical economists and their successors in orthodox economics, the neoclassicals, regarded all crises and problems of such an economy as temporary disruptions of the essential balance of the system, which sooner or later could be overcome by the self-healing forces of the market — if the market forces were allowed to operate without outside intervention.

In fact, in the history of the leading capitalist economies, so far, not only were all pure economic crises overcome sooner or later, but the economies also developed almost continuously. However, that did not always happen only as an effect of the market forces in operation, but often also through the effects of colonialism and imperialism or through the interventions of the state in the market economy, i.e., through protectionism, subsidies, devaluation of the national currency, etc. Powerful states have even helped their corporations with wars. Thus, in the mid-nineteenth century, Western imperialist powers sent gunboats to Japanese ports to force the country to open its markets for Western traders. Again in the mid-nineteenth century, Britain and France waged two wars against China to compel its government to allow selling imported opium to Chinese citizens. In 2003, the USA invaded Iraq to gain control over its oil wealth. It was only with the works of Marx and Engels that the notion gained currency that capitalism is, *by its inner logic*, a crisis-prone system. Their thinking revealed that economic crises are not just relatively harmless, periodic, and cyclical, but that there is also an absolute barrier within the capitalist economic system. The real barrier to capitalist production is, according to Marx, capital itself.

Nowhere in Marx's works is there a systematic discussion of this topic, and since his comments on and analyses of this issue are scattered over the three volumes of *Capital* and some other texts, his followers, the later Marxists, have had to systematize or develop the Marxist crisis theory. This was not an easy task, particularly as Marx's theory is very abstract, at times unclear and difficult to understand, and often not convincing. For that reason there have been different Marx interpretations and also some controversies among later Marxists. For this short presentation, I make the task easier for myself by mainly resorting to the presentations and analyses of some renowned Marx experts (Sweezy 1942; Mandel 1971; *Lehrbuch* 1972).

Anyone can observe the phenomenon of cyclical economic crises in capitalist economies. In their early work, *The Communist Manifesto* (1848), Marx and Engels referred to the "commercial crises that by their periodical return put the existence of the entire bourgeois society on trial, each time more threateningly" (quoted in Sweezy 1942: 133). But later on, these clear statements of their earlier work were not taken all too seriously, neither by Marx nor by the Marxists. Evidently, they regarded these crises as part of the normality of the capitalist mode of production, in the same manner as the bourgeois economists did. Although economic crises cause human suffering and destruction or waste of wealth and production capacity, they cease in time and are followed by a new upturn. At the very least Marxists saw in such crises no serious threat to the existence of capitalism. Ernest Mandel wrote:

> Crises make possible the periodical adaptation of the amount of labour actually expended [by individual firms] in the production of commodities to the amount of labour which is *socially necessary* [i.e., corresponding to the stage of technological development], the individual value of commodities to their socially determined value.... Because capitalist production is not consciously planned and organised production, these adjustments take place not *a priori* but *a posteriori* [i.e., afterwards]. For this reason they necessitate violent shocks.

Mandel also wrote that the general significance of the phenomenon economic cycle lies in the fact that it functions "as a periodical readjustment of the conditions of equilibrium of capitalist reproduction" (Mandel 1971: 349).

Elmar Altvater (1992) regards cyclical economic crises, which he calls "small crises," as banal. However, a series of small crises can become uncontrollable within existing institutions. When that happens protracted and deep social, political, and economic transformations begin to take place. The institutions themselves are then affected. A process of this type signals the end of an era. A series of such crises can be termed a crisis of the social formation. Capitalism can overcome such crises too: thus it was able to weather the great world economic crisis of 1929–1933, fascism, and World War II. It was able to transform itself into the social formation called "Fordism."

But in the Marxist economic theories we find the more significant notion that in the course of its development some inherent, logical contradictions of capitalism must result in an absolute inner barrier, which could lead to the breakdown of the system. Marx and Marxists have summarized these contradictions of capitalism in four concepts: tendency of the rate of profit to fall, under-consumption, realization crisis, and pauperization of the working class.

## 1. The Tendency of the Rate of Profit to Fall

Since the main objective of capitalist production is to make the maximum possible profit, a tendency of the rate of profit to fall, should this be a fact, must constitute a great problem for entrepreneurs. And if this tendency applies to the whole of the economy — if the average rate of profit has a tendency to fall — then it becomes a problem for capitalism. In order to understand and examine the validity of this statement, which has been elevated to the status of a law, readers who are not familiar with Marxist economic theory have to learn beforehand, and ideally uncritically at first, a few basic elements of this very abstract theory. In the following I present these elements in brief, simplified versions.

In Marxist economic *theory* only labor can create *value*. The value of a commodity is not its market price, which can fluctuate wildly, but the labor that is necessary to produce the commodity. But this value is not even the *actual* labor expended in each particular case, but the amount of labor that is *necessary on the average* according to the state of the technology in a given society. The measure of labor and thus the measure of value is labor-time. It makes no difference whatsoever whether for the production of a commodity only hands were used, or a hand axe, or a machine, because hand axes, machines, and the materials necessary to manufacture them were also gathered or produced by means of labor. Marx often calls a commodity simply *"value."*

If a shoemaker, for instance, sells his goods — a pair of shoes — in the market, and can buy ten shirts with the proceeds, then we learn something about the *exchange value* of shoes and shirts. What this exchange ratio tells us is that the value of a pair of shoes is ten times the value of a shirt. In other words, for producing a pair of shoes one needs ten times as much labor as for producing a shirt. In this way all commodities have a relative exchange value with respect to other commodities. Only through exchange transactions (with or without the help of money) in a normal, stable market — free from price fluctuations generated by external factors — can one learn what the value of a commodity is *in the eyes of society,* not before that. Exchange value is therefore the outward form or the way of expression of the value contained in a commodity.

In the short term, influenced by other factors (e.g., by difficulties in importing better machines), exchange value may oscillate within certain limits. However, in the long term, it cannot be too far removed from value, which represents, so to speak, the stable center of gravity of exchange value.

In capitalism, the value of a commodity (call it X) is made up of three components. The first component is the *proportional* value of the materials and machinery (means of production) that have been used to produce X. This component is called "constant capital" ($c$). Further on I will explain why here the attribute "constant" is used. The second component is the proportional value of the labor *power* that has been used to produce X. This component is called "variable capital" ($v$), for reasons that will be stated below. As we know, in a real capitalist economy an entrepreneur does not use for these capital expenditures this abstract thing called *value,* but money: money to buy machines and materials ($c$) and money for wage payments ($v$). The entrepreneur pays for all of this before he can sell the produced commodity X. This is his investment. In order for a worker to be able to work 8 hours, her labor power must be (re)produced through food intake, lodging, clothing, and more (this is why she receives a wage). But the value of all these necessary things taken together is, say, 4 labor-hours. That means the entrepreneur has obtained more value from the worker than what he has given her (the wage). The difference ($8 - 4 = 4$), which is appropriated by the entrepreneur, is the third component of the value of X. It is called surplus value ($s$). The value of the commodity X is then $c + v + s$. The *rate of surplus value* ($s'$) is 100% (4:4).

The worker creates surplus value with her labor power. The portion of capital used to buy her labor power ($v$) becomes larger, so to speak. That is why it is called variable capital. According to Marx, this does not happen with $(c)$, the portion of capital used to buy the means of production (machinery and materials). $(c)$ cannot vary. The value of the worn-out and consumed part of the means of production $(c)$ is transferred unchanged to the new commodity produced with their help. That is why it is called constant capital.

When the entrepreneur has sold commodity X at its full value, he has *realized* the appropriated *surplus value*. In other words, he has made a profit $(p)$, $(p = s)$. However, for him the most important magnitude is the *rate of profit* $(p')$. It is calculated, logically, on the basis of the *total* capital, therefore $p' = s : (c + v)$. Part of the realized surplus value (that is, of the profit) is needed by the entrepreneur for his own consumption. The rest is generally invested, is turned into capital. That means, the original capital grows. This is how the process of *capital accumulation* goes on.

Now we can understand how the law of the tendency of the rate of profit to fall is substantiated. It is an historical fact that alongside the accumulation of capital there has been, so far, a progressive mechanization and automation of the production process. Marxists have always believed that this process would go on forever. The same amount of labor, which is provided with more and more plentiful and more and more effective technical equipment, can process more and more material and produce more and more commodities. That is, *productivity of labor* grows steadily. This has an additional effect: the ratio between the investments of the entrepreneur in machinery and materials $(c)$ and his total investments $(c + v)$ — which Marx calls "*the organic composition of capital*" $(q)$, i.e., $c: (c + v)$ — shows a steadily growing trend. From this it follows that if we assume the rate of surplus value $(s')$ to be constant, then with a growing $(q)$ the rate of profit $(p')$ must fall. Now, it is a historical fact that in the capitalist development $(q)$ has a rising trend; therefore, the rate of profit $(p')$ must at least have a falling tendency. Marx illustrates this claim, his law of the tendency of the rate of profit to fall, with the following example:

If with a variable capital $(v)$ of £100 goods worth £200 are produced, then the surplus value $(s)$ is £200 − £100 = £100, and the rate of surplus value $(s')$ is 100%. Now,

If $c = 50$,  $v = 100$,  then $p' = 100 : 150 = 66\frac{2}{3}\%$

If $c = 100$,  $v = 100$,  then $p' = 100 : 200 = 50\%$

If $c = 200$,  $v = 100$,  then $p' = 100 : 300 = 33\frac{1}{3}\%$

If $c = 300$,  $v = 100$,  then $p' = 100 : 400 = 25\%$

If $c = 400$,  $v = 100$,  then $p' = 100 : 500 = 20\%$

(Marx 1977c: 221)

For Marx this law "possessed great significance. It demonstrated that capitalist production had certain internal barriers to its own indefinite expansion. ... [T]he falling rate of profit ... must ultimately choke up the channels of capitalist initiative" (Sweezy 1942: 96–97). Sweezy then quotes Marx:

> [T]he rate of profit, the stimulating principle of capitalist production, the fundamental premise and driving force of accumulation ... [is] endangered by the development of production itself. And the quantitative proportion means everything here. ... It is here demonstrated, ... from the standpoint of capitalist production itself, that it has a barrier, that it is relative, that it is not an absolute but only a historical mode of production. (Marx, quoted in Sweezy 1942: 97)

After reading the exposition up to here, the critical reader will invariably ask why an entrepreneur should then progressively mechanize production at all, when that leads to a growing $(q)$ and a falling $(p')$. The current Marxist answer to this question is usually: competition. When a new technique is introduced in a particular enterprise, the productivity of labor in that enterprise increases and the production costs for the entrepreneur fall in comparison to the average production costs. For him this difference constitutes an *extra profit*. The will to increase labor productivity and reduce production costs spurs investment in more and better technologies, which are normally more expensive (see *Lehrbuch* 1972: 349ff.). As a consequence, constant capital $(c)$ increases. Later on, other entrepreneurs follow the pioneering one, and consequently the aggregate $(c)$ and $(q)$ of the whole economy increase. Marx acknowledged this process with the following statement:

> The development of the productive forces of social labor is the historical task and privilege of capital. It is precisely in this way that it unconsciously creates the material requirements of a higher mode of production. (Marx, quoted in Sweezy 1942: 97)

But the average rate of profit $(p')$ of the whole economy falls.

A progressively growing $(q)$ is not the only possible cause of a falling $(p')$. The entrepreneur also may not be able to sell his commodity for its full value. For different reasons, the market price can temporarily fall below the value of the commodity. In that case, there is a smaller profit or no profit at all. This unfortunate event can befall a commodity, an entrepreneur, or a branch of industry. If this happens to a sufficiently large number of industries, the result is a general fall in the rate of profit.

If the average rate of profit of the whole economy falls, and if this does not happen gradually, which would otherwise make it possible for entrepreneurs to adjust to it, an economic crisis can ensue. A drastic fall in the rate of profit may lead some entrepreneurs to refrain from investing. They may either decide to invest less, or postpone the reinvestment of the profit, or even quit the field altogether. As a consequence, other producers (their suppliers) will not be able to sell their goods. This is then a crisis of overproduction or of overcapacity, which results in a contraction of the economy. Profit does not necessarily have to disappear or the rate of profit to be negative for a crisis of this type to unfold. It only takes the rate of profit to fall below its usual level to trigger such a crisis.

## 2. Dissatisfaction with the Law of the Tendency of the Rate of Profit to Fall

Bourgeois economists reject Marxist economic theory altogether. But even at first sight *anyone* can see that the claim of the falling rate of profit is not very convincing. As stated above, in the answer usually given by Marxists to the question of why an entrepreneur invests more in (c) at all, it is argued that in this way he can reduce his production costs. However, in the Marxian example quoted above there is no reference to this argument. Quite on the contrary, production costs rise, and then only due to more investment in (c); for the production of the same amount of surplus value (100), the same amount of (v) and increasing amounts of (c) are being consumed. This is the cause of the falling rate of profit.

Some Marxists are not satisfied with this theory — Sweezy, for instance. For Sweezy the law of the tendency of the rate of profit to fall is very problematic. He does not dispute the existence of such a tendency. Already before Marx the great bourgeois economist David Ricardo had discovered this phenomenon, and he deemed it perturbing. Mandel quotes some historical data collected by the US Department of Commerce in order to show that the rate of profit of the American manufacturing industry fell between 1889 and 1919 from 26.6% to 16.2% (Mandel 1971: 166). Sweezy has doubts only about the tenability of the Marxian explanation of this phenomenon.

Marx himself enumerates some factors that counteract this law: (1) Along with the spread of mechanization of production comes the mass production of machines, which leads to a drop in the price of the elements of constant capital (c). That is to say, although the *physical volume* of (c) grows steadily, its *value* does not grow to the same extent. In exceptional circumstances its value can remain the same or even fall in spite of the growth in its physical volume. (2) The entrepreneur can make the worker produce more value by lengthening the working day and/or intensifying labor. Since the value of her labor power ($v$) remains unchanged and the mass of surplus value ($s$) grows, the rate of surplus value ($s'$) rises. Marx calls this possibility "raising the degree of exploitation of labor." (3) Additionally, the entrepreneur can at times "drive down wages below the value of labor." (4) The increasing use of machinery, that is, the growing ($q$), makes workers redundant and thus creates a "relative overpopulation" or an industrial reserve army, which pushes wages down. This allows entrepreneurs to set up new industries that need less ($c$). Of course, they then need more labor power, but because of falling wages total ($v$) does not rise or it does not rise enough to offset the savings in ($c$). This means that the organic composition of capital ($q$) declines. If we now assume that the rate of surplus value ($s'$) remains the same (actually, one can also assume that $s'$ now rises), this leads to a higher rate of profit ($p'$). For now either ($c + v$) has fallen while ($s$) has remained the same, or ($c + v$) has remained the same while ($s$) has risen. If one now calculates the average of the relatively high profit rates of these industries and the profit rates of the older industries, then it could well be that the profit rate of the economy as a whole rises. (5) Foreign trade often facilitates import of raw materials and food that are cheaper than similar domestic products. This reduces ($c$) and, to the extent that wages depend on the price of food, also ($v$). In this way, the rise in ($q$) can be kept low and ($s'$) can be kept high. These counteracting factors were clearly the reason why Marx formulated his law cautiously, as a general tendency.

In addition to these factors mentioned by Marx, Sweezy mentions some others that have the effect of raising the profit rate: the power of employers' organizations, export of capital, formation of monopolies, and intervention of the state in favor of capital. Labor unions and intervention of the state in favor of labor have the effect of reducing the profit rate.

Sweezy thinks that the Marxian analysis of the tendency of the rate of profit to fall is neither systematical nor exhaustive. The Marxian explanation thereof is based on the assumption that the organic composition of capital ($q$) grows steadily while the rate of surplus value ($s'$) remains constant. But a rising ($q$) normally goes hand in hand with rising labor productivity. If ($s'$) were to remain constant, says Sweezy, then it must be assumed that the worker partakes in the increased productivity of her labor in the same measure as the capitalist. Of course, there is no logical objection to this assumption. But, usually, alongside the rising productivity of labor effected by a rising ($q$) an industrial reserve army comes up. And that exercises a depressing effect on wages, thus elevating the rate of surplus value (Sweezy 1942: 100f.).

Marx, of course, considered this reality to be a counteracting factor. "But it seems hardly wise to treat an integral part of the process of rising productivity separately and as an offsetting factor; a better procedure is to recognize from the outset that rising productivity tends to bring with it a higher rate of surplus value" (Sweezy 1942: 101).

Also, the aforementioned belief shared by many Marxists, namely, that entrepreneurs increase investments in $(c)$ because they can thus reduce production costs, simply means that then workers can be made redundant, wages reduced, and $(v)$ cut down, all of which leads to an increase in $(s')$.

In order to make it all more complicated, Sweezy shows that Marx knew this all along. He quotes the following passage from *Capital*, volume 1: "But hand-in-hand with the increasing productivity of labor goes, as we have seen, the cheapening of the laborer, therefore a higher rate of surplus value even when the real wages are rising. *The latter never rise proportionally to the productive power of labor*" (101f.; emphasis added by Sweezy). Then Sweezy concludes: "Marx was hardly justified, even in terms of his own theoretical system, in assuming a constant rate of surplus value simultaneously with a rising organic composition of capital" (Sweezy 1942: 102).

With these considerations in mind, Sweezy argues that if both $(q)$ and $(s')$ are appropriately assumed to be variable, the direction in which the rate of profit $(p')$ will change becomes indeterminate. In the same vein, he also rejects one possibility, which could support the usual Marxian explanation for the tendency of $(p')$ to fall, namely, that normally the increase in $(q)$ will be relatively so much larger than the increase in $(s')$ that the former will dominate the movements of $(p')$. Sweezy thinks that the rapidity of growth in $(q)$ is generally exaggerated. In *physical* terms it is surely correct that the *quantity* of machinery and materials per worker grows very rapidly. However, $(q)$ is an expression of *value*. Since labor productivity steadily rises, growth in the *volume* of machinery and materials per worker cannot be regarded as an index of growth in $(q)$. For with growing labor productivity, machines and materials can be produced with less and less labor. For all these reasons Sweezy concludes that the Marxian formulation of the law of the tendency of the rate of profit to fall "is not very convincing" (104).

Sweezy's alternative, also Marxist, explanation for the tendency of the rate of profit to fall begins with the process of accumulation (growth). It is not only that existing enterprises and branches of industry expand; new ones are also founded, such as the railways in the nineteenth century (and mobile telephony nowadays). The first effect of accumulation of capital is increased demand for labor, which leads to a shrinking of the industrial reserve army and, consequently, to a rise in wages. In the first instance, this results in a reduction in $(s')$, which, in turn, causes the rate of profit to fall. Just the chain of causation up to here can account for a lasting tendency of the rate of profit to fall. It is not necessary to posit a rising $(q)$ for that result.

However, entrepreneurs do not suffer a reduction in $(s')$ and a falling $(p')$ without countermeasures. By introducing machinery and other labor-saving devices they endeavor to bring the rate of profit back to its former level or even to raise it well above it. Naturally, this is something they attempt to do on an individual basis — for their own enterprise. But, over time, all entrepreneurs do the same. This is where the rising $(q)$ comes into play. "Whether their actions will succeed in restoring the rate of profit, or whether they will only act to hasten its fall[,] is an issue which cannot be settled on general theoretical grounds" (105f.).

A factor I miss in this discussion is population growth. Maybe not in the short term, but in the middle and long term entrepreneurs benefit greatly from population growth, which keeps the industrial reserve army sufficiently large, as is the case in most developing countries. Also, when the laborers who have recently arrived in the labor market find work, the number of buyers for the products of an expanding economy also grows. Sweezy thinks it is almost certain that the rising $(q)$ will tend toward restoring the former $(s')$. And because now more and better machines will process more materials and hence produce more goods, the *mass* of surplus value $(s)$ will exceed the magnitude it would have achieved had $(q)$ not increased.

At this point I can complete the answer to the question posed above, namely, why entrepreneurs mechanize production, invest more in $(c)$, if by doing so they only cause the rate of profit to fall. Although the rate of profit $(p')$ *can* fall due to a rising $(q)$, the *mass* of surplus value $(s)$ grows, and with it grows the *mass* of profit $(p)$, even if the $(s)$ cannot be realized entirely. This is a sufficiently strong motive for accumulation. What else can entrepreneurs do with their accumulated profit? (Speculation in the stock market, finance market, and so forth can only make one speculator richer at the expense of another. It is a zero-sum game.) Besides, after some time, they start regarding the lower rate of profit as the normal one.

In capitalism, accumulation cannot be planned at the macroeconomic level. For this reason, its development is always accompanied by sharp fluctuations in the accumulation *rate*, fluctuations that are sometimes caused by technical revolutions and that sometimes lead to them. This results in cyclical economic fluctuations and often in severe crises. However, as stated above, these are not system-threatening crises.

### 3. The Marxist Under-Consumption Theory of Crisis

It has been stated above that capitalists may sometimes have to sell their goods below their value. Sometimes portions of their goods cannot be sold at all. In this case, they cannot realize the whole surplus value that has already been produced. This also leads to a fall in the rate of profit. But why is it that this happens? The answer is that in capitalism there is a contradiction between two tendencies: the tendency towards unfettered production and the tendency to limit consumption of the masses (by keeping their wages and salaries as low as possible). The consuming power is

> not determined either by the absolute productive power or by
> the absolute consuming power, but by the consuming power
> based on antagonistic conditions of distribution, which reduces
> the consumption of the great mass of the population to a variable
> minimum within more or less narrow limits. The consuming
> power is further restricted by the tendency to accumulate, the
> greed for an expansion of capital and a production of surplus
> value on an enlarged scale. (Marx, quoted in Sweezy 1942: 175)

The purchasing power of the masses is often not sufficient to buy up all produced goods. The periodical crises in capitalism then appear as realization crises. But they could also be called "under-consumption crises."

There are doubts about and objections to the under-consumption theory of crisis, which have stopped many Marxists from accepting it as a significant aspect of the crisis problem (186). Marx himself is partly to blame for this. Sweezy quotes passages from Marx's writings that give the impression that the under-consumption theory is *the* Marxian crisis theory. For instance:

> The last cause of all real crises always remains the poverty and
> restricted consumption of the masses as compared to the

tendency of capitalist production to develop the productive
forces in such a way that only the absolute power of consumption of the entire society would be their limit. (Marx, quoted in
Sweezy 1942: 177)

Sweezy also quotes a passage from *Capital*, volume 2, that, intriguingly,
shows that Marx expressly rejects the under-consumption theory:

It is purely a tautology to say that crises are caused by the
scarcity of solvent consumers, or of a paying consumption. The
capitalist system does not know any other modes of consumption but a paying one. . . . If any commodities are unsaleable, it
means that no solvent purchasers have been found for them. . . .
But if one were to attempt to clothe this tautology with a
profounder justification by saying that the working class receive
too small a portion of their own product, and the evil would be
remedied by giving them a larger share of it, or raising their
wages, we should reply that crises are precisely always preceded
by a period in which wages rise generally and the working class
actually gets a larger share of the annual product intended for
consumption. . . . It seems, then, that capitalist production
comprises certain conditions which are independent of good or
bad will and permit the working class to enjoy that relative
prosperity only momentarily, and at that always as a harbinger
of a coming crisis. (Marx, quoted in Sweezy 1942: 150f.)

Sweezy wrote that Marx never really developed a detailed under-
consumption theory. His statements on this theory are scattered in different parts of his work. Therefore, one could think that Marx regarded
under-consumption as an aspect — but, on the whole, not a very important aspect — of the crisis problem (1942: 176, 178). Sweezy himself does
not reject the under-consumption theory. However, he tries to formu-
late it "carefully." I shall here briefly present and explain his more careful
formulation.

Sweezy assumes that all production capacities are continuously utilized
in full. Under this condition, surplus value and total profit increase. Since
capitalists strive to become as rich as possible, they also aim at accumulating as much of the surplus value as possible. The share of accumulation in
total surplus value rises (compared to the former level). The Marxian concept of accumulation includes both the money that is paid to additional

hired workers (additional $v$) and the money spent to buy additional means of production (machinery and materials) (additional $c$). In modern business cycle theory, only this second part of accumulation is called *investment*. Investment in means of production (additional $c$) as a proportion of total accumulation rises (compared to the former level). All the while, consumption rises too, because capitalists increase their own consumption and, as is generally assumed, the additional hired workers consume away their entire wages ($v$) (i.e., they do not save). However, and this is the decisive point, the share of growth in consumption of capitalists in the total surplus value gradually declines, and so does the share of growth in the total wage bill in total accumulation. From this it follows that the rate of growth in consumption is less than the rate of growth in means of production (growth in $c$). In other words, *the ratio of the rate of growth in consumption to the rate of growth in means of production declines.* "This is a result which flows logically from the characteristic pattern of capitalists' behavior" (Sweezy 1942: 182).

In a second step of his argumentation Sweezy maintains, on the basis of statistical evidence, that in a "reasonably well-developed capitalist economy" the relationship between the mass of consumed means of production and output has a "remarkably high degree of stability." He thinks "that over long periods a given percentage increase in the stock of means of production will generally be accompanied by approximately the same percentage increase in output." On this basis he feels entitled to assume that "if we start from a position of equilibrium, ... a given rate of increase in means of production will be accompanied by an equal rate of increase in the output of consumption goods. In other words, *the ratio of the rate of growth of the output of consumption goods to the rate of growth of means of production remains constant*" (182). The essence of Sweezy's formulation of the under-consumption theory can be briefly presented as follows (183):

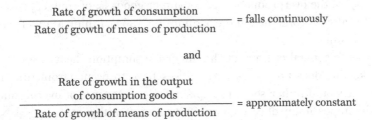

$$\frac{\text{Rate of growth of consumption}}{\text{Rate of growth of means of production}} = \text{falls continuously}$$

and

$$\frac{\text{Rate of growth in the output of consumption goods}}{\text{Rate of growth of means of production}} = \text{approximately constant}$$

Therefore, growth in consumption has an inherent tendency to lag behind growth in output of consumption goods.

### 4. Dissatisfaction with the Under-Consumption Theory of Crisis — The Disproportionality Theory of Crisis

Ernest Mandel criticizes the "shallowest" version of the theory, according to which the origin of the crisis lies in the fact that workers receive a wage that is equivalent only to a part of the new value that they produce:

> The crudest defenders of this idea ... forget that the other part of this value [the part the workers do not receive] corresponds to the purchasing power of the bourgeois class (capitalist families and firms).... The workers are not at all expected to buy all the commodities produced. On the contrary, the capitalist mode of production implies that a part of these commodities, namely, capital goods, is never bought by the workers, but always by the capitalists. (Mandel 1971: 361)

Mandel should not have addressed his critique to the "crudest defenders" of the under-consumption theory, but to its author, namely, Marx, who wrote: "The last cause of all real crises always remains the poverty and restricted consumption of the masses ... " (Marx, quoted in Sweezy 1942: 177). And it was Marx who wrote about the "antagonistic conditions of distribution" (see quote further above) as being one aspect of the cause of the realization problem of capitalists.

Mandel also criticizes other proponents of the theory who tried to give it a more subtle form: "these various 'models,' arithmetical or algebraic, of under-consumption all suffer from a common weakness. They always *beg the question* by regarding as already shown, in their exposition of the problem, the solution which they wish to offer" (Mandel 1971: 363). Sweezy's more careful formulation of the theory is also among these models. Mandel comments: "If one starts from this assumption [Sweezy's assumption that all production capacities are being continuously utilized in full], the 'necessity' of the overproduction of consumer goods is, of course, proved, since it is already contained in the assumption" (364). I think Mandel's critique is justified.

Mandel's general critique of the under-consumption theory says: "An idea like this does not explain why crises have to occur [from time to time] — it would rather serve to explain the *permanence* of overproduction, the impossibility of capitalism" (361). I agree with him.

Unlike Mandel, the (unknown) authors of the Soviet *Lehrbuch Politische Ökonomie* (1972) (*Textbook of Political Economy*) accept under-consumption as a cause of crisis, but only as "one of the most important links in the mechanism that unleashes the crisis." Furthermore, they write:

> However, the contradiction between production and consumption [too much production, too little consumption] cannot itself explain the inevitability of crises in capitalism, although the form of a crisis *itself*, namely, the impossibility of selling all the produced goods, at first sight appears to corroborate the correctness of such an explanation. (471)

They give two convincing arguments for their position. First, like Mandel, they argue: "The theorem that under-consumption is an autonomous cause of crises inevitably results in the conclusion that crises must have a chronic and steady character." In reality, though, their course is different. They are neither chronic nor steady in character. Secondly, they argue: "Under-consumption cannot explain the periodicity of overproduction crises. It is well known that in periods of upswing (boom), which precede crises, the purchasing power and consumption level of the working class is usually higher than at any other time" (472). Marx himself wrote "... crises are always prepared by a period in which wages generally rise, and the working class actually does receive a greater share in the part of the annual product destined for consumption" (Marx 1978: 486–487).

One of the early critics of the under-consumption theory of crisis was Mikhail Tugan-Baranovsky, who submitted an alternative theory of crisis, namely, the disproportionality theory. He tried to show that even with continuous accumulation the supply of commodities need not necessarily exceed the demand, no matter how low society's consumption might be. This cannot happen as long as total production is divided up among the various branches of industry in the right proportions (which calls for flexibility). This claim contains two theses: that under-consumption is not the cause of crises, and that disproportionality is the real cause thereof.

Disproportionality as the cause of crises is a part of common knowledge of every economist. When capitalists invest and produce they do not know beforehand what the right proportions are. Everyone produces for a market whose dimensions can be estimated only on the basis of very incomplete knowledge. As a result, sometimes "too little" is produced, sometimes "too much." This is reflected in prices, which sometimes lie above the value of the commodity, and sometimes below it. In the subsequent period the production of some goods will be cut down and that of others increased. If consumers' wishes, labor productivity, production methods, etc., never changed, the right proportions could eventually be found by means of trial and error. And from that moment on, there would be no unsold goods anymore, and all prices would reflect the value of goods. And, therefore, from then on, there would be no crisis anymore. In the real world, however, these conditions change all the time. Disproportionalities that are rooted in the unplanned, erratic, and anarchic nature of capitalist production come up all the time.

Marx had also realized that such partial disruptions of the production and circulation process can unleash a crisis that can spread and turn into a general crisis. And his followers never disputed this cause of crises. However, Marx devoted only passing attention to disproportionality as a cause of crises, and his early followers turned a blind eye to it. But later Marxists have taken disproportionality as a cause of crises more seriously. The authors of the Soviet *Lehrbuch* wrote:

> In every system of commodity production based on private property we can observe a disproportionality in the development of social production. . . . But under capitalist relations, owing to the social character of the production process, the anarchy engulfs the whole social production — not only in individual countries, but in the whole world. . . . There are too many value- and materials-related proportions that are required to be correct in order that, under extended capitalist reproduction, the social product is realized. Because of the anarchy of production, they become as many sources of disproportion. (1972: 472)

They updated the disproportionality theory by including also the credit system in it. The authors regard disproportion between production and consumption as one aspect of the general disproportionality in capitalism. Sweezy too highlights the point. He wrote:

> [I]t is incorrect to oppose "disproportionality" to "under-consumption" as a cause of crises; . . . For it now appears [here he refers to his own formulation of the under-consumption theory] that under-consumption is precisely a special case of disproportionality — disproportionality between the growth of demand for consumption goods and the growth of capacity to produce consumption goods. This disproportionality, however, in contrast to the kind envisaged by Tugan, arises not from the uncoordinated and planless character of capitalism, but from the inner nature of capitalism, namely [here Sweezy quotes Marx], "that capital and its self-expansion appears the starting and closing point, as the motive and aim of production; that production is merely production for *capital*. (Sweezy 1942: 183f., Marx quote from 1981: 278)

Almost in the same vein the authors of the *Lehrbuch* write:

Just as the contradiction between production and consumption cannot explain how the possibility of a crisis becomes the reality of a crisis, so also disproportionality cannot in itself — i.e., without reference to the contradiction between the social character of production and the private-capitalist form of appropriation — explain this process. (473)

Mandel too thinks that disproportionality, on its own, cannot account for the phenomenon of crisis in capitalism: "The anarchy of capitalist production ... cannot be regarded as a cause in itself, independent of all the other characteristics of this mode of production, independent in particular of the contradiction between [too much] production and [too little] consumption which is a distinctive feature of capitalism" (Mandel 1971: 367).

We thus see that all three — Sweezy, Mandel, and the authors of the *Lehrbuch* — sought the same way out of the jumble of contradictory and problematic, that is, unsatisfactory, Marxist crisis theories: integration of the under-consumption theory into the disproportionality theory. Mandel speaks of a synthesis "undertaken in Marxist terms" (368). He wrote:

> The collapse of the boom is thus the collapse of the attempt to maintain the former level of values, prices and rates of profit with an increased quantity of capital. It is the conflict between the conditions for the accumulation of capital and for its realization, which is merely the unfolding of all the contradictions inherent in capitalism, all of which enter into this explanation of crisis: contradictions between the great development of production capacity and not-so-great development of the consumption capacity of the broad masses; contradictions arising from the anarchy of production resulting from competition, the increase in the organic composition of capital and the fall in the rate of profit; contradictions between the increasing socialization of production and the private form of appropriation. (371)

## 5. So Where Is the Final Crisis *of* Capitalism?

As we have seen above, Tugan-Baranovsky, in connection with his disproportionality theory of crisis, posited the *theoretical* possibility that, under certain conditions, capitalism could become crisis-free, if the right proportions between the different branches of industry could be achieved. He did not think a problem could arise if, given a state of ideal proportionality, consumption, and thus the production of consumption goods, stagnated or fell. Even then, the overall supply of goods would not necessarily exceed the overall demand. For then there could be a greater demand for means of production (machinery, materials, etc.), and thus further means of production could be produced. Then there would be neither an overproduction crisis nor stagnation, since capitalists could then perpetually create a market for themselves by buying means of production from one another. Of course, from the workers' point of view the situation would be increasingly bad, but, Tugan-Baranovsky reminds us, capitalists created capitalism for themselves, in order to increase their wealth. From their point of view, there is no problem.

Thus far, I can follow Tugan-Baranovsky's line of reasoning to some extent. In order to keep the economy somehow afloat, capitalists need not buy only means of production from one another. They can also increase their own consumption and that of their managers and executives. They can have streets, bridges, and parking lots built for their large number of big cars. For their own luxury needs they can have many big and beautiful houses built in many different cities and holiday resorts. They can have more golf courses built for their sport and recreational needs, more museums for their cultural needs, and so on and so forth. For all of that they will also need more means of production.

In order to make the point absolutely clear, Tugan-Baranovsky takes the logic of his reasoning to its most extreme conclusion:

> If all workers except one disappear and are replaced by machines, then this one single worker will place the whole enormous mass of machinery in motion and with its assistance produce new machines — and the consumption goods of the capitalists. The working class will disappear, which will not in the least disturb the self-expansion process [*Verwertungsprozess*] of capital. The capitalists will receive no smaller mass of consumption goods, the entire product of one year will be realized and utilized by the production and consumption of the capitalists in the following year. Even if the capitalists desire to limit their own consumption, no difficulty is presented; in this case the production of capitalists' consumption goods partially ceases, and an even larger part of the social product consists of means of production, which serve the purpose of further expanding production. For example, iron and coal are produced which serve always to expand the production of iron and coal.

The expanded production of iron and coal of each succeeding
year uses up the increased mass of products turned out in the
preceding year, until the supply of necessary minerals is
exhausted. (Tugan-Baranovsky 1905, quoted in Sweezy 1942: 168)

This conclusion, which only makes sense in abstract-logical terms and is
deliberately exaggerated, may seem absurd. But the theoretical problem is
not an abstract one. It is very relevant, especially for the current predicament. As we've known for a long time now, workers are being replaced
by machines, millions of people in the capitalist countries are without
employment, and labor unions as well as economists from the left repeat
like a mantra that more jobs have to be created and that workers should
receive higher wages in order to increase their consumption, or else there
will be no end in sight for the recession/stagnation. But the capitalists and
their economists ignore these demands with utmost calm. What is worse,
they continue to lay off further workers in the thousands and even demand
wage cuts. They do not see therein any threat to capitalism. We will deal
with this current situation in detail further on.

In the early twentieth century, contemporary Marxists reacted to
Tugan-Baranovsky's provocation with exasperation. Sweezy summarizes
their reaction as follows:

[But] none could stomach the idea that production could
expand indefinitely without any regard to the level or trend of
consumption. ... Behind all these criticisms of Tugan's theory
lies one single idea, namely, that the process of production is
and must remain, regardless of its historical form, a process of
producing goods for human consumption. Any attempt to get
away from this fundamental fact represents a flight from reality
which must end in theoretical bankruptcy. (Sweezy 1942: 169, 172)

Let me quote Karl Kautsky, who was regarded at the time as an authori-
tative spokesperson of Marxism, vicariously, for all other Marxists. In his
review of Tugan-Baranovsky's book he wrote:

The capitalist may equate men and machines as much as he
likes, society remains a society of men and never one of
machines; social relations remain always relations of man to
man, never the relations of men to machines. It is for this
reason that in the final analysis human labor remains the
value-creating factor, and it is for this reason also in the final
analysis that the extension of human consumption exercises the
decisive influence over the expansion of production. Production

is and remains production for human consumption. (*Die neue Zeit*, vol. 20, part 2, quoted in Sweezy 1942: 170)

Six decades later, Tugan-Baranovsky's conclusion was not a closed chapter. The renowned economist Michal Kalecki examined his thesis in the 1960s. Leszek Kolakowski summarizes his view as follows:

> There is nothing absurd, in capitalist terms, in production being undertaken simply in order to increase production: on the contrary, production regardless of need *is the strength of the system*. But, Kalecki observes, Tugan-Baranovsky overlooked the fact that a system that entirely ignored the level of consumption would be very unstable, since any drop in investment would mean a decrease in the use made of the existing apparatus of production, hence a further drop in investment, and so on in a vicious spiral. (Kolakowski 2005: 413; emphasis added)

In all these critiques of and comments on Tugan-Baranovsky's abstract thesis I see, firstly, that he has been partly misunderstood, and, secondly, that some possibilities to theoretically develop his ideas have been ignored.

Tugan-Baranovsky does not at all say something as absurd as that society could one day be a society of machines. Nor does he dispute the fact that production is and will remain production for *human* consumption. Karl Kautsky only alleges that Tugan believed both. Actually, Tugan says only that capitalist production can continue to exist, and in fact grow, even if the number of *workers* and their consumption decline drastically. The hypothetical single worker would not only produce new machines but also consumption goods for capitalists.

If the *working class* were to disappear, it would not mean that *people* would disappear. When Marxists speak of a classless society as their goal, they, as everybody knows, mean only that workers should no longer constitute a class below the capitalist class, but that all of them together should become "owners" of all the means of production, maybe through state ownership.

Tugan-Baranovsky's error consists in the notion that if a single worker with the help of machines is able to produce everything, the rest of the population, the great majority of the people, are capitalists. This is clearly absurd. If the working class were to disappear, there would be one of the following three possible forms of society: (1) A classless socialist society; (2) a society, also classless, where all people, as self-employed farmers and craftspeople owning modest means of production, produce everything; or

(3) a society in which people are organized in big cooperatives (or collectives) and produce everything with the aid of big machines in collective ownership of some kind, and where working hours are reduced substantially. In none of these three scenarios realization and expansion (valorization) of capital takes place. Moreover, in such scenarios it is also likely that production would be deliberately curtailed, out of environmental considerations, for instance, or due to scarcity of resources. Then there would simply be no economic crisis in the present-day sense of the word.

The hypothetical situation in which a single worker can set a monstrous mass of machinery in motion is no longer unimaginable for us. TV reports nowadays often show almost deserted factory floors during working hours. But this has not turned the great majority of the population into capitalists or rentiers. The great majority is made up of neither workers nor capitalists. It consists of workers and white-collar employees, students, unemployed people, welfare recipients, schoolchildren, toddlers, and pensioners. They cannot live solely on the proceeds of shares and securities, which they may also own. Moreover, labor-intensive industries have not vanished. They have only been relocated to cheap-labor countries like China, India, Bangladesh, etc.

In the quote above, Kautsky wrote that it is human labor that, in the final analysis, remains the value-creating factor. But the issue is not as simple as that. For then, common sense raises the question: How are value and surplus value created in factories almost devoid of laborers? I have touched on this question in the preface, and I will discuss it in detail in chapter X.

As the preceding paragraphs show, there is no clear-cut, convincing Marxist answer to our starting question, namely, whether there could ever be an economic crisis so severe that it would result in the end of capitalism. And the disproportionality theory of crisis, which is not a specifically Marxist theory, but rather a part of general bourgeois economic thought, explains only benign crises, which can be overcome by restoring the right proportions. Furthermore, some of Marx's statements on crises give the impression that he thought that crises and depressions did not in themselves constitute a threat to the capitalist system. We still do not know why capitalism should not be able to survive in the long run. Where lies, then, the possibility of a big crisis that could bring about the end of capitalism and pave the way for another, better system? The authors of the Soviet *Lehrbuch* write, as an answer to this question as it were, that crises only correct the disproportions "violently and temporarily" (478). Later on, they write about the "increasing depth of crises" and state that the development of capitalism "aggravates further the contradictions between the social character of production and the capitalist form of appropriation" (483). And then the authors express the following hope:

> The crises *aggravate the contradictions between labor and capital*, for capital strives to find a way out of the crisis at the expense of the working class — by reducing the wages, increasing the intensity of labor, and laying off a part of the workers. It is mainly the working class that has to bear the brunt of the crisis. Not only does the struggle between the working class and the bourgeoisie for their share of the national income escalate as a result of the various effects of the crises. The crisis also teaches the workers *that only the overthrow of capitalism* can eliminate crises and the suffering of the masses resulting therefrom. (484;
> italics are partly in original, partly added)

In addition to this hope that the working class would overthrow capitalism, there has been among Marxists another hope, namely, that capitalism would break down when it hits its barrier — a hope that Marx himself nourished.

## 6. The Controversy over the Breakdown Theory

In volume 3 of *Capital* — in a passage on the process of centralization of capital — Marx wrote: "This process would soon bring about the collapse of capitalist production ... "[2] (quoted in Sweezy 1942: 191). But this passage, according to Sweezy, is nothing more than a description of a tendency, since Marx speaks in the same breath about "counteracting tendencies which continually have a decentralizing effect by the side of the centripetal ones" (192). Nowhere else did Sweezy find in Marx's works a "doctrine of the specifically economic breakdown of capitalist production." Nevertheless, some early Marxists thought one could read such a doctrine in his works. Actually, this doctrine can be logically derived both from the law of the tendency of the rate of profit to fall and the under-consumption theory.

   Eduard Bernstein, the leading theoretician of the revisionists in the German Social Democratic Party at the time, claimed that Marx and Engels indeed had a breakdown theory — breakdown in the sense of a great, all-embracing economic crisis. He, however, wanted to refute that theory. In his view, the economic developments since Marx's death — growth of the world market, the emergence of cartels, perfection of the credit system, etc. — knocked the bottom out of the breakdown theory. Back in 1899 he identified in capitalist development a trend towards improvement, and concluded that Marx's breakdown theory was no longer tenable. He also claimed that the magnitude of crises and the severity of class struggle were diminishing. The practical political objective of the whole exercise was to reject — together with the refutation of the breakdown theory — the necessity of a revolution. He firmly believed that persuasion and education were the means to achieve socialism.

Karl Kautsky, who at the time was the leading voice of the orthodox Marxists, disputed that Marx and Engels had a breakdown theory. According to him, although the two masters believed that the crises would increasingly aggravate, they thought that the decisive factor for the transition towards socialism was "the growing power and maturity of the proletariat" (quoted in Sweezy 1942: 194). Unlike Bernstein, Kautsky saw in 1899 no diminution in the severity of crises. With respect to the strategy of social democracy, Kautsky seemed to be unsure. He believed in being prepared for any eventuality.

Three years later, in 1902, Kautsky appeared to have overcome his uncertainty. He claimed that the crises intensified and expanded more and more. In general, he regarded crises and depressions as a signal for the demise of capitalism. However, he did not want to advocate a breakdown theory. Instead, he thought that capitalism was in for a period of chronic depression. He argued that the capitalist mode of production needed constant and fast expansion, but that very soon it would become impossible for the world market to expand faster than the growth of the productive forces of society. Then overproduction would become chronic for all industrialized countries (this is then a chronic depression).

According to Kautsky, continuation of capitalist production would be feasible even under such circumstances. However, he thought that "it becomes completely intolerable for the masses of the population; the latter are forced to seek a way out of the general misery, and they can find it only in socialism.... I regard this forced situation as unavoidable if economic development proceeds as heretofore" (quoted in Sweezy 1942: 198). Kautsky expected the victory of the proletariat to take place before the forced situation arose. Should that not happen, then class conflict would be aggravated.

Kautsky saw not only the aggravation of domestic class conflicts coming, but also the aggravation of international conflicts, as in the face of a chronic depression each industrialized nation would increase its efforts to enlarge its share of the international trade to the detriment of other nations. As we know, colonial conquests, protective customs duties, cartels, and the like were already in place as means of resolving conflicts. As to perspective on the future, he thought that the coming decades would bring humankind crises, conflicts, and catastrophes of all kinds.

### a) *The Pauperization Theory*

In the quote above, Kautsky speaks of intolerable general misery of the population at large. That is a clear reference to the pauperization theory of Marx and Engels. The concept "pauperization" does not necessarily mean material pauperization, which, indeed, has occurred in extremely bad times. In the last hundred years, however, in the developed capitalist countries, the material standard of living of the working class has, generally speaking, improved. Nevertheless, even with increasing real wages the situation of the working class can *relatively* deteriorate — in the sense that its share of the gross domestic product falls.

A relative deterioration of this kind, however, cannot make the situation of workers unbearable. Marx and Engels rather highlighted other aspects of pauperization:

> [A]ll means for the development of production undergo a
> dialectical inversion so that they become means of domination
> and exploitation of the producers; they distort the worker into a
> fragment of a man, they degrade him to the level of an append-
> age of a machine, they destroy the actual content of his labor by
> turning it into a torment; they alienate [*entfremden*] from him
> the intellectual potentialities of the labor process; ... they
> deform the conditions under which he works, subject him
> during the labor process to a despotism the more hateful for its
> meanness; they transform his life-time into working-time, and
> drag his wife and child beneath the wheels of the juggernaut of
> capital. (Marx 1982, vol. 1: 799)

Marx knew that the organization of workers and their resistance counteracted pauperization. Yet, "what is certainly growing is the uncertainty of existence" (Marx, quoted in Lotter et al. 1984: 348).

Except for the period of the long boom after World War II, in which workers could — before taking up a job and afterwards through the trade unions — set conditions, this description of pauperization fully applies to all eras of capitalism. Moreover, in the present era of neo-liberal globalization real wages are falling even in the developed industrialized countries — in some cases even nominal wages are falling. One would think this was an unbearable situation. But the working class does not intend to try to topple capitalism.

### b) *Rosa Luxemburg: Limits to Accumulation*

Towards the end of the controversy over the breakdown theory, the majority of orthodox Marxists accepted Kautsky's position. Among the few who did not was Rosa Luxemburg. In her book *The Accumulation of Capital*, published in 1913, she wanted to remove any doubt about the inevitability of the fall of capitalism *on economic grounds*. This was important to her. For, she wrote, "if we assume, along with the 'experts,' the limitlessness of capital accumulation, then the solid soil of objective historical necessity is cut from under the feet of socialism" (quoted in Sweezy 1942: 207). Marx's work, too, gives grounds for one to think that he believed that in capitalism, theoretically, limitless accumulation is possible. Luxemburg wanted to redress this error of Marx and to state more precisely the economic conditions for the fall of capitalism.

For this purpose she could have cited Engels. In 1892 he republished — in the preface to the English translation of his early work *The Condition of the Working Class in England* — an article he had first published in 1885. In it he wrote:

> Capitalist production *cannot* stop. It must go on increasing and expanding, or it must die. Even now the mere reduction of England's lion's share in the supply of the world's markets means stagnation, distress, excess of capital here, excess of unemployed workpeople there. What will it be when the increase of yearly production is brought to a complete stop?
>
> Here is the vulnerable place, the heel of Achilles, for capitalistic production. Its very basis is the necessity of constant expansion, and this constant expansion now becomes impossible. It ends in a deadlock. Every year England is brought nearer face to face with the question: either the country must go to pieces, or capitalist production must. (Engels 1892/1976b: 449f.)

Luxemburg wanted to show why one day this necessary expansion would no longer be possible.

In general, her theory is labeled as one of "automatic breakdown of capitalism," which may imply that she recommends a wait-and-see attitude rather than a revolutionary one. According to Kolakowski, however, Luxemburg herself never used the term "automatic breakdown." On the contrary, she was convinced that the revolution would triumph long before capitalism was exhausted (see Kolakowski 2005: 407).

In what follows I have briefly presented Luxemburg's argumentation as laid out in Kolakowski (2005), Sweezy (1942), and Predrag Vranicki (1972, vol. 1).

In the beginning, there is the old question: With continuous accumulation (extended reproduction), how are capitalists able to realize all the created surplus value? They themselves consume only a part of it (let us call this part $s1$). Only if the other part (let us call it $s2$) is realized (i.e., sold at its full value) can it be accumulated (i.e., invested) in the next period of production. Once this accumulation has taken place, it has the effect of correspondingly increasing the mass of goods. This means that the condition for continuous accumulation (extended reproduction) is continuously expanding demand for the produced goods. The question is: From where does the demand for the mass of goods come, which represents in physical form that part of the surplus value ($s2$) that is to be realized and accumulated?

As we have seen above, no one was prepared to accept Tugan-Baranovsky's claim that the problem of under-consumption need not necessarily arise, that capitalists could create an endless market for themselves by buying means of production from one another. If this were possible, then there would be no realization problem. But this is not possible. It only makes sense to produce means of production if at the end of the chain consumer goods are produced that are also consumed. Furthermore, in case of extended reproduction consumption must also be extended. To produce goods just for the sake of producing is, from a capitalist point of view, total nonsense.

According to Luxemburg, in a pure, i.e., closed, capitalist system — the assumption from which Luxemburg and Marx both started their argumentation — there is, for the *totality of* capital, no solution to the problem of finding demand for ($s2$). She thought that Marx's reproduction formulae did not prove the possibility of extended reproduction. Population growth is no solution to the demand problem. For an increase in the number of capitalists is already considered in the absolute magnitude of the consumed part of the surplus value ($s1$), while the consumption of the working class is always contained in wages ($v$) (workers exhaust their wages through their consumption; they cannot consume more). The consumption of the unproductive strata — landowners, bureaucrats, military, independent professionals, etc. — is included either in ($s1$) or in ($v$) (salaries and wages). Foreign trade is no solution either, since the analysis of extended reproduction is based on the assumption of a single capitalist world market, which amounts to all countries constituting one domestic market.

In Luxemburg's view, the only solution to this problem is to drop the aforementioned assumption of a single world market. That part of the surplus value that is to be realized and accumulated ($s2$) can only be realized by selling goods to people who live outside the capitalist system of production. These can be people in underdeveloped countries, where pre-capitalist economic forms prevail, or sections of the population of capitalist countries that have remained outside the capitalist system — for instance, small farmers and craftspeople.

So, on the one hand, capitalism has to expand all over the world. On the other hand, it is exactly through its expansion that it finds its limits. Slowly but surely, the expansion of capitalism does away with pre-capitalist economic forms, which it needs for the realization of ($s2$). It also destroys the small producers in crafts and agriculture. When this process is completed throughout the world and when the economy of the whole world has been transformed on the pattern of this system, then it will no longer be possible to accumulate any further. In this way, Luxemburg thought she had theoretically demonstrated that the demise of capitalism was unavoidable. We should note that this conclusion is based on the assumption (or definition) that an economy in which no capital accumulation takes place and which does not expand is not a capitalist one. Is it then impossible to imagine a capitalism that functions at a high level, but without accumulation (with simple reproduction)? Luxemburg wrote:

> Capitalism is the first form of economy with a drive to expand, a form with a tendency to spread itself over the whole world and push away all other forms of economy, a form that does not tolerate any other at its side. But, at the same time, it is the first form of economy that cannot exist without other forms, ... a form which, simultaneously with the tendency to become a global form, crashes against its inner inability to be a global form of production. (Quoted in Vranicki 1972: 331f.)

Luxemburg's accumulation theory was almost unanimously rejected — not only by the revisionists, but also by other orthodox Marxists. The reason for this was not just that her orthodox Marxist critics had gradually aligned themselves to revisionism. True, the revisionists needed a theory that confirmed the ability of capitalism to expand without limit, not a breakdown theory. But Luxemburg's theory was simply not convincing.

However, I find the criticism leveled at her theory to date equally not convincing.

## c) *Critique of Luxemburg's Theory*

Sweezy and Kolakowski criticize Luxemburg's assumption that in a capitalist society wages will always lie close to the subsistence level. Kolakowski wrote that Luxemburg erroneously assumed that "although the laws of exploitation might be weakened from time to time they would 'in the last resort' always prevail over working-class resistance, so that a genuine increase in workers' consumption was unlikely to occur" (Kolakowski 2005: 413). That is the reason, according to Kolakowski, why she thought that workers' consumption would never be enough to realize the whole surplus value. From here it was only a short step for Luxemburg to conclude that accumulation of capital (increasing fixed capital assets) was pointless. *In reality*, however, accumulation of capital typically entails growth in variable capital ($v$). History has demonstrated this time and again. This increase in ($v$) is usually spent on additional consumer goods, and in this way *a part* of the surplus value is realized.

This critique can be further supported by quoting a comment made by Engels in 1885, long before Luxemburg wrote her book:

> The truth is this: during the period of England's industrial monopoly the English working class have, to a certain extent, shared in the benefits of the monopoly. These benefits were very unequally parceled out amongst them; the privileged minority pocketed most, but even the great mass had, at least, a temporary share now and then. And that is the reason why, since the dying-out of Owenism, there has been no Socialism in England. (Engels 1892/1976b: 450)

Of course, any one country's *industrial monopoly* in the world market cannot exist in pure form in pure capitalism, which, again, exists only in the imagination of economists. Yet, a quasi industrial monopoly of England did exist in *history*, in the then actually existing capitalism. This monopoly of England and, later on, that of the few industrialized countries of the world lasted, as we know, very long — until approximately the beginning of the 1980s. During this long period of time the working class of the few industrialized countries partook in the advantages of their industrial monopoly, not now and then, but continuously — except in the war years and during the Great Depression. During this time wages did not always lie close to the subsistence level — which is in any case a relative concept — but considerably higher.

Nevertheless, I am not satisfied with this critique on the following grounds: Firstly, even if a part of the surplus value could be realized through a certain growth in wages and salaries $(v)$, the problem posed by Luxemburg remains unsolved. In the formula value $= c + v + s$, $(v)$ now becomes larger and $(s)$ slightly smaller. However, $(s)$, at least $(s2)$, is still there, as is the problem of realizing it. Secondly, Kolakowski wrote the sentences quoted above in the mid-seventies. *Today*, we must say that Luxemburg was not far off the right track with this assumption of hers. Technological development, automation, rationalization, and other factors have brought about high levels of unemployment and have very much weakened the resistance of the majority of the working class. For quite some time now labor unions have been acquiescing to decreasing real wages and falling net income. They are also being compelled to agree to longer workweeks and job-cutting.

The right critique of Luxemburg's theory should be something different. Sweezy concedes in his own, reformulated Marxist crisis theory (see earlier on) that a portion of the surplus value remains unrealized. This presses the rate of profit downwards and also presses the business cycle to a lower level. Both of these are enough to make the economic development in a closed capitalist system crisis-prone. From time to time that leads to recessions; it can also lead to chronic depressions or stagnation (as low growth rates are called nowadays). In such situations, some enterprises can go bankrupt. But capitalism can live on with all that. None of such crises leads to the collapse or demise of capitalism.

Capitalists themselves consume a part of the surplus value $(s1)$. The remaining surplus value $(s2)$ is never entirely accumulated (that is, invested in machinery and materials). Part of it remains in bank accounts waiting for investment opportunities. When this idle sum of money does not find a profitable investment opportunity in the real (productive) economy, it is often used for speculation — in the stock, finance, and commodities market or in the real estate market. All speculators hope to be able to make a good profit at the expense of other speculators. When speculators suffer big losses, due to a crash for example, a lot of *fictitious* capital/ assets ("hot air," such as inflated stock value) is destroyed. Capitalism can also live on with such things. Capitalist production as a whole does not fall apart. After each crash and each crisis there is a recovery. If Rosa Luxemburg still lived today, she would have to explain why capitalism has not collapsed in spite of the big crises of the past.

The second point in Sweezy's criticism appears at first sight to be convincing. He argues as follows: If Luxemburg's analysis were correct, then consumers from the non-capitalist sectors of the economy and non-capitalist countries would not change the situation either. Who would buy the goods that would be imported from non-capitalist regions into capitalist regions as payment for the exports of the latter? If in a capitalist country there had been no demand for the exported goods, then there could be no demand for the imported goods either.

This particular criticism, as well as Luxemburg's argument, which draws the criticism, are somewhat flawed. The purpose of exporting goods is not merely to realize the surplus value, but also to obtain, by importing, such goods and services that are not available, not available in sufficient quantities, or not available cheaply enough in the domestic market (goods like raw materials, tropical fruits; services like cheap call center work, software and back-office services; even cheap labor). If such goods were offered for sale in the capitalist countries, then most likely capitalists themselves and working people would invest/consume more. Let us think of Ricardo's theory of international trade (see chapter VIII). However, even in this case some unrealized surplus value ($s2$) would remain, and with it would remain the demand problem and the problem of realizing the rest ($s2$).

Kolakowski downplays the political value of Luxemburg's analysis by saying that her scenario in which capitalism would necessarily collapse is totally unrealistic. It presupposes a capitalism that is a single market spanning the whole world, that is, a pure capitalism, in which in respect of the rate of profit there is no difference between different countries. This is a scenario

> in which there is no difference in economic development between the Congo and the USA. One may imagine a world as uniform as this, but it scarcely affords a solid basis for economic predictions. Not only is this prospect remote and unreal, but it ignores the fact that the gap between developed and backward nations is getting larger rather than smaller. (Kolakowski 2005: 412)

Sweezy goes even further in his critique:

> The whole distinction between "capitalist" and "non-capitalist" consumers is, in this context, quite irrelevant. If the dilemma were a real one, it would prove more than she bargained for: it would demonstrate, not the approaching breakdown of capitalism, but the impossibility of capitalism. (Sweezy 1942: 205)

I think Sweezy goes too far. Luxemburg indeed stated under which conditions, in her view, capitalism was feasible: it was feasible in a world with many underdeveloped countries such as Congo, India, Bulgaria, etc., and a few highly developed countries like the USA. Today she would probably say capitalism has not collapsed yet exactly because there is still this class difference between the countries of the world. What we need to carefully examine is her thesis that in an assumed closed, pure, single capitalist world economy further accumulation is not possible.

The fact that capitalism with extended reproduction has continued to exist since 1913 — even in the era of neo-liberal globalization, which is indeed the closest approximation to her pure, global capitalism — is the definitive proof of the assertion that Luxemburg's accumulation theory is wrong. Of course, there are still underdeveloped countries and some non-capitalist areas in capitalist countries. But since 1913 their number and size have drastically decreased. If Luxemburg's theory were correct, capitalism would be long dead.

The reason why this has not happened so far is that after the Great Depression of the 1930s (see the next chapter!) — which to some extent confirmed Luxemburg's theory that ($s2$) can largely remain unrealized — the demand problem could be more or less solved. Firstly, ever larger amounts of short-, medium-, and long-term consumer credit, which had already been introduced in the 1920s, made it possible for working people of all strata to consume more than the equivalent of their wages and salaries ($v$). They hoped that their future income would be continually rising. Capitalists themselves made that possible by granting credit through banks. That is clearly part of pure capitalism. But, obviously, in 1913 Luxemburg could not visualize this solution of the problem. Secondly, the economy was no longer solely dependent on working people's income and consumer credit for realizing ($s2$). The state too became involved and created demand when necessary. It also intervened in other ways to help the economy. This, however, cannot be regarded as a criticism of Luxemburg's theory, as in the pure capitalism she imagined there is no room for state intervention. In the following chapters I shall present these aspects of the crisis problematic in the context of the big crises of the twentieth century and the crisis theories of the more important bourgeois economists such as Keynes, Schumpeter, Friedman, and others.

My own explanation for the fact that capitalism has not collapsed yet, and my answer to the question of whether that will ever happen, has little to do with the capitalist economy being a closed or an open system, or with differences in the stage of development between different countries or between parts of the population of the same country. Actually, these things have nothing at all to do with the issue of limits to capital accumulation. They have a lot to do with the limits to resources and the sinks of nature (i.e., the capacity of nature to absorb human-made pollution and environmental degradation). This topic will be dealt with in chapter X.

## II.

# The Great Crash
# and the Great Depression

In publications on the problems of the economies of the industrial societies, the term "crisis" is used in a rather careless manner. Even in the case of a recession, i.e., when the gross domestic product (GDP) has fallen two quarters in a row, they speak of a crisis. Even when an economy has grown for several years, but at a yearly rate lower than the previous year, there is talk of a crisis. One also speaks of a crisis when the growth rate lies under 2 percent, and even more so when the economy does not grow, in other words when it stagnates. Such "crises" are not really worth talking about; they come and go. They are not crises, but only a part of the normality of capitalism. One should use the term crisis only if, after a recession, the economy for a relatively long time stagnates at a level lower than that before the recession, or when the recovery takes a long time to come — in other words, in case of a depression. Such a state of the economy, a very deep and long depression, afflicted capitalism in the 1930s, especially in the years from 1929 to 1933. In order to understand this crisis, however, we must first have some information on the development of events in the 1920s.

## 1. The 1920s

To the readers of today, capitalism in the 1920s presents a complicated picture. In the first years of the decade, the crisis had the form of high inflation in many countries. Taking the price level of 1913 as 100, wholesale prices in 1920 stood at 226 in the United States and 307 in the United Kingdom, while in France, in 1925, they stood at 584 (Kurz 1999: 423). This was the situation of the economies of the victors of World War I; in the countries that lost the war and in Eastern Europe, hyperinflation prevailed. Prices reached absurd heights. John Kenneth Galbraith wrote of a US congressman who visited Germany in 1923 "receiving 4 billion mark in exchange for seven dollars, then paying 1.5 billion mark for a restaurant meal and giving a 400-million-mark tip" (Galbraith 1994: 37). "At the end of this process prices had risen, in comparison to those before the war, by fourteen thousand times in Austria, twenty-three thousand times in Hungary, two-and-a-half million times in Poland, four billion times in Russia and one trillion times in Germany" (Aldcroft 1978, quoted in Kurz 1999: 424). Curiously, in the literature of those days one also reads of a severe depression, which in the 1920s was referred to as "the world economic crisis" (Predöhl 1962: 23). It took place almost simultaneously with the hyperinflation (actually between 1920 and 1921).

After the end of the inflation period, there followed a few years of very good economic conditions, which started in different countries at somewhat different times. Galbraith wrote on the USA:

> [T]he twenties in America were a very good time. Production and employment were high and rising. Wages were not going up much, but prices were stable. Although many people were still very poor, more people were comfortably well-off, well-to-do, or rich than ever before. Finally, American capitalism was undoubtedly in a lively phase. (Galbraith 1955: 7)

In Germany, inflation came to an end, or rather, it was brought to an end, in November 1923. And the period between 1924 and 1928 was one of "unprecedented economic boom" and "great increase in public sector consumption, namely, at the municipal level." All this was mainly sustained by American loan capital (Predöhl 1962: 24). By 1928, in Germany, both industrial and agricultural production had again reached the level of the pre-war period. And although structural unemployment was high, wages rose substantially from 1924 onwards (von Freyberg et al. 1977: 127f.). It is said that the prevailing "Zeitgeist" of the time was one of steadfast optimism. The 1920s were called "the golden years" — at least in the USA, but partly also in Europe. The average economic players at the time firmly believed — particularly in the USA — that an era of everlasting prosperity was dawning (Predöhl 1962: 8). Some economists played a role in generating this optimism as well.

There was, however, an exception. The economy of the United Kingdom was afflicted with a depression. The cause thereof was that the country returned to gold standard in 1925 with the parity of the pre-war era, which led to an overvaluation of the pound sterling and consequently to a fall in exports. In spite of that, Sweezy wrote that, speaking generally, world capitalism had reached a "relative stabilization" in the 1920s (Sweezy 1942: 207).

Against this backdrop and also in view of his newfound sympathy for revisionism, it is easy to understand that in 1927 Kautsky, who was until then the most prominent orthodox Marxist, rejected his own earlier forecast of a chronic depression: "The expectation that crises (*Absatzkrisen*) would someday become so extensive and long-drawn-out as to render the continuation of capitalist [mode of] production impossible and its replacement by a socialist order unavoidable finds no more support today." In the same year, Rudolf Hilferding, the other great theoretician of social democracy of that time, said that "[T]he overthrow of the capitalist system is not to be fatalistically awaited, nor will it come about through the workings of the inner laws of the system, but it must be the conscious act of the proletariat" (quoted in Sweezy 1942: 208). Only two years later, in 1929 — what an irony of history — the Great Crash in the New York Stock Exchange triggered the Great Depression. It was a deep depression, which extended to the whole world and lasted through the decade, leaving millions of people without work. And yet, the working class did not topple capitalism.

The hyperinflation, the catastrophe of the beginning of the decade, cannot be regarded as the outcome of the inexorable internal laws of capitalism. It was caused by the exogenous factor of the world war, which was an extraordinary event. The huge costs of this destructive enterprise were financed through debt that could not be paid back after the war except through an enormous inflation, which was consciously brought about by printing money on a large scale. But both the great crash of 1929 and the subsequent Great Depression, which really came to an end only with the beginning of World War II, were results of the workings of the inner laws of capitalism.

To follow I give a brief account of these two big events of economic history based largely on the works of Galbraith (1955, 1994) and Charles P. Kindleberger (1973). This will help us understand the present crises of capitalism.

## 2. The Boom and the Delirium

Against the background of the promise of everlasting prosperity mentioned above, it is understandable that many did not want to wait for this promise to come true. They wanted to see this future prosperity materialized in the present, and speculating on the stock exchange offered them a possibility. They were not all bad people. A noted economist of that time, Joseph Lawrence of Princeton University, characterized speculators as a "cultured, conservative, innocent, honest, intelligent and public spirited community" (quoted in Galbraith 1955: 44–46).

The stock exchange boom that preceded the crash lasted for five years. Stock prices fell countless times during this period. Still, this did not have any negative effect on the general euphoria. In the fall of 1929, however, uncertainty was widespread. People oscillated wildly between optimism and pessimism until the crash occurred on October 24 (on October 25 in Europe).

In the beginning, this boom had a solid real-economic basis, but in the end the rise in share prices turned into a speculative boom. Galbraith described this development thus:

> As to the national mood, there was the picture of great, enduring and deserved prosperity so admirably articulated by President Coolidge. Sustaining it was the vision of a new world of industry and technology, dominated by automobile manufacture with its still widely admired assembly lines and, especially, by the new communications world of radio. The speculative favorite of those years was RCA, the Radio Corporation of America. Its future was indeed before it; RCA had never paid a dividend.
>
> In keeping with this mood and justified by it was, as ever, the self-sustaining power of the speculative boom. ... the improving prices of stocks brought in the buyers who bought and sent prices still higher, thus supporting in a very persuasive way their previous decision to buy. (Galbraith 1994: 62f.)

This brief description of the situation in the 1920s shows that the dynamics of the stock exchange in our times is in principle not much different from that in those days. The parallels are all the more clear when one remembers the stock prices boom in the 1990s, especially in the high-tech industries and the so-called dot-com branch. One need only think of the billions paid by telecommunication companies (Deutsche Telekom, for instance) for one of the UMTS licenses, although the technology was not fully developed at the time. The price of shares of Amazon.com, one of the very big dot-com companies, rose continuously, although it had not made any profit yet (see Bello 2003: 45). Now let us go back to 1929.

In his book *The Great Crash 1929*, published in 1955, Galbraith rendered a very detailed description of the events that took place on the stock exchange. According to him, in the USA of the 1920s there were good reasons for the prices of normal shares to go up. The companies were making good and increasing profits and the outlook was positive. Moreover, in the early 1920s the share prices were low and the yields good. Therefore it was no surprise that in 1924 the share prices began to rise. However, in 1927 the upward trend became alarming, for the share prices rose from day to day and from month to month. The gains were not very high, but the crowd of investors, which had in the meantime become quite big, could count on steadily growing stock prices. For in that year only two months out of the twelve saw no growth in share prices.

Economic historians have an explanation for the fact that in 1927 the (until that time) warranted rise in share prices turned into an unwarranted stock market boom. That year the US central bank (called the Federal Reserve System, or the "Fed," which is composed of twelve Federal Reserve banks), following a request from European finance officials, changed its monetary policy to one of cheap money: it made a large amount of liquid money available and lowered the interest rate in order to make loans cheaper. The latter step, moreover, reduced the attraction of government bonds and other fixed-interest securities. All of this strongly motivated people to invest in stocks. Up to this point there was nothing extraordinary about this. But very soon the character of the boom changed. "The mass escape into make-believe," "the true speculative orgy", was clearly under way (Galbraith 1955: 16). Now and then share prices also fell, but they went up again — often on the very same day. In the spring of 1929, share prices began to rise in big leaps. Within a few months, for instance, the price of the shares of Radio Corporation of America shot up from $85 to $420, although the company had not yet paid any dividend.

Many people, indeed, thought that the boom would be over before the end of 1929, simply because every boom has to end sometime. Many were concerned about the wild speculation that resembled a delirium and feared that a bad crash was coming. They believed something needed to be done to stop speculation.

> For these people, however, every proposal to act raised the same intractable problem. The consequences of successful action seemed almost as terrible as the consequences of inaction, and they could be more horrible for those who took the action.
>
> A bubble can easily be punctured. But to incise it with a needle so that it subsides gradually is a task of no small delicacy. ... The real choice was between an immediate and deliberately engineered collapse and a more serious disaster later on.
> (Galbraith 1955: 30)

Why was the choice so difficult to make?

There are not only savers who invest their savings in stocks, but also speculators who buy shares, also with borrowed money. Whereas a saver-investor expects good dividends and, in the long term, growth in the value of his shares, the speculator expects that a buyer will soon buy his shares at a price higher than what he has paid. He hopes that the difference between these two prices will be much larger than the interest on the money he had borrowed and that he can thus make a good profit. Quite often, speculators sell away their shares before they have received the first dividends, and with the proceeds they buy other more lucrative shares with the same objective. It is very likely that the new owners of the shares are also speculators, who do the same with the same expectations. But at some point there are no more speculators who think that the share prices will keep on rising. Then the share prices also stop going up. But the market does not then stabilize. Quite on the contrary: it then no longer makes any sense to hold on to shares that have been purchased with borrowed money. One will then only make losses, for interests will have to be paid. Then all speculators try to sell away their shares as fast as they can — and the share prices slump.

The basis of all hopes of investors at the stock market is the expectation that the real economy will grow in the long term. However, it is also widely known that the economy includes the phenomenon of crisis, and that even in times of general economic upswing individual enterprises can undergo a crisis. While saver-investors are normally prepared to endure those crises, as they are generally cyclical, i.e., temporary, in nature, speculators cannot bear them as they have debt commitments to meet. When they sense that a crisis is imminent, they quickly dispose of their shares, ideally before other speculators see it coming. They might even make a profit, or at least they avoid suffering a loss. But the buyers — if they are also speculators — cannot make a profit anymore, as in the meantime everyone knows that a crisis is unfolding. They then try to sell away their shares with as small a loss as possible. But as many speculators now try to sell their stocks, their prices do not cease to fall. In order to make a good bargain, potential buyers with sufficient capital of their own wait until they see the end of the downturn. Naturally, everyone can miscalculate and make wrong decisions in this process, and some can enrich themselves at the expense of others. But when a long recession sets in or when the real economy is undergoing a general crisis, or when a large corporation (such as Deutsche Telekom, whose shares have become people's shares) is stuck in a crisis, usually many lose out. Just not receiving dividends is a loss.

The severity of the crash and the extent of the losses depend on the proportion of speculative transactions in the total stock market transactions. In 1929 on Wall Street, this proportion was very high. At the time the stock exchange played a very important part in the life of Americans. Even very ordinary people tried to get rich by trading in the stock market. Of a total of 120 million inhabitants and some 30 million families, over 1.5 million Americans were participating in stock exchange transactions. Approximately 600,000 among them bought stocks with borrowed money. But the total number of "active speculators" was higher, although probably lower than a million. Of course, 1.5 million may not seem like a large figure today, but it should be kept in mind that this was the situation in 1929 (all figures from Galbraith 1955: 83). No wonder the people in authority were afraid of being held responsible for the bursting of the bubble.

Even before the boom, Wall Street had developed mechanisms to make it easy for speculators to borrow money: they could buy stocks "on margin." The speculator bought stocks, but did not have to pay the full amount. He paid only a percentage of the total price; the broker paid the rest. The speculator became the owner of the shares, which, however, were held by the broker as collateral. The broker, in turn, borrowed the money for this transaction from a bank; and the same shares were used again as collateral for this loan. Thanks to this mechanism, a speculator, who himself had, for instance, only $100, could buy stocks worth, for instance, $1000. The advantage of this kind of transaction was that whereas the amount of the loan remained the same, the value of the stocks was expected to rise sharply. This speculators at least hoped. This factor was one among several that fueled the boom.

At the peak of the boom, even the total savings of all Americans did not suffice for meeting the credit demands of the speculators. Although banks can create money by giving loans, there are limits to it. Creating money in this way is limited by the total savings of the people and the rules of the central bank. So banks began also to attract rich investors from abroad. They offered a high rate of interest: at the end of 1928 it was 12 percent, and the capital was still 100 percent secure. Even industrial corporations found this rate very attractive. Some decided to put a part of their working capital in the financing of stock market speculation. In addition, banks had a simpler possibility: they could borrow money from the central bank, the Fed, at a 5 percent interest rate and then lend it as overnight credit at 12 percent.

At the peak of the boom, it was said that the economy did not have enough stocks to meet the demand. Therefore, a larger supply of stocks was created. New companies were set up, and existing companies expanded their production capacity. For both, new shares were issued. In addition, holding companies, which pushed forward merger processes, issued shares in order to raise funds for acquisitions. But all of them together only had a limited capacity to absorb new capital.

What made it possible for investors and speculators, notwithstanding these limits to capacity, to invest money in stocks was the creation of investment trusts. These trusts did not set up new companies, nor did they expand existing ones; they merely acquired stocks of a great variety of existing companies. They raised the money for this by selling their own shares to investors and speculators, who, in this comfortable way, got the possibility of indirectly owning shares of different companies producing goods and services. The crucial trick in this innovation was that investment trusts sold their own shares much in excess of the shares of other companies they bought. The surplus was invested in the overnight money market or in real estate; a portion of it also went into the pockets of the trust founders. In this way, the volume of stocks in the economy completely lost the relation it ought to have had to the total worth of all companies. The value of the former could amount to many times the latter. This completely cleared the way for speculation in the stock market. What made the matter more explosive was that at the peak of the boom there were investment trusts that set up new investment trusts. The shareholders of the parent investment trust, which owned the majority of the shares in the subsidiary trust, could thus make profit from the business of many investment trusts (leverage effect).

The amount of overnight lending by brokers to speculators was a good indicator of the extent of speculation at the stock exchange at the time. In the early 1920s, the amount involved was between $1 billion and $1.5 billion. Shortly before the crash it amounted to over $7 billion. The interest on loans that speculators were prepared to pay can be regarded as an indicator of their profit expectations at the time. It generally ranged between 7 and 12 percent. Once it even reached 15 percent (all figures from Galbraith 1955: 25–26, 72–73). More than half of these sums, enormous for that time, was supplied by industrial corporations and private persons, from the United States and from abroad. As in those days such loans appeared to be almost 100 percent secure and liquid, and, as they were easy to manage, they were attractive all over the world. It seemed as if Wall Street was about to absorb all the surplus cash in the world.

### 3. The Crash

There is always an end to a boom, but an end need not become a crash. An end can be gentle, and the subsequent downtrend can be short. But in 1929 a crash took place, and it became a catastrophe. Never before had capitalism experienced anything like it.

In the period leading up to the crash, once people became aware of the speculative boom, many experts had been issuing warnings, which however fell on deaf ears. There had earlier been some smaller and bigger slumps, the latter being followed by obituaries. But the market recovered every time. Influential people predicted sustained prosperity, which was actually part of a ritualized incantation, the purpose of which was (and still today is) to work on the psyche of the speculators and influence the market positively. But in September 1929, the boom came to an end. Although some share prices still rose, the market was no longer as confident as before. And again it was the time for Cassandras and ritual conjurers of optimism. A renowned stock market analyst, Roger Babson, predicted not only the crash but also the subsequent Great Depression.

Even the most optimistic experts no longer radiated unmitigated optimism. A Boston investment trust predicted slight setbacks, but it also reassured the public by stating that these were just temporary *"indentations in the ever ascending curve of American prosperity"* (quoted in Galbraith 1955: 91). A leading and powerful banker, Charles E. Mitchell, said that "the industrial condition of the United States is absolutely sound," and "the markets generally are now in a healthy condition.... [V]alues have a sound basis in the general prosperity of our country" (99). Professor Irving Fisher, a famous economist, stressed that the dividends were rising. He said: "There may be a recession in stock prices, but not anything in the nature of a crash"; he spoke of a "permanently high plateau" and said that he expected "to see the stock market a good deal higher than it is today within a few months" (91, 99). So, in spite of some ups and downs, there was no end in sight to the speculative zeal. New investment trusts were still being set up, new speculators were still coming to the market, and overnight loans of brokers were still rising. "The end had come, but it was not yet in sight" (92).

Talking up the economy, however, did not help. Between October 19 and 23 there was a wave of selling. Share prices tumbled, even those of first-rate, safe securities. Brokers started sending margin calls, i.e., they demanded more cash from borrowers — namely, the speculators — since the falling value of shares, which served as collateral for the overnight loans taken from them, could no longer cover the loans. In spite of this, some people still tried to instill hope into the market. They said the market would receive "organized support," namely, from the big players at the stock exchange, especially from the investment trusts. They surely would not all put up with a plunge in stock prices. And they purportedly had enough cash to buy up stocks, the prices of which had lately fallen considerably. Moreover, the well-known ritual conjurers of optimism did whatever they could: Professor Fisher said that the drop in stock prices represented only a "shaking out of the lunatic fringe." He even maintained that the stock prices had not reached their real value during the boom and hence they would soon rise again. Mitchell asserted that the economic conditions were "fundamentally sound," and that the market "would correct itself if let alone" (all quotes in Galbraith 1955: 102).

But the speculators no longer listened to the likes of Mitchell and Fisher. On Wednesday, October 23, there was another wave of selling. In the last trading hour alone, a phenomenal 2.6 million shares were sold, and the prices slumped rapidly. That was the beginning of the panic, confusion, and chaos that broke out in the morning of October 24, the "black Thursday." That day, 12.9 million shares were sold — at prices that pushed thousands into bankruptcy. Blind, endless fear prevailed. There was a wave of suicides; eleven well-known speculators had already taken their lives. This was not just the continuation of a downward trend; this was the crash.

Three sentences from Galbraith's description of these events make the difference between this day and the preceding one clear: "Of all the mysteries of the stock exchange there is none so impenetrable as why there should be a buyer for every one who seeks to sell. October 24, 1929, showed that what is mysterious is not inevitable. Often there were no buyers and only after wide vertical declines could anyone be induced to bid" (Galbraith 1955: 104).

In the afternoon of this day the most powerful bankers in the United States met. The "organized support" was coming. They announced that they had decided to improve the situation. And the announcement was followed by action: The incumbent president of the stock exchange appeared personally at the market and began purchasing stocks of different companies, outbidding other bidders. This move helped; further losses were averted. At the end of the day prices even went up.

Over the next two days the usual optimistic mantras were repeated. Even President Hoover joined in by saying that "the fundamental business of the country, that is production and distribution of commodities, is on a sound and prosperous basis" (quoted in Galbraith 1955: 111). At Sunday church services, in some of the sermons, it was asserted that the crash was God's punishment for those who had neglected spiritual values in their single-minded pursuit of money. They, it was expected, had now learned a lesson. This expectation of the preachers was, however, unfounded. For almost all people involved believed that the worst was now over and that the speculation business could resume. Stock prices were now very low and brokers expected the speculators to buy them en masse.

But the opposite happened. Monday and Tuesday, October 28 and 29, were devastating — worse than October 24. This time there was no organized rescue operation by the banks. They preferred to make sure there was order in the market, where stock prices were determined by supply and demand. So the prices were allowed to fall. The supply was so large that for many stocks there were no buyers at all. The Times Industrial Average plummeted to levels so low that all the gains made in the twelve preceding, booming months were obliterated.

And so it went on. The organized efforts to create an optimistic mood made the speculators sway between hope and despair. Rumors spread that the large banks — those that had organized support on October 24 — were now themselves selling off shares. Also industrial corporations and regional banks, many of which had in the good times lent their surplus cash to Wall Street, were now demanding their money back. The investment trusts, which shortly before had been expected to support the market with their huge liquid reserves, were themselves in great trouble. They were busy trying to support the price of their own ordinary shares by buying them back at a certain price. But they were buying with cash stocks that had already become worthless. That was self-destruction. Those shares could hardly be sold to others.

## 4. The Great Depression

The story of the stock market crash was hardly over when the story of the Great Depression began. In the USA, months before the crash, the real economy was showing signs of a downturn. Already in March production and orders in two of the most important branches of the economy — car manufacturing and house building — had begun to decline. In June, the Industrial Production Index began to fall. That is why Charles P. Kindleberger (1973: 117f.) agreed with the view that the crash was less a cause of the depression than a signal for the need to pause for some time and redeploy. In Germany and the United Kingdom, the economic downturn became apparent in April and July respectively.

In November, shortly after the crash, there was more bad news on the fundamental data of the American economy. Now there was also a slump in the commodities market. There were big losses in cotton, and in the wheat market there was once a downright panic as the price seemed to go into free fall. Production of steel, coal, and cars was declining. The Industrial Production Index continued to drop rapidly. Consumers spent less and less; purchase of costly goods especially declined sharply. Sales of radios had halved since the onset of the crash.

By mid-November, the stock prices seemed to have reached the trough. In the following months there was a moderate to substantial recovery. But in June 1930, there were again big losses. "Thereafter, with few exceptions the market dropped week by week, month by month, and year by year through June of 1932. The position when it finally halted made the worst level during the crash seem memorable by contrast. On November 13, 1929, it may be recalled, the Times Industrials closed at 224. On July 8, 1932, they were 58" (Galbraith 1955: 146).

The year 1932 was in the middle of the Great Depression. But before that there had been a number of organized attempts to reassure the market, in which even the US president took part. But, as a leading politician expressed it, "every time an administration official gives out an optimistic statement about business conditions, the market immediately drops" (quoted in Galbraith 1955: 148).

If the crash was not the cause of the depression, but only aggravated it, can it then perhaps be said that it only reflected the downturn in the real economy that had already begun? Galbraith rejected this explanation of the crash. But before embarking on explanations of these events and — in the following chapters — on general theories of crisis, we should have a short overview of the course and other aspects of the Great Depression.

The stock market crash in the United States led to a serious crisis of the banking system. When the shares pledged as collateral for bank loans rapidly lost value, the latter became bad debts. In order to avoid bankruptcy, the concerned banks resorted to measures that aggravated not only the stock market crisis but also the downturn. In granting credit, they became overcautious. Some loans were also recalled before they were due for repayment. Freezing of installment sales extended the crisis into every part of the economy. Furthermore, American banks began to demand from their debtors abroad redemption of loans that had been given for a short term but that had been invested in long-term businesses. Europeans, especially, were affected by such demands.

Although in those days the degree of interconnection between the national economies was not as high as it is today, it was high enough to let the crisis spread from the United States to Europe and other economies that were integrated in the world market. As mentioned above, the economic upturn in Germany in the second half of the 1920s was mainly based on loan capital from the United States. That is why the premature recall of loans given by American banks hit Germany particularly hard. In 1931, some leading banks of the country collapsed. In Austria, as well, two big banks went bankrupt.

The banking crisis in America and then in Europe disrupted both the domestic and the international chain of credit, on which a highly developed capitalist economy rests. In all, international capital loans fell by more than 90 percent (Kurz 1999: 435). On the one hand, there was a run on banks; foreign creditors as well as domestic savers and investors wanted to quickly withdraw their money. On the other hand, due to the economic downturn, industrialists and businessmen had difficulty servicing their debts, especially as banks were very unwilling to give new loans. All that together led to a general decline in investments. This and the cautious spending behavior of scared consumers led in turn to a rapid decline in production.

Also international trade was badly hit by this development. Almost all countries tried to protect or promote their national production. They used customs duties to reduce imports, i.e., they either raised existing tariffs or introduced new duties. Also quantitative limits to imports were imposed. Devaluation of the national currency was used as an instrument of export promotion, the necessary consequence of which was the abolition of the gold standard. But as every country tried to achieve the same effect by the same means, there were only losers. Furthermore, these measures led to a drastic decline in international trade, the total value of which dropped by more than 50 percent by 1932 (*Encyclopedia Britannica* 2001). Their debt burden — domestic as well as foreign — was so heavy that many countries could not honor their international payment obligations. Some countries even shifted to some sort of barter trade in order not to let any liabilities in gold reserves or foreign currency arise. All of this further deepened the depression; all this gave a fresh impetus to a policy of autarchy.

A factor that in the USA, but partly also in the rest of the world, heavily contributed to the general economic depression was the state of agriculture, which usually tended to overproduction. One has even asked whether it was not really the depression in American agriculture — going on independently of the rest of the economy — that, at least partly, caused the stock market crash, the Great Depression, and the bank crisis.

The cause of overproduction in agriculture lay in the structural changes that had resulted, to a great extent, from World War I. While the war raged in Europe and, as a consequence, agriculture there suffered severely, the cultivated area outside Europe grew considerably. This was facilitated by immigration to Australia and Canada. After the war, however, agriculture in Europe recovered and the cultivated area there grew again. Another important structural change was the mechanization of agriculture — especially in wheat cultivation — which, in the USA, made it possible to move agricultural production to the Great Plains, thus significantly reducing costs. Moreover, mechanization of agriculture freed a lot of land from growing horse-feed crops. From 1925 onwards, overproduction resulted in growing stocks and falling prices. Producers of rubber, coffee, sugar, and (to some extent) cotton also faced similar overproduction problems.

Of course, not in Western Europe, but in other countries — in the Eastern European countries, the United States, Argentina, Uruguay, etc. — agriculture was a very important sector of the economy. In the United States, for instance, it employed in those days a quarter of the working population. Two fifths of the world trade was trade in agricultural products. And just in this very important sector prices fell drastically — and along with them fell the income of farmers and their employees. An index of world market prices for agricultural products, for which the price level of 1923–1925 was taken as 100, showed for the period between July and October 1929 a decline to 70 (Kindleberger 1973: 86). While this situation, with its negative impact on the various branches of industry that supplied inputs to agriculture, partly caused the Great Depression, the latter itself exacerbated the predicament of the already over-indebted farmers. In 1932, prices for agricultural products covered only 57 percent of the costs (Galbraith 1994: 76). The situation in Germany was similar. In the United States, unsalable foodstuffs and cotton were destroyed in order to save at least the storage costs. In Brazil, a huge amount of coffee had to be destroyed.

There was also overproduction of minerals like silver, zinc, and copper, which led to a steep decline in their prices. The trade in mineral raw materials amounted in those days to a fifth of the world trade (86). Underdeveloped countries, which heavily relied on the export of such commodities (but also of agricultural products), were hit hard.

If one takes the average total value of industrial production in the period 1925–1928 as 100, then this value reached its lowest point in the USA in 1932 with 58; in Germany in 1932 with 66; Austria in 1933 with 72; France in 1933 with 79; and the United Kingdom in 1931 with 88 (Brusatti 1967: 234).

The index of average *world* industrial production (1925–1928 = 100) was as follows: 1929 = 102; 1930 = 100; 1931 = 89; 1932 = 78; 1933 = 88. These world production figures should be taken with a pinch of salt, because they included the high values of the non-capitalist Soviet Union (1931 = 274), which did not suffer at all from the depression. Also the good figures of Japan (1931 = 107), which was able to overcome the crisis quickly due to a Keynesian policy pursued before Keynes's time, made the world figures look better than they really were (all figures quoted here from Brusatti 1967: 234).

The crisis pushed thousands of industrial companies into bankruptcy. Until 1933, 11,000 out of the 25,000 banks in the United States went bankrupt. (Only the special, decentralized structure of the American banking system can account for these unusually large numbers.) Unemployment soared by leaps and bounds. In the United States the figure reached more than 14 million people in 1933, 25 percent of the workforce; in the United Kingdom, 25 percent in 1931; in Germany, 31 percent in 1932, with over 6 million people unemployed; and in Austria, 600,000 people were unemployed in 1933. (These rounded-off figures are from different sources: Brusatti 1967: 237, 239; Kurz 1999: 435; *Encyclopedia Britannica* 2001; Hardach 1976: 51.) Furthermore, in every country there were several million unregistered unemployed and partially unemployed people.

By 1936, some recovery had begun in most of the aforementioned countries. However, according to some historians, the Depression lasted the whole of the 1930s and really ended only with the outbreak of World War II. Thus, in the United States, in 1937, when the business cycle was at its peak, there were still 7.5 million unemployed people. Then there was again a setback and a depression, that of 1937–1938. In the United Kingdom, throughout the period between the two world wars, the unemployment rate rarely fell under 10 percent (figures from Dillard 1972: 22). The *Great* Depression was over, but clearly not the depression.

## 5. Explanations

There had been economic crises and depressions before. Historians regard the crisis of 1857–1859 as "the first world economic crisis of the modern ages" (Wehler 1976: 56) and the long period of depressions from 1873 to 1896 as "*the* Great Depression" (Kindleberger 1973: 20). There were many similarities between this depression and the Great Depression of 1929–1933. What was unusual about the latter was its great geographical spread and its depth. Not only the industrialized countries of Western Europe and North America were hit by it, but also countries much farther afield, such as Japan, Argentina, and India. The depression of 1929–1933 was also much deeper than the deepest of the three depressions of the period 1873–1896, namely, the one of 1873–1879. Ravi Batra compares the lowest points of the recessions and depressions between 1790 and 1980 against a hypothetical long-term growth trend represented by a horizontal straight line stretching from the beginning to the end of said period (i.e., the average of the yearly growth rates of the whole period is taken as the trend. Recessions and booms in this period are shown as deviations from the trend, i.e., from the horizontal straight line). While in the depression of 1873–1879 the deviation of the lowest point from the trend was minus 12 percent, for the depression of 1929–1933 it was minus 50 percent (Batra 1987, 108–112).

Also the duration of the Great Depression — four years (for some historians, the whole decade of the 1930s) — was unusual, if we ignore the long period of depressions from 1873 to 1896. All of this could not be accounted for with the usual business-cycle theories. That is why there are very different explanations for these events.

The easiest aspect to explain is the far greater geographical spread of this crisis compared to many others. As a result of colonialism and imperialism, international trade had increased a great deal, as had interdependence and interconnectedness of the economies and finances of the countries hit by the crisis. In addition, thanks to technological progress, communication between distant places had dramatically improved.

As for the depth and duration of the depression, the explanation was fairly simple for both Keynesians and those who had demanded or introduced Keynesian-like measures. According to them, a very normal downturn turned into a catastrophe because, in the beginning, and in spite of the worsening situation, those in power clung tenaciously to orthodox economic policies. When in the USA tax revenue dropped as a result of the downturn, the reaction was to increase taxes — in the name of balanced budgets. All these politicians were adherents of laissez-faire politics (a policy of not intervening in the economy). Even Franklin D. Roosevelt, who from 1933 onwards, as president of the United States, did intervene in the economy, supported this policy in the beginning.

Kindleberger (1973: 23), a Keynesian, wrote of the "failure of economic policy," and of "economic illiteracy." "Deflationists are found everywhere — Hoover [in the USA], Brüning [in Germany], Snowden [in the United Kingdom], Laval [in France]. Examples abound of bad judgment — the British decision to return to the gold standard at par [with the pre-war rate] in 1925. . . . Often no one in authority had any positive idea of what to do, and responded to disaster in the policy clichés of balancing budgets, restoring the gold standard and reducing tariffs."

In some countries, some relief measures for agriculture had already been in place. In the USA, other measures were also taken to halt the downturn. But every time a deficit-financed measure was taken, the government affirmed that it would return as soon as possible to a "healthy" fiscal policy, that is, to a balanced budget. In Germany, the Brüning government, in fact, took drastic steps to reduce government expenditure. It directly induced deflation by ordering cuts in prices, rents, wages, salaries, and interest rates. Although along with wage cuts prices were also reduced (prices had been falling anyway), the outcome of this policy was all in all a massive fall in real wages. As for the unemployed, many of them received no unemployment benefits at all. And those who did received only meager ones. Such benefits had also been cut several times during the crisis. All this further weakened demand and only strengthened the downturn. (More on Keynesianism in chapter III.)

This explanation may seem plausible, yet it is not fully satisfactory, as it would still be necessary to explain why in the pre-Keynes era not every downturn turned into a catastrophe of such proportions.

Galbraith (1955: 95) rejects the explanation that the crash only reflected the downturn in the real economy, which had already begun and was an expected stage in the normal course of a business cycle. According to him, the said downturn was very modest. Until the crash, one could justifiably expect that the downturn would soon give way to a recovery, like other downturns before. Only after the crash were there plausible reasons to expect a rather long depression, for instance, the lack of confidence among investors. So the explanation for the crash remains the real task.

Kindleberger (1973: 19) mentions an explanation Paul A. Samuelson gave in a TV debate in 1969. Samuelson thought that the Great Depression had been the result of a "series of historic accidents." Kindleberger does not say which accidents Samuelson referred to. But indeed, there had been a number of serious "accidents" before the crash. In September 1929 the fraudulent business practices of a very large British industrial and financial empire, built up by a certain Clarence Hatry, were exposed. Not only had he issued unauthorized shares, he had also forged share certificates. Subsequently his empire collapsed. A further accident was the unusual refusal of authorities to allow Boston Edison, a gas light company, to split each of its shares into four. Even worse was, firstly, their decision to examine the company's prices and, secondly, their statement that the company's shares were highly overvalued. These "accidents" were said to have severely shaken the speculators' confidence. But simply a spontaneous decision by a few of them, who probably reacted to a negative assessment of the situation, may also have triggered off the crash. In any event, the boom had to end sooner or later.

Joseph Schumpeter's explanation for the unusually great depth and duration of the depression cannot be put under the category of "accidents," but it can be put under the category of coincidence. Schumpeter sees in economic history three different types of cycles of different periodicity (wave length) proceeding simultaneously. According to him, in the four years between 1929 and 1933 the depression phases (the low stretches) of all three cycles (waves) met coincidentally, which turned the depression into a catastrophe (see Kindleberger 1973: 22). (More on Schumpeter's theory in chapter III, section 2.)

Why was the Fed unable to do anything to curb the stock market boom and effect a return to sensible share prices? The Fed, in fact, tried to do that, but to no avail, as it only sent out warning signals and expressed concern. It hinted, for instance, that it would forbid the misuse of Fed loans for speculation purposes. But at the same time it affirmed it would not meddle with the business practices of commercial banks so long as the twelve Fed banks remained unaffected. It also used two instruments of practical monetary policy: manipulation of the discount rate, and the sale of bonds in large amounts in order to take liquid cash out of the money market and, thus, out of the stock market. But it did both half-heartedly, so they didn't work. The Fed feared that through excessive action it could also starve the real economy of the needed money supply. It could have tried to make share purchases on margin more difficult. That is, with the approval of Congress, it could have laid down the margin at a level higher than the then prevailing 50 percent, which was already a high level for the time. But by so doing it could have possibly itself caused a severe crash. What all of this really meant was that the Fed only wanted to protect itself from being made responsible for the imminent stock market meltdown. The policy of calming and coaxing, innuendoes and half-hearted actions, failed.

In spite of this very cautious policy, the Fed was severely criticized by the business world. They accused it of throwing a monkey wrench in the works of prosperity. A critical voice said, "If buying and selling stocks is wrong the government should close the Stock Exchange. If not, the Federal Reserve should mind its own business" (quoted in Galbraith 1955: 44).

The leading American banker Charles E. Mitchell, who was also director of the New York Federal Reserve Bank, regularly thwarted the Fed's endeavors. At one point, as it looked like the market would crash, he declared that he would lend money generously to stabilize it. And he defied the Fed by declaring that for this purpose his bank would also borrow money from the New York Federal Reserve. The Fed said nothing in reply and withdrew from the affair. It realized "that while the hysteria might be somewhat restrained, it would have to run its course, and the Reserve Banks could only brace themselves for the inevitable collapse. More accurately, the Federal Reserve authorities had decided not to be responsible for the collapse" (46).

There simply was no way out of the dilemma. Even leading personalities of the ruling elite were caught in it. They, too, dared not publicly denounce the speculators, or say the stock prices were too high. Besides, many of them were themselves speculators, such as the aforementioned Charles E. Mitchell.

I have referred above to the collapse of international trade, disruption of the international credit chain, protectionism, prohibitive import duties, and competitive devaluation of national currencies. In his own explanation for the great depth and spread of the Great Depression, Kindleberger places great emphasis on these aspects of the crisis, especially on the international monetary mechanism. He narrates how all international efforts — meetings, conferences, dialogues, etc. — aimed at restoring some balance in the international finance system and stabilizing the world economy failed due to the selfishness of the countries involved. He notes that the United States was not prepared to take on a leadership role involving sacrifices. According to him, the various shocks inflicted on the system, including the crash of October 1929, were not as bad as they appeared to be. In the past, equally great shocks had been coped with satisfactorily. He wrote:

> The world economic system was unstable unless some country
> stabilized it, as Britain had done in the nineteenth century and
> up to 1913. In 1929, the British couldn't and the United States
> wouldn't. When every country turned to protect its national
> private interest, the world public interest went down the drain,
> and with it the private interests of all. (Kindleberger 1973: 292)

The catastrophe at the stock market made the development of the incipient downturn in the real economy into the Great Depression inevitable. This thesis asserting a connection between the two phenomena is more convincing than that of Kindleberger. It appears particularly convincing when one reads a report on some comments made by the German Bundesbank on the stock market crash that took place in installments between 2000 and 2002 and which was accompanied by a slowdown in the world economy.

> Private consumers are induced to reduce their spending by one
> or two Euro on average, when their wealth in the form of share
> certificates goes down by €100. As share prices in Germany
> have fallen by 40% over the past year, growth of consumption
> could, purely arithmetically, have been 0.2 to 0.4 percent lower
> than expected. . . . This would amount to a drop in total con-
> sumer spending of 2.4 to 4.8 billion Euro. Moreover, according
> to the monetary authority, the stock market slump may have

contributed, through other effects, to the "pronounced restraint in consumption."

An equally negative effect ... of the slump in share prices is that it has practically brought venture capital investment to a standstill.[3] (*Frankfurter Rundschau*, 18 March 2003)

The selfishness of nations deplored by Kindleberger is nothing out of the ordinary in capitalism; it is rather the rule. It is of little value for explaining the Great Depression.

Seventy years later, at least the more intelligent and more historically aware players and observers of the stock market boom of the 1990s must have foreseen the crash of 2000–2002. But precisely the inner laws of capitalism prevented them from putting the foot on the brake. Perhaps it is right to conclude that this system lacks a brake mechanism altogether.

# III.

# The Saviors of Capitalism

## 1. Keynes and the Keynesians

The Great Depression made it again possible to raise the system question. It was not the social democrats who did this, but Marxists, communists, and other socialists, who hoped that this crisis would convince all sensible people that capitalism, if not overcome, would bring civilization to an end. For instance, in 1934, after the Nazis had captured power in Germany, the British Marxist John Strachey wrote:

> The condition of the world compels us to attempt the discovery of the causes and remedies for our mounting ills. For all around us we see man's newly won power and knowledge being used to destroy our civilization and us with it. ... [It] is not ... an academic or ideal issue. It involves *our* destruction or *our* development. (1935: 9)

In the United States, among those who between 1933 and 1939 worked for the realization of the New Deal program (see further on), there was a "small but highly articulate ... group," who agreed that it was necessary "to abolish the system entirely — accept that capitalism was a failure. Communism was the obvious alternative" (Galbraith 1994: 84). But bourgeois economists too were very disturbed about this development. Looking back upon that time Predöhl (1962: 9) wrote: "The crisis *in* the system turned into a crisis *of* the system."

As we know today, this severe crisis did not bring capitalism to an end. The programs of the New Deal in the United States, the job creation measures undertaken by the state in Germany and in other countries (e.g., construction of highways), and/or simply the normal course of a business cycle, in which a depression is followed by a recovery and then a boom, averted the collapse of the system.

### a) *Crisis of Orthodox Economics*

For Strachey, economics was simply divided into two schools: "the capitalist and the Marxist." The non-Marxist economists all belonged to one group, at least in the sense that they all wanted to defend or save capitalism. This capitalist school — it was called the orthodox (or classical or neoclassical) school — had serious problems during the Great Depression.

According to orthodox economic theory there can be no serious crisis in a well-functioning capitalist market economy. Although there can be slight deviations from full-employment equilibrium, they are soon corrected by the market forces, and full-employment equilibrium is restored. Some exponents of this theory, however, concede that in the economy there is an "unexplained residue" of facts that their discipline does not analyze satisfactorily. Lionel Robbins, a renowned orthodox economist of the time, wrote:

> The best example of the unexplained residue is provided by ...
> the trade cycle. Pure equilibrium theory ... does not provide any
> explanation of the phenomena of booms and slumps. ... It
> explains fluctuations which are in the nature of orderly adaptations. But it does not explain the existence within the economic
> system of tendencies conducive to disproportionate development. It does not explain discrepancies between total supply
> and total demand in the sense in which these terms are used in
> the celebrated law of markets [of J.B. Say]. Yet unquestionably
> such discrepancies exist, and any attempt to interpret reality
> solely in terms of such a theory must necessarily leave a residue
> of phenomena not capable of being subsumed under its generalizations. (Quoted in Strachey 1935: 16)

The *pure* equilibrium theory of orthodox economics assumes that in a well-functioning market economy wages and prices are flexible. Orthodox economists believe(d) that also in the real-life economy wages and prices are normally flexible *enough* to justify finding this equilibrium theory tenable. According to Professor Pigou, a leading exponent of orthodox economics at the time, this assumption also agreed with the reality in the period up to the beginning of World War I. In those days, unemployment was very low, except during cyclical downturns (see Dillard 1972: 23). So if sometime, for whatever reason, aggregate demand declines, companies will, of course, not be able to sell as much as before and they must then reduce production and investment, leading to a fall in aggregate income of society. But this adjustment will last for only a short time. As a consequence of the drop in aggregate demand, first the prices of goods and services fall and then, as a consequence of the fall in production, the demand for labor falls, which leads to a fall in wages. If both wages and prices of consumer goods fall evenly, the majority of consumers can buy again as many goods and services as they did before, in spite of the drop in their income. After the stock of goods has been sold out, entrepreneurs can again produce as much and employ as many workers as they did before. Full-employment equilibrium will then be restored. What will remain from the effects of the original disruption are low prices and low wages. From this line of thought, orthodox economists conclude that in a well-functioning capitalist market economy there can be no *involuntary* unemployment, and that, in terms of production capacity and labor force, such an economy should practically almost always be at full employment.

The Great Depression shook this belief. Orthodox economics had been able to survive all earlier crises. For, firstly, after each recession or depression there had always been, sooner or later, again an upturn. Secondly, there was no other *bourgeois* theory that could explain the crisis phenomena better (see the Robbins quote above). And thirdly, as a simple explanation for the serious disruptions in the equilibrium, orthodox economists could always fall back on the shallow argument that the market could not function well because of the imperfections and rigidity of the real economy, for instance monopolies (especially the trade unions) and state interventions. Thus, in 1933, when in the United States unemployment reached 25 percent, Pigou wrote in his book *The Theory of Unemployment*: "With perfectly free competition there will always be a strong tendency toward full employment. Such unemployment as exists at any time is due wholly to the frictional resistances [that] prevent the appropriate wage and price adjustments being made instantly" (in Samuelson and Nordhaus 1998: 694). Orthodox economics was simply unable to explain the unusual depth and duration of the Great Depression. It was bankrupt.

### b) *The Non-Marxist Crisis Management*

While bourgeois politicians tried to save capitalism by way of practical policies, the system needed to be saved in theory as well. For, as we have seen in chapter I, the question of whether capitalism is at all viable in the long run had already been posed since Marx's time. Bourgeois economics and its beliefs desperately needed a new theoretical ground.

One proposal of such a theoretical ground already existed. Joseph Alois Schumpeter, whose main work *The Theory of Economic Development* had been published in 1912, but whose role as a theoretical savior of capitalism could not be recognized earlier, had presented the brilliant thesis that, in capitalism, depressions — far from being regrettable and inscrutable tragic accidents — are exceedingly necessary elements of the economic *development* process. What takes place in depressions is "creative destruction," without which a capitalist economy could not develop.

In 1936 came another proposal. In his main work, *The General Theory of Employment, Interest, and Money*, John Maynard Keynes declared depressions to be a totally unnecessary and easily avoidable suffering. The timing could not have been better. It not only became a bestseller among economists, but it also started a revolution in economic theory. Because of its chronological closeness and direct reference to the Great Depression, I shall present the Keynesian crisis theory first. A presentation of Schumpeter's crisis theory follows in the subsequent section. But first I must tell the story of the attempts to manage the great crisis undertaken by some bourgeois politicians before 1936, some of which (as we shall see below) were Keynesian in content.

In 1932, Franklin D. Roosevelt, the presidential candidate of the Democratic Party, promised the American people a "New Deal" for the "forgotten man." Soon after taking office in early 1933, he started working towards overcoming the Great Depression and its devastating effects. He took a series of measures that implemented the idea of an economy regulated by the state.

He set up authorities that created jobs by commissioning construction of office buildings, bridges, and other elements for infrastructure. They distributed emergency assistance, short-term grants, and temporary jobs; they organized youth work in national parks, etc. The biggest job-creating measure in this program was the dam project in the Tennessee River Valley. In addition to such measures, in 1935 and 1939, social security bills were passed that provided modest old-age and widow pensions, unemployment benefits, and disability insurance.

The Roosevelt administration also took measures that enabled the state to regulate the economy (which however no Keynesian would recommend). In order to stop the devastating drop in prices caused by the Great Depression, companies were allowed to fix prices in agreement with one another (thus creating cartels). The government believed that if the dramatic drop in prices could be stopped, then the downward wage-price spiral could also be stopped; and this, in turn, could jump-start the recovery. At the same time, the administration made founding workers' unions easier.

In order to help the farmers, the government tried to lift the prices of agricultural products by controlling production levels and giving subsidies and price guarantees. A system of deposit insurance was created in order to protect savers from losing their money when banks go bankrupt. A commission was set up to protect shareholders from fraudulent stock market practices. Furthermore, a large number of industries were regulated. Authorities fixed prices, set security standards, etc.

It is clear that this wave of regulations also meant an attack on orthodox, conservative economic policy. The old dogma, that the best government was the one that governed the least, was no longer valid. Even the sacred principle of competition in a free market was being undermined. And the confidence in the self-healing power of a capitalist economy no longer existed.

Orthodox economists and the conservative political opposition bitterly fought against the New Deal. Since the criterion for success of the job-creation measures was, above all, the number of jobs created, and not what and how much was being built at what cost, they were denounced as a pure waste of money. Even the more modest social security measures were ferociously attacked. A conservative congressman said: "Never in the history of the world has any measure been brought in here so insidiously designed as to prevent business recovery, to enslave workers, and to prevent any possibility of the employers providing work for the people." Another politician said on a more dramatic note: "The lash of the dictator will be felt" (both quoted in Galbraith 1994: 94). Generally speaking, the New Deal as a whole was depicted by its opponents as a socialist program, which in the United States of that time amounted to slander. Roosevelt was branded "a traitor to his class" (quoted in Hardach 1976: 68). Those whose business was adversely affected by these measures went to court. Some New Deal laws were declared unconstitutional by the Supreme Court; others were enforced.

In Germany, the Nazi regime took resolute and authoritarian measures to overcome the crisis. It pursued policies strongly directed towards job creation, which comprised public works or subsidized construction projects such as construction of canals, railroads, public buildings, housing colonies, highways, etc. Later, rearmament served the same purpose. Mandatory, unpaid labor service, compulsory military service, propaganda against women going to work, statutory preference for manual work and part-time jobs, expansion of state and party bureaucracy — all this brought relief to the labor market and created jobs.

These measures were financed by borrowing money. Long-term bonds were sold to insurance companies and savings banks. Since this was in the end financed through a decline in consumption by savers and insurance takers, inflation was no real threat. The inflation of the previous years had almost eliminated the public debt.

These policies and measures were very successful, and by 1936 a sort of full employment was achieved. But this kind of success was attained by annulling to a large extent the rules of a market economy. Private ownership of means of production was left untouched, but almost the whole economy was controlled by the state. Consumption, investments, and the labor market — everything was steered by the state. It was, so to speak, a "command capitalism" (facts on Germany from Hardach 1976: 68ff.).

Less known but much more successful were Japan's efforts to overcome the crisis. Its recipe was a combination of monetary, fiscal, and currency (exchange rate) policy. However, the main means was expansion of state spending (a large portion of which was military spending), which grew at a yearly rate of 20 percent between 1932 and 1934. The share of public spending in the net domestic product rose from 31 to 38 percent. By devaluing their currency yen, the Japanese were also able to substantially increase their exports. In this way, Japan reached full employment by mid-1938 (see Kindleberger 1973: 166f., 284).

### c) *The Keynesian Revolution*

The idea of promoting public works in times of excessive unemployment was by no means new, nor was the Keynesian strategy of saving less and consuming more (see Higgins 1965: 468f.). Lawrence R. Klein (1949: 31) noted: "It was not his theory which led him [Keynes] to practical policies, but practical policies devised to cure honest-to-goodness economic ills which finally led him to his theory." Keynes's great achievement in his *General Theory* was actually to provide a more detailed and convincing substantiation of this practical economic policy.

A basic assumption of the orthodox theory, namely, of a capitalist market economy with "perfectly free competition" (Pigou, see quote above), was totally unrealistic. Because of trade union activities there was no free competition in the labor market. Wages were not so flexible; they could not be reduced at will every time a recession set in. Nor were prices in reality as flexible as the orthodox economists assumed them to be. According to Keynes, and as one could observe, prices were very "sticky," i.e., they adjusted rather slowly. The economy reacts to changes in aggregate demand with adjustments in quantity rather than with adjustments in prices. For entrepreneurs can themselves decide how much to produce, while prices are determined by market forces. But even if wages and prices were totally flexible, there would still be, according to Keynesian theory, the possibility of involuntary mass unemployment.

Another basic assumption of orthodox theory, which led to the conclusion that there can be no involuntary unemployment in a capitalist market economy, was Say's Law of Markets, also known as Say's Theorem. This law assumes that

> [n]o man produces but with a view to consume or sell, and he never sells but with an intention to purchase some other commodity which may be useful to him, or which may contribute to future production. . . . Productions are always bought by productions, or by services; money is only the medium by which the exchange is effected. (J.B. Say, quoted in Haberler 1965: 173)

The law says, in other words, in an economy in which goods and services are produced in order to be sold, every supply of a product involves the demand for another one. This also says that additional supply creates additional demand. Therefore, normally, if the market is considered as a whole, whatever is produced can also be sold. Of course, it can also happen that a producer cannot sell a newly produced commodity or cannot sell it at a profit, or that he has produced too many pieces of a particular good and is not able to sell them all at a profit. But this mistake is soon corrected. The producer changes his program to goods and quantities that he can sell at a profit. So, according to Say, there can be no overproduction crisis in the economy. It is profitable to increase production up to the point where all available production capacities, including resources and labor, are fully used (i.e., until full employment is attained). There is only one condition for this, namely, that suppliers do not demand a price for a commodity above that justified by productivity.

Up to this point, the line of reasoning of Say's law sounds as though one is talking about what happens in a barter economy. Say himself assumed that the seller of a product was keen to spend the proceeds immediately, "for the value of the money is also perishable" (quoted in Haberler 1965: 174n). But, naturally, the proponents of his theorem knew that in a monetary economy a supplier might not spend the sales proceeds on the purchase of other goods right away, that he might save part of the proceeds in order to spend it later on. One might think that when workers and other non-entrepreneurs save, they cause an imbalance to arise between supply and demand (when entrepreneurs save, they normally buy investment goods for future production), and thus Say's law is refuted. But it is not. Orthodox economists also assumed that the saved money was always borrowed by entrepreneurs and spent for investments (in the real world also common people borrow money for consumption), so that the demand for investment goods always offset the deficit in demand for consumer goods. In their opinion, just as in the case of goods, the assumed flexibility of prices guaranteed equilibrium between supply and demand, so the flexibility of interest rates ensured equilibrium between savings and investments. Low interest rates motivated borrowers to borrow more and, at the same time, dampened the motivation of savers to save. The opposite happened with high interest rates. It was thought that there would always be an interest rate level at which all savings would also be borrowed. This thesis, namely, that all savings would sooner or later be invested, was based on the assumption that there could never be a shortage of profitable investment opportunities.

In contrast to the thesis that full employment is the normal state in a market economy, Keynesian theory holds fluctuating employment levels (also fluctuating levels of use of other means of production) to be the normal state. In the economy there can be full employment for some time, but there can also be underemployment and massive unemployment. Typical of a "mature" (i.e., highly developed) capitalist industrial economy is a level well under full employment. "Indeed it seems capable of remaining in a chronic condition of sub-normal activity for a considerable period without any marked tendency either towards recovery or towards complete collapse" (Keynes 1973: 249). Keynes regarded full employment, the assumed normality of which constituted a foundation of orthodox economics, as a rare special case.

Critics of Keynesian economics have often expressed the view that it is only a special theory, not a general one, and that it is an economics of depression. Of course, Keynes mostly dealt with the situation of an economy in depression. But his followers have demonstrated that his analytical model can provide convincing explanations for all phases of the business cycle, and also for inflation (see Klein 1949: chapter 6).

In the nineteenth century, most of the basic assumptions of orthodox economics largely agreed with economic reality. The multitude of small businesses and the nearly perfect competition in a relatively free market guaranteed the flexibility of prices. There were no trade unions, or they were still rather weak, and the population grew rapidly. So there really was competition in the labor market. Moreover, thanks to the territorial expansion achieved by colonialism and imperialism, there were enough investment opportunities for newly accumulated capital. Orthodox economic theory was, therefore, *at the time*, not totally unrealistic. Nevertheless, the long depression of 1873–1896 came about. By the 1930s, however, this time was long gone. Monopolies, cartels, and trade unions had in the meantime emerged and grown strong. Price and wage flexibility was no longer as great as in the nineteenth century. But orthodox theory lived on, until it experienced its big crisis in the 1930s. The Keynesian revolution freed economics from its ivory tower and freed politics from the fetters of laissez-faire ideology.

### THE ORTHODOX AND THE KEYNESIAN EXPLANATION OF BUSINESS CYCLES

The main objective of *The General Theory* was to explain how employment levels were determined. Keynes wrote only some "notes" to explain the business cycle (in chapter 22). But from these notes a Keynesian theory of business cycles could be easily derived. It differs significantly from the pre-Keynesian theories.

The relatively convincing theories among the pre-Keynesian ones are, of course, based on the assumptions of Say's theorem. Once a deviation from the normal state (full-employment equilibrium) has taken place, irrespective of the direction, it is aggravated over a certain period of time due to the multiplier effect.[4] An initial rise in production creates new income, which — according to Say's theorem — is entirely spent. This creates an optimistic atmosphere and motivates entrepreneurs to increase production even more. As they expect demand to grow in the near future, they feverishly invest in capital goods, particularly during the later phase of the upturn. Something similar happens also in the case of a deviation in the opposite direction, i.e., in the downturn. An initial drop in production diminishes income, which causes the aggregate demand to drop and a pessimistic atmosphere to spread. Particularly the demand for capital goods then declines drastically. This movement too intensifies until it reaches the cycle's lowest point. One of the basic assumptions of the orthodox economists was that the prices follow such movements of aggregate demand.

But how are the all-important turning points of the business cycle to be explained? Pre-Keynesians and Keynesians have different answers to this question.

Pre-Keynesians imagined limits which the upturn or the downturn could reach, or they found external factors which could stop an otherwise accelerating movement. One such limit, according to them, was the lending capacity of the banking system. In the course of the boom, lending reaches an excessively high level, and bank reserves fall to a precariously low level, for which bankers cannot accept responsibility. Moreover, for the rising level of business transactions, the economy needs a rising level of liquid funds, which adds to the strain on bank reserves. At this point, banks are no longer willing to lend more; the interest rates go up. As a result of all that the credit volume shrinks. This brings about a decline in aggregate demand, which triggers the cumulative process of the downward movement. Pre-Keynesians also referred to the possibility of a sudden shortage of one or more of the production factors — e.g., labor or a raw material — that significantly slows down production in a branch of the economy, which then has a stronger negative impact on the whole economy.

An explanation for the turning point at the lower end of the cycle, i.e., after a recession, is as follows: after some time, part of the equipment is worn out; then new equipment is ordered, and this brings about an upturn. (It has not been explained why part of the equipment in a large number of companies should wear out at around the same time, when it is actually a continuous process.) Another explanation sees the origin of the turnaround in the increasing lending capacity of the banks. Both contribute to the other cause of the turnaround, namely, return of business confidence, which enhances the willingness to invest.

In the Keynesian explanation, objective upper and lower limits or external factors play a secondary role at best. The turning points come long before the limits suspected by the pre-Keynesian can come into play. (The following presentation of the Keynesian business cycle theory is based on Metzler 1965 and Dillard 1972.)

Keynes rejected Say's Law. He did not believe that aggregate demand rose automatically with aggregate supply. And when it did, Keynes did not think it rose to the same extent as the latter; he saw aggregate demand as determined by other factors. Here it is necessary first to get acquainted with the Keynesian employment theory.

According to Keynes, in the short term, the supply side of the whole economic process is relatively stable. Producers are always willing and able to supply the demanded quantities of goods and services at remunerative prices. And their understanding of what a remunerative price is for a certain production level is also relatively stable, because that depends on the physical conditions of production and on the state of technology. In scientific jargon one says: in the short term, the supply curve is given. Therefore, current production volume and employment level are determined by the current aggregate demand, which is not given. When this fluctuates, then production and employment volume also fluctuate, and so does the aggregate income with them.

However, the movements of demand for *consumer* goods are relatively predictable. For it is based on custom (habits), income distribution in society, and the tax system — that is, on already established factors, which are difficult to change. That means that demand for consumer goods varies with changes in aggregate income in a regular manner. In scientific jargon one says: the consumption curve is relatively stable. Keynes introduces at this point a new analytical tool, namely, the "propensity to consume." It is the ratio between aggregate income and aggregate consumption. Keynes postulated — and he claimed to have found evidence for this in empirical research — that although aggregate consumption increases with increasing aggregate income, it does not increase to the same extent as the latter. Furthermore, the gap between aggregate income and aggregate consumption widens with increasing aggregate income, because rich households spend a progressively decreasing portion of their increasing income for consumption. This means that the upturn cannot become a self-reinforcing cumulative process if this ever-widening gap is not filled with ever-increasing investment spending (the other component of aggregate demand) on the part of entrepreneurs.

The demand for investment goods, however, is not predictable. It can violently fluctuate, as it is determined by uncertain expectations, irrational fears, and dubious assessments of future prospects — in other words, by such psychological factors as optimism and pessimism. That is why fluctuations in the employment level depend mainly on fluctuations in the volume of investment. Keynes here introduces another analytical tool: the "marginal efficiency of capital," which is nothing other than the expected profit rate on new investment. The key to understanding business cycles is, therefore, the unstable nature of the marginal efficiency of capital. To this instability is added financial and stock market speculation.

At this point one could ask why it should be impossible to keep filling the gap between aggregate income and aggregate consumption with increasing investment spending. The answer is as follows: when the gap becomes ever wider, it dampens the profit expectations of businesspeople. They can no longer hope to continue to make enough profit by investing further. In the final analysis, all investment is made, directly or indirectly, to produce consumer goods (and consumer services). Additional amounts of the latter, however, result in tougher competition in the market. Then suddenly the marginal efficiency of capital collapses, and a situation arises in which it is lower than the rate of interest. At this point, it is no longer profitable to invest in means of production. The boom collapses, and the downturn sets in.

According to Keynes, the Great Depression, too, began in this way. The demand originating from investments collapsed, and, through the multiplier effect, this brought about the rapid decline in income and demand for consumer goods. All of this together caused the downward spiral in the economy.

Keynes of course conceded that rising interest rates resulting from the rising unwillingness of banks to give new credit could play a role in the end of a boom—worsening it, sometimes even initiating it. But he asserted that the main cause of the downturn was, as a rule, a sudden collapse of the marginal efficiency of capital. If the latter collapsed *suddenly*, then the interest rate could not fall fast enough to reverse the change in mood. The interest rate was not as flexible as the orthodox school deemed it to be. Rather, it was sticky, and it tended to remain high. Once set into motion, the downturn continued following the pattern described above.

There is also a Keynesian explanation for the recovery from a depression. When aggregate income sinks during a downturn, aggregate consumption spending also sinks, but it does not sink to the same extent as the aggregate income. At the beginning of the downturn, the warehouses of the wholesalers are overstocked. They want to and have to considerably reduce their inventories. As at the lower stages of the downturn the drop in consumption is not as strong as at the upper stages — after a certain degree of drop it cannot drop any further — a point comes at which the inventories are again normal in relation to sales. Wholesalers' orders to manufacturers stabilize. Then also the marginal efficiency of capital stabilizes. The downturn eases. In the meantime, the interest rates have fallen somewhat, and the marginal efficiency of capital improves, so that it now lies above the interest rates. The capacity and willingness of banks to give more credit are restored, although this does not play a decisive role. Slowly the recovery gains traction.

The Keynesian theory of business cycles can also be presented with the help of another analytical tool: the propensity to save. The propensity to consume and the propensity to save are two sides of the same coin. Whatever is not spent on consumption is saved. When consumption is low, savings are high and vice versa. The former is stable, and so is the latter.

However, when one tries to understand the business cycle with the help of the propensity to save, one finds that Keynes created a lot of confusion in this matter. In *The General Theory* (1973: 63) he wrote: savings and investments "are necessarily" (i.e., always) equal. But if that were so, there could not be any business cycle. Something like that is what the orthodox economists also believed! Keynes's followers later disentangled the confusion (see Lerner 1965 and Dillard 1972: chapter 4). This assertion of

Keynes can be paraphrased as follows: It can sometimes be that the people *want to* save more than before. They consume less, save more, take their savings to the bank, and buy with that money fixed-interest securities thinking they are investing the money. Entrepreneurs, however, had not planned to invest more; and they are now even less inclined to do so, as they observe that, lately, people have been saving more. What is worse, since now the people are consuming less, demand drops, and the marginal efficiency of capital falls. Now entrepreneurs invest less than before, and less than they had planned for. They employ fewer workers, and the aggregate income of the people falls. But since consumption cannot drop proportionally, people now save less. Soon aggregate savings reach the same level as aggregate investments. In other words, there is again overall economic equilibrium, but at a level below full employment. This means that savings are in this way *brought* to a level equal to that of investments.

The fact that the aggregate income of a people drops when they save more than they usually do, and that they thus become poorer, is an instructive paradox, called in Keynesian jargon "the paradox of thrift."

Once the people save less than the planned investments of entrepreneurs, demand for consumer goods rises. Entrepreneurs then increase their investments (with the commercial banks creating the necessary credit by borrowing from the central bank). Employment rises, and aggregate income rises too. But since consumption does not increase proportionally, savings increase and soon equal investments.

If one carefully reads Keynes, one actually finds that he himself intimated this elucidation. He wrote: "The equivalence between the quantity of saving and the quantity of investment emerges ... " (Keynes 1973: 63). The equivalence *emerges*, it is not always there. The difference in this regard between orthodox theory and Keynesian theory lies in the factor that brings about equalization. For orthodox economists it is the fluctuating interest rate; for Keynes it is the fluctuating aggregate income.

The most important point in the Keynesian explanation of business cycles is the notion that the boom can end before the economy reaches full employment. According to Keynes, the system can be in equilibrium at different employment levels. This means the economy can for a long time be in equilibrium well under the full employment level. This was precisely the situation in most of the industrialized countries, especially in the United States, in the 1930s after the worst was over and the Great Depression had given way to a modest recovery.

Another important point is the view that in recessions and depressions lowering the interest rate alone is not sufficient as a counteracting measure and that, generally speaking, monetary policy is — except in the case of inflation — not a good stabilizer. In order that the all-important marginal efficiency of capital rises, there must be primarily good prospects of an increase in aggregate demand.

### SECULAR STAGNATION

Most interesting for our question put at the beginning of the book is a train of thought in Keynesianism that says that a state of secular (long-term) stagnation could become a characteristic feature of "mature" capitalist market economies. We have seen above that Keynes spoke of the possibility of "a chronic condition of sub-normal activity for a considerable period" in mature capitalist economies (Keynes 1973: 249).

He thought that capital assets could cease to be scarce within one or two generations (see Dillard 1972: 154), and that simultaneously profitable investment opportunities would gradually decrease. However, he did not make a dogmatic prognosis in this respect.

Concerning the duration of a recession, he argued that the recovery could not begin until the marginal efficiency of capital improved, and that this could not happen until the stock of capital was reduced through amortization (see Metzler 1965: 448). That means, costs and useful life of equipment play an important part in this matter. Equipment with a long useful life is a disadvantage for the process of overall economic recovery.

However, the marginal efficiency of capital may not improve at all if no new profitable investment opportunities are available. The former can even worsen in the long run if the latter decrease. Keynes thought exactly this could happen in mature capitalist market economies, even if all kinds of short-term measures were taken to stimulate the economy.

The reason why the economy developed so rapidly in the nineteenth century — in spite of some recessions and depressions — was for Keynes "the growth of population and of invention, the opening-up of new lands, the state of confidence and the frequency of war over the average" (Keynes 1973: 307). Especially epochal inventions such as the steam engine, the railroad, electricity, and the automobile — which created opportunities for large investments — were, against the background of the other factors mentioned here by Keynes, very profitable. Territorial expansions in America, Asia, and Africa (particularly in the United States) led to opening up of new lands for investments, and population growth taking place all around the world created a market for the products of new investments. Together with the high propensity to consume, these factors were enough to maintain the willingness of the wealthy to invest. In the period between the end of World War I and the beginning of World War II, however, these external factors were missing, and the technological developments of this period were rather of the capital-saving type (see Dillard 1972: 155),[5] which meant that the demand for investment goods was low.

In addition to this, with growing national wealth the gap between aggregate income and aggregate consumption becomes larger. Keynes thought the typical quantities of real investment were not sufficient to fill this gap. The reason for this is very simple: Every additional investment brings additional products onto the market, and these products compete with those of the already existing capital. This reinforces the trend towards low prices, which pushes the return expectations on additional invest-ments (i.e., the marginal efficiency of capital) downwards. It is of course possible that in the long run, with increasing savings, interest rates for loans to entrepreneurs will have a downward trend, which will result in decreasing production costs. But even then, the expected marginal revenue would not exceed the marginal production costs; in other words, the mar-ginal efficiency of capital would be negative. But the process of *real* capital accumulation can go on for only as long as the marginal efficiency of capi-tal is higher than the interest rate.

In 1930 Keynes wrote:

> Great Britain is an old country. ... The population will soon
> cease to grow. Our habits and institutions keep us ... a thrifty
> people, saving some 10 percent of our income. In such condi-
> tions one would anticipate ... that, if Great Britain were a closed
> system, the natural rate of interest would fall rapidly. In the rest
> of the world, however (though the United States may find
> herself in the same position as Great Britain much sooner than
> she expects), the fall in the rate of interest is likely to be much
> slower. Equilibrium under laissez faire will, therefore, require
> that a large and increasing proportion of our savings must find
> its outlet in foreign investment. (Quoted in Sweezy 1965: 428)

Later he wrote: "Today and presumably for the future ... the marginal effi-ciency of capital is ... much lower than it was in the nineteenth century" (425). Keynes commented:

> This analysis supplies us with an explanation of the paradox of
> poverty in the midst of plenty. For the mere existence of an
> insufficiency of effective demand may, and often will, bring the
> increase of employment to a standstill *before* a level of full
> employment has been reached. ...

> Moreover the richer the community, the wider will tend to
> be the gap between its actual and its potential production; and
> therefore the more obvious and outrageous the defects of the
> economic system. (Keynes 1973: 30f.)

This was, however, not a very new idea. Some of his predecessors —
Adam Smith, David Ricardo, Karl Marx, and John Stuart Mill — believed,
for different reasons, in the tendency of the rate of profit to fall. Keynes
only gave this thesis a new technical name: the tendency of the marginal
efficiency of capital to fall (see Dillard 1972: 153). We already know Marx's
explanation for this phenomenon. For Ricardo and Mill the explanation
is the niggardliness of nature, in the sense that we must get food for a
growing human population from soil with progressively diminishing productivity. For Keynes, as for Adam Smith, it is the increasing stock of capital — an explanation that bears a certain resemblance to that of Marx. Also
Keynes's thesis of insufficiency of effective demand is similar to Marx's
under-consumption theory. (This presentation of the theory of secular
stagnation is mostly based on Sweezy 1965 and Dillard 1972.)

Alvin Hansen, who had accepted Keynes's new theory, thought it necessary to correct Keynes on one point. In his analysis of empirical data he
did not find any evidence for Keynes's claim that the share of consumption
in national income diminishes with the growth of prosperity of a society.
Secular stagnation cannot therefore be explained through a falling propensity to consume. The explanation lies rather in the other factors (see
Deutschmann 1973: 53ff.).

A phenomenon that refuted the Keynesian thesis of secular stagnation,
namely, the twenty-five-year-long economic boom after World War II,
which had only brief interruptions, was ascribed by many observers precisely to the application of Keynesian economic policies. However, when
this long era came to an end and the phenomenon of stagflation (the
simultaneous occurrence of stagnation and inflation), unknown to that
date, emerged, economists were puzzled. Many blamed Keynesianism for
the misery, and all politicians abandoned it. But in the beginning of the
twenty-first century a large part of the highly developed capitalist world
again suffered from a relatively long stagnation. In its monthly report of
July 2003, the German Bundesbank (central bank) expected "sustained
stagnation" and could not predict any improvement in the near future
(*Frankfurter Rundschau*, 22 July 2003). Many people asked themselves:
Was Keynes right after all with his careful prediction? We will deal with
this issue in the later chapters.

## KEYNESIAN ECONOMIC POLICY

The foregoing exposition indicates that Keynes had great doubts about capitalism's ability to heal crises by itself. Evidently, he also had doubts about the system's long-term ability to survive. Hence, he thought capitalism needed to be helped.

Until 1930, Keynes recommended mainly monetary measures to overcome the depression. But gradually he started having doubts about the effectiveness of applying monetary policies only. In 1931, he recommended that the state should carry out investments in housing, city redevelopment, modernization of the main industries, etc., and subsidize the electrification of the railroads. He also suggested the state itself should carry out domestic investments for building up capital, and incur debts in order to do so. He called such debts "nature's remedy ... for ... a slump," and he argued that they were better than debts "for the purpose of paying doles" (quoted in Higgins 1965: 471). He also denounced the British government's austerity program as wrong and stupid.

Three strategic variables emerge from the Keynesian problem analysis in *The General Theory*: the interest rates, the marginal efficiency of capital, and the propensity to consume. Keynes defined the task thus: "Our final task might be to select those variables which can be deliberately controlled or managed by central authority in the kind of system in which we actually live" (Keynes 1973: 247). Three main categories of possible political recommendations result from this: (1) The interest rates should be kept low by a strong monetary authority (cheap money policy), in order to create incentives for private investments. (2) Such incentives are generally insufficient. When a boom has collapsed, profit expectations of entrepreneurs can be lower than the lowest possible interest rates. That is why such incentives must be complemented by public investment expenditures; Keynes actually demanded that the state control/direct overall investment — including private investments. This is perhaps what he meant when he spoke of a "somewhat comprehensive socialization of investment" (378). (3) A progressive tax system should be set up. In order to counteract the low propensity to consume, it should tax the portion of income that is normally saved more heavily than the portion that is normally spent.

Of course, theoretically, the gap between aggregate income and aggregate spending could be filled by just reducing the tax burden on the lower income groups, who spend most of their income on consumption, and increasing it on the higher-income groups, who save most of their income. But Keynes thought that in developed capitalist societies, with their characteristic large income gaps, the propensity to save is so high that it is very difficult to raise the propensity to consume to a sufficient extent. The task must then be performed mainly by increasing public spending.

In Keynesian economic policy it is particularly underscored that the state should, as a measure to fight depressions, spend money on *investments*, and not on producing consumer goods. The merit of investment spending lies in the fact that in this way income is created, which in turn creates demand for consumer goods, whereas, if the opposite is done, immediately more consumer goods will come to the market and seek buyers who are simply not there.

But how is higher public investment spending to be financed? According to Keynesians, through budget deficits, no doubt. If such spending is to counteract a depression, it must be new spending. If the government tries to finance such spending through tax revenues, the undertaking would probably defeat its purpose. For in that case, most probably, a large portion of the money that would otherwise have been spent in the private sector would now be spent in the public sector. That does not result in any increase in aggregate demand. Now, one could suggest or even demand, as many leftists do, that only the rich and upper-middle-class people, who do not consume away all of their excess income, should be asked to pay higher taxes. But, firstly, in the case of such intentions there are always *political* limits to state power, and, secondly, there are also economic limits to it. The additional sums that could be raised by such means without damaging the economy — e.g., by provoking flight of capital, flight to tax havens, and tax evasion, or by causing a fall in motivation to perform — would not be sufficient for the purpose. If, instead, the state borrows money for the purpose, additional demand is generated.

The argumentation in favor of financing public investment spending through budget deficits has a second thread: any attempt to boost consumer demand through a *general* tax cut can have the desired effect only if the usual state expenditures are not reduced at the same time. This, however, is only possible if the resulting deficit in the budget is financed through new loans. To grant tax cuts to citizens and to keep the budget balanced by means of austerity measures is, according to Keynesians, counterproductive. Such a policy actually leads to a drop in aggregate demand. For the people's relatively stable propensity to consume ensures that not all the additional money in their pockets is spent. As evidence of the counterproductive effects of this policy, present-day Keynesians point to the economic stagnation in Germany during the coalition government of Social Democrats and the Greens in the years 1998–2003. Instead, they advocate a combination of tax cuts for the lower income groups and an increase in state expenditures financed through budget deficits (see Stiglitz 2006).

Orthodox economists have criticized this policy in the name of solid state finances. To that Keynesians reply that orthodox economists cannot differentiate between a private household or a company on the one hand, and a national economy on the other. They say that with productive resources lying idle, it is in any case useful for the national economy to employ an unemployed person, who is presently producing nothing, as long as she can produce something. Any production of this kind is a 100 percent contribution to the growth of national income, while *for society* the marginal costs of employing an unemployed person are nil or close to nil. As Keynes said in 1933, 100,000 new apartments are a national asset and 1,000,000 unemployed persons a national liability. The danger of the state going bankrupt, orthodox economists' main fear, does not exist in the eyes of Keynesians *as long as the state borrows money from its own citizens*. Unlike private households or companies, a national economy cannot spend more than it earns (not considering debts run up abroad). National debts within the country can always be serviced, since the state, which borrows money in the interest of all citizens, can, if necessary, collect higher taxes from its citizens for servicing the debts.

Many conservatives think that the national income is maximized when the profits of companies are maximized. One need only think of the American saying: What is good for General Motors is good for America. Keynesians, though, do not agree. Company profits are only a relatively small part of the national income. Only the latter is the key criterion for national welfare.

Conservatives, who, as everybody knows, do not like the state to be economically active, can say that weakness in consumer demand can also be counteracted by social security spending. In practical politics, Keynesians, of course, object to cuts in social security payments, but they do not demand their increase either. Such expenditures are merely transfer payments; they do not create any new job, nor new income. It is therefore obvious that investment spending is preferable.

In a polemical note Keynes even argued in favor of wasteful construction projects for combating unemployment. He wrote:

> In so far as millionaires find their satisfaction in building
> mighty mansions to contain their bodies when alive and
> pyramids to shelter them after death, or, repenting of their sins,
> erect cathedrals and endow monasteries or foreign missions,
> the day when abundance of capital will interfere with

abundance of output may be postponed. "To dig holes in the ground," paid for out of savings, will increase, not only employment, but the real national dividend of useful goods and services. (Keynes 1973: 220)

In another passage he wrote:

[T]he above reasoning shows how "wasteful" loan expenditure may nevertheless enrich the community on balance. Pyramid-building, earthquakes, even wars may serve to increase wealth, if the education of our statesmen on the principles of the classical economics stands in the way of anything better. (128f.)

But, Keynes also wrote: "It is not reasonable, however, that a sensible community should be content to remain dependent on such fortuitous and often wasteful mitigations when once we understand the influences upon which effective demand depends" (220).

Finally, Keynesians see their fiscal policy as compensatory fiscal policy. While they advocate budget deficits as a means of counteracting depressions, they call for a balanced budget or even budget surpluses during a boom. When the boom goes beyond full employment and the inflation rate rises, the state should increase the tax rates — not only to curb inflation but also to utilize the opportunity to reduce the accumulated national debt. But Keynesians regard monetary policy as a more suitable tool than tax increases, if the purpose is only to curb inflation.

### d) *Keynes versus Marx*

For those who nowadays might generally be called social democrats, Keynes was the ideal political economist; for many, he still is. Somewhere in their program they might still have had a declaration saying they intended to abolish capitalism and build a socialist society. But in reality they had long lost the courage to make a revolution, or they regarded their declared goal as practically unattainable. So they dropped Marx and became reformers of capitalism and followers of Keynes, whose theory and policy recommendations promised to make capitalism crisis-free and a little more just. Keynesianism was a good alternative to Marxism.

Many conservatives, however, believed Keynes was a socialist. This was a misunderstanding, but there were grounds for this belief. For example, Keynes advocated a "socially controlled rate of investment" (Keynes 1973: 325). And demand management was, in any case, the most important part of his policy recommendations. He had never wholeheartedly accepted capitalism. He thought that capitalism "in itself is in many ways extremely objectionable" (quoted in Dillard 1972: 300). But he still supported this system. He regarded "the enlargement of the functions of government ... as the only practicable means of avoiding the destruction of existing economic forms in their entirety and as the condition of the successful functioning of individual initiative" (Keynes 1973: 380).

He also believed that "capitalism, wisely managed, can probably be made more efficient than any alternative system" (quoted in Dillard 1972: 300). This belief constituted the basis of his whole involvement in practical economic policies. The fact that he supported public works and state regulation of the economy "was in no sense intended to be an entering wedge for socialism. On the contrary, public works as well as monetary control were part of the liberal program [of Keynes] for avoiding socialism" (310).

Keynes did not think much of Marxism. He wondered "how a doctrine so illogical and so dull can have exercised so powerful and enduring an influence over the minds of men, and, through them, the events of history." He wrote further, "How can I accept a doctrine which sets up as its bible, above and beyond criticism, an obsolete economic textbook which I know to be not only scientifically erroneous but without interest or application for the modern world?" (both quotes in Dillard 1972: 322).

Nevertheless, in respect of analysis, there is some common ground between the two thinkers. Keynes's secular stagnation because of secularly low marginal efficiency of capital is comparable to Marx's law of the tendency of the rate of profit to fall. The Keynesian notion of weakness of the propensity to consume in mature economies is comparable to the Marxian notion of under-consumption. In regard to this last point of similarity, both thought that inequality in distribution represented a major problem for capitalism. But whereas Marx considered this problem to be an unsolvable inner contradiction of the system and, hence, strove for a revolution, Keynes believed it could be defused by means of the new economic policies he recommended. He regarded greater equality of income as an important condition for progress. Paul Mattick, who found the conclusions of Marx and Keynes "quite similar," referred to "inconsistent socialists" who "attempted to blend Marx with Keynes, accepting Keynes's theories as the 'Marxism' of our time" (Mattick 1971: 2, 21).

Keynes rejected class conflict as a category of politics. But if it should come to a conflict, he wrote, "the *class* war will find me on the side of the educated bourgeoisie" (quoted in Dillard 1972: 319). The relationship between him and the working class was clearly not a friendly one. His policy recommendations for overcoming unemployment were, of course, received by the working class with enthusiasm, but not his ideas on the wage issue. He did not recommend wage increases as a means to overcome a depression, but he was also against reductions in nominal wages in such times. When, in 1940, he suggested that for financing the war the payment of a part of the wages should be postponed until after the end of the war, a group of Labour politicians reproached him for fighting on the side of the capitalists (321).

There was indeed some truth in the statement, though not in the sense of this reproach. Keynes sided with the industrial capitalists, but the opponents were not the working class, but rather the rentier class, finance capitalists, and speculators, who gained a share of the national income without having performed any productive work.[6] What Keynes would have liked the most was to enforce a policy that would make the rentier class disappear — these "investors without any function," this "dead hand of the past," as he sometimes called them. For this purpose, as well as for the purpose of supporting industrial capitalists in their productive work, he advocated reduction of interest rates on long-term credit and a moderate inflation. But for eliminating the parasitical rentier class there was, according to Keynes, no need for a revolution. Finance capital fetches an income because it is scarce. In the future, when, according to Keynes, it would no longer be scarce, income derived from it would disappear, and along with it the rentier class. As we know, Marx also wanted to eliminate the class of industrial capitalists, because, in his view, their only function was to organize the exploitation of the working class.

### e) *The Rise of Keynesianism*

The long boom period between the end of World War II and the beginning of the 1970s is generally termed "the Keynesian era." In the early 1950s someone made the statement: "We are all good Keynesians now." It was a little exaggerated. For Keynesianism did not become popular in all developed capitalist countries, but mainly in the Anglo-Saxon ones. And even in these countries, in practice, there was quite a tug-of-war between the new doctrine and the old orthodoxy.

Keynesianism spread quickly among academic economists who were looking for a new approach after the Great Depression. They also made it intelligible for students. The more capable among them contributed with great enthusiasm to its further development. Eventually, even the fiercest critics and the most resolute opponents of the early years gave way and became the "loyal opposition" (see Hansen 1966/1993: 419). However, it cannot be said that orthodox economics disappeared altogether. After all, Keynes had little to say about microeconomics. In this area the old doctrines remained valid. So, many regarded the new Keynesian economics as an enrichment of, or as an important complement to, orthodox economics; and in the course of time a theoretical synthesis of the two emerged.

For the world outside academia, Keynes's policy recommendations were the most important. Already in 1943, Keynesianism could achieve its first success in official economic policy. The *Beveridge Report* on the reform of the social welfare system, which was submitted to the British government, incorporated Keynes's ideas. In its White Paper on Employment Policy presented in May 1944, the British government advocated a wholly Keynesian policy: "[T]he first step in a policy of maintaining general employment must be to prevent total expenditure ... from falling away" (quoted in Hansen 1966/1993: 420). Within a few months after the presentation of the said report, two bolder works written by Keynes's followers were published: *Full Employment in a Free Society* and *The Economics of Full Employment*.

In 1944, in his State of the Union message, US president Roosevelt outlined an economic bill of rights, in which he proposed a right to "a useful and remunerative job." In that same year, the Republican presidential candidate also declared that the government had a duty to create jobs, if necessary. However, when the idea became law in 1946 (the Employment Act), the wording "full employment" gave way to "maximum employment." It became a duty of the government to ensure production and purchasing power.

The turn could also be perceived on the international stage. At the Bretton Woods Conference (United Nations Monetary and Financial Conference) of 1944 the idea of a well-considered government policy to replace the automatic functioning of the economy prevailed. The Charter of the United Nations, proclaimed in 1945, includes a call to promote full employment (Article 55a).

In 1945, the Canadian government took the matter even further. It declared it would not only tolerate large budget deficits but would also consciously plan them whenever there was a danger of high unemployment. In fact, it really practiced a strictly Keynesian economic policy.

The ascent of Keynesianism in Europe had an additional background. John Gray wrote: "It took the catastrophe of the Second World War to jolt economic orthodoxy into accepting Keynesian ideas." And, further:

> The managed economies of the post-war period did not arise
> from an intellectual conversion from laissez-faire [to Keynes-
> ianism]. ... They grew out of a horror of the economic collapses
> and dictatorships that had led to the Second World War and
> from the resolute refusal of voters in Britain to return to the
> social order of the interwar years.
>
> The idea of a self-stabilizing international economic order
> perished in the totalitarian dictatorships, forced migrations,
> Allied saturation bombing and the measureless horror of the
> Nazi genocide. In Britain, the idea was killed by the experience
> of a war economy, far more efficient than that of Nazi Germany,
> in which joblessness was unknown and nutritional and health
> standards higher for the majority than they had been in
> peacetime. (Gray 1999: 15f.)

The long post-war period of growing prosperity (the long boom) in
the industrialized countries led many people to believe that it had been a
consciously pursued Keynesian economic policy that brought about this
prosperity. However, this is at best only half true. Alvin Hansen, a leading
Keynesian himself, wrote in 1966:

> Ever since the Second World War the American economy has
> done moderately well compared with earlier times. This may,
> however, have had little to do with the Employment Act or
> Keynesian economics. The post-war scarcities, the huge defense
> budget, the government contracts, the new technologies, the
> rapid population growth, the mass market for consumer
> durables of all kinds — these spontaneous forces, not govern-
> ment intervention, held the stage. (Hansen 1966/1993: 421)

But there is no doubt that during the long boom there existed a consensus
in the industrialized countries that the authorities in an economy, in which
not everything was left to the market and which was steered by the state in
the Keynesian sense, would be able to attenuate the regular business-cycle
fluctuations, overcome recessions quickly, and limit unemployment and
inflation. Many people thought that a real crisis was no longer possible.

## KEYNESIANISM IN PRACTICE

The ascent of Keynesianism in practical politics was much more difficult.
By no means had all politicians become good Keynesians, nor had all those

governments that had professed to have accepted Keynesianism. There were ups and downs.

In spite of the 1946 Employment Act, the US government did not assume any responsibility for full employment. The Congress as well as the influential media were still too conservative and too anti-Keynesian to support that. In situations in which Keynesian remedies should have been applied — namely, in recessions, which had also taken place during the long boom, e.g., in 1949–1950, 1953, and 1958 — the government in each case did not take any action or only acted half-heartedly. There were ditherers and supporters of the old politics in both parties and their administrations. They feared inflation more than they feared high unemployment. They often expressed their continued faith in the self-healing power of the economy and tended to minimize government's responsibility for the economy. The balanced-budget principle was still the norm for many. In the case of the 1958 recession, after the bottom had been hit and the first signs of recovery were visible, the government reduced state spending in 1960, which led to a new recession. The result of these successful attempts to balance the budget was that a semi-stagnation persisted until 1963.

However, a full return to fiscal orthodoxy was no longer possible. Moderate Republicans saw the need for a conservative version of Keynesianism. They advocated leaving anti-cyclical measures to a mechanism of built-in stabilizers still to be created. They believed that a tax structure was needed that would automatically guarantee a balanced budget at full employment. According to this idea state expenditures should not vary anti-cyclically, but rather along a trend line. Also the tax rates should be adjusted from time to time along a trend line. At the time, this idea seemed plausible to many people. In view of the budget amounts that had enormously increased in the previous decades, it could be expected that automatic fluctuations in revenue and expenditure would have a stabilizing effect on the economy.

Keynesianism attained true hegemony in American *thinking* on economic policy only in the 1960s, during the presidency of the Democrats Kennedy and Johnson. But in *practice*, it was the conservative version of Keynesianism that came into effect. The emphasis lay on tax rates, not on state expenditures. The authorities thought that by reducing or manipulating tax rates they could achieve two Keynesian objectives: full employment and relative price stability. However, when social priorities were the issue, and when it came to correcting blatant imbalances between the private and the public sector, then, of course, increased state spending was preferred.

In 1964, when the economy was in the middle of a recovery phase and the budget was still in deficit, a tax reduction was undertaken. This amounted to a radical break with the fiscal policy tradition. This measure was very successful; it pushed the long expansion phase up to a growth rate of 5.5 percent.

In Europe, the Keynesian consensus of the post-war years found an early power-political expression in the election victory of the British Labour Party in 1945. Hansen's explanation for the long post-war boom in the United States (see quote above) also applies to the so-called "economic miracle" in Europe. The latter was, however, set in motion by the so-called Marshall Plan, which, though conceived as an anti-communist measure on the part of the United States, was in all respects a typical Keynesian measure. Between 1948 and 1952, $12 billion was distributed under this plan among the Western European countries. The direct state investments in repair, expansion, and improvement of the infrastructure financed through this aid money were exactly what Keynesians wanted. Also, building up and developing the welfare state in the following years — whatever its motive might have been, to relieve poverty or to contain communism — indirectly had an effect commensurate with Keynesian objectives. The automatic increase in total welfare benefits with every increase in unemployment retarded the drop in aggregate demand. Due to full employment in this period, employees were able to push through higher wage demands, which in turn enhanced aggregate demand and counteracted any incipient recession. This, too, was a part of Keynesian thinking.

In West Germany, Ludwig Erhard, the Minister of Economics, was no follower of Keynes.

> As recipe against recession Erhard thought of a cartel-like agreement among leaders of the economy. The latter should agree, voluntarily and together, to produce more even though current demand was not sufficient to justify that. Erhard thought additional demand would … come as a result of producing more. [This was Say's theorem in pure form.] Erhard's rejection of Keynesian recipes had its roots in his general skepticism about state interventionism. (Hallwirth 1998: 37f.)

During the so-called economic miracle, i.e., up to 1967, there was no need to apply Keynesian economic policies. Hence there was also hardly any discussion on this subject.

However, West Germany was a special case and two extra factors should be added in the explanation for the long boom. The required demand came to a large extent from abroad. The undervalued Deutsche mark in the then-obtaining regime of fixed and stable exchange rates was of great advantage to the economy. This "had the effect that the growth of aggregate demand in the USA also befell West Germany, as though it were a state of the USA" (Hallwirth 1998: 39). Furthermore, at the time there was a national consensus on distribution. The capital side accepted continuously rising real wages, which were however lower than those in the neighboring countries, as well as further development of the welfare state. And the trade unions, on their part, provided a strike-free atmosphere. These circumstances can also be interpreted as the readiness on the part of the capital side to accept the Keynesian principle implicit in the national distribution consensus: growth through strengthening demand. Moreover, against the background of what had happened in the crisis of the 1930s, business decisions were anyhow oriented towards demand and capacity utilization (see Hein 1998: 827).

As in the USA, Keynesianism got its chance in West Germany in the 1960s, after measures taken to fight inflation led to the first recession there. In the winter of 1966–1967 nearly 700,000 working people were unemployed. That was when the Social Democrats, who favored Keynesian policies, came to power, as partners in a grand coalition. In June 1967, the Law for the Promotion of Economic Stability and Growth was passed. It obliged the government to pursue through its economic policy four macroeconomic goals: price stability, full employment, foreign trade equilibrium, and steady/continuous and adequate growth.

Two economic stimulus programs financed through budget deficits were implemented. However, with respect to income policy, the government tried — by means of quantitative orientation data and a new institution called "Concerted Action" — to persuade employers and employees to reach reasonable wage tariff agreements. In plain words, employees were asked to keep their wage demands within reasonable limits, which they also did. This policy was highly successful. In 1968 the economy recovered quickly; in 1969 the growth rate was 7.5 percent. However, this time it was exports that gave the decisive impulse — not domestic demand.

Sweden has a special place in the history of Keynesianism in practice. Until roughly the mid-1980s, it was the model of the Keynesian, social-democratic welfare state. Social Democrats had come to power there in 1932, and they formed the government for most of the next sixty years. Their very first budget, that of 1933, included, following Gunnar Myrdal's ideas, public works projects worth 160 million kronor that were to be paid for in four years with the revenue from increased inheritance taxes. Budget deficits, therefore, remained modest (see Kindleberger 1973: 182). After this first budget of the Social Democrats, even after the Great Depression was over, Sweden pursued a cautious and flexible conservative-Keynesian full-employment policy. That also included generous social welfare policies, such as health, education, and kindergarten services for all, financed with tax revenues. Even old-age pensions were largely paid by the state. Later on, generous allowances were introduced that were determined on the basis of income: allowances for all sick, unemployed, disabled, infirm, and other types of dependent people. Until the beginning of the 1980s, the rate for such allowances was 90 to 100 percent of an individual's previous income. Myrdal said, "social welfare policies were not a cost factor, but a productive investment" (quoted in Perger 2005).

In order to not stoke inflation, trade unions showed restraint in their wage demands. The government also shaped its monetary and fiscal policy in such a way that the demand for labor always remained less than the total supply. Most of the few unemployed — 1.5 percent in 1990, for instance — got a job in a public works project or were trained or retrained until they found a job in the regular economy.

Unlike the Labour governments in the United Kingdom, the Swedish Social Democrats never considered the nationalization of companies. Moreover, they were adherents of free international trade. Inefficient or obsolete industries and companies with low productivity were not protected from international competition — they were left to their fate, i.e., closing down. The retrenched workers were cushioned in the manner described above until they found employment in growing, more productive, and internationally competitive industries. The government gave managers free rein; nevertheless, it retained overall control by passing appropriate laws. For instance, private as well as public sector banks and their dealings were subject to strict regulations.

These policies were extraordinarily successful. There was always full employment and great harmony prevailed between labor and capital. There were no strikes. The country became wealthy, and the wealth was distributed very equitably, at least within the working class. In other words, the wage differential was very small. The Swedes saw their society as a *"Volksheim"* (people's home), in which the citizens were well looked after from the cradle to the grave.

For most moderate leftists in the rest of the world, who were looking for a third way between capitalism and socialism, Sweden was until the mid-1980s "the most successful society the world has ever known" (Toynbee 2005). For moderate leftists, the Swedish model proved that a social democratic government could work, that it could combine a high degree of equality with high growth rates. Later, however, there were also many skeptics, who thought that the Swedish welfare system was overdeveloped and, hence, unsustainable. (This description of the Swedish model is largely based on Stretton 1999: 796–808.)

## 2. Schumpeter's Transfiguration of Crises: Creative Destruction

When I classify Schumpeter under the category "saviors of capitalism," I do so not in the same sense in which I put Keynes under this category, not in the sense that he, like Keynes, gave policy recommendations for preventing or limiting economic crises. He "saved" capitalism by, so to speak, transfiguring economic crises as something good for the system. Unlike Keynes, who was rather critical of capitalism, Schumpeter defended the system.

In 1918, after the Communists had eliminated capitalism in Russia and when the German Socialists tried an uprising in their country, Schumpeter published *The Crisis of the Tax State* (*Die Krise des Steuerstaates*). In this essay he explored the problem of conversion of a war economy into a peace economy. He wrote:

> If the free market economy succeeded ... in adapting to the war, then it would *a fortiori* also succeed in adapting back to peace. Here we do not want to reopen the old question whether management of the economy by the state can make one exert one's whole personality, can release that desperate energy that alone can lead to success in the foreseeable future and that exactly characterizes the achievements of private enterprise.... It suffices to assert that the organizational form of competitive economy, just the way it has in essence been created by modern national economy, can also reconstruct it [the competitive economy] after the war. (Quoted in Müller 1990: 47f.)

Of course, this conversion problem is not one that only capitalism can have. But it bears a strong resemblance to the, in Schumpeter's view, normal course of capitalism. During the transition to a war economy, the means of production that were being used in the pre-war period for producing capital goods (which would be needed for the supply of future goods) had to be used for the production of present-day goods (consumer

goods). After the war, therefore, the task was again to go in more strongly
for capital formation for the capital goods industry. According to Schumpeter, this amounted to the act of saving, struggling against the impulse
to satisfy immediate consumption needs — a task for which private entrepreneurs were the most qualified people. For Schumpeter, however, the
entrepreneur played a much more important, a more essential, role in capitalism, which I will take up further on.

In his obituary on Keynes, written in 1946, Schumpeter characterized
the Keynesian model as one of *static* equilibrium:

> The exact skeleton of Keynes's system belongs ... to macrostat-
> ics, not to macrodynamics. In part this limitation must be
> attributed to those who formulated his teaching rather than to
> his teaching itself which contains several dynamic elements,
> expectations in particular. But it is true that he had an aversion
> to "periods" and that he concentrated attention upon consider-
> ations of static equilibrium. (Schumpeter 1947: 92f.)

Keynes's own words — "In the long run we are all dead" — confirm this
judgment of Schumpeter.

In contrast to Keynes, Schumpeter focused on macro*dynamics*, on economic *development* over a series of periods, which he regarded as the normal (general) state of the economy. That is why he disputed that Keynes
had, with his famous book, presented a general theory. In Schumpeter's
view, Keynes's "general theory" actually only discussed "very special cases"
(Schumpeter 1947: 96).

Whereas Keynes regarded sustained full employment as the key criterion for a well-functioning economy, for Schumpeter it was economic
*development*. For this was the main factor that brought about the prosperity of capitalist societies and that could guarantee the same in the future.
Whereas in Keynesian economic policy the most important role in attaining and maintaining full employment should be assigned to the state and
its fiscal policy, in Schumpeter's view it is dynamic entrepreneurs and their
innovations that play the key role in the process of economic development.

### a) *Schumpeter's Theory of Business Cycles*

His stress on dynamics and development makes it easy for Schumpeter to
view business cycles as something good, as the unavoidable form of development in the capitalist system. For him crises are "the necessary complement of the continual emergence of new economic and social forms

and of continually rising real incomes of all social strata" (Schumpeter 1934: 255). They are necessary because economic development is not possible without periodic destruction of the old. Destruction of the old does not only mean that large amounts of old means of production (factories, machinery, etc.) have become unusable and that part of the productive forces (technologies) have become obsolete. It also means destruction of the previous inner proportionality of the reproduction process. It is *"creative* destruction."* For it is followed by the new, the new and higher-level productive forces, production methods, means of production, etc., which boost the economy and, sooner or later, lift it to a higher production level. Both the boost and the "sinking in the social scale (*Deklassierung*) of businesses, individual positions, forms of life, cultural values and ideals" ... "are theoretically and practically, economically and culturally, much more important than the economic stability (*die Existenz relativ konstanter Besitzpositionen*)" (255). The main actor, indeed the driving force, of this process is the *dynamic* entrepreneur who introduces innovations in the economy. Schumpeter's main contribution to the defense of capitalism is the glorification of this type of entrepreneur.

Schumpeter starts out from the conviction that, firstly, in the future, just as in the past, there will always be a steady stream of potentially economically relevant inventions and discoveries, and that, secondly, in every society there are some people who possess a high degree of entrepreneurial ability. In times when it is possible to reliably assess risks—i.e., in times in which the economy is temporarily in equilibrium or in a stationary state—these people, who are sometimes called dynamic entrepreneurs, pioneers, or innovators, set about utilizing the new inventions and discoveries. In other words, they introduce innovations.

Schumpeter defines "innovation" in very general terms as "new combinations of productive means" (Schumpeter 1934: 66) and, later, as "any doing-it-differently in the whole area of economic life" (quoted in Bass 1998: 28). In concrete terms, he names five types of innovations: (1) "The introduction of a new good ... or of a new quality of a good" (product innovation); (2) "The introduction of a new method of production, that is one not yet tested by experience, ... which need by no means be founded upon a discovery scientifically new, and can also exist in a new way of handling a commodity commercially" (process innovation, e.g., Taylorization of production); (3) "The opening of a new market"; (4) "The conquest of a new source of supply of raw materials or half-manufactured goods"; (5) "The carrying out of the new organization of any industry, like the creation of a monopoly position ... or the breaking up of a monopoly position" (Schumpeter 1934: 66).

Of course, Schumpeter did not present a totally new theory of business cycles, but his work put a specifically Schumpeterian stamp on the existing theory. Starting from a temporary stationary equilibrium at full employment (before 1936 the Keynesian notion of an equilibrium below full employment did not exist), Schumpeter explains the upturn phase of a business cycle as the result of the introduction of innovations by droves of dynamic entrepreneurs who see therein a temporary opportunity to make some extra profit. After the first innovations have been introduced, the less bold and less capable entrepreneurs try their luck and imitate the pioneers. Now also the multiplier effect begins to work. It is now less risky to place orders because the new product(s) has (have) already been introduced to the market. Then follows the second round of innovations, which are often results of combining the original individual innovations.

At the beginning of the innovations wave, when the economy is in a stationary equilibrium at full employment, there is no unutilized production potential. That means that total production cannot rise in the short run, which, therefore, necessarily results in a change in the existing demand structure in favor of the industries producing means of production. This, in turn, leads to a rise in prices, especially in prices of means of production. The interest rates for bank credit, through which, according to Schumpeter, innovations are normally financed, also rise. Now, gradually, the calculation basis for further innovations becomes insecure. Consequently, the confidence of would-be innovators planning to introduce new innovations diminishes, and along with that diminishes the profit expectations from further innovations. This is a sort of built-in mechanism that slows down or even halts the innovation wave such that one can speak of an innovation cycle.

According to Schumpeter, these changes do not occur gradually. Economic development is no gradual, continual growth. It proceeds in jerky, shock-like jumps. There are also counter-movements, setbacks, and collapses, all of which can be summarized in the concept "crisis." The causes of crises can lie outside the economy, for instance, in a war [or, as we know, in a stock market crash], but also within the economy itself. "[T]he counter-movements and setbacks of which we are speaking here are frequent, so frequent that upon first consideration something like a necessary periodicity seems to suggest itself" (Schumpeter 1934: 216).

An upswing destroys the hitherto existing macroeconomic equilibrium. However, it does not merely bring about a new equilibrium with an *increased social product*. Often there is a speculative boom leading to overconsumption and utilization of inefficient production facilities, which compete with the efficient ones. Then there is overproduction. Subsequently the new equilibrium is followed by a movement below the equilibrium level, and finally a depression sets in. But in Schumpeter's model, a depression, however unwelcome it may be, also has a systemic task, which it can fulfill only if prices, wages, and interest rates can also freely move downwards (Predöhl 1962: 37). A depression is a time of creative destruction. It is a time in which extensive destruction of unprofitable and obsolete capital takes place. The economy is cleared of such capital, rearranged, and then prepared for a recovery towards the next equilibrium and then for a new upswing towards a new and higher peak. However, after the upswing comes again a crisis, which puts an end to the upswing, but at a higher level of the development process.

Given this business-cycle theory and this understanding of crises/ depressions, it is no wonder that Schumpeter did not regard the Great Depression and the general depressed state of the economy in the 1930s as something exceptionally dramatic or exceptionally abnormal, as other economists did. Schumpeter opined that — at least in the United States — the business cycle in that decade and in the preceding years had largely followed the usual pattern: the period between 1925 and 1929 was the upswing phase, from 1929 to 1930 was the downswing, then depression for two years, and finally the recovery phase from 1932 to 1934. The new cycle began in 1935, and the upswing phase, which, however, was relatively weak, lasted until 1937. But the then expected downturn did not follow the pattern. It was a strong setback, which led the US economy unexpectedly rapidly into a deep depression.

Schumpeter's explanation for this strong setback, which eluded the usual pattern, was that an exogenous factor, namely, large state expenditures in the preceding two years, had pushed up the cycle anomalously. In the USA there was also a setback in 1933, i.e., in the middle of the recovery phase. But, according to Schumpeter, this was not atypical after such a strong depression. Moreover, it was probably caused by a new series of bank failures.

So, in Schumpeter's view, the New Deal did not play any essential role in the recovery from the Great Depression and in the subsequent economic upswing. The New Deal, of course, supported the upswing, but it did not bring it about. The New Deal had also overridden parts of the automatic mechanism of the business cycle and replaced it with other factors. But seen from a macroeconomic standpoint, it had only a corrective rather than a constructive effect. (This presentation of Schumpeter's interpretation of the business cycle in the 1930s is based on Predöhl 1962: 28–34.)

### b) *The Long Waves*

A special aspect of Schumpeter's business-cycle theory is his three-cycle schema. According to Schumpeter, economic development proceeds in a wave-like pattern, i.e., in the form of a series of business cycles, and more precisely, as the wave-like pattern *resultant* of three types of cycles with different wave lengths: the Juglar cycles, the Kitchin cycles, and the Kondratiev cycles — all named after their discoverers. The Juglar cycles with a duration of eight to ten years are the well-known business cycles. Schumpeter divides a Juglar cycle into three Kitchin cycles, each with a duration of approximately forty months. Kitchin cycles can also be called "inventory cycles of the industry." "This is a wave which is formed by the fact that the industry builds up its inventory for a certain period, and subsequently reduces it for a certain time, so that the inventory functions as a buffer between preliminary production and final processing" (Predöhl 1962: 20). The Kitchin cycles were purportedly discovered by economic statisticians. But I do not understand why all or most entrepreneurs should want to increase or reduce their inventory at the same time. Logically, without this simultaneity there can be no industry-wide wave! Be that as it may, Kitchin cycles are not important for our subject matter.

Far more important for understanding the long-term development and dynamics of a capitalist economy are the long waves named after the Russian economist and statistician Nikolai Kondratiev. These waves, which are overlaid with several readily perceptible Juglar cycles, have a length of fifty to sixty years. What makes them specially interesting for us is that they are seen as connected to great, fundamental technological developments and innovations that gave a wide range of opportunities to dynamic and innovative entrepreneurs as described by Schumpeter.

Ernest Mandel wrote in 1973 about four long waves known until that time:

1. The wave starting at the end of the eighteenth century and lasting until the crisis of 1847. It is characterized by the gradual dissemination of the steam engine — manufactured first by skilled craftsmen and later in manufactories.

2. The wave from the crisis of 1847 to the beginning of the 1890s. It is characterized by the dissemination of the steam motor *manufactured by means of machines*. This is the period of the first technological revolution. Other authors mention here also the development of steel and the railway.

3. The wave from the 1890s to World War II. It is characterized by the widespread use of the electric motor and the internal combustion engine. This is the period of the second technological revolution. It is also characterized by electrification, the automobile, and broad use of chemicals.

4. The wave that started in North America around 1940, and in the rest of the industrialized nations between 1945 and 1948. This wave is characterized by widespread use of *steering* of machines by means of *electronic devices*. (Mandel 1973: 113; see also Müller 1990: 43)

Each long wave can be divided into two phases: the first phase of accelerated growth and the second one of retarded growth. The first phase is the one in which technology is really revolutionized. That takes place in the sector that produces the means of production. This is where, in the first phase, there is rapid capital accumulation, high growth, and high profit rates. Here, at the same time, a rapid devaluation of old capital takes place in favor of new capital (creative destruction). In the second phase, after the technological revolution has already taken place, it is only a question of using the new methods and means of production in a generalized way in all branches of the economy and, especially, in all branches of industry. In this phase capital accumulation slows down; also, the growth and profit rates are lower.

The long waves influence the Juglar waves. In the first, expansive phase of a long wave, the upswings and peaks of the Juglar waves are longer and more intense, while their recession and depression phases are shorter and less deep. Conversely, in the second, stagnation phase of a long wave, the upswings and peaks of the Juglar waves are shorter and less intense, while the recession and depression phases are longer and deeper. Altogether, an observer can perceive long-term trends — an expansive one and a stagnating one.

The twenty-five years of the "economic miracle" after World War II can easily be regarded as the expansive phase of the fourth long wave, and the years since 1974 as its stagnating phase. As of 2003–2005, with widespread and persistent stagnation in many highly industrialized countries, it seemed the economies of the developed world had reached the end of this long wave. Then, after a short period of upswing, came the crash and the great recession of 2008–2011. Whether a new long wave can soon set in, and if yes, with which basic technological inventions and innovations, is a question we can only answer with intelligent speculation. This issue will be explored in chapter X.

### c) *Demise of Capitalism*

Schumpeter did not only save capitalism, *ideologically*, by declaring crises (recessions and depressions) to be necessary elements of the economic development process and reinterpreting economic destruction as creative destruction. He also defended it by using two well-known standard arguments, namely, (1) that the motivation mechanism of capitalism and the stimulating atmosphere of inequality generate economic activities and guarantee rising standard of living, and (2) that rising standard of living secures, despite occasional crises, the *longer term* stability of society. In support of this view, Schumpeter could refer to the concrete historical success of capitalism. However, like Keynes, he was objective and honest enough to recognize and state openly that one could not be sure on this issue. In the last phase of his life he thought that the golden age of capitalism could soon be over. In his book *Capitalism, Socialism, and Democracy*, published in 1942, he discusses the question of the possible demise of capitalism.

According to Schumpeter, there is no problem as long as one can assume perfect competition. Social welfare policies are then not only not necessary, they can even be counterproductive, as the state could damage the motivating force of capitalism by taxing profit excessively. But perfect competition is only a fiction. In reality, especially in developed capitalism, monopolies and monopolistic competition prevail. But even a capitalism of this sort, which functions sub-optimally, is, according to Schumpeter, efficient and can raise the standard of living of the working people, although it cannot rule out involuntary unemployment. Hence, there is no danger of competition being increasingly restricted, as economic liberals fear.

Schumpeter also disagrees with the reasoning behind the Keynesian thesis of secular stagnation. He sees no limits to investment opportunities since, according to him, needs are variable. And with respect to excessive saving, i.e., too little consumption, he thinks it can worsen a crisis, but no more than that.

However, Schumpeter believes there are factors that give rise to doubts about the long-term stability of capitalism. These factors can be found outside the economic system as such — partly in the institutional structure of capitalist society, partly in social and cultural domains. In his view, the system of large corporations that arose from the capitalistic concentration process renders the type "dynamic entrepreneur" superfluous. Such corporations are totally bureaucratized entities, and they are run by hired managers who are not entrepreneurs in the Schumpeterian sense. Since in a capitalism of this type innovations also largely become impersonal, the entrepreneurial function has become obsolete. In addition, consumers have gotten used to frequent arrival of new products on the market, so that in this respect too the assertiveness of a pioneering entrepreneur is no longer necessary.

The large corporations, Schumpeter argues, edge out or even expropriate the small and medium-size firms. The owners of these firms and their family members — that is, the petty bourgeois class whose existence is threatened — question the legitimacy of the capitalist system. There is no point in telling them that this system will, generally speaking, be more successful in the long term although it is making their existence more insecure at present.

Moreover, modern capitalism weakens the family as an institution, which hitherto played an important role in the functioning of capitalism, namely, as the motivating force of capitalist ethics "... that enjoins working for the future irrespective of whether or not one is going to harvest the crop oneself" (Schumpeter 1943: 160). The application of cost-benefit analysis to decisions on starting a family — the sacrifices made for raising children versus the benefits from descendants — eliminates this motivating force.

Schumpeter also refers to the cultural factor that inequality of wealth and the possibility of involuntary unemployment — two of the main principles on which capitalism is based — finds less and less acceptance, especially among intellectuals.

From these facts Schumpeter concludes that "... there is inherent in the capitalist system a tendency toward self-destruction" (1943: 162). He at the same time believe that a socialist economic system — a system based on a planned economy and state ownership of the means of production — can function and is, therefore, a practicable alternative. His argument for this belief is no part of the subject matter of this book. Suffice it to indicate briefly how he envisages an evolutionary transition: "... socialization means a stride beyond big business on the way that has been chalked out by it" (1943: 195f.). However, in his view, the substitution of capitalism by socialism is not guaranteed.

All that does not mean that Schumpeter was actually a socialist, something some of his opponents thought. He reportedly said once that it was annoying that capitalism did not believe in itself. And Bass, the Schumpeter expert, thinks that "Schumpeter perhaps secretly hoped that this [his statement on the self-destructing tendency of capitalism] would turn out to be a *self-destroying* prophecy" (Bass 1998: 54). Schumpeter himself wrote: "The capitalist or any other order of things may evidently break down — or economic and social evolution may outgrow it — and yet the socialist phoenix may fail to rise from the ashes" (1943: 56f.). This remark, made in 1942, appears in our time as a prophecy coming true. More and more, the world seems about to sink in chaos, anarchy, or even in a new barbarism. And still, nowhere around is a socialist phoenix in sight.

### d) *Schumpeterian Economic Policy*

Since for Schumpeter "neither profits in a boom nor losses in a depression are meaningless and functionless," but rather represent "essential elements of the mechanism of economic development" (1934: 252f.), and since capitalism, in his view, "cannot do without the *ultima ratio* of the complete destruction of those existences which are irretrievably associated with the hopelessly unadapted" (253), one cannot expect him to advocate an economic policy that would prevent crises. Any attempt to do so would have no chance of success; it would only paralyze economic development. "[No therapy can permanently obstruct the great economic and social process by which businesses, individual positions, forms of life, cultural values and ideals sink in the social scale" (255).

Nevertheless, the early Schumpeter, who fully believed in the efficacy of the market, made suggestions to mitigate crises: "improvement of business cycle prognosis," "postponement of new construction by government enterprises or by great combines to periods of depression," etc. The latter is aimed at "moderation of the consequences of the swarm-like appearance of new combinations and ... attenuation of the inflation of the boom and the deflation of the depression" (253). This sounds very much like anti-cyclical (compensatory) investment policy.

Although Schumpeter is always skeptical about state intervention, he does not object to state intervention in extreme cases of crisis, out of *social* (as opposed to business-cycle) considerations. He can also accept that the state, in an exceptional situation, grants credit to a company. Such a company may have been affected by "secondary circumstances" of a crisis, which have nothing in common with the actual process of "creative destruction." However, these are only secondary thoughts of Schumpeter (see Bass 1998: 36).

Surprisingly, in his later work *Capitalism, Socialism and Democracy*, Schumpeter also advocates a sort of conscious industrial policy. The structural change that becomes necessary after a wave of creative destructions should proceed in an orderly manner. For this purpose, private companies should be allowed to build cartels and impose other restrictions on free competition. The state can also play a part in this process. Schumpeter wrote: "[T]here is certainly no point in trying to conserve obsolescent industries indefinitely; but there is point in trying to avoid their coming down with a crash and in attempting to turn a rout, which may become a center of cumulative depressive effects, into orderly retreat." This is, so to speak, care for the terminally ill old industries. Schumpeter also speaks of an "orderly advance" (Schumpeter 1943: 90). This is assistance at the birth of new industries (Bass 1998: 36).

Intellectuals interested in economic theory have been deeply impressed by Schumpeter's business-cycle theory, his rediscovery of the long waves, his brilliant formulation "creative destruction," his underscoring of the role of dynamic entrepreneurs and their innovations, and his emphasis on development (not equilibrium) as the main characteristic feature of capitalism. But his ideas on economic *policy* did not find any resonance among politicians during his lifetime. This was partly because his thoughts on policy were hardly any different from those of contemporary orthodox economists, and partly because his advocacy of state intervention and help in special cases was half-hearted and, hence, was considered by his contemporaries as only secondary thoughts. Towards the end of the 1930s and after World War II Keynesianism was all the rage. But when, towards the end of the 1970s and against the background of the special kind of crisis called stagflation, the disappointment with Keynesianism became widespread, some theoreticians rediscovered Schumpeter. In the beginning of the 1980s, when politicians became aware of a structural crisis and of the need for structural reforms, some circles started talking about a "Schumpeter renaissance," and some economists wondered whether Schumpeter would not be *the* economist of the 1990s (see Stolper 1984 and Neumark 1984). But nothing like that happened. Instead, monetarism and supply-side economics (generally speaking, neo-liberalism) came up to gain the upper hand. However, various elements of Schumpeter's work have found a place in supply-side economic policies. I shall take up this matter in the next chapters.

# IV.

# Stagflation — The Decline of Keynesianism and the Rise of Neo-Liberalism

In the mid-seventies, the long boom — and with it the "golden age" of capitalism — came to an end. In the previous twenty-five years one could emphatically assert that the question "capitalism or socialism?" had become irrelevant, and that, thanks to Keynesianism, there could not be any serious economic crisis in capitalism anymore. But now there was again a serious economic crisis, and soon thereafter the Keynesian era also came to an end. In 1986, Will Hutton, a Keynesian, lamented: "Keynesianism is now seen by many as close to the root of all economic evil" (Hutton 2001: 140). This was also understandable. The so-called neo-liberal "counterrevolution" was in full swing. It consisted of government policy in the United States, the United Kingdom, and many other developed countries. The theoretical basis of this policy was made up of a combination of monetarism, neo-liberalism, and supply-side policies (see further on) that has generally been termed "neo-liberalism." By the mid-nineties, all economic policy makers of the world and almost all economists were adherents of neo-liberal economic policies and theory.

Already in the first half of the 1990s there were many doubters in many countries, who questioned the wisdom of pursuing a neo-liberal economic policy. There were also many protest actions by concerned and affected people, e.g., against the proposed World Trade Organization (WTO), which was installed in January 1995. In 1997, in several OECD countries there were protest movements against the proposed Multilateral Agreement on Investments (MAI), with the result that the idea was dropped. By the middle of the first decade of the new millennium, neo-liberalism was no longer regarded as the last word on economics. This was because, since a few years earlier, stock exchange crashes, recessions, stagnation, mass unemployment, and downscaling of the welfare state had been afflicting several capitalist countries. But before we delve into the controversies of the new millennium, we need to understand how and why the Keynesian era came to an end and the neo-liberal era began.

## 1. Stagflation

What dealt a mortal blow to Keynesianism was the until then unknown phenomenon "stagflation," i.e., stagnation occurring simultaneously with inflation. Marxist author Jacob Morris wrote: "This is a one-word characterization of the worst of all possible capitalist worlds.... 'Stagnation,' though it is a more ominous sounding word than 'recession,' is still only a euphemism for that dreaded non-word 'depression'" (Morris 1974: 1).

In his anti-capitalist zeal Morris exaggerated a little. The term "depression" is usually considered to mean "a prolonged period characterized by high unemployment, low output and investment, depressed business confidence, falling prices, and widespread business failures" (Samuelson and Nordhaus 1989: 970). Most of the attributes used here are rather vague and relative. In 1974, three countries of the G7 group notched up good growth rates of the real GDP, and only three recorded slightly negative rates. Although all *growth rate* figures were lower than those of the previous year, in four countries the real GDP grew after all. Also, no country suffered from hyperinflation. Such a situation cannot seriously be called "the worst of all possible capitalist worlds." Below are the figures for the seven most industrialized countries (G7) and for the OECD (Organisation for Economic Co-operation and Development) as a whole:

|  | Growth rate of real GDP | | | | Growth of inflation rate (in %) | | | |
|---|---|---|---|---|---|---|---|---|
|  | 1973 | 1974 | 1975 | 1976 | 1973 | 1974 | 1975 | 1976 |
| USA | 5.7 | −0.9 | −0.8 | 4.7 | 6.2 | 11.0 | 9.1 | 5.8 |
| Japan | 8.8 | −1.0 | 2.3 | 5.3 | 11.7 | 24.5 | 11.8 | 9.3 |
| Germany | 4.7 | 0.3 | −1.6 | 5.4 | 6.9 | 7.0 | 6.0 | 4.5 |
| France | 5.4 | 3.2 | 0.2 | 5.2 | 7.3 | 13.7 | 11.8 | 9.6 |
| United Kingdom | 7.6 | −1.0 | −0.7 | 3.8 | 9.2 | 16.0 | 24.2 | 16.5 |
| Italy | 7.0 | 4.1 | −3.6 | 5.9 | 10.8 | 19.1 | 17.0 | 16.8 |
| Canada | 7.5 | 3.5 | 1.1 | 6.1 | 7.6 | 10.9 | 10.8 | 7.5 |
| Whole G7 | 6.3 | 0.0 | −0.4 | 5.0 | 7.5 | 13.3 | 11.0 | 8.0 |
| Whole OECD | 6.1 | 0.5 | −0.2 | 4.8 | 7.8 | 13.4 | 11.3 | 8.6 |

(Source: OECD 1985: Annex)

As for the unemployment rate, it is neither an important nor an unambiguous indicator of *economic performance*, for some other factors also play a part in it. Moreover, definitions of the term are sometimes unclear, or they, as well as registration practices, differ from country to country.

Nevertheless, some figures, as standardized by the OECD, are useful for understanding the situation at the time.

| | Standardized unemployment rate (in %) | | | |
|---|---|---|---|---|
| | 1973 | 1974 | 1975 | 1976 |
| USA | 4.8 | 5.5 | 8.3 | 7.6 |
| Japan | 1.3 | 1.4 | 1.9 | 2.0 |
| Germany | 0.8 | 1.6 | 3.6 | 3.7 |
| France | 2.6 | 2.8 | 4.0 | 4.4 |
| United Kingdom | 3.0 | 2.9 | 4.3 | 5.7 |
| Italy | 6.2 | 5.3 | 5.8 | 6.6 |
| Canada | 5.5 | 5.3 | 6.9 | 7.1 |
| Whole G7 | 3.4 | 3.7 | 5.4 | 5.4 |
| 16 OECD countries | 3.2 | 3.5 | 5.1 | 5.2 |

(Source: OECD 1985: Annex)

The dramatic fall in the growth rates of real GDP or, in some cases, stagnation (i.e., only a mild rise or fall in output) in the years 1974 and 1975, and the strong rise in the unemployment rates in 1975 — all these together were perceived, against the backdrop of the long boom of the preceding twenty-five years, as a severe crisis.

The prevailing economic theories at the time saw inflation as a possible concomitant of an upswing. Keynes had accepted the possibility of a moderate inflation as a side effect of implementation of his recommendations against recession or depressions. He had even favored an inflation of this kind as a way to reduce real labor costs when nominal wages went up. In the long boom period, entrepreneurs could also accept the advice to not oppose the wage demands of workers too strongly. But in the mid-seventies, a two-year recession set in and, at the same time, inflation got out of control. Between 1965 and 1972, the inflation rate in the industrialized countries varied between 2.6% and 5.7% (OECD 1985: Annex). Thereafter it shot up, as the table on the previous page shows.

With respect to production (real GDP), the economies of the industrialized countries recovered in 1976, and they recorded good or normal growth rates until 1979. But the inflation rate could be reduced only marginally and it stayed high until 1982. So the terms "stagnation" and "stagflation" are justified only for the years 1974 and 1975. For the following years it was inflation that was the disturbing element.

This stagflation caused the end of Keynesian economic policy. For restrictive monetary and/or fiscal policy measures would have caused unemployment to rise, and expansive measures would have further stoked inflation. This was a very bad economic policy dilemma.

The oil price shock of 1973 — the price had quadrupled in the last quarter of the year — was, via the resulting rise in production costs, certainly the most important cause of the sudden jump in the inflation rate. But it was not the only cause. The inflation rate had actually begun to rise earlier on. The well-known usual factors played their usual roles in the matter: the wage-price spiral and the expansive monetary policy.

Here we must note a difference between the effects of the internal and external causes. Because the higher nominal wages that the working people received in those inflation years were mostly spent or invested within the country, they generally did not lead to a decline in production. They possibly even contributed to growth in production. Only the prices rose. The fourfold rise in oil prices had, however, different consequences. A larger portion of the industrialized countries' GDP flowed away into oil-exporting countries. And these countries did not spend all of this additional income on imports from industrialized countries. This is in my view the only way in which the phenomenon of stagflation can be explained.

### DEVELOPMENTS IN THE FEDERAL REPUBLIC OF GERMANY

As an illustration of the developments in that era, I give here a short account of those in West Germany.

Inflation can also be a result of income policy, i.e., a result of struggles between the social classes for their share of the gross national product. Until the end of the 1960s, the German trade unions showed restraint in their wage demands. However, in 1969 the period of restraint ended. The trade unions made high wage demands, and there were even wildcat strikes. In 1970 wages rose on average by 15.5%, and in the following years too there were double-digit wage increases (Hallwirth 1998: 44). Through the mechanism of the wage-price spiral these developments necessarily led to a high inflation rate. It rose from 1.9% in 1969 to 5.5% in 1972 (OECD 1985: Annex). The oil price shock of 1973 further worsened the situation.

Then came another shock. In the early seventies, the system of fixed exchange rates between the various currencies, which had been established in 1944 at Bretton Woods, fell apart. The exchange rate of the Deutsche mark, which had until then been undervalued, rose considerably. As a consequence, West Germany lost part of its export advantages of

the previous years. The German Bundesbank, which could now act autonomously, decided to fight inflation and heftily applied the brakes. Within
a year, growth in money supply was halved. The negative effect of this
measure on economic growth was equally strong. Here a combination of
inflation and a drastic demand squeeze enforced through monetary policy
came into play. Company profits dropped and unemployment exceeded
one million.

After the strong recovery in 1976, the growth rate dropped again
in 1977 and 1978 — to 3% and 2.9% respectively — and unemployment
remained almost as high as before (OECD 1985: Annex). The government
tried to stimulate economic growth and employment by means of several
fiscal expansion programs. But these measures were like a flash in the pan
and their employment effect was very modest. The Keynesians ran out of
ideas, particularly because the costs of their experiments were becoming
too high. The budget deficits doubled, and the state indebtedness almost
quadrupled (Hallwirth 1998: 45). There was no room left for any further
fiscal policy experiments.

The second oil price shock of 1979 — a threefold increase in the price of
oil in the first half of the year — pushed the inflation rate up from 2.7% in
1978 to 6.3% in 1981. This oil price shock was not the only event to negatively impact employment. There was also the drastic decline of economic
activity in the USA, an important buyer of German exports, resulting from
a severely restrictive monetary policy from 1979 onwards (see further on).
The unemployment rate in Germany rose from 3.5% in 1978 to 8% in 1983
(all figures from OECD 1985: Annex).

## 2. The Neo-Liberal Counterrevolution

In the second half of the 1970s, the political climate began to change,
mainly in the Anglo-Saxon countries. In 1979 Margaret Thatcher came to
power in the United Kingdom, in November 1980 Ronald Reagan in the
USA. In both countries, the economy had been hit by recession and high
inflation in the election year, which may have caused the defeat of the hitherto ruling party (see further on). The economic policy of both the newly
elected governments was determined by conservative ideologues, who traditionally idealized the private sector and demonized the public sector.
They incessantly advocated a small government and less state spending.
They were convinced that governments were inevitably inefficient and
that state regulation could only worsen the problems. Their objective was
continual growth without inflation, which in their opinion could only be

attained if the economy was left to the invisible hands of the market. The two governments abruptly changed course and introduced neo-liberal economic policies, which prevail to this day.

It is true that opponents of Keynesianism took advantage of the crisis, but even Paul Samuelson, who, as is well known, had made Keynesian theory acceptable to the standard economics of the time, wrote in 1974: "Economists are more conservative than they were ten years ago because they have seen interference with the market system that has fulfilled their worst foreboding" (quoted in Morris 1974: 4). The Keynesians were now, to say the least, unsure of themselves, were no longer convinced that their theory was right. Hutton reports that they no longer defended the fundamental teachings of their master with conviction, and that they either remained silent or their reply to the neo-liberal offensive sounded very feeble. According to Hutton, they now tried to explain the economic problems of the time with the orthodox teachings rather than with the Keynesian theory (Hutton 2001: XVI).

In the realm of government policy the change had already begun in 1976, namely, in the United Kingdom. The Labour Prime Minister at the time, James Callaghan, said that it had clearly become impossible "to spend our way out of a recession" (quoted in Willke 2002: 165), and that the pursuit of full employment through Keynesian policies of economic management was no longer feasible (see Gray 1999: 24). Callaghan did not try this — not because he had been influenced by the propaganda of the neo-liberal counterrevolutionaries, but rather because he was under the pressure of imperative conditions imposed by the International Monetary Fund (IMF) (see Gray 1999: 16). Britain had problems with its balance of payments, which had compelled the government to request credit from the IMF. And it was a Labour government that undertook, even before the Thatcher era, the first privatization in the United Kingdom, namely, the selling of a part of the state's share in British Petroleum (see Gray 1999: 27).

In the United States, in October 1979, the Fed started a drastic tight-money policy in order to vigorously fight inflation, which had risen from 5.8% in 1976 to 11.3% at the end of 1979. By the end of 1980, it had climbed further to 13.5%. In 1978, the economy had grown by 4.7%; after the U-turn in monetary policy the rate dropped to 2.6% at the end of 1979 and further to –0.4% in 1980. The unemployment rate increased accordingly. Whereas unemployment had dropped from 7.6% in 1976 to 5.8% in 1979, it rose by the end of 1980 to 7% (all figures from OECD 1985: Annex).

Although Reagan hailed the Fed's anti-inflationary policy, the economic crisis was inconvenient for him. In order to overcome it he prescribed a "Program for Economic Recovery," which was to embody the rupture with Keynesianism. The program consisted of hefty tax cuts, a strict limit imposed on (the growth of) state spending, and a reduction in the extent of regulation. What motivated Reagan to adopt this policy was not only the economic problems he faced at the time, but also the economic philosophy of the conservatives described above. The Republicans did not simply think that substantial tax cuts would stimulate the economy. That view was, to a certain extent, reconcilable with Keynesianism, for then the lower income groups, if their taxes were also reduced, would be able to increase their consumption. What set the Republicans apart from the Keynesians was the belief of the former that the (in their opinion) steep progression in income and corporation tax rates were to blame for the economic woes. Accordingly, they reduced the top tax rate for personal income and corporate profit from 70% to 28% and from 48% to 34%, respectively (Tigges 2004). Another difference with the Keynesians was that the Republicans, following orthodox economic teachings, did not place a high value on short-term revitalization of the economy. They rather wanted to improve the basic economic framework in the middle- and long-term. In order to do this, they also accepted the possibility of a recession caused by their restrictive monetary policy. They considered stable prices to be more important in the *long run* for economic growth and stability.

This policy of the American neo-liberals was soon successful — in their own sense. By 1983, the inflation rate had fallen to 3.2%. But, as expected, the growth rate fell too — after an interim peak of 3.4% in 1981 to -3% in 1982. And, expectedly, unemployment too began to rise again. In 1982 it reached 9.5% and remained at that level in 1983. From 1983 onwards, the economy recorded positive growth rates, and unemployment fell from 1984 onwards (all figures from OECD 1985: Annex). At the end of the presidency of Reagan (1988), this economic policy was on the whole regarded as a success, in spite of the big stock exchange crash of 1987. In 1988, the growth rate was 4.2%, the inflation rate 4.1%, and the unemployment rate 5.5% (OECD 2000: 211, 226, 231).

But at the same time, there were a few negative sides to this administration. Reagan fueled the Cold War. The massive rearmament that he pursued devoured at its peak 6.2% of the GDP. The tax cuts benefited only the rich, inequality in society increased, and the poorest became even poorer (this, however, had been already happening since 1973). The crime rate and the percentage of the population behind bars were amongst the highest in the world (see Stiglitz 2003: 34f.). Reagan's foreign trade policy was also criticized because of the numerous protectionist measures that his administration took.

Although generally successful, Reagan's economic policy also suffered a few failures. He did not succeed in reducing state spending, and also tax revenues lagged behind expectations in spite of satisfactory growth rates since 1983. The hoped-for self-financing of the tax cuts did not material-ize. He did not manage to present a balanced budget in any single year. The massive increase in military expenditure had to be financed through massive budget deficits.

Yet another negative aspect of the Reagan presidency was the real estate bubble, which was caused by some tax concessions granted in the early years. In 1986, when he had to annul them under the pressure of public criticism, the bubble burst. As a consequence, many banks came close to bankruptcy, and his successor, George H.W. Bush, had to salvage them with over $100 billion of taxpayers' money.

Now let us consider the United Kingdom during the same period. Margaret Thatcher came to power in 1979. She finally put an end to the until then existing Keynesian quasi consensus on British economic policy. Moreover, she also reversed the trend towards more state intervention in the distribution of the national income and for protecting the interests of the poor, a trend that had existed, with ups and downs, since 1851. For this purpose, she followed a policy similar to that of the US government under Reagan — a tight-money policy side by side with a substantial reduction in state spending. As in the USA, fighting inflation and reducing the tax rates became top priorities of Thatcher's government policy. She privatized a series of state-owned companies, some of which had earlier been nation-alized by Labour governments. In the later years of her rule, which lasted until 1990, she extended the "Thatcher Revolution" to the area of social policy. That is, she also initiated the privatization of the education, health care, and housing systems. Like the other neo-liberals, she too was against too much interference of the state in the economy and for independence of the individual from the state.

Thatcher was successful in fighting inflation, which went down from 18% in 1980 to 8.6% in 1982. In the following years of the 1980s it fell even further. But the price the British people had to pay for this suc-cess was very high. The growth rate of the real GDP fell from 2.2% in 1979 to −2.3% in 1980 and to −1.4% in 1981. Accordingly, the unemploy-ment rate shot up from 5.1% in 1979 to 9.9% in 1981. Thereafter, until 1989, the economy recorded positive, often good, growth rates. However, unemployment kept growing; it reached 13% in 1984 and then remained high (all figures from OECD 1985: Annex). And a large underclass arose.

A special feature of Thatcher's policy was the attempt — successful in her view — to debilitate the trade unions. She did this by subjecting them to stricter and more restrictive laws. Striking coal miners, whose jobs were threatened by closure of coal mines, were beaten up by the police. In addition to that, a large number of companies and individuals went bankrupt.

## 3. The Theoretical Foundation of Neo-Liberal Policies —
Monetarism versus Keynesianism

The oldest version of what is nowadays termed "neo-liberalism" is monetarism. It had already arisen in the heyday of Keynesianism — as theory, as critique of and theoretical alternative to Keynesianism. Even in the 1950s Keynesian *theory* was a little weakened. On the basis of their theory, Keynesians had thought that right after the end of World War II, when the huge state spending boom caused by the war would come to an end, a new great depression would set in. That was also the reasoning behind their strong plea for a Keynesian economic policy. As we have seen in chapter III, until the mid-sixties governments of the industrialized countries did not follow their advice consistently. Despite this, instead of the feared depression came the beginning of a long boom. The cheap money policy (lower interest rates), which, as we know, is also a part of Keynesian economic policy, led to inflation in many countries.

During the long boom, recessions and unemployment were not a big problem. The attention of creative economists, therefore, shifted to the phenomenon of inflation, which had gradually become a serious problem. Over and above this, the personal ambitions of young economists played a part in the shift, since they saw no "chance" in the already established Keynesian new economics "to jump onto the front — and not the rear — of an academic bandwagon" (Johnson 1971: 6). This was a further reason why in the 1950s and 1960s not all economists had become Keynesians.

In the 1980s, monetarism exerted great influence on the economic policy of the US and British governments. Milton Friedman was its main theorist and proponent. Although there were also some differences among monetarists, their theoretical and political positions can be presented as a single tenet. "Monetarism ... views the role of money as central to macroeconomic theory and policy. More precisely, monetarism holds that the money supply is the major determinant of short-run movements in nominal GNP and is the prime determinant of prices in the long run"

(Samuelson and Nordhaus 1989: 355). Naturally, this definition is very reduced and does not cover all aspects of monetarist thought.

In contrast to Keynesians, who think the market economy is inherently unstable, monetarists, who are conservative in their *Weltanschauung* (worldview), think, just like the orthodox economists, that the private sector is in itself stable. They believe that if the market economy is left to its own devices, there can at most be minor and unimportant deviations from the potential production.[7] That in reality big crises do happen cannot of course be denied. But in the view of the monetarists their origins do not lie in the market economy itself. When the state and/or the central bank start meddling, the economy only gets destabilized. This causes either inflation or unemployment. And, all in all, such interventions make the private sector feel unsure and thus weaken private initiative. Monetarists are therefore advocates of the smallest possible government and more market. They regard governments, in general, as inefficient. Personal freedom is for them a value of the highest order. Friedman once said: "If free market economy were not the most efficient system, I would even then want it — because of the values it stands for: freedom of choice, facing challenges, taking risks" (quoted in Heuser 1993: 101f.; retranslated).

In contrast to Keynesians, monetarists think there is a natural rate of unemployment, which is the result of market forces, search processes, adaptation problems, the level of real wages as well as the wage structure, etc. Moreover, in their view a large part of unemployment is voluntary unemployment. Therefore, they think inflation, not unemployment, is the greatest foe of the economy. They do not think it is possible to permanently eliminate natural unemployment by means of an interventionist fiscal and/or monetary policy. Therefore, their foremost economic policy objective is not full employment, but rather stability — not stagnation, but stable growth and price stability.

The controversy between Keynesians and monetarists (and conservatives) is not only one over worldviews: more state or more freedom. It also arises from different theories and analyses of economic events. Monetarists, moreover, think they can cite results of empirical research in support of their theory. In what follows I shall try to briefly present their theoretical and analytical arguments for their views and their differences with the Keynesians.

Keynes and the Keynesians thought (and still do) that the Great Depression of the early 1930s, in the final analysis, was caused by the collapse of demand from investments. They also thought that in the case of this depression the recipe against economic crises that had been applied up to that time, namely, a flexible monetary policy, had failed and that monetary policy in general was of little use against economic crises of this kind. With the help of extensive empirical research on American monetary policy of the years in question, Friedman showed that the Fed, by pursuing a wrong monetary policy, let a crisis that otherwise would probably have been a short and relatively harmless recession become the Great Depression. "From 1930 to 1933, a series of bank runs and bank failures were permitted to run their course because the Federal Reserve failed to provide liquidity for the banking system, which was one of the main functions the designers of the Federal Reserve system intended it to perform"(Friedman 1970: 16). A third of all American banks had to close down. As a result, the amount of money circulating in the economy fell by one third, and the Fed allowed this to happen, although it "had it within its power to prevent the decline in the quantity of money and to produce an increase" (17). The Great Depression was therefore, according to Friedman, actually a "tragic testament to the effectiveness of monetary policy, not a demonstration of its impotence"(11f.). He firmly believed that "if Keynes had known the facts about the Great Depression as we now know them, he could not have interpreted that episode as he did" (17) and that "if Keynes were alive today he would no doubt be at the forefront of the counter-revolution" (8). With respect to business cycles in general, Friedman interpreted them — as did Irving Fisher, the father of the modern quantity theory of money — as "the dance of the dollar" (9).

Why do monetarists think that the private sector is stable *in principle*? In contrast to Keynesians, monetarists are mainly interested in long-term stable growth. Logically, therefore, the *long-term* development of aggregate income and aggregate demand are more important for them. They, therefore, work with (1) *life income* of a person from all types of assets including human capital, which yields an earned income over a period of time, and (2) *average permanent life income*. They are of the opinion that people's consumption plans depend on their expected life income. *Current* income is only a part of the average permanent life income, and it, therefore, does not play any decisive role.

That is convincing. For a long time now, people have been buying cars, homes, and much more on credit and paying for them in many installments. Monetarists think that for this reason people would not restrict their consumption at all or would do so only minimally if their current income were to drop temporarily. If this is true, then one must conclude that aggregate demand develops in the long term relatively smoothly and that the whole private sector is therefore relatively stable. The multiplier

effect then loses some of its importance. Exogenous disturbances or politically motivated changes in fiscal and/or monetary policy do not set any
*cumulative* processes in motion but only induce small and temporary
effects.

Another reason why monetarists believe that the private sector is in
principle relatively stable is the alleged fact that the velocity of circulation of money $(V)$[8] is relatively stable and predictable *in usual situations*.
(In unusual situations such as high inflation or deep recession, it is obviously unstable.) According to them, what makes $(V)$ relatively stable is
that the time intervals in which incomes are received and spent remain
the same over long periods. This is the reason why monetarists think that
variations in money supply $(M)$ alone cause the short-term fluctuations
in employment and aggregate income and the long-term movements in
prices. "Only money matters," they pithily say. Therefore, if the money supply or the growth rate of the money supply is kept stable, the private sector also remains stable.

But what happens when the money supply $(M)$ is not kept stable?
Keynesians think that when the money supply $(M)$ is discretionally
increased, most of the additional money remains unused. This is the so-
called liquidity trap (you can lead a horse to the water, but you can't make
it drink). Then $(V)$ drops. Conversely, when, in a situation of growing
economic activity, the money supply remains unchanged, or is perhaps
reduced, then the market players spend money faster than usual, and $(V)$
rises. In both cases, the product of $(M) \times (V)$, the really decisive macroeconomic quantity, remains relatively unchanged. What Keynesians want
to say with all this is that the course of economic events cannot be influenced much by means of discretionary variations in money supply (that is,
through monetary policy). Particularly the probability that policy makers
can pull an economy out of a deep recession by increasing the money supply is, according to them, not very high. It is more likely that the inflation
rate can be reduced by drastically reducing the money supply. They say,
money supply policy is like a string that can be pulled downwards, but not
pushed up. The right role of monetary policy is, in their view, to keep the
interest rates low. For the rest, it all depends on demand.

According to Friedman, however, empirical data show that

> the movements of velocity [of circulation] tend to reinforce
> those of money instead of to offset them [what Keynesians
> believe]. When the quantity of money declined by a third from
> 1929 to 1933 in the United States, velocity declined also. When

the quantity of money rises rapidly in almost any country,
velocity also rises rapidly [which leads to inflation]. Far from
velocity offsetting the movements of the quantity of money, it
reinforces them. (Friedman 1970: 17)

With these facts and remarks, Friedman wanted, firstly, to say that variations in the money supply have strong macroeconomic effects. And secondly, he wanted to give a monetarist explanation for inflation. Later, economists calculated $(V)$ for the period between 1929 and 1988 on the basis of historical statistical data. The results confirm Friedman's claims (see Samuelson and Nordhaus 1989: 356f.).

For monetarists, therefore, a good money supply policy is sufficient for overcoming economic crises and instabilities. But, for this purpose, is it not advisable to use *also* fiscal policy?

Monetarists think the problem of unemployment cannot be solved by means of fiscal policy measures, and that the latter can possibly even worsen the macroeconomic situation. They differentiate between two ways of financing additional state expenditures:

1. When the state raises money by taking more credit, private entrepreneurs are crowded out of the capital market. Consequently, they invest less. The employment programs of the state are then by and large ineffective. Moreover, when private people lend the state more money, consumption decreases. That means, according to the monetarists, a credit-financed stimulus program of the state does not achieve any increase in aggregate demand. It only results in a redistribution of the same between the public and the private sector.

2. When, instead, the state gets more money printed for the same purpose, then it is, according to the monetarists, not really fiscal policy, but money supply policy. This indeed would have an effect — but what sort of an effect? An *unexpected* and large expansion of the money supply would cause inflation. Cases of galloping inflation and hyperinflation in world economic history support this view.

Keynesians can easily refute the first argument. Since they start out from the fact that in highly industrialized countries in a situation of underemployment equilibrium too much savings remains unutilized, no crowding out can take place if the state borrows more at the capital market. For the same reason, this also cannot reduce private consumption. However, inflationary pressure can result if hitherto unutilized savings are transformed into demand through state actions, and if output does not increase

quickly. But, in any case, Keynesians do not think that a moderate inflation is a problem. Friedman himself did not think that credit-financed
state spending caused inflation. He viewed inflation as a purely monetary
phenomenon.

A relevant question here is also whether an expansion of the money
supply exceeding the normal extent brings only inflation or (also) an
upswing. Friedman's answer is: it only sets off inflation. As stated above,
Keynesians do not believe that such a measure is a very effective means to
bring about an upturn. But they do not deny the effectiveness of reducing the money supply as a means to fight inflation. Monetary policy can
thus easily find a place in their conception of anti-cyclical economic policy, especially because they are prepared to accept a moderate degree of
inflation in order to attain full employment. This is also the case in current times. Two crucial questions thereby are: (1) whether in the case of
a strong expansion of the money supply inflation can be kept at a moderate level, and (2) whether the rise in employment level, possibly attained
through these measures, would also persist at the attained high level when
the measures are wound up.

Friedman's view that a large expansion of the money supply only causes
inflation is based on two assumptions: (1) that prices and wages are not
as sticky as Keynesians believe them to be, that they are actually relatively
flexible; and (2) that the private sector generally sustains production close
to the potential production level (since it is, in their view, relatively stable).
That means the private sector cannot substantially increase output in the
short term. Hence, any unexpectedly large expansion of the money supply
would only cause high inflation.

Some other monetarists think that a large expansion of the money supply can, of course, also bring about an upswing, but that it can only last for
a short time, between two to five years. For the rising inflation rate takes
by surprise both workers and lenders, who cannot increase their wage and
interest demands quickly enough because of existing contracts. As a consequence, *real* wages and *real* interest rates fall, thus generating an impulse
to increase output if the capacities are not already fully utilized. However,
as soon as wages and interest rates have caught up with the increased
inflation rate, output and employment return to their "natural" level. The
upswing will then have been only a flash in the pan.

We see, then, the distance between the two schools on this issue is
much smaller than one might have thought. Not fully utilized capacities — that exactly is the situation in which, and only in which, Keynesians
would recommend their measures to stimulate the economy, whether fiscal

or monetary! Moreover, they would also be satisfied with an upswing for two to five years.

The response of these other monetarists presented above shows that they think nothing of the Keynesian thesis of the liquidity trap. They think that for economic players liquid funds are only a transit station. The liquid money initially held in excess will soon be transformed into financial investments. And since the individual branches of the market are networked, these financial investments will eventually enter the production-income cycle and have a positive impact on demand. That is why, according to them, it is not necessary for the state to create demand or to pursue a special fiscal policy in order to fill a supposed demand gap (see Senf 2001: 250ff.).

TWO "EXPERIMENTS"

In connection with the controversy over the relative importance of fiscal and monetary policy, Friedman (1970: 19ff.) reported on two "nice experiments" that took place in the real economy of the USA. In the mid-sixties the government pursued an expansive fiscal policy. However, the Fed, which is an independent institution, saw inflation picking up in 1966 and curbed the expansion of the money supply in the spring of that year. As a result, it did not increase at all in the last nine months of the year. The result of this jumble of a situation — expansive fiscal policy and restrictive monetary policy — was that in the first half of 1967, economic growth slowed down markedly. Thereafter, the Fed abruptly changed course by 180 degrees. It started "to print money like mad," which caused, with a slight delay, a fast expansion of economic activity.

The second "experiment" took place in 1968. That summer, on the recommendation of the president, Congress passed a supplementary tax of 10 percent on income in order to fight inflation. Even Keynesians, advocates of primacy of fiscal policy, thought it was excessive and feared, as did the Fed, that this would lead to a stagnation. Thereupon the Fed rapidly expanded the money supply. In this way, again, there arose a situation in which two contradictory policies were being pursued — this time, restrictive fiscal policy and expansive monetary policy. Monetarists predicted that the result would be a continuation of inflation, and they were right. Thereupon, in December 1968, the Fed began to reduce the money supply, which brought about a slowing down of growth in the next year. For monetarists the results of these two "experiments" were the definitive evidence of the greater effectiveness of monetary policy against fiscal policy.

### 4. Monetarist Economic Policy

Not all monetarists are of the opinion that the central bank should fine-tune the economy with its monetary policy. Friedman opposed this vehemently. He had no confidence in the ability of officials of central banks to correctly assess the economic situation at particular times. He thought they always reacted too late and too heftily. Reacting too late, they may expand the money supply when the recovery has already begun after a recession, so that their action brings about inflation. Or they may reduce the money supply too early and thus stifle an incipient upturn. What additionally makes fine-tuning very difficult, according to Friedman, is that it takes a few quarters for monetary measures to take effect. "That is why it is a long road to hoe to stop an inflation that has been allowed to start. It cannot be stopped overnight" (Friedman 1970: 23). Friedman's explanation of the Great Depression and the two "experiments" described above seem to support his view.

Nevertheless, some monetarists think that central banks should perform fine-tuning of the economy by means of monetary policy. Firstly, for ideological reasons, they are against state intervention in the economy. And, secondly, on the basis of their analysis, they regard fiscal policy as relatively ineffective. Hence they rely on monetary policy. However, they say monetary policy should not be pursued as interest-rate policy, because interest rates are, in their view, a "highly misleading guide" for policy makers. For the same change in money supply can have, in different situations, countries, and periods, different effects on the interest rates. Moreover, understanding them is difficult because of the distinction between nominal and real interest rates (25f.).

Friedman and most monetarists advocate a fixed rate of growth in money supply to be laid down by law for a long period — e.g., 3 to 5 percent per year. They believe this will give the economy a stable and secure monetary framework and also do away with arbitrary and politically motivated changes in monetary policy. They maintain that if this stable rate of expansion of the money supply matches the expected growth rate of potential production, then there will be no more excessive inflation and the economy can grow steadily over a long period. However, how the economy will then actually develop will depend on some other real factors: "the enterprise, ingenuity and industry of the people; the extent of thrift; the structure of industry and government; the relations among nations, and so on" (Friedman 1970: 24). It is striking that in this enumeration of real factors there is no mention of the propensity to consume, a factor so important to Keynesians. It is also striking that there is a similarity between the first three factors in Friedman's list and the traits of the Schumpeterian entrepreneur.

The theoretical positions of monetarists, e.g., the alleged basic stability of the private sector, have much to do with the fact that they ignore the actually existing imperfections of the market. As soon as they face up to this reality, they have to concede that there can also be self-generated disruptions in the private sector. For this reason, some monetarists endorse the position that the central bank should counteract these disruptions by means of its monetary instruments.

This brings them a little closer to Keynesianism. That is why one may say that "monetarists and Keynesians are not two irreconcilable camps opposing each other; 'pure monetarism' and 'pure Keynesianism' are rather two conceptual endpoints of a spectrum, within which most economists take their place" (Felderer and Homburg 1991: 236). In a simplified form, one can describe their differences as those between two schools, the *priority* areas of whose theoretical work are different and whose economic policy priorities are therefore also different. There are *political* reasons for these differences. Both schools want(ed) to protect capitalism from dangers. However, whereas the one regards high inflation as the greater danger, the other sees it in mass unemployment. That is why there are also conciliatory words on both sides. I have mentioned above that Friedman had said in 1970 that had Keynes lived then, he would have become a monetarist. Also, two Keynesians — Alan S. Blinder and Robert M. Solow — wrote: "Since we all are now Keynesians in the short run, those of us who are not dead in the long run are at least half monetarists" (quoted in Felderer and Homburg 1991: 254, retranslated).

However, as regards positions related to worldview, the differences are serious. It is not for nothing that Keynes was denounced by some of his opponents as a socialist. Whoever pleads for state-sponsored employment programs, which benefit mainly the unemployed and can cause the inflation rate to rise, is not on the same side of the class divide as the monetarists, whose policy of prioritizing the fight against inflation benefits mainly the owners of large money capital.

The anti-inflation policy started in the United States in 1979 was an application of the monetarist economic policy. This time, the Fed did not want to directly push the interest rates upwards, namely, by fixing a higher prime rate. This time, it laid emphasis on slowing down the expansion of money supply by other means, for instance, by laying down a higher mandatory cash reserve holding for credit given by commercial banks. The Fed hoped that the slower expansion of money supply would cause a rise in the interest rates at the capital market. This strategy was quite successful, as we saw earlier on. However, the argument of the monetarists that a stringent and credible money supply policy is a cheap anti-inflationary strategy was not confirmed by facts. The price paid for this success was high: recession and high unemployment.

## 5. Neo-Liberalism and Supply-Side Economics

For many years now, one has hardly heard of monetarism. The reason for this might lie in the fact that all over the world central banks have returned to the policy of fine-tuning the economy by changing the prime interest rate. They had to do that because in the 1980s and 1990s one of the main assumptions of monetarism — namely, that the velocity of circulation of money $(V)$ is stable — no longer held. $(V)$ became very unstable due to some innovations in the world of finance, such that central banks could no longer rely solely on the regulation of money supply. A second reason could have been that the other aspects of monetarism were subsumed under "neo-liberalism," which came up later. Since the early 1980s, in the public discourse, we have heard more of neo-liberal economic policy and supply-side economics.

Neo-liberalism in the narrower sense is a revival and modernization of Adam Smith's classical liberalism. According to Smith, the state should play only one role, that of a "night watchman." It should not intervene in the economic process, but only guarantee that economic subjects abide by the contract law. For, left alone, the market can best regulate everything else through competition: serve the interests of consumers, increase prosperity, etc. Neo-liberalism has, however, learned a lesson from history and realized that the market is neither a perfect nor a stable system. It therefore demands that the state should prevent the emergence of monopolies and formation of cartels and ensure fair competition in the market, e.g., by eliminating subsidies. Neo-liberals think that too much bureaucracy blocks investment and, hence, hampers job creation and the starting of new businesses, which the state should actually facilitate. For this purpose the jungle of rules and regulations should be thinned out; in other words, the business world should be deregulated. For the rest, the state should only lay down the basic regulatory framework for the economy and provide and/or improve the infrastructure. Neo-liberals do not contest the assertion that market economies also have negative effects, such as involuntary unemployment and poverty. The state has to correct them, but at the same time it should reduce total state spending and privatize state-owned enterprises. Neo-liberals often express their views and demands in a pithy slogan: as much market as possible, and only as much state as absolutely necessary.

Unlike monetarism, supply-side economics, which also played an important role in the economic policies of Reagan and Thatcher, focuses on fiscal policy and other state policies. However, it does not share the demand-orientation of Keynesianism. Supply-siders reproach Keynesians for pursuing only a business-cycle policy, that is, for almost exclusively concentrating on the *short-term stability* of the economy and ignoring its *long-term vitality*. Supply-side economics maintains that it is only the degree of willingness of the people to work and to save that sets a limit to an economy. It therefore stresses the importance of structure policy, that is, the importance of long-term improvement of the supply conditions of the factors of production: of capital, of entrepreneurship, and of labor. In this way, government policies can foster growth of *potential* production. From this perspective, fine-tuning of the economy by means of frequent changes in some variables is detrimental to long-term growth. According to supply-siders, during the dominance of Keynesianism the economy became too addicted to state stimulus programs for growth. In contrast, supply-side economics advocates more faith in market forces, an anti-inflation policy, and a return to balanced budgets. This is actually a revival of the classical/orthodox approach to economic policy.

Supply-side economics aims at giving strong incentives to suppliers of factors of production, that is, good net yield (i.e., yield after tax deduction) from savings, investments, and labor. This should be achieved through low tax rates; this is the task of fiscal policy. According to supply-siders, high taxes eliminate these incentives. The higher the taxes, the less people will save, invest, and work, so that — in the end — not just production but also tax revenue will fall. Hence, the effect of taxes on the incentive structure, that is, the supply side, should be the focus of analysis, rather than their effect on aggregate demand. If the government reduces taxes on labor, interest income, and dividends, then the savings and investment rates and, consequently, the economic growth rate can rise. Then, moreover, tax revenue will increase and budget deficit will fall.

Savings is the area where the difference between supply-side economics and Keynesianism can be seen most clearly. In the former, there is no such thing as the paradox of thrift. Quite on the contrary, people should be encouraged to save more, because the problem is not too much savings, but too little. Also, for supply-siders the function of tax cuts is not to stimulate consumption but rather to encourage more investments. Arthur Laffer, a prominent representative of this school, maintained that, at the time, the tax rates in the United States were too high and that a drastic reduction in tax rates would result in an increase in tax revenues. The Reagan administration, which followed this advice, expected in fact that its huge tax cuts would finance themselves. But this expectation did not materialize. Moreover, since the government could not reduce state spending, it had to increase the budget deficit, especially because spending on arms increased. Therefore, in the 1990s (the Clinton era), tax rates had to be raised. Keynesian Joseph Stiglitz (2003: 17) labeled Laffer's thesis "Voodoo economics."

Besides tax reductions, supply-siders had some other ideas for increasing net yields from investments (rate of profit). They demanded a cutback in budget deficits, from which they expected a fall in the long-term interest rates, which, they thought, would in turn encourage entrepreneurs to invest more. They demanded wage flexibility, deregulation of the labor market, and curtailment of the power of trade unions. In order to eliminate hurdles to investment, they demanded that bureaucracy and the number of regulations be reduced.

Supply-siders also voiced a more general criticism of the economic conditions at the time, which, they thought, were generally impairing the efficiency of the economy. They criticized the "hardening" and "ingrained rigidities" of the economic structure, the lacking mobility of the economic subjects, the inertia of the institutions, the inflated social security system, the subsidies for dying industries, protectionism, etc. (see Hallwirth 1998: 49). They lashed out against the public sector in general and demanded privatization of state-owned enterprises.

In those days, in connection with the term "efficiency of the economy," one often thought of productivity increase and an "innovation-friendly atmosphere." These phrases are reminiscent of Schumpeter. Indeed, one can say that supply-side economics took over many of his ideas.

# V

# Why Keynesianism Failed—
# Explanations of Professional Economists

The great majority of professional economists believed that Keynesianism had failed beyond repair by the end of the 1970s, but even then many Keynesians refused to accept this point of view. In this chapter I shall present some explanations given by Keynesians and other professional economists for the "failure" of Keynesianism in the 1970s.

## 1. A Political Decision

James Tobin, Nobel laureate for economics, after whom the "Tobin tax" demanded by the movement of critics of globalization was named, published in 1977 a paper entitled "How Dead Is Keynes?" In this paper he vindicated both the Keynesian crisis-diagnosis and the Keynesian policy recommendations.

He succinctly stated what in his view caused the recession in the United States: "The 1974–75 recession was the result not of double-digit inflation but of the quixotic measures taken by the Fed to oppose an externally generated bulge of specific prices. It was not the first recession generated by anti-inflationary policy" (Tobin 1977: 277).

In defense of Keynesianism he enumerated four central theses of Keynes's *General Theory* (here paraphrased, in italics) and claimed that the events of the mid-seventies did not refute them.

First thesis: *Prices and wages are sticky. They only react slowly to increases in demand and supply. They react particularly slowly to oversupply.* Tobin pointed out that between 1974 and 1977 wages and prices continued their spiraling inflationary trend of the previous years in spite of the recession, high unemployment, and overcapacity in the economy. In this specific case, when demand increased after some time, output and employment also increased and a slow recovery ensued, but inflation did not accelerate. He saw in these facts a confirmation of the logically derived conclusion from the above thesis, namely, that it is actually output and employment that react promptly to changes in supply and demand, not prices.

The second thesis follows from the first: *In developed capitalist economies involuntary unemployment continues for long periods. Unemployed persons who are willing to work for wages lower than the prevailing ones do not find jobs because they are not able to signal their willingness effectively.* Tobin thought this was clearly the case in 1974.

Third thesis: *Investments are dependent on profit expectations; expectation of stable prosperity is an important stabilizer of investments; when such an expectation is eliminated, a mild cyclical recession can become a long persistent stagnation.* Tobin thought this was how the Great Depression of the early 1930s came about. And as to the 1974–1975 recession, he pointed out that in 1977 investments were still 7 percent lower than in 1973.

Fourth thesis: *Even if wages and prices were not sticky, they would still not be able to stabilize the economies exposed to supply-and-demand shocks.* This was the Keynesian thesis that opposed the orthodox doctrine that claimed market mechanisms were inherently self-correcting and self-stabilizing. The purported demonstration of the validity of this orthodox doctrine within certain *individual markets* was for Keynes not convincing in respect to the *whole economy.* That is why he thought demand management was an easier method of stabilizing the economy than wage level management, even if the latter were a realistic option. Tobin wrote that price adjustments in interwoven free markets, in which competition prevailed, were a very complicated affair and that on this issue there was hardly any data that could serve as conclusive evidence. So Keynes's skepticism with respect to this orthodox doctrine was justified.

In conclusion, Tobin maintained that the economic situation at the time did not contradict any of these four Keynesian theses. Actually, the situation in the mid-seventies fit the Keynesian theory much better than the situation in any other post-war period — with the exception of the early 1960s. Tobin also discussed many questions of detail of the time and convincingly pointed out the errors of critics of Keynesianism.

Tobin maintained that Keynesian recipes against recession and stagnation were by no means rendered obsolete by subsequent developments in macroeconomic theory. He criticized that opponents of an expansive fiscal policy opposed it with arguments that would make sense in a situation of full employment but that would be nonsensical in the case of underemployment of labor and capital. When the US federal government incurred new debts in 1975 and 1976 — partly also because their regular tax revenue had fallen due to the recession — there was panic amongst orthodox economists, who criticized this move with the old, fallacious crowding-out argument (see chapter IV). Monetarists also opposed the expansion of the money supply, because they considered it to be an intrinsically inflationary measure.

Tobin criticized the cautious "go-slow recovery policy" pursued by the US government since 1974 as too expensive: $50 billion worth of goods and services not produced for each additional percentage point of unemployment. But the government and the Fed had a different priority, namely, to combat inflation. Against that, Tobin would have preferred the goal of a "sustainable and complete recovery," for which he considered an expansive monetary policy to be necessary. "In an economy suffering from insufficiency of demand ... more labor and capital services will be supplied, if demanded, along the ongoing path of wages and prices, without accelerating their increase" (1977: 277). In plain English, Tobin was prepared to relinquish the fight against inflation as long as the existing inflation rate was not exceeded. He recommended an active "incomes policy," that is, regulatory measures, as "the only way" to prevent a further rise in the inflation rate. Tobin knew all the usual arguments against his position. But "the microeconomic distortions of incomes policies would be trivial compared to the macroeconomic costs of prolonged under-employment of labor and capital" (280). He pointed out that, after publishing his *General Theory*, Keynes too had acknowledged the need for a sort of direct wage/price policy.

But even in 1979 Keynesians seemed to have capitulated. A very prominent British Keynesian, Joan Robinson, wrote with resignation in an article entitled "Has Keynes Failed?":

> At any moment there are a great number of contradictory ideas
> being advocated by various economists. The establishment
> picks out the one that suits them at the moment. In 1945, the
> promise of abolishing unemployment was what the authorities
> needed so that Keynes was the favorite. Now inflation is seen as
> the greater evil and Milton Friedman is all the rage.

What Robinson wrote in this article on an aspect of Keynes's thinking, unknown until then, is highly interesting. After meeting with his converts in Washington, Keynes purportedly said to a friend: "I was the only non-Keynesian there" (Robinson 1979/1983: 397). This suggests how overzealous early Keynesians were, and reminds me of a very similar statement by Marx, who once allegedly said: "All I know is that I am not a Marxist" (quoted in Bettelheim 1978: 503). Robinson further wrote:

> In fact Maynard Keynes himself was somewhat skeptical about
> the possibility of achieving permanent full employment. ... It

was his British disciples, rather than he, who drafted the white
paper in 1944 which proclaimed that it is the responsibility of
government to maintain a high and stable level of employment.
Keynes said: you can promise to be good but you cannot promise
to be clever. Moreover he foresaw that if a long run of near-full
employment was achieved, inflation through rising money wage
rates would present an awkward political problem though he
did not suggest how to solve it. (Robinson 1979/1983: 397)

Some other early Keynesians were also worried about the danger of
inflation as a result of full employment.

Nevertheless, wrote Robinson, Keynes was convinced that his new theory would have a great practical significance. Robinson thinks Keynes had
overestimated the power of reason. He had believed in the "dominance
of ideas over vested interests." This was, in Robinson's view, "an illusion"
(ibid.).

After the experience of war-time full employment, the Treasury
View could not be revived, but the only moral that was drawn
from the new theory was to allow budget deficits as a prophy-
lactic against recessions. The main consequence was the
hypertrophy of the military-industrial complex in the USA.
Useful government expenditure was branded as socialism but it
was always possible to get a vote for "defense." (1979/1983: 398)

Robinson also criticized the Keynesians among economists and politicians who had turned Keynesianism into a "new orthodoxy." According
to her, the economists had avoided undertaking a radical examination of
the whole corpus of the traditional orthodox doctrine, a move that Keynes
had actually called for. As for teaching economics, only an "emasculated
version" of Keynesian theory was being taught (ibid.). She also found fault
with Keynesian theory itself, namely, that it left aside the problems of the
long term.

Finally, Robinson also stated the *political* root cause of the failure of
Keynesianism. Keynes, no anti-capitalist, had tried to save the system
from itself by attempting to remedy its defects. But, to orthodoxy, "even to
mention that it has defects appears to be dangerous" (ibid.).

What Robinson meant by the expression "emasculated version" was
the so-called Keynesian-neoclassical synthesis (KNS) created by some
renowned Keynesians but rejected by true and leftist Keynesians. These
were two very opposite lines of thought. "On the one hand the Keynesian

approach: macroeconomic, demand-oriented, emphasis on overall economic imbalance and underemployment. On the other hand the classical approach: microeconomic, supply-oriented, postulates of equilibrium in sector markets and full employment of all resources" (Willke 2002: 146). This synthesis made Keynesian theory acceptable to professional economists: it was made innocuous, stripped of its thorns, namely, its criticism of the defects of capitalism.

According to Hutton, this reduction of Keynesianism to a harmless theory could happen because of the strong liberal and, above all, individualistic tradition in the politics, economy, and society of Anglo-Saxon countries. In the liberal tradition, social well-being results from the actions of individuals. Keynesianism goes too much against the grain of this tradition (Hutton 1986/2001: 197).

> In fact the integration of Keynesian economics back into the main stream of economics has meant that the "Keynesian Revolution" has lost almost all its meaning. We are left with the slogans and empty theoretical categories; but the insights that filled them have been lost in the process of integration. The Keynesian economics that we are told has nothing to offer us today has little to do with the economics of Keynes. (xviii)

In practical politics, this reduction and integration of Keynesianism meant that towards the end of the 1970s the responsibility of the state as the guarantor of common good, and especially of full employment, was ignored or even denied. That the monetarist notion of inflation being the greatest danger for the economy and society could prevail was likely also a result of this integration.

## 2. Is Inflation a Major or Rather a Minor Evil?

Joan Robinson made it clear that it was a *political* decision to regard inflation as a greater evil than high unemployment. But why? Robinson spoke of "vested interests" that dominated politics. Richard Douthwaite — a British professional economist, but one who is very close to the activists of TOES (The Other Economic Summit) — calls these vested interests by name. Otherwise, he takes a Keynesian stand on inflation, which also goes beyond standard Keynesianism.

Douthwaite (1992: chapter 5) gives an explanation for the high inflation rates in the 1970s in the industrialized countries, especially in the United Kingdom: (1) A massive increase in the US current account deficit[9] in 1970 and 1971 (partly because of the armaments purchase all over the world during the Vietnam War) flooded the world with US dollars. This intensified the boom in most of the industrialized countries, which was not only welcomed but also supported by the politicians of these countries because many of them were running for election at the time. (2) Then, in 1973, came the final breakdown of the Bretton-Woods system of fixed exchange rates. Since then, governments thought they did not need to control their spending as carefully as before, because the exchange rates were now being determined only by the foreign exchange market. (3) This was still the time when Keynesianism prevailed. Douthwaite reports that Anthony Barber, then British Chancellor of the Exchequer, had seen in this situation "a rare opportunity to secure a sustained and faster rate of economic expansion over a considerable period of years" (1992: 58). He also took measures for a "growth spurt." In 1972, he reduced taxes and increased the budget deficit by £1.2 billion — at a time when the inflation rate in the United Kingdom was already at 7 percent. (4) At the same time, he freed banks from the controls that regulated the granting of loans — controls that had been in place since World War II. All this led to a massive increase in credit given to the private sector — in one year by 345 percent, totaling £6.4 billion. This fueled the inflation.

Douthwaite wrote that by then the long boom had already caused a scarcity of some raw and basic materials, including foodstuffs. As a consequence, production costs and cost of living had gone up, unleashing an inflationary wage-price spiral. Despite this, Barber's fiscal measures alone would not have had too great an aggravating effect on inflation. But the credit expansion in the private sector was just too much.

(5) Moreover, there was the oil price shock of 1973. Since in industrial economies oil is in different degrees a production input for almost all goods and services, the shock led to a general and strong increase in production costs. Further price increases in several steps had to be undertaken in order to adjust the economy to this increase in costs. Together, the last two events pushed up the rate of inflation in the United Kingdom to 15.9 percent in 1974 and 24.2 percent in 1975.

According to Douthwaite, "the dust had settled" in 1977 and "everyone was pleasantly surprised by how quickly the world's economies had returned to their pre-crisis condition, particularly in view of the pessimistic predictions made when the crisis broke" (1992: 58). This remark of Douthwaite's is difficult to understand. We know that the US authorities had to take drastic action in 1979 in order to curb inflation. And in the early 1980s several industrialized economies suffered from recession or stagnation resulting from their preceding anti-inflationary policies (see section 3 of this chapter and chapter VI). Maybe he means that the people stoically accepted all the consequences.

Be that as it may, Douthwaite does not consider inflation to be a major evil. On the contrary, he thinks inflation plays a positive role in society, and is a fine "balancing mechanism." He explains his stance thus: "[I]f the rate of inflation (say 4 percent) plus the rate of GNP growth in real terms (say 3 percent) is equal to the rate of interest (say 7 percent), the division of national income between borrowers and lenders stays constant" (1992: 64). Moreover, since trade unions make sure by means of collective bargaining that wages keep up with inflation and productivity increase, workers' share of the cake also remains the same. Thus, though the three social groups do not get an equal share of the newly created wealth, this wealth is distributed in the same ratio as in the previous year. If at some point the profit margin of most entrepreneurs in an industry falls below the acceptable level, they will try to increase the prices. And they will be successful if there is no foreign competition. The inflation caused thereby reduces the *real* interest rates, the *real* wages, and the *real* prices that entrepreneurs have to pay their lenders, workers, and suppliers. This way their profit margin rises again. On the other hand, if the profits of the entrepreneurs increase above the acceptable level, they will invest more, and this will normally lead to more demand for labor and capital. Both tend to push wages and interest rates up, which increases the workers' and lenders' share in the national income. However, for this nice adjusting mechanism to work, the government has to adopt a relaxed attitude towards inflation.

The attentive reader must have noticed that this is nothing other than the usual equilibrium theory of orthodox economists, who advocate a noninterventionist posture of the state towards the ups and downs of business cycles. What is new in Douthwaite's approach is his argument for tolerating inflation: it should be tolerated because anti-inflationary actions generally lead to recession and unemployment. But, unlike orthodox economists, he does not support a relaxed attitude toward rising unemployment.

Douthwaite concedes that two social groups lose out with inflation: fixed-interest savers, and pensioners who live by a fixed life annuity. But, according to him, for protecting these two groups no general anti-inflation policy, which harms the economy as a whole, is called for. The state can help these two groups through special measures instead.

Douthwaite claims to have observed that in the 1950s and 1960s the British public had a relaxed attitude towards a moderate inflation (at the time, 3.2 percent on average). In the 1970s, they were naturally worried about the two-digit inflation rate. But the driving forces behind the anti-inflation policy of the British and American establishments were the banks and holders of large money capital, whose capital loses, as a rule, some of its value with inflation (whereas borrowers benefit from it). These are the "vested interests" Robinson referred to.

In the 1970s, the banks in the UK were in a very dangerous position. After controls on bank loans had been lifted, several small banks had given too many loans to construction companies. Soon there was an oversupply of housing property and the prices plummeted. Panic spread amongst the concerned banks, because real estate was the security for many of those loans. Of course, big banks rescued the small ones in trouble, but then doubts on the solvency of the rescuers arose. In order to defuse the situation the government lifted the then existing freezing of commercial rents, which led to a certain rise in such rents and thus made the concerned loans somewhat more secure. But that again lured investors into the real estate market. This crisis of the banking system was not limited to the United Kingdom. In Germany, the Herstatt Bank declared bankruptcy (1974), and in New York, the Franklin National Bank just managed to escape the same fate.

Douthwaite thinks the second oil price shock should have been allowed to cause a round of inflation, as the first had been, so that the economy could adjust to the higher production costs. But the banks, who had become wiser through the previous crisis they had just barely managed to overcome, put pressure on the political class and persuaded them to not undertake the necessary corresponding expansion of the money supply.

Douthwaite (1999: 59) alleges that also after World War I the British banks had "forced" the then government to restore the gold standard for the pound sterling at the pre-war parity, which was done in 1925. Through this action the British pound became highly overvalued; this severely harmed the rest of the British economy, which was mainly export-oriented. The banks, however, profited from this measure. For, as a result, the value of their capital increased, and London could again establish itself as the center of international finance. Also in 1979, the Fed's decision to fight inflation with tough measures was the result of pressure from the US banks, according to Douthwaite (60).

Inflation can also be fought by increasing taxes, which results in citizens having less money to spend. But that is loathsome for all taxpayers. If direct taxes are raised, with progressive tax rates in place, the rich have to pay much more than do ordinary people. That is why the rich would rather have a tight-money policy for fighting inflation.

## 3. Public Campaigns

As stated above, public opinion in the United Kingdom had changed: the mood was no longer relaxed; there was anxiety about the double-digit inflation. Douthwaite reports that in the 1970s, a flood of books and articles presented inflation as a great danger and as the main problem of the economy. An author who had worked for the IMF earlier on wrote: "The ills of such inflation fall most heavily on the poorest but the great majority of people are increasingly harmed in many different ways. Among its victims are national objectives of satisfactory levels of growth, employment and income distribution" (quoted in Douthwaite 1992: 61). Douthwaite also reports that the economist George L. Bach found no evidence that inflation had any negative effect on growth and employment. But, according to Douthwaite, Bach was a solitary exception.

Nevertheless, it cannot be said there was a consensus among economists that inflation was an evil. According to reports, opinions among economists ranged from thinking "the costs are trivial" to believing "the costs are enormous and include an eroding of the social fabric." However, at the time, except for Professor Bach, hardly anybody among the economists, who saw no danger in inflation, expressed that opinion publicly. Douthwaite criticizes this behavior as a "shameful failure." Then, in 1981, 364 economists published a letter in *The Times* (London) expressing the view that the conservative policy of fighting inflation would "deepen the depression, erode the industrial base of our economy and threaten its social and political stability" (Douthwaite 1992: 61). But it was too late; vested interests had already established their hegemony over the economic policy of the USA and the United Kingdom a few years earlier.

While Tobin put the blame for the downfall of Keynesianism on the Fed's "quixotic measures," and Robinson and Douthwaite on vested interests, Susan George, a leading personality of the Attac movement, thought retrospectively in 1999 that the theoreticians and ideologues of the capitalist class had fought for this political change. She suggested a conspiracy of these ideologues when, in a speech, she explained the triumph of neo-liberalism over Keynesianism in the following words:

> [O]ne explanation for this triumph of neo-liberalism ... is that
> the neo-liberals had bought and paid for their own unscrupulous
> and retrograde "Great Transformation." They had understood —
> in contrast to the progressives — that ideas have consequences.
> Starting from a small cell at the University of Chicago, to which
> the economic philosopher Friedrich von Hayek and his students

like Milton Friedman belonged, the neo-liberals and their financiers had built up a huge international network of foundations, institutes, research centers, journals, scholars, writers and public relations hacks, in order to develop and pack their ideas and doctrine and to beat the drum for it.

They had built up this extraordinarily efficient ideological cadre, because they had understood something about which the Italian Marxist thinker Antonio Gramsci had spoken when he developed the concept of cultural hegemony: If one can occupy the heads of the people, their hearts and hands will follow. . . . [T]he ideological and propaganda work of the rightists had been absolutely brilliant. They had spent hundreds of millions of dollars.[10] (George 1999: 5)

## 4. Some More Objective Explanations

Susan George's explanation is not very convincing. It sounds more like a conspiracy theory. In the 1970s, and also afterwards, Keynesians were working in universities, research institutes, trade unions, and governments in very large numbers, and at high levels. There was no shortage of money and opportunities for them. Why couldn't they organize a counter-campaign? The only plausible explanation for this is that they were no longer very sure about their views (see chapter IV).

Roughly in the same vein, Will Hutton, looking back on those years, mentioned a characteristic feature of applied Keynesianism that he considered to be a cause of the latter's defeat, namely, the lack of efforts to influence the world of finance. At least in the United Kingdom, the lenders (banks, insurance companies, the central bank, etc.) were very conservative in their lending policy. The banks, in his view, always wanted to sit on a thick liquidity cushion, thus undermining attempts to stimulate a stagnating economy (see Hutton 1986/2001: chapter 7).

Some other authors, who also wanted to save Keynesianism and the welfare state, gave another, more convincing explanation. They simply acknowledged that mistakes had been made. For example, Hugh Stretton wrote:

Continuing growth and full employment led governments to dismantle some of the controls which were actually contributing to the growth and full employment. (Because the controls had been associated with temporary war organization or postwar reconstruction, their value as permanent aids to growth and stability was not widely understood). (1999: 117)

The removal or loosening of controls and steering measures — for instance, the lifting of controls on the lending business of British banks in 1972 — had most probably contributed to accelerating the inflation. It could well be that powerful people with vested interests had in those years pushed the governments to do this. It could also be that in the second half of the 1970s the banks and owners of money-capital had pushed the government towards fighting inflation. But this time they had public opinion on their side, with the prevailing perception that a double-digit inflation was bad. Douthwaite wrote:

> The main asset the banks had in persuading the politicians to take such a drastic action on their behalf was the public perception that inflation was harmful. The popular prejudice was based on highly colored accounts of the German hyperinflation in the wake of the First World War in which people were said to have needed wheelbarrows to carry their money when they went out shopping. It had strengthened during the fifties and sixties, when the main economic problem the [British] governments had faced had been keeping the British inflation rate in step with rates in other countries so that the pound's fixed exchange rate could be maintained [that was agreed upon at the Bretton Woods conference]. The whole postwar period [in the United Kingdom] seemed to have been an endless series of inflation-induced balance-of-payments crises cured by cutting state spending, imposing pay pauses and import controls, and restricting the outflow of capital and the use of hire purchase. (1992: 60)

In those years, these restrictive direct measures did not lead to any severe recession. At most, they caused a few small dents in the long boom. In the second half of the 1970s and beginning of the 1980s, however, the situation was far worse. Consequently, drastic anti-inflation measures had to be taken.

But these explanations too are unsatisfactory. It can very well be that the conflict between the two objectives — full employment and the fight against inflation — is simply unsolvable. A lower inflation rate could only be had at the price of a recession or stagnation. "The inflation could only have been fought [also in accordance with Keynesian anti-cyclical policy] with restrictive measures and the unemployment caused by stagnation only with expansive measures — an unsolvable dilemma" at a time marked by stagflation (Willke 2002: 164).

## 5. The Objective Compulsion to Restructure the Economy —
   Why Keynesianism *Had* to be Buried

That it is necessary to address the issue of inflation with a relaxed attitude in order to avoid recession was (and still is) for most people an unconvincing argument that is much too abstract.

John Gray's explanation for the political change in the United Kingdom goes deeper and is therefore more plausible. On the IMF intervention in British economic policy in 1976 (see chapter IV) he wrote:

> The declining productivity and social and industrial conflicts of British corporatism were the catalysts for the intervention of the International Monetary Fund. ... That intervention began the swift unraveling of Britain's post-war Keynesian economic consensus which culminated with Margaret Thatcher's rise to power in 1979. (1999: 16)

Regarding Thatcher's policy, Gray continued:

> [It] was an attempt to impose a *much needed modernization* on the British economy. ... In its initial policy agenda nothing was more important [to Thatcherism] than trade union reform [i.e., the unions' weakening]. Thatcher understood that British corporatism — the triangular coordination of economic policy by government, employers and trade unions — had become an engine of industrial conflict and strife over the distribution of the national income rather than an instrument of wealth creation or a guarantor of social cohesion. (24f.; emphasis added)

On New Zealand, another Anglo-Saxon country, Gray wrote that in the early 1980s, New Zealanders feared that their country could lose its status as a First World economy — a result of "quickening relative economic decline." As was the case in other countries, "New Right thought seemed compelling in having radical solutions for economic *problems that could not go untreated for much longer.*" And as in the United Kingdom, it was Labour governments that between 1984 and 1990 undertook the elimination of "New Zealand's inheritance as an egalitarian social democracy and a socially cohesive Keynesian managed economy." This work was only completed by the (conservative) National Party (39f.; emphasis added).

Gray comments on the outcome of this policy as follows:

> In strictly economic terms, the neo-liberal experiment achieved many of its objectives. It forced a restructuring of the economy which, though it could have been achieved without some of the social costs imposed by neo-liberal policies, *would have been necessary in any case* [because of the ongoing globalization of the world economy]. (44; emphasis added)

In order to make the value of these assessments clearly understood, I must add that Gray was for a while an advisor to the Thatcher government. Later, also in the book I have here quoted from, he vehemently criticized neo-liberal globalization.

## 6. Macro-Politics

Let us return to the inflation issue: Why were politicians in the industrialized countries not prepared to ignore the double-digit inflation, or why couldn't they accept the advice of, for instance, James Tobin? Were there also some more convincing grounds than pressure from powerful people with vested interests and the negative public perception of inflation?

Some reasons have been mentioned that even Keynesians cannot possibly deem wrong. For them expectations play a very important part in the decision-making process of economic subjects, particularly in regard to investment decisions of entrepreneurs. In the Keynesian era there was practically a general expectation that the state would see to it that full employment prevailed. That induced trade unions as well as entrepreneurs to make such decisions and act in such a way (excessive wage demands and price increases) that the already ongoing inflation caused by other factors was further fueled. Worse still, all market participants perceived budget deficits as a permanent inclination of state policy and framed their own long-term price policy accordingly. Occasional attempts by governments to curb inflation were half-hearted and temporary. That undermined the credibility of Keynesian anti-cyclical economic policy.

On the other hand, any inflation rate perceived as too high makes entrepreneurs expect that now measures will be taken to cool down the overheated economy. This expectation results not just from the usual practice of central banks, but also from the anti-cyclical economic policy propagated by Keynesians. This leads to a cautious attitude to new investments that does not end with equilibrium at full employment but leads to recession, which can turn into a depression. What Tobin, Robinson, and Douthwaite have written on the issue suggests that this is exactly what happened in the second half of the 1970s and beginning of the 1980s.

It is important to stress the difference between the Keynesian policy of *limiting* inflation and the neo-liberal policy of *fighting it*. What the Keynesians advocate can be well described with the term "fine-tuning," that is, using the tools of economic policy for the purpose of attaining and maintaining a permanent "quasi boom" with moderate inflation. Why did the then ruling governments, who were still under the influence of Keynesians, fai to successfully apply this fine-tuning in the 1970s?

One reason was that the Keynesians have never been the only ones who could influence economic policy. Another reason, a general lesson of history, is that when striking a balance between the interests of different classes does not succeed, then it is the rich who have more pull. After all, under capitalism, money rules the world. Douthwaite wrote in general terms:

> The richest half of the community she [Thatcher] represented
> *felt* that progress towards greater equality had gone too far,
> even though the distribution of both income and wealth had
> not shifted against it for a generation. Striving for harmony was
> out; readiness for confrontation was in ... conflict was inescap-
> able." (1992: 57; emphasis added)

But this is only one side of the answer. The other side can be summarized thus: In an era in which not only full employment but also *continuous* economic growth, steadily rising standard of living, and welfare state had become goals of the state, effectively limiting inflation was *politically* very difficult. In the upswing phases, the state should have drastically reduced its expenditures and built up budget surpluses in order to pay off the debts incurred during the downswing phases. But by the mid-sixties all welfare-state spending financed largely through budget deficits had become irrevocable rights of the beneficiaries. And since for political reasons it was not easy to further raise taxes and charges to an adequate level, budget deficits became a permanent feature of state policy. More and more new debts were incurred, often only to service the old ones. Even some Keynesians complained about "the *inertial feature* of public spending" and the fact that it "has an inbuilt tendency to increase," which leads to rising state indebtedness (Hutton 1986/2001: 214). That is why hardly any measure was taken to contain inflation — quite on the contrary.

That means, right from the beginning there has never been a consequent anti-cyclical policy, but only a half one, that is, a pro-boom and preventive *anti-recession* policy. The consequence was a permanent distribution struggle and continuously rising unit labor costs; wages and prices rose also in downswing phases. The final outcome of all this could be nothing other than stagflation. What has been depicted here as, so to speak, a political compulsion, can also be considered clientele politics and misuse of Keynesian policies by politicians.

However, limiting state spending alone would not have been sufficient for limiting inflation. In the Keynesian era, during the long boom, the private sector too had enormously expanded. If the Fed hadn't taken strong action in 1979 to curb that expansion (see chapter IV), the high inflation of those days could not have been contained.

High private-sector indebtedness might be bad for the whole of the economy (think of the subprime mortgage crisis in the USA from 2008–2009). But why should it be bad if public debt increases or is too high? In well-functioning First World countries, the state, unlike private sector firms, cannot break down if it has solvency problems for some time. It can, after all, increase taxes, duties, and charges, or cut state spending if necessary! Lower-ranking states, as long as they have not ceased to function, can request that creditors allow them to extend the term of repayment. This was and still is the reason why Keynesians did not (and still do not) see any great problem in high levels of public debt. And why should it be bad if the ratio of public spending to GDP is too high? Whether an amount of money is spent by the state or by private economic subjects is, seen macroeconomically, irrelevant, since demand is created in any case.

However, what is seen macro-*economically* as irrelevant can be or become macro-*politically* very problematic. That was and still is the case with the public spending ratio. The hegemony of the welfare state ideal and Keynesian thought in the post-war period led to an increase in the public spending ratio. During the long boom, citizens could easily bear the burden of increasing taxes and charges, especially as they themselves, even the well-to-do, benefited from the public services that were becoming larger and better. But that changed in the 1970s. Firstly, parallel to rising wages and salaries all labor-intensive public (as well as private-sector) services (e.g., education, medical care, etc.) became more and more expensive. Ever costlier technological innovations, such as new medical equipment, also contributed to the rise in costs. The costs of social security benefits for a now growing number of unemployed people and for pensioners, who now lived longer, rose too. This required a larger public-spending ratio and led to conflicts over tax rates. In some countries there were tax rebels, some of whom founded their own protest parties.

Secondly, there were changes in the social composition of the population. The proportion of classical workers and other low-income earners in it — that is, the traditional voters of the Keynesian social democrats with their welfare-state orientation — was continuously dwindling. Also the character of the middle class, a large minority, gradually changed. It can be said about the middle class of the 1950s and 1960s that their consciousness was molded by the depression of the 1930s and the "total war," so that they had a strong sense of social solidarity. On the middle class of the 1970s and 1980s Stretton wrote:

> The fast growth of incomes, of household capital and of helpful
> public services was increasing the numbers of contented and
> [therefore] potentially conservative voters. And the elite
> schooled in depression and war and Keynesian economics
> was giving way to a well-off generation who had led liberation
> movements and other campaigns against government in the
> 1960s, then lost faith in economic policies that betrayed
> expectations by allowing the simultaneous rise of inflation
> and unemployment. (1999: 117f.)

So it was not only powerful forces with vested interests, like the banks and the financial aristocracy, that pushed through the political transformation, but partly also the prosperity generation, the majority of the population. After all, Thatcher and Reagan were elected! By the beginning of the 1970s, in the industrial countries, the poor and the unemployed were a small minority. So it can perhaps be said, not without some justification, that through its successes — the welfare state and the near full employment — Keynesianism dug its own grave.

# VI.

# The Crises in Globalized Neo-Liberal Capitalism

With Reagan and Thatcher in the United States and the United Kingdom and, later, with Helmut Kohl in West Germany, the era of neo-liberalism started in the beginning of the 1980s, and it soon spread to the rest of the world. Since the early 1990s, after the demise of the communist regimes, it has also gained a foothold in the territory of the former Soviet Union and in Eastern Europe. Under the political rule of a supposedly communist party, large parts of the Chinese economy work according to nearly neo-liberal rules. The early 1990s can be regarded as the beginning of an era termed "globalization," which was made possible through fast developments in information technology and very low transportation costs. The *internationalization of production* (by means of international division of labor among the industrialized countries and their interdependence) had begun a little earlier. Globalization does not just mean the worldwide, i.e., geographic, expansion of these phenomena. It is also qualitatively different; it is *neo-liberal* globalization. It comprises: (1) Free trade. Import duties and other trade barriers are being progressively scaled down. The market is becoming a global market, and competition is becoming global competition. (2) Market players are not only trading in goods, but also in services and capital. Unlike in the past (except the colonial past), when mainly credit was given to states and companies abroad, large-scale private investments including financial ones are now being made in foreign countries. National borders are progressively losing importance. Investments are being made not just for producing goods, but also for producing services. Such investments are being progressively deregulated; that is, rules and regulations governing them are being relaxed. (3) These developments lead to competition between alternative locations for industry and services, since large and medium-size companies can now either themselves produce their goods in many countries or get them produced there by local companies (outsourcing). This leads to strong capital mobility. (4) That results in a much stronger growth of world trade than that of world goods production. (5) The above developments make it necessary for billions of dollars to move across borders. That has brought a global foreign currency market as well as a global securities market into being, where large-scale speculation with many negative effects takes place.

In this chapter, I shall briefly present some of the most important crisis phenomena and events of this era, which stretches up to the present time. I shall do this in order to convey a more comprehensive picture of the *crisis-proneness* of present-day capitalism — I want to show that fluctuations in the market are problematic and not just the harmless ups and downs of business cycles and unemployment figures.

## 1. From the 1970s to the End of the 1980s

### a) *The Debt Crisis of the Developing Countries*

When addressing the crises of capitalism in this era, it is no longer possible to limit the discussion to the industrialized countries. Now we must also include in our reflections the developing countries, for whom — unlike for the industrialized countries — the main objective of economic policy was not to avoid recession, depression, stagnation, and inflation, but to promote rapid economic development. And they were successful, to a certain extent. In the 1970s, per capita income in the developing countries grew by 3.5 percent per annum (UNCTAD [United Nations Conference on Trade and Development], quoted in Welzk 1988: 72). In the beginning of the 1980s, however, for many such countries, this era of continuous economic development came to an abrupt end.

The debt crisis of the developing countries, which broke out in 1982/1983 with Brazil's and Mexico's insolvency, was the main crisis phenomenon of globalized neo-liberal capitalism in that decade. In the 1970s, the industrialization process of these countries as well as the import of modern consumer goods were largely financed through increasing amounts of (initially) low-interest credit from the big international banks. Enormous amounts of so-called "petrodollars" — the OPEC countries' export surplus after the first oil price shock — as well as lack of profitable investment opportunities in the industrialized countries due to the stagflation had made it easy to get that credit.

Easier credit led to an enormous growth in the foreign indebtedness of these countries. Their ruling elites had believed in the "thesis of the debt cycle": "A country takes credit, uses it in a productive way, can increase its exports and earn foreign exchange, with which it can pay back the debt and then even transform itself into a creditor country" (Altvater et al. 1987: 26). Actually, this was not an unusual belief at the time. However, a chain of events in the new era disappointed these expectations:

1. The two oil price shocks of 1973 and 1979 made it very difficult for countries without sufficient oil resources of their own to pay the higher oil import bills without incurring new debts abroad.

2. Then the interest rates for commercial bank credit, which were flexible from the very beginning, rose enormously — partly as a result of the anti-inflation policies pursued in the creditor countries (see chapter IV).

3. In the United States interest rates also rose as a consequence of the enormous debts incurred by the Reagan administration, with which it financed massive rearmament as well as tax reductions for the rich and corporations. This had negative effects on the credit requirements of developing countries.

4. In addition to this, the exchange rate of the US dollar, in which most credit taken by the developing countries was denominated, skyrocketed. This happened because foreign money-capital owners, lured by high interest rates, wanted to invest their money in the United States. The high exchange rate of the US dollar made it more difficult for borrower countries to service their debts (that is, to pay interest and repayment installments in hard currency).

5. In the G7 industrialized countries there was a strong recession from 1980 to 1982. In sum, real GDP growth fell there from 3.6% in 1979 to –0.3% in 1982. In the same period, the growth rate in the United States — the largest market for the exports of the indebted countries, especially for those of the Latin American countries — was negative to very low: –0.5%, 1.8%, and –2.2% in 1980, 1981, and 1982, respectively (OECD 1994: A4). This resulted in a decline in demand for the export goods of the developing countries and, consequently, in a fall in their prices. As a result, the export earnings of these countries also fell.

The debtor countries had given too little thought to the economics of their industrialization project, and so they had now to export many more goods to be able to service their debts, which grew continuously and much faster than before. Some data, collected unsystematically, can illustrate this situation. In the beginning of the 1970s, the external debts of all developing countries taken together amounted to approximately (in US dollars) $150 billion, in 1980 to $604.6 billion, and in 1986 to approximately $1,000 billion — a really galloping indebtedness (see Wolf 1987: 12).

Although all developing countries had borrowed abroad, the indebtedness was not equally high everywhere. It was the highest in Latin America, where in 1986 40% (US$400 billion) of the total external debts of the developing countries had accumulated; 45% of this continent's export earnings had to be used to service the debts (see Wolf 1987: 14f.). For the African states the figure was 25%; that for the Asian countries was just 10%. Nevertheless, it cannot be said that the debt crisis had been a purely Latin American phenomenon. In the 1970s, the pace of indebtedness in the forty-four sub-Saharan African countries was higher than that in Latin America. In the period 1980–1985, their payments for debt-servicing totaled about $50 billion (Altvater/Hübner 1987: 22), quite a high sum for the poorest among the developing countries.

The crisis was most evident in the three biggest debtor countries — Brazil, Mexico, and Argentina — that purportedly stood at the threshold of rising to the status of "developed industrialized countries." In the beginning of the 1980s, in the wake of the strong recession in the G7 countries, there was also a severe economic crisis in Brazil (foreign debt in 1986 US$109 billion) and Argentina (foreign debt in 1986 $52 billion). From 1984 to 1985, the economy recovered in both countries, but the recovery proved to be a flash in the pan. From 1986 onwards growth slowed down. But still the governments did not manage to contain the high inflation (in Brazil 200%). The trade surplus was declining. Both countries had enormous difficulties in servicing their foreign debts. Austerity measures on the part of the state followed, and the people reacted with great protest demonstrations, riots, and general strikes. In 1987, Brazil declared temporary insolvency in respect of its foreign debts; Argentina threatened to follow suit.

The problems of Mexico, an OPEC country (foreign debt in 1986: US$102 billion), began with the decline of crude oil prices in the first half of the 1980s. Export earnings fell drastically, and the country went through an economic crisis in 1986. The GDP fell by 4%, industrial production by 6%. The inflation rate rose to 115%. However, unlike Brazil, Mexico did not formally declare insolvency, but tried to get more loans from the creditor banks to refinance the outstanding debts. (All figures in the above two paragraphs from Wolf 1987: 12, 16–18.)

The above description of the situation in Latin America can also be generalized for all developing countries. Between 1982 and 1990, the debtor countries of the South transferred to the creditor countries of the North on average US$12.45 billion every month towards interest payment and repayment of principal (see George 1992: xiv). In view of the poverty in these countries, Susan George finds it justified that one compares this process with "extracting blood from a stone" (xv). "The debtors' lack of unity ensures the draining of their economies and a continuing South-to-North resource flow on a scale far outstripping any the colonial period could command" (xvii).

But in spite of the enormous sums — altogether US$1,345 billion — that were paid between 1982 and 1990 to service the debts, the debtor countries could not free themselves from their debts. Quite on the contrary; in 1991, their total indebtedness was 61% higher than that in 1982. The total debt of sub-Saharan African countries grew in this period by 113% (xvf.).

In the same period, US$927 billion was transferred from the North to the South (George 1992: xv). In the North, this was denoted by the blanket term "development aid." But included in it were all kinds of transfers: credit, which had to be repaid (with interest), from states as well as from institutions such as the World Bank, export credit, private commercial credit, credit from the big banks of the industrialized countries, direct private investments, and also some donations from states and charities. It is difficult to find out how much of such total transfer figures were donations, which alone deserved to be called aid. One figure is available on the poor countries of sub-Saharan Africa. Between 1975 and 1977, of all new transfers 30% were donations, but by 1983 the ratio had dropped to 15% (Altvater/Hübner 1987: 22).

In respect of the usual figures on resources transfer from the South to the North, it should also be noted that they do not include some transfers that ought to be taken into account: royalties, dividends, transferred profits of foreign companies, payments for raw materials below world market price, etc.

The difference between US$1,345 billion and $927 billion — $418 billion — is then a grossly understated figure. Even if we consider only this figure, it is six times greater than the Marshall Plan aid that post-war Europe received from the United States (14 billion 1948 US dollars are equivalent to 70 billion in 1991) (George 1992: xvf.).

A purely political decision of the industrialized countries, namely, their protectionism, additionally worsened the crisis in the debtor countries. On the one hand, the latter were urged to export more to the industrialized countries in order to achieve higher export surpluses necessary for servicing their debts. On the other hand, exactly this was made more difficult for them through protectionist measures. Raw materials were welcome, but not higher-value finished goods like agricultural products or clothing. Agricultural subsidies given by the European Economic Community (EEC) and the United States enabled their farmers to outcompete the agricultural producers of the South in the world market.

The crisis in the developing countries was to a greater extent the result of a purely market-economic development of this era, namely, the deterioration of the terms of trade of these countries vis-à-vis the industrialized countries. Here are a few examples: In the period between 1961 and

1964 Tanzania needed to export 7.5 kg of coffee in order to import a Swiss watch. In the period between 1971 and 1974 it had to export 14.2 kg of coffee to import a similar Swiss watch (Strahm 1981: 46). In 1985 the value of a German truck delivered at the German border equaled that of 93 bags of coffee, 44 tons of bananas, 7.6 tons of cocoa or 49 carpets. In 1990, with the quality of the goods remaining the same, the figures were: 302 bags of coffee, 58 tons of bananas, 29 tons of cocoa or 90 carpets (*Frankfurter Rundschau*, 24 July 1991). The prices of the collective category "raw materials" had dropped by 1986 to the lowest level since the end of World War II. Just in the short period of 1980–1986, they fell by 30% (Wolf 1987: 10). Already in 1985, *The Economist*, an important mouthpiece of British capital, had put the great significance of this development in a nutshell:

> Just as yesterday's dearer oil twice brought stagflation to the rich countries, so today's cheaper raw materials can now help them kill inflation and boost economic growth.... Most of the rich countries have not yet understood ... how much of [this opportunity] ... is *a gift from poor countries*. In the past twelve months, the world price of food ... has fallen by 10%.... [The] price of metals has dropped by 15%, that of oil by 5½%. These declines ... mean that consumers [in the rich countries] are now paying about $65 billion a year less for the same amount of raw materials than they did 12 months ago." (*The Economist*, 6 December 1985: 13; emphasis added).

So, at least during this period, neo-liberal globalization did not create a win-win situation, but a win-lose one. *The Economist* estimated at that time that the US$65 billion mentioned above amounted to 0.7% of the GDP of all OECD countries. According to a UN resolution, the rich countries were to give the poor countries exactly this percentage of their GDP as development aid.

Once the debt crisis had unfolded, the IMF and the World Bank got the opportunity to intervene in the management of the economies of the over-indebted developing countries. Their debt managers' responsibility was to ensure that the debtor countries remained able to service their debts, nothing else. In terms of their neo-liberal articles of faith, their recommendations were also very logical. In order to be able to further pursue a debt-financed export-oriented industrialization, these countries had to maintain or restore their credit-worthiness. For this purpose, they had to continue to service their debts despite their many problems. For this reason again, they needed to earn much money in hard currencies. In order to be able to do that, they had to increase their exports and decrease their imports. In order to be able to increase exports they had to devalue their currency. They also had to massively reduce state spending, particularly spending for public services benefitting the population at large. In order to make the economy more efficient, they had to privatize state-owned enterprises. Most of the debtor countries accepted such advice (or rather dictates), which was the condition for debt rescheduling or further credit. These debtor countries implemented draconian measures, the so-called "structural adjustment programs" (SAP), and they destroyed their environment by ruthlessly exploiting their natural resources so as to export more raw materials. But the crisis remained. The only economic result of these programs was mass unemployment, real wage reductions, and further impoverishment. In Latin America, between 1980 and 1985, per capita GDP fell on average by over 10% (Altvater/Hübner 1987: 27). Susan George wrote in 1992:

> Clearly, the economic policies imposed on debtors by the major multilateral agencies — policies packaged under the general heading of "structural adjustment" — have cured nothing at all. . . . [T]he debt managers would be hard pressed to point to a single third world success story. Economically, socially and ecologically speaking, "structural adjustment" has been a disaster. (George 1992: xvi–xvii)

But perhaps the debt managers' mission was not to look after the economic recovery of the debtor countries, but rather to assist in the pillage of their resources and exploitation of their labor force by the countries of the North. If so, then their work was highly successful, their mission accomplished.

For most of the developing countries the 1980s were "the lost decade," but this was certainly not the case for all citizens of these countries. Members of the elite could see to it they did not have to suffer under the SAP. The entrepreneurs benefited from the falling real wages, and the rich could keep their money in the banks of industrialized countries, where they were protected from successive depreciations of the local currency. This kind of flight of capital assumed enormous proportions. Morgan Guaranty Trust, one of the big creditor banks, itself estimated that in the period of 1976–1985 about US$200 billion of capital of this category was transferred abroad (Wolf 1987: 22). When state-owned enterprises were privatized, the owners of such money-capital in hard currency were able to acquire the best pieces at bargain price. No wonder then that they cooperated with the debt managers.

For some time after the debt crisis broke out, there were fears, for good reason, that the international system of commercial finance would collapse. Firstly, just the extent of indebtedness of the developing countries — especially that of the larger Latin American countries — was alarming. Secondly, too large a portion of that was made up of credit from private banks; in 1980 this portion amounted to 27%. Thirdly, such banks had been very imprudent in their lending practices — especially the American private banks. Some of them had engaged themselves in such business with amounts that far exceeded their own capital assets (Nohlen 2002: 856). However, in the following years, the collapse could be averted through several measures directed toward reducing the debt burden — through rescheduling, partial remission of the debts of the poorest countries, reducing the interest rates, debt-for-equity swaps (debts were converted into share-ownership in firms in the debtor countries), building up reserves in the endangered banks, etc. Since the mid-1990s there has not been any more talk of a generalized debt crisis that could lead to some kind of collapse. (This however radically changed in 2008; see the last chapter.)

### EFFECTS ON THE INDUSTRIALIZED COUNTRIES

The crisis also had negative effects on the economies of the industrialized countries — though not to the same extent. It aggravated the recession in these countries and caused in other ways economic losses for the population. For the developing countries tried to reduce imports from the industrialized countries in order to attain export surpluses. As a result, exports of the latter to the former either dramatically fell or their growth rate dropped markedly.

The fact that the industrialized countries could cope with this dramatic fall or stagnation in their exports to the developing countries without too much difficulty had two explanations. Firstly, trade among industrialized countries kept on growing, and secondly, their exports to developing countries — if one leaves out the OPEC countries — did not constitute too large a portion of their total exports. In 1981, for the European Economic Community (EEC) it amounted to only 10%, for North America 23%. Only for Japan was this figure high, 31% (George 1992: 105). Nevertheless, the decline in their exports to developing countries caused a considerable loss of jobs — even in the EEC.

North Americans, especially the USA, had to accept running large trade deficits in order to enable the debtor countries to service their debts. That also happened. While in 1980 the United States had a trade surplus of $166 billion, in 1988 they piled up a deficit of $500 billion (101f.). The latter was also partly due to Japan's efforts to greatly increase exports to the USA in order to compensate for the loss of markets in the developing countries. According to one estimate, in the period between 1980 and 1984 this development caused in the United States job losses (and loss of potential employment) to the extent of 3.2 million employment-years (97).

The assumption that all OPEC countries were super rich is wrong. Some of them — Nigeria, Indonesia, Venezuela, and Algeria, but also a few somewhat rich Arab OPEC countries — belonged to the group of heavily indebted developing countries. They, too, had to reduce imports due to the burden of debt-servicing, particularly because their oil export earnings had considerably decreased due to the steep fall in the world market price of oil in the 1980s.

With great effort, the bigger debtor countries like Brazil and Argentina managed to flood the world market with their agricultural products. Particularly US farmers, whose exports to Latin America had already fallen by 30% due to the debt crisis, suffered greatly under this new development. For the export offensive of the developing countries pushed down world market prices of their products. US farmers were also in distress at home. Cargill, the large US grain trading corporation, threatened them with the intention to import wheat from Argentina, where the prices were lower than in the USA. In this situation, many US farmers experienced their own debt crisis; they could not service their debts and went bankrupt. The incidence of suicide, divorce, and mental illness increased. At the same time, hunger and undernourishment spread in the food-exporting debtor countries.


Now it could be said there has always been exploitation in capitalism — of individuals and classes as well as of whole countries and regions. That is part of its fundament. Nevertheless, in the history of capitalism there have been long periods of growing and fairly widespread prosperity. During the long boom after World War II, some countries of the South also enjoyed some economic development. Then how can their exploitation by industrialized countries lead to a crisis of capitalism? According to apologists of capitalism there can therefore be a degree of exploitation (they however do not call it so; they call it "distribution ratio") that can be compatible with a crisis-free capitalism and in the framework of which poor countries can also attain a certain level of prosperity. This is the stance of Keynesianism and social democracy as well. But is it so? I shall deal with this issue in chapters VIII and IX.

## b) *The Stock Exchange Bubble and the Crash of 1987*

Another big crisis event of the 1980s was the stock exchange crash in the industrialized countries that took place in October/November 1987. As already mentioned in chapter IV, the beginning of the era of neo-liberal capitalism in the USA and the United Kingdom was accompanied by a recession. The widespread implementation of tight-money policy to fight inflation and the strong 1980–1982 recession in the United States, the largest market in the world, also caused recession or stagnation in some other industrialized countries. In Germany, for instance, the growth rate of real GDP fell from 4.2% in 1979 to 1%, 0.1%, and –0.9% in the years 1980, 1981, and 1982, respectively. The official unemployment rate in 1982 was 6.4%. In Japan, to take another example, the growth rate first fell steeply, and then it stabilized at a modest level for Japanese standards. From 5.5% in 1979, it fell to 3.6%, 3.6%, 3.2%, and 2.7% in the years 1980, 1981, 1982, and 1983, respectively. The official unemployment rate increased slightly, from 2% to 2.7%. In the G7 countries taken together, the growth rate fell by 1982 to –0.3% (all figures from OECD 1994: A4, A23).

The so-called "armaments Keynesianism" of the Reagan administration, however, quickly brought about a strong rise in demand and pulled the United States out of recession. The economy grew there by 3.9%, 6.2%, and 3.2% in 1983, 1984, and 1985, respectively. That soon caused the exports of both Germany and Japan to boom, which also enabled these two countries to recover from the recession or stagnation of the early 1980s. Then came an upswing. By 1985 Japan's growth rate had climbed to 5%. In Germany too the economy grew, but until 1987, due to the government's anti-inflation policy, the growth rate remained well under 3%. In the G7 countries as a whole, by 1985 the growth rate had reached 3.3% (OECD 1994: A4).

By 1985 the recession was overcome. Yet the US government decided to move further to improve the competitiveness of the US manufacturing industry vis-à-vis its superior main competitors from Japan and Germany. The US successfully put pressure on the governments of the two countries and pushed through the so-called Plaza Agreement, in which the five topmost industrialized countries committed themselves to take measures to cause the US dollar's exchange rate to fall. This agreement attained its goal; the US dollar experienced a more or less continuous and strong devaluation vis-à-vis the Deutsche mark and the yen. This led to a recovery of the competitiveness of the US manufacturing industry and to an accelerated growth of its exports. As an unavoidable consequence thereof, the strongly export-dependent German and Japanese economies suffered diminished competitiveness, and their export surpluses dwindled sharply.

The Japanese perceived this development as a serious crisis. The government and the central bank met it with a strategy of extremely cheap money. Interest rates were drastically reduced, and real estate construction companies and share-broker firms were generously granted cheap loans. The idea was as follows: speculation should push up real estate and security prices, which in turn should artificially increase the value of real estate property and securities-assets of corporations. That should make it easier for them to borrow more money, and the low interest rates should reduce the costs of borrowing. Taken together, they should constitute an incentive for the corporations to invest more in increasing competitiveness. The authorities also expected that, at the same time, consumers — encouraged by the increasing value of their stocks and lower interest rates — would save less and consume more. This policy was successful. The GDP growth rate, which had fallen from 4.4% in 1985 to 2.9% in 1986, rose again, to 6.2% in 1988. Also, the trade balance surplus grew again.

Against the backdrop of these developments, the great stock market crash of October–November 1987 took place in the industrialized countries. Once the 1980–1982 recession was overcome, the upturn in the USA was accompanied by a stock market bubble. As we have seen above, in Japan too a stock market and real estate bubble developed. Since all bubbles must eventually burst, these ones burst too. On October 19 — the so-called "black" or "bloody" Monday — the Dow Jones index fell by 22.6% compared to the figure of the previous Friday. Thereafter, the index of the London stock exchange fell by 14.2%, that of Paris by 4.7%, that of Frankfurt by 6.2%, and that of Amsterdam by 8.2%. On October 20, the index of the Singapore stock exchange fell by 12.1%, that of Hong Kong by 10.1%, and that of Tokyo by 2.4%. No index of the important stock exchanges of the world was spared. Panic broke out. People were reminded of the crash of 1929. Just like in that case, a campaign to calm share-owners was launched, as were rescue operations — there were well-directed massive stock purchases by big banks and leaders of the finance industry. As a result thereof the very next day there was a rush of countless small investors who thought they could now buy stocks at very low prices. This interim boom stabilized the stock markets. However, it lasted only one day, and the stock prices continued to fall. To make a long story short, until November 11 stock indexes fell in Frankfurt, Amsterdam, London, and Zurich by about a third (compared to the index on October 16); in Hong Kong, Singapore, and Sydney they fell by almost half. In New York, however, there was a recovery. On November 11 the index there was only 15.5% lower than that on October 16 (all figures from Welzk 1988: 16ff.).

It is interesting to inquire how this crash could happen, given that since the mid-1930s all people in authority had repeatedly said they had learned the right lesson from the crash of 1929 and, therefore, something like it could never happen again. It is easy to explain why and how a bubble that keeps getting bigger and bigger bursts. But, actually, it is more interesting to fathom the mechanism through which the big bubble, that is, the stock market boom prior to October 19, 1987, developed.

Paul A. Samuelson gave a simple explanation. He asserted there wasn't any connection at all between a stock market boom and a subsequent crash, on the one hand, and the condition of the real economy, on the other. According to him, the behavior of stock market speculators was just irrational and, moreover, the basic data showed that the real economy then was healthy (see Mandel 1988: 87).

But Ernest Mandel (1988) contradicted him and gave a convincing explanation for the crash. Unlike Samuelson, he did see a connection between the developments in the real economy, on the one hand, and the stock market boom and the subsequent crash, on the other. In spite of the four-year-long upswing since 1983, there was overcapacity in all large productive sectors of the real economy. Nonetheless, company profits were very high, partly because of relatively low wage increases, a consequence of the preceding recession. In France in 1982, the government had even decreed a halt to wage raises. The two developments — overcapacity and high company profits — led to over-accumulation of capital that could not be invested in the real economy. In West Germany, for instance, in the period 1982–1986, the part of the profits that was productively invested was only half of the figure for the period 1972–1981. Of course, the upswing in the real economy also contributed to the stock market boom, but the main factor in the process was the flow of the accumulated excess money-capital into the stock exchange aimed at making speculative profits. Towards the end of the boom, stock prices in New York and Tokyo reached heights at which the dividend rates, *measured on the basis of current stock prices*, were lower than the interest rate on a simple term-deposit at a bank. This madness could not go on for much longer. The market plunge was unavoidable.

Some other factors also contributed to the formation of the bubble. The net resource transfer mentioned in the previous section and the flight of capital from developing countries into industrialized countries stoked the stock market boom at the international financial centers, since there were not enough productive investment opportunities for the money coming from these sources. In addition to this, banks paid less tax when they held hundreds of millions of dollars in reserve for their huge and extremely risky loans, which they could enter in their books as losses even when the loans did not have to be written off or written off totally. These tax savings by banks also landed in speculative business at the stock exchange.

Some aspects of the American real economy of the time played a big part in forming the stock market bubble. The Reagan administration liberalized the rules for the economy. Among other things, it liberalized the anti-trust law and the finance market. This facilitated hostile takeovers and friendly acquisitions of entire companies by other companies. In both cases, large packets of stocks of the target company had to be bought up. Those that resisted such takeovers tried to protect themselves by purchasing large numbers of their own stocks. All such moves pushed up the price of the stocks in question and attracted speculators. The banks, for reasons stated above, had no problem granting the huge credit needed for such maneuvers. In addition to this, large sums came from Europe and Japan, the owners of which wanted to make large profits speculating at the New York Stock Exchange.

The tax benefits that the rich and the corporations received from the US government also played an important role in the stock market boom. The alleged purpose of those benefits was to induce economic subjects to invest in the real economy. But they did not serve this purpose. Instead, they acted as an incentive to mergers, acquisitions, and hostile takeovers, which were not real investments but were the only means through which some of the tax benefits could be realized. The huge budget deficits caused by these tax benefits led to a rise in interest rates. This discouraged the entrepreneurs, who would have otherwise tried to make profits through real investments.

Some secondary factors made the crash much worse than what it would have been without them: (1) Several financial innovations of that time — futures trading, options, etc. — were too complicated for normal speculators. Even the chairman of the New York Stock Exchange at the time said that no one could fully understand the mixture of securities and commodity futures trading that was developing (Welzk 1988: 18). (2) The fact that powerful big companies operating at the stock exchange had to pay with their own money only 5 percent of the total price for share options (the rest they could borrow) made it easier for them to pour hundreds of millions of dollars into highly risky speculative transactions. (3) The use of computers and highly complicated software specially developed for speculative stock market business intensified every move at the market. In this way, often a slight price fluctuation led to a large profit or a large loss.

Among the financial innovations there was also one whose purpose was to protect investors from losses: it was called "portfolio insurance" or "computerized hedging." In 1986 and 1987, investors were very keen on this tool. This promise of protection only whetted the appetite of speculators. However, it turned out to be only hot air when the crash happened. A stock market expert wrote with hindsight (retranslated/paraphrased): "When the investors hurried to cover themselves against plummeting stock prices, they only intensified the process further, which in effect transformed a bad situation into a full-blown crisis. In other words, in the final analysis, the instruments for risk management made the world a more risky place" (Tett 2007).

There were many similarities between this stock market crash and the one of 1929. George Soros, already a big speculator in 1987, said at that time: "[T]echnically, this is 1929" (quoted in *Financial Times*, 19 October 2007). That is why immediately the question arose whether, this time too, a big economic crisis would follow the crash. From the word go, politicians and other influential people of the economic establishment tried to calm the public, but everyone was alarmed for some time to come. Social democrats and Keynesians, e.g., author Stefan Welzk (1988), warned that a severe economic crisis could unfold if states and central banks did not undertake something to stop it. Quite a few representatives and mouthpieces of capital were worried as well. The *International Herald Tribune*, for instance, wrote: "The whole future depends on one question: Will the uncontrolled market forces plunge the world into a dreadful crisis or will the prudent and coordinated interventions of the governments succeed in avoiding it?" (quoted in Mandel 1988: 90; retranslated). *The Economist* also saw in 1988 a recession coming (87). Marxist economists (Mandel 1988, Wolf 1988) spoke of the possibility of a severe recession.

These warnings and concerns were understandable. If prices of stocks and other securities collapse, businesspeople and private consumers who own such securities can offer less collateral for their credit applications. Banks then grant less credit, which leads to a fall in aggregate demand, production, and employment. So there indeed is a connection between developments at the stock exchange and the state of the real economy.

In the immediately following years, there was neither a dreadful crisis nor a recession. The economic growth rate in 1988 was 4.2% in the United States, 3.7% in West Germany, 6.2% in Japan, and 4.5% in the whole of the OECD (OECD 2000: 211). However, the absence of a crisis in the real economy was no clear proof of superiority of neo-liberal economic policies. For what happened in the economy after the crash was not simply left to the market. The Fed intervened massively in order to avert a crisis. Its new chief, Alan Greenspan, was of the opinion that a financial crisis should not be allowed to damage the real economy. In the morning of October 20, the Fed announced its intention to provide the real economy and the financial markets the liquidity needed to avert the crisis. It supplied billions of dollars to the financial system by means of open market operations,[11] and, soon thereafter, reduced the prime rate (the interest rate at which banks borrow from the Fed) by 1.5% (see Guha 2007; and Western 2004: 157f.). The other leading central banks followed the example of the Fed. They did all that with such largesse that soon thereafter stock market speculation was flourishing again.

It must be said in this connection that Reagan's economic policy was not in every respect a neo-liberal one. A combination of massive tax cuts and large budget deficits — a policy continued by his successor, Bush Sr. — could also pass as Keynesian economic policy. Reagan did not pursue this policy in order to lead the economy out of the recession. He had actually accepted the recession in order to enable the Fed to fight inflation. He pursued this policy, firstly, to make the rich richer, and, secondly, to massively rearm the United States. But the effect of this rearmament-Keynesianism was indeed an economic recovery. Economic historian Robert Brenner wrote:

> [T]his partly offset the ravages of monetarist tight credit policy
> and kept the economy ticking over. The ensuing record federal
> deficits, and the unprecedented trade and current account
> deficits that accompanied them, proved indispensable, as had
> their predecessors of 1970s, in providing the injections of
> demand that were needed not only to pull the world economy
> out of the recession of 1979–82, but also to steer growth
> forward at home and abroad through the remainder of the
> decade. (2003a: 36)

## 2. The Turbulent 1990s

### a) *The Neo-Liberal Democrats in the USA*

The feared great crisis after the stock market crash of 1987 could be averted, but a recession came after all, only with a little delay. During the post-1987 boom, which was probably caused by the enormous amounts of money that had earlier been poured into their economies by the central banks, inflation had increased in some industrialized countries. That is why, in the early 1990s, the authorities in these countries took successive deflationary measures. These resulted not only in a drop in prices but also in a recession, which led to a financial crisis and even to some bank failures. These latter events aggravated the recession. Some figures on the successive recessions in the G7 countries help illustrate the situation:

**Growth rate of real GDP (in %)**

|      | France | Germany | Italy | UK   | USA  | Japan | Canada |
| ---- | ------ | ------- | ----- | ---- | ---- | ----- | ------ |
| 1989 | 4.3    | 3.6     | 2.9   | 2.1  | 3.5  | 4.8   | 2.5    |
| 1990 | 2.6    | 5.7     | 2.0   | 0.7  | 1.8  | 5.1   | 0.3    |
| 1991 | 1.1    | 5.0     | 1.4   | -1.5 | -0.5 | 3.8   | -1.9   |
| 1992 | 1.3    | 2.2     | 0.8   | 0.1  | 3.1  | 1.0   | 0.9    |
| 1993 | -0.9   | -1.1    | -0.9  | 2.3  | 2.7  | 0.3   | 2.3    |

**Unemployment rates (in %) (following country-specific definition)**

|      | France | Germany | Italy | UK   | USA  | Japan | Canada |
| ---- | ------ | ------- | ----- | ---- | ---- | ----- | ------ |
| 1989 | 9.3    | 6.9     | 10.2  | 6.1  | 5.3  | 2.3   | 7.5    |
| 1990 | 8.9    | 6.2     | 9.1   | 5.9  | 5.6  | 2.1   | 8.1    |
| 1991 | 9.4    | 5.4     | 8.6   | 8.2  | 6.8  | 2.1   | 10.3   |
| 1992 | 10.4   | 6.3     | 8.8   | 10.2 | 7.5  | 2.2   | 11.2   |
| 1993 | 11.7   | 7.6     | 10.2  | 10.3 | 6.9  | 2.5   | 11.4   |

(Source: OECD 2000: 211, 231)

Here a few comments could help explain the situation: (1) In the years between 1989 and 1993, in six out of the seven countries, production fell in only one year. In Japan it did not fall in any year. In the rest of the years it had actually grown in comparison to the previous year. What happened before production really dropped was merely a fall in the *growth rate*, which for some economists and politicians feels like a crisis. It should be added here that, while for calculating the growth rate the GDP figure for the year in question is usually compared with that from the same month one year before, one speaks of recession when the GDP has fallen in two consecutive quarters. It can therefore be that within a period of twelve months the GDP has fallen in two consecutive quarters (recession), but that it has increased in comparison to the year before (positive growth). (2) In the years 1990 and 1991 — contrary to the trend — there was strong growth in Germany. This was due to a special event: the strong growth in demand after the reunification of the country. (3) There is no regular and simple correlation between the growth rate of an economy and the unemployment rate (which is often defined arbitrarily). In the United Kingdom, for instance, the unemployment rate rose in 1992 by two full percentage points, although the economy recovered only slightly in that year. Obviously, the unemployment rate depends on several other factors too.

In the years 1993–2002, the developments in the US economy were in many respects unusual. Bill Clinton — a president from the Democratic Party, which is traditionally thought to have a social, liberal, and Keynesian slant — let it be known that he did not want to allow the huge public debt left by his predecessors to grow any further. On the contrary, he wanted to reduce the budget deficits. His advisors persuaded him that "without deficit reduction, financial markets would punish him, and without the support of finance, he could not accomplish the rest of his agenda" (Stiglitz 2003: xiii).

During the election campaign Clinton had summarized his program with the slogan "Putting the people first." Most members of the inner circle of his staff knew what they wanted: Joseph Stiglitz, head of Clinton's council of economic advisors, wrote: "We were against Reagan conservatism. We knew that there needed to be a larger and different role for government, that we needed to be more concerned for the poor and for providing education and social protection for all, and we needed to protect the environment" (2003: 25). Yet, during his eight-year presidency all these good resolutions were thrown overboard — in favor of a policy of deficit reduction and focusing on the world of finance.

After the recession of 1990–1991 had given way to a slow recovery, halfway through 1993 a robust growth began, which was of a new type in that, unlike the growth phases of the 1970s and 1980s, it did not need the help of a deficit-spawning budget policy. It is not as if the Clinton administration did not want to help the economy. It did, but in a different way. It wanted to help the latter reduce costs, at least by not letting them rise too high. It wanted to end the dependence of the economy on budget deficits and to force it to orient itself more towards export. Growth, thus, was to come not so much from high domestic consumption demand but rather from investments and exports. Until 1995, the Clinton administration used economic diplomacy — especially the negotiations of the Uruguay Round, which led to the creation of the WTO — to aggressively promote the interests of American corporations and investors. It served especially the interests of the finance sector and the rentier class, which together had in the meantime conquered the central place in the US economy. These interest groups needed an anti-inflation policy that would prevent the value of the credit they gave and that of their money-assets from being eroded by inflation. For the same purpose the Clinton administration continued the deregulation policy of the previous Republican governments. And it reduced social welfare as well as unemployment insurance benefits, from which, moreover, many more workers were excluded. As for tax policy, unlike the previous Republican administrations, it raised the income tax rates for the middle and upper middle classes (1993), but reduced tax rates on capital gains (1997), from which mostly super-rich speculators profited. It was neo-liberal policy through and through. This about-turn in policy induced the Democrats to henceforth informally call themselves "The New Democrats," in the same way as later the Labour Party of the United Kingdom called itself informally "New Labour." [The information on the USA, Japan, and East Asia presented in this section are largely take from Stiglitz (2003), Brenner (2003a), and Henderson (1998).]

This policy was very successful. Between 1992 and 1997 the budget deficit fell from 4.7% of GDP to zero (Brenner 2003a: 75), and at the end of the Clinton presidency — by the end of 2000 — the budget even showed a surplus. In the economy too things were looking up. In 1994, it registered a growth of 4%, and growth expectations were several times revised upwards. However, the Fed regarded this as a sign of overheating and thought that full employment had been achieved, although in 1994 the unemployment rate amounted to 6.1%. It saw the danger of inflation looming and stopped economic growth by raising the prime rate step by step (Brenner 2003a: 76; OECD 2004: 215, 203). But at the end of 1995 the Fed returned to the policy of cheap money, and, after a brief interruption, the economy recovered its dynamics.

A central campaign slogan of Clinton had been "Jobs! Jobs! Jobs!" During the eight years of his presidency eighteen million jobs were created (Stiglitz 2003: 6). It was termed a "job miracle" (although most of them were low pay and low level jobs). And then there was another miracle: although unemployment fell steadily—from 5.6% in 1995 to 4% in 2000—the inflation rate remained moderate—on average 2.5% for the same period (see OECD 2004: 215, 220). It seemed both recession and accelerating inflation had now become things of the past.

This success totally contradicted some basic tenets of standard economics—of both Keynesian and neo-liberal provenance. Of course the recovery in the US economy had already begun in 1992, but it was a jobless recovery. In the first quarter of 1993, the economy shrunk again (−0.1%) (Stiglitz 2003: 40). Then the new government that had begun work in January 1993 raised taxes—a violation of neo-liberal economic policy—and began to reduce state spending—a violation of Keynesian economic policy. And by so doing it was even very successful.

Stiglitz—a Keynesian—regards this success, a quasi miracle, as an exception, a special case, the result of two "lucky mistakes." He explains the "mistakes" as follows: By raising taxes and reducing state spending the government was able to reduce new borrowing. As a result, long-term interest rates fell from above 9% to under 6%. That had the effect that market prices of long-term fixed-interest bonds that had been issued earlier at higher interest rates went up considerably. This improved the balance sheets of banks that had massively bought such securities in the period before this development. At the time in question, however, because of the decrease in interest rates, new securities of this type became unattractive. So banks returned more and more to their original activity, namely, lending money to business. This made the decisive difference. The "mistake" of excessively reducing state spending produced in this way an unintended good effect. The direct negative effect of reducing budget deficits on the economy was in this way overcompensated for by the indirect positive effect on investments, and that despite tax increases. The second lucky "mistake" was made by the Fed. In the early phase of the recovery, in 1993, it refrained from raising the prime lending rate, contrary to what it had always done before (Stiglitz 2003: 36ff., 44ff., 51).

This explanation of Stiglitz's leaves one question unanswered: Where did the demand for new credit, which the banks were now ready to give, come from? The answer is probably as follows. Until 1995/1996, this demand came from the increased willingness of American companies to invest, which was the consequence of a rise in the profit rate and international competitiveness resulting from the Plaza Agreement. And, from

1996 onwards, it also came from the increased willingness to consume on the part of the public, which followed the rise in value of their securities resulting from the stock market boom.

Some economists made a general theory out of this specific US experience, and the example caught on, but only half of it. During the crises in East Asia and Latin America (see below and section 3 of this chapter), the US-dominated IMF forced governments that were asking for help to reduce their budget deficits. This had devastating consequences. In Germany, when the Social Democratic Party (SPD) came to power, deficit reduction became the new mantra. No one, however, dared raise taxes as Clinton had done. On the contrary, taxes were reduced.

## b) *Recession and Stagnation in Japan*

While the US economy grew considerably from 1992 onwards, the Japanese economy experienced throughout the 1990s an unprecedentedly long period of recession and stagnation. The decline began in 1991. It was set off by the abrupt end of the "bubble economy" that had been created and stoked by the Japanese authorities themselves (see section 1 of this chapter). Between May 1989 and August 1990, the central bank raised in several steps its prime lending rate, from 2.5% to 6%. The purpose thereof was to *gradually* let some hot air out of the overheated bubble by making credit more expensive. Another purpose of this measure was to stop the flight of capital that had been taking place because of the low interest rates. But this strategy failed, and the bubble burst. From almost 40,000 points in 1989, the Nikkei Index of the Japanese stock exchange fell to 14,309 in August 1992 — a drop of 63%. Building site prices fell to a third of their peak. According to the then chairman of McKinsey and Company — a business consultancy company — at the peak of the real estate bubble the total value of all real estate in Japan came to two and a half times the value of all real estate in the US (Garnreiter et al. 1998; Schmid 2001). In the beginning of the 1990s, a square meter of top quality building site in Ginza (Tokyo) cost US$300,000 (Impoco 2008).

This development had effects on the real economy. Economic growth sank. In 1990 and 1991, it was still 5.1% and 3.8%, respectively. From 1992 to 1995 it was just 1.0%, 0.3%, 0.6%, and 1.5%. In 1996 the growth rate suddenly shot up to 5.1%. But, according to observers, this jump was only the effect of the reconstruction efforts and other tasks connected with the Kobe earthquake of 1995. In 1997, the growth rate fell again to 1.6% (figures from OECD 2000: 211). This result of the end of the "bubble

economy" is easy to explain. Companies had made their investment decisions on the basis of the assumption that the consumption and investment
boom given rise to by the "bubble economy" would continue, albeit curbed
a little by the central bank measures. But when assets worth billions of
yen disappeared into thin air owing to the bursting of the bubble, the consumption frenzy abruptly came to an end, and with it many investment
plans too. Fear spread. Companies were suddenly left sitting on enormous
building and industrial overcapacities. Private persons saw their old-age
provisions endangered. Panic saving set in. In spite of the steep fall in the
incomes of private households, their saving rate in the crisis years 1993–
1996 was higher than in 1988. This naturally aggravated the economic situation (Schmid 2001: 18; OECD 2000: 234).

These developments led to numerous bankruptcies of both companies
and individuals. Even those companies that managed to hold out had difficulties in servicing their debts. Japanese banks suddenly found themselves
sitting on a huge mountain of bad debts. According to official statistics,
they amounted to the equivalent of DM 1,130 billion (ca. €565 billion) and
threatened to double within a short time. That would have amounted to
30% of Japan's GDP (Gassner 1999: 123).

Apart from the immediate cause of the crisis, the bursting of the bubble,
there were also some structural problems that contributed to causing the
long stagnation. Japanese manufacturing industry had long been strongly
oriented towards exports, and at the same time the country imported too
little. This had led to Japan having for a long time surpluses in both the
balance of trade and the current account.[12] To a certain extent, the latter
surplus came about also because the Japanese invested a large portion of
their capital abroad and received profits, interests, and dividends on it.
This had the effect that, since 1971, the exchange rate of the yen had been
showing a chronic upward trend, which is detrimental to exports. This was
especially the case after the Plaza Agreement of 1985 (see section 1).

With enormous effort and by accepting large cuts in prices and profit
margins, the Japanese could of course continue exporting their products
all over the world. But the growth rate of the export volume slowed down
considerably. From 15.8% in 1984, it fell between 1985 and 1991 on average to 3.1%. Another period of rise in the exchange rate of yen began in
1991 and lasted until 1995. This caused a further weakening of the growth
rate of exports, which, between 1992 and 1996, amounted on average to
1.26% per year (OECD 2000: 248). At the same time, the appreciation of
the yen led to an increase in imports and, thus, to increased competition
for Japan's manufacturing industry in the domestic market. This development also pressed the GDP growth rate downwards.

There was another structural factor: the mutual support system warranted by the government, which protected key industrial and financial corporations from having to file a bankruptcy petition or from being compelled to close down or lay off workers for reducing production in factories temporarily suffering from insufficient orders. All such things are otherwise usual practice in capitalism, and they normally help solve common crises originating in overcapacity in a very short time. Because of this system, unprofitable units also remained in business. That caused profits to fall and prolonged the stagnation.

The crisis was also intensified by the developments in the United States, Japan's largest export market. Both the 1990–1991 recession there and the policy of rigorous deficit reduction pursued throughout the Clinton era led to a contraction of demand for Japanese exports.

Already in the second half of the 1980s, the Japanese economy had begun to relocate the technologically less demanding parts of production, trade, and finance in East Asia. In 1990–1991, when the investment climate in Japan again worsened, this process was intensified. In the first half of the 1990s, Japanese investments in East Asia enjoyed three times more profitability than at home. By 1996, stimulated by this relocation process, Japanese exports to East Asia (mostly investment goods) made up 40% of all Japanese exports. And by that same year, the share of East Asia in direct Japanese investments in the manufacturing industries of foreign countries reached approximately the same percentage (Brenner 2003a: 117). This development, however, soon reached a point in which its negative effects on production and employment in Japan (and therefore on its GDP) could not be overlooked. "[T]he gains from increased exports of capital and component parts to Japanese subsidiaries abroad were more than counterbalanced by the losses due to the substitution of production abroad for Japanese exports, as well as the increase in imports from [their own] foreign subsidiaries" (118).

### c) *Rescue Effort for Japan; About-Turn in the USA*

In the mid-1990s, the outlook for Japan was grim, for the exchange rate of the yen to the dollar kept creeping up. The situation was regarded as dangerous: a collapse of the world's second largest economy could have bad general consequences for the world economy. For the United States in particular, the effects could be especially bad, for Japan was not only its largest trade partner but also its largest creditor. If the Japanese — being in difficulties due to the crisis — were to massively sell US bonds in their possession, that could cause a hike in the effective interest rates in the United States, which — in turn — would stifle the incipient upturn.

Americans could not just stand and watch this possibility becoming reality, particularly shortly after a sudden and severe financial crisis in Mexico had caused turbulence in the whole of Latin America as well as in the rest of the world (see next section). Hence, in the summer of 1995, a new agreement between the United States, Japan, and Germany was constructed, the so-called "Reverse Plaza Accord," the purpose of which was to push up the exchange rate of the US dollar and bring down that of the yen (and the Deutsche mark) through interventions in the finance markets, both of which occurred. As a consequence, the US economy lost, one after the other, both the motors of its growth dynamic: the deficit-running state expenditures (due to Clinton's fiscal policy) and the low exchange rate of the dollar.

According to what until that time usually happened in the world economy in such situations, the United States should now have been in great trouble. With the appreciation of the US dollar, the advantages and improvements the US economy had experienced since the 1985 Plaza Agreement came to an end. The profit rate of industry soon began to fall.

In the meantime, both governments and companies around the world had accepted the tenets of supply-side economics and introduced measures to reduce costs. In general, that had become essential for companies in view of the pressure of international competition, the worldwide overcapacity and overproduction, and their sluggish earnings. In most of the EU states, in order to prepare themselves for the new currency, the Euro, governments introduced a rigorous policy of limiting budget deficits. All of this, taken together, resulted in a weakening of demand — at least in the highly developed industrialized countries.

Yet, the US economy seemed to be able to withstand it all. It continued to grow in full swing. How could this be? For a while, the manufacturing industry could sustain the production and export boom by cutting prices and accepting lower profit margins. This, however, could not have been sustained for long. The solution to the puzzle: the swing came from the stock exchange and the support given by the Fed.

As expected, the boom in the real economy was accompanied by a boom in the stock market. But soon the latter seemed to be developing into a stock market bubble. In 1996 alone, the Dow Jones index rose by 1,500 points. In a famous speech, the president of the Fed, Alan Greenspan, cautioned against "irrational exuberance." However, he undertook nothing to gradually let some air out of the bubble. He feared that by trying to do so, the Fed would cause the collapse of the boom in the whole real economy. In 1997, the government drastically reduced the capital gains tax, which brought a flood of capital into the stock market. Shortly thereafter, Greenspan changed his opinion. He almost seemed to be encouraging speculators at the stock exchange when he said that the so-called "New Economy"[13] heralded a new era of growing productivity. Brenner describes and explains the outcome of this development with the following words:

> Simultaneously, the US stock market took off on the greatest ascent in its history, leaving underlying profits in the dust. Finally, by making possible the explosive growth of household and corporate indebtedness [by means of the wealth effect][14] the expanding equity price bubble facilitated an eventual decisive shift in the engine driving the US economic expansion — from the recovery of US manufacturing in the world market toward the growth of US domestic consumption, as well as investment aimed at the home market. It thereby maintained, and even accelerated, the US boom. (2003a: 130)

But how did this change come about exactly? As planned in the Reverse Plaza Agreement, the Japanese bought large numbers of US securities in order to push up the exchange rate of the US dollar. Also some other East Asian countries did the same in their own interest. So the objective was met. However, this operation had three further effects: (1) It effected a strong rise in the prices of US securities. (2) The enormous flow of money-capital into the securities market — from overseas alone about US$1 billion per day, year after year (Stiglitz 2003: 17) — pushed the long-term interest rates down. The Fed had already lowered the short-term interest rates. Because of the low interest rates and the wealth effect of rising securities prices, incurring debts became cheaper and easier. (3) And the high exchange rate of the US dollar made imports cheaper, which in turn, via competition, pushed down the prices of domestic products. The two related effects together worked as a great stimulus for consumption. This development brought about a strong boom in the United States and, ultimately, a huge stock market bubble. The NASDAQ (the stock market index for high-tech industries), for instance, which stood at 500 points in April 1991, had risen to 5,132 points by March 2000 (5). Thereafter, the bubble burst. Before that, however, the world economy had to struggle with some big crises at the periphery, which I describe below.

## d) *Crises in the "Emerging Markets"*

A few of the so-called Third World countries succeeded in growing out of the status of an underdeveloped country. They were therefore given different markings: "emerging markets," "Asian tigers," "baby tigers," "newly industrialized countries." From the mid-1990s to 1998, some of them were shaken by severe crises, which were a strange tangle of serious problems difficult to unravel — problems of the real economy and currency crises caused by attacks by speculators. In the following, I shall describe briefly the crises in Mexico and East Asia, which to a certain extent also spilled over to the rest of the world.

MEXICO

In the early 1990s, Mexico enjoyed a good reputation in the world economy. The disgrace of insolvency and inflation (140.7% in 1987) of the 1980s was overcome. The economy stood again on solid ground. State spending and top bracket tax rates had been reduced. State enterprises had been privatized and foreign trade liberalized. In order to eliminate inflation the central bank had seen to it that the interest rates remained high. The Mexican peso had been pegged to the US dollar in 1988, and since then its exchange rate was allowed to fall in a controlled way within a certain fluctuation range. The results of this stabilization program were very good. Between 1989 and 1992, annual economic growth averaged out at 4.3%. In the four years prior to that, it was on average only 0.5%. The inflation rate fell in 1992 to merely 14.4% (all figures from OECD 2000: 211, 224). In 1993, Mexico became a founding member of NAFTA (North American Free Trade Agreement). International investors had great confidence in the health of the economy. It was said the country had reached the status of a First World nation and it attracted large masses of international capital.

However, there were also two problems: (1) Because the peso was pegged to the US dollar and was allowed to fall only within a narrow fluctuation range, it was, against the backdrop of inflation, overvalued. The result was a balance of trade deficit. Since, at the same time, foreign investments in Mexico grew rapidly and more and more payments (interests, dividends, profits, etc.) had to be made to foreign investors, Mexico's current account deficit also grew. In 1994, it amounted to US$29.7 billion (OECD 2000: 259). That was 8% of the GDP, which was too high according to the World Bank (Henderson 1998: 63). (2) This current account situation also had a negative effect on economic growth, which fell from 5.1% in 1990 to 2% in 1993. After that, the government loosened the fiscal discipline that had been in place since the early 1990s. The central bank increased the money supply as well. These measures proved effective. The growth rate increased again, to 4.5% in 1994. However, inflation did not wait long. It shot up from 8.5% in 1994 to 38% in the following year (all figures from OECD 2000: 211, 224).

The current account deficit was partly defused by the ongoing flow of foreign capital — a fact that entailed an unpleasant dependence. Such a solution of the problem can work only as long as the country in question and its economy do not lose the confidence of foreign investors. But exactly this happened to Mexico. On January 1, 1994, the indigenous population of Chiapas revolted. On March 23, 1994, the reform-friendly presidential candidate of the ruling party was murdered. And then, after another reformer had been elected president in August, the general secretary of the ruling party was murdered in September. These incidents were proof of internal political conflicts in the country and within the ruling party, in which resistance to neo-liberal reforms was strong. These incidents were perceived by alarmed international investors as signs of political instability. It seemed as if the President was losing control of the situation and the reform process was going to be stopped. Mexico appeared to be losing its newly attained First World status.

As mentioned above, in 1994 the economy, on the one hand, boasted a good growth rate; on the other hand, the current account deficit grew, which made a larger inflow of foreign capital necessary. But the Fed prevented that by raising the prime interest rate, thus making it more expensive for US investors to take new credit. In this situation, three things were necessary for reducing the current account deficit: exports had to be increased, imports had to be curtailed, and, in general, peso transfers to foreign countries had to be reduced. For all three, it was necessary to devalue the peso. But this brought the country into a quandary. It was precisely the stability of the value of the currency that was so important for the confidence of foreign investors, on whose investments Mexico depended so much.

Under the pressure of a growing current account deficit it became all the more necessary to buy US dollars in the currency market. As a result, the exchange rate of the peso fell below the previously set fluctuation range, and so the central bank had to intervene, that is, it had to buy pesos in order to keep its exchange rate above the lower limit of the fluctuation range. That set off a rapid depletion of the central bank's foreign currency reserve. In April 1994 alone, it fell by US$11 billion (Henderson 1998: 67). Such a situation was practically an open invitation to currency speculation.

### DIGRESSION: CURRENCY SPECULATION

The business of currency speculators is not easy to understand. It is understandable that a small speculator quickly sells her money held in currency X, i.e., changes it into, for example, US dollar, when the exchange rate of X is likely to fall soon. It is also easy to understand that she exchanges a lot of US money into X, that is, she buys X, when she thinks the exchange rate of X has reached its lowest point, for she now expects the exchange rate of X to rise soon. In such cases, the speculator is only taking advantage of a trend in the currency market that is not of her own making.

However, big currency speculators — George Soros, for instance — "attack" the currency of an *ailing economy*, let us now call it Y, with the aim of pushing down its exchange rate. They sell millions of Y, which they hold on their account (i.e., they convert it to, say, US dollars). But what benefit do they draw when they themselves try to push down the exchange value of the millions of Y they hold? The answer is: if they succeed, they can later, at the right moment, buy even larger sums of Y, which has now become much cheaper — in the hope that its exchange rate will soon go up, for instance after an economic recovery or after an improvement in the current account balance of the country in question. But the exchange rate of Y was already, before their "attacks" began, higher than now. Then why did they "attack" the currency at all?

The answer to the riddle is that the few speculators who start the attack sell their money held in Y at the *beginning* of the process, when Y is obviously overvalued, i.e., the exchange rate of Y is much higher than its expected exchange rate at the bottom of the process. They expect that after their massive sales, thousands of other holders of Y will panic and also sell away their Y quickly. After all, doubts about the solidity of the economy of the country, whose currency Y is, has already been expressed. These panic sales will lead to a further drop in the exchange rate of Y. At the bottom of the process, Soros and co. can buy millions of Y at the cheapest price with the dollars they have acquired at the beginning by selling their holdings in Y. They now have much more Y than they had in the beginning.

What is, however, very difficult to understand is that big speculators generally borrow beforehand the millions of Y with which they start the attack from banks at a certain interest rate. Such a speculation-action can also fail. The interest burden can turn out to be higher than the speculative profit. The exchange rate of Y may not fall low enough because the concerned central bank defends its exchange rate with determination and, eventually, succeeds. In such a case the speculators may suffer great losses. What is even more difficult to understand is why banks are willing to lend hundreds of millions of Y for such high-risk speculative actions. In one notorious case, the hedge fund Long-Term Capital Management (LTCM) borrowed from banks US$120 billion on the basis of investor capital of only US$2.3 billion (see Garnreiter et al. 1998: 36).

If the currency speculator is also an industrial investor, she can exchange dollars for now much cheaper Y and buy up stocks of ailing companies in Y country. Also in this way large European and American corporations can acquire whole companies in emerging-market countries. In fact, speculative investors — hedge funds, investment funds, private equity companies, etc. — are nowadays acquiring entire industrial groups, even in Europe and America, breaking them up, revitalizing the lucrative parts, and selling them at a high profit.


Let us now return to Mexico. In April 1994, speculators attacked the peso. So the Mexican central bank raised interest rates in order to make the costs of borrowing money higher for speculators. Also Mexico's NAFTA partners helped by lending the country large sums of US dollars, which raised the central bank's foreign currency reserve. These defense measures were successful. But in autumn the situation deteriorated again — partly, as stated above, because of political instability. Since the economic situation — with falling growth rate of exports together with high growth rate of imports and softened fiscal and monetary policies — was regarded as problematic, international investors again became nervous. An exodus from Mexican stocks and securities began. When foreign investors wanted to convert their money into US dollars, the central bank had to tap its foreign currency reserves. While such reserves stood at approximately US$17 billion in November, they fell to approximately US$10 billion by mid-December (Henderson 1998: 68). On December 19, a US investment fund sold pesos worth US$20 million, which scared all market players. The next day, the central bank announced it would accept a fall of the exchange rate of the peso down to 15% below the set fluctuation range. That set off a wave of selling, and the central bank had to intervene repeatedly in order to stop the collapse. As a result, its dollar reserves were almost fully eroded. On December 22, the central bank gave up and let the peso float freely, that is, its exchange rate was now left to be entirely determined by market forces.

The consequence of this decision was a free fall of the exchange rate. In March 1995, US$1 cost 122% more pesos than in December 1994 (69). Stock and security prices also plummeted. The interest rates had to be raised in order to induce unnerved investors to stay in the country, but that action retarded investment in equipment. Since the foreign currency reserves were very low, there was a renewed danger that Mexico would, as in the 1980s, fail to service its debts. In concrete terms, a series of government bonds were due for repayment in the first quarter of 1995, and it looked like Mexico would not be able to pay them back.

In this situation, help came from the USA, which could not allow the collapse of a NAFTA partner. The IMF and some other industrialized countries were mobilized, and also some Latin American countries helped. An aid packet of US$49.8 billion — in the form of credit guarantees — was put together. Mexico's president also appealed to the citizens to put up with some sacrifices, for state spending had to be cut drastically.

These measures helped. By June 1995, both the peso and the stock exchange had stabilized. The mature government bonds could be repaid. In order to further stabilize the economy and eradicate inflation, the central bank drastically raised the interest rates, which also led to a contraction of imports. The fall in imports, in turn, contributed to an improvement in the balance of trade and hence also in the current account balance. Mexico, however, had to pay a high price for this stabilization. A deep recession ensued. The growth rate fell from 4.5% in 1994 to –6.2% in 1995, and the unemployment rate rose from 3.5% in 1994 to 5.8% in 1995 (OECD 2004: 203, 215). Wages fell, there were many demonstrations against the government, and the crime rate rose sharply.

In 1996, the crisis was overcome. The economy grew by 5.1%, and unemployment fell to 4.3% (OECD 2004: 203, 215). Also the national budget recorded a surplus. The foreign currency reserve reached the normal level, and the confidence of foreign investors was restored.

### e) *The Great Crisis in East Asia*

From 1985 to mid-1997, all East Asian countries boasted a very dynamic growth — often above 8%. One spoke of an economic miracle. Wim Duisenberg, at the time director of the Bank for International Settlements (later president of the European Central Bank) said in June 1997, just about one month before the crisis broke out in July: The outlook on the world economy "today is perhaps better than it has been for a long time. A particularly positive aspect is the strong economic expansion in the emerging markets" (retranslated; quoted in Jakob 1999: 15). International banks almost wanted to force credit on them.

The rapid economic growth was based on exports. The share of goods from the "Asian tigers" (South Korea, Taiwan, Hong Kong, and Singapore) in US imports grew from 1.6% in 1963 to 6.7% in 1973 (Jakob 1999: 20). From 1985 onwards, the region's exports grew even faster. They were no longer just raw materials and simple products such as textiles, but also industrial and high-tech products such as automobiles, office machines, semiconductors, etc. This had a lot to do with the Plaza Agreement of 1985, which prompted the Japanese to move a large part of their industry and financial investments to these countries. Thanks to this industrialization process, the low labor costs, and the low exchange rates of its currencies, which were pegged to the falling US dollar, this region could rapidly increase its exports to many other countries as well.

When, in the early 1990s, Japan slid into a recession, the above-mentioned process of relocating Japanese industrial investments in the other East Asian countries was accelerated. And the import of consumption goods from these countries into Japan grew rapidly. But in certain periods in the 1990s, there was also recession or weak growth in the USA and the rich European industrialized countries. A large part of the surplus savings and cheap credit in these countries, which could not find sufficiently profitable investment opportunities at home, flowed into the emerging-market countries. For there the interest rates and — because of the economic boom — the profit opportunities were much higher. From 1995 onwards, the European banks also got into this business in a big way. All of this made an intensification of the export-led boom in the region possible.

Except in the case of South Korea and Taiwan, whose development had been largely the result of their own efforts, the fast development of this region would not have been possible without massive capital import — although the domestic savings rate in these countries was quite high. Between 1986 and 1996, the savings rate in Thailand, Malaysia, South Korea, and Indonesia came on yearly average to over 33% of GDP (see Huffschmid 1999: 162). Towards the end of the 1980s, in order to attract more foreign investments, these countries had to largely deregulate their financial markets. To this same end, they simultaneously ensured the stability of the exchange rate of their currency by pegging it to the US dollar. This meant that the exchange rate was allowed to fluctuate only within a set narrow range. By buying and selling US dollar and their own currency in the open currency markets, the central banks prevented the exchange rate of their own currency from crossing the limits of this fluctuation range.

This endeavor was very successful, especially in the 1990s before the crisis broke out. During that period of general enthusiasm for emerging markets, private capital totaling US$420 billion was channeled to such Asian countries, mostly as short-term loans. Some of them had a maturity time of just three months (Goldstein 1998: 13, 19). In spite of this, there seemed to be no problems. On maturity, these loans could easily be renewed or rescheduled. Portfolio investments (stocks and other securities) could, of course, be sold immediately, but there were always new buyers for them. The countries of this region had a very good reputation. They had successfully integrated themselves into the world market, and their governments pursued a disciplined fiscal policy. Some countries had a budget surplus, which meant that if individual financial institutions ran into trouble, they could count on state help.

But already during this boom, its foundation began to crumble, for three reasons. (1) The recessions in the industrialized countries — in the mid-1970s, in the beginning of the 1980s, and in the first few years of the 1990s — had caused growing overcapacity and overproduction in the manufacturing industries worldwide, which further increased with the rapid industrialization of the East Asian emerging countries. In addition to this came, a little later but in massive proportions, the export-led industrialization of China. (2) The demand for East Asian manufactured products gradually dwindled, because of three developments: (a) the US government under Clinton gave up the policy of large budget deficits, (b) thanks to the revival of competitiveness and higher productivity, the US manufacturing industry could regain a large share of the world market, and (c) some European countries followed an austerity policy, particularly after the Maastricht Treaty of 1993. (3) Then came in 1995 the Reverse Plaza Agreement, which led to a gradual revaluation of the US dollar, and with it a revaluation of the currencies of the above-mentioned Asian countries that were pegged to the dollar. This brought along a considerable deterioration of the competitiveness of the exports of these countries, because precisely the currencies of their competitors — Japan, Mexico, and China — were now considerably devalued, which gave the latter an advantage in exports.

Under these circumstances, the East Asian governments could have given up the pegging of their currencies to the US dollar and let them float. Had this been done, the exchange rate of these currencies would have fallen and reflected their true market price; that would have restored the competitiveness of these countries. But they held on tightly to the peg to the US dollar. This decision was made on sound grounds. The stable exchange rate of their respective currencies had been an important factor in the antecedent economic boom, particularly in making their economies attractive to foreign investors and lenders — an advantage they were not willing to relinquish. They also needed a continuous inflow of foreign capital in order to finance their mounting current account deficits. These deficits arose in spite of the export boom — firstly, because high interests and yields had to be paid to foreign creditors and investors and, secondly, because large quantities of both investment and consumption goods were being imported at high prices. Moreover, stability of the exchange rate was not the only matter of importance, because in that case, stability at a lower exchange rate would have been acceptable too. All countries, naturally, *also* wanted to get the highest possible amount of money in hard currency for a given amount of their national currency — for that reduced import costs. This was also a reason they resisted a devaluation of their currency.

The East Asian enterprises wanted to solve the problems that had arisen due to the revaluation of their currencies through greater effort to increase exports. For the prospects for solving the problem through a quick reorientation towards an underdeveloped domestic market were meager. Moreover, payment of interests and transfer of profits and yields to foreign creditors and investors had to be made in hard foreign currency. For some time, exports grew further at a satisfactory pace, but only in respect to *volume*. To maintain the competitiveness of their products, they had to reduce prices. The growth of export *proceeds* was, therefore, not satisfactory: it fell from over 30% per annum in early 1995 to nil in mid-1996 (Brenner 2003a: 161). This had, of course, a negative impact on the profit rate.

In spite of these problems the flow of foreign capital into the region continued for some time. Only speculative motives could explain that: the rising exchange rates of their currencies promised good gains to early foreign investors who bought assets in local currency.

In the region itself, governments (or central banks) relaxed their monetary policy in order to let their currency's exchange rate fall a bit within the set fluctuation range (they may have done it to promote exports). The relaxed monetary policy, however, also reinforced the credit boom that was already under way. The expansion of credit generated a speculative bubble in stock and real estate prices, although — this exactly is one of the absurdities of capitalism — the foundation of the economic growth, namely, a steep rise in exports, was already undermined.

In 1997, the crisis broke out. Capacity utilization levels fell rapidly. Because of ensuing losses the region's companies had increasing difficulty servicing their debts. Real estate and stock prices dropped. Defaults on payment spread. In early 1997 a series of bankruptcies erupted among South Korea's industrial conglomerates (chaebol). The same happened in Thailand. In the banks bad debts were accumulating. Suddenly, current account deficits, which until then were regarded as "good deficits" (because they could be balanced off without problem), became a risk factor. Then the international investment funds began to leave the region. Between April and June, foreign banks withdrew 30% of their credit (Brenner 2003a: 163) (this was obviously short-term credit). And then stock prices too started to plummet.

At this point a wave of currency speculation began, which worsened the negative image of the economic situation. This time speculators tried to take advantage of both the expected strong devaluation of the currencies and the end of their pegging to the US dollar. Indeed, they wanted to cause such things to happen. In order to stop the flight of capital, the central banks raised interest rates. But this increased the difficulty of the real economy to get credit, which led to a further decline in stock and real estate prices. And this, in turn, led to more flight of capital. In the course of 1997, the situation worsened dramatically: from a net inflow of US$93 billion in 1996 to a net outflow of US$12 billion in 1997 (163). It was a state of total panic. All foreign lenders and investors wanted to get out.

The debtors of the region — companies and banks — had an additional problem: they had to repay in foreign currency all their debts denominated in foreign currency (mostly in US dollars). For this purpose they had to acquire hard foreign currencies by exchanging their money in national currencies, which had undergone a drastic devaluation. Since July 1997 central banks, one after the other, had given up the battle to defend the exchange rate of their currencies and had allowed them to float freely. That had always led to immediate strong devaluation of the currency in question. This went on until well into the year 1998. The situation worsened more and more.

The following table provides data on the two most important aspects of the financial crisis.

**Cumulative, percent change between June 30, 1997, and May 8, 1998**

|  | of the exchange rate of the local currency in relation to the US dollar | of the local stock price index |
|---|---|---|
| Thailand | −36.0% | −26.7% |
| Malaysia | −33.6% | −46.2% |
| Indonesia | −73.8% | −40.0% |
| The Philippines | −33.0% | −21.3% |
| South Korea | −36.2% | −50.0% |
| Taiwan | −13.8% | −9.1% |
| Singapore | −11.6% | −28.5% |
| Hong Kong | 0.0% | −33.8% |

(Source: Goldstein 1998: 2f.)

## CASE STUDY THAILAND

After having made a general presentation above, I would now like to give a somewhat detailed example. Once the East Asian crisis broke out in Thailand, the Thai crisis worked like a catalyst for the crises in the other East Asian countries. Hence, Thailand can serve as a good example.

In the period between 1980 and 1990, the Thai economy grew on average by 7.6% per year (Jakob 1999: 39). The falling exchange rate of the Thai baht (along with the US dollar) — a consequence of the 1985 Plaza Agreement — provided the basis for an export-led economic boom. The low Third World wages also played an important role in it. However, this export boom could no longer, as the earlier one, be based mainly on agricultural development, the possibilities of which had been exhausted. For this reason, the state directed its promotion efforts towards developing the manufacturing industry.

That was also the time when Japanese corporations made massive investments in the East Asian countries in order to circumvent the negative effects of the Plaza Agreement. Thailand was one of these countries. Big Japanese banks also lent large sums of money to Thai companies. Western corporations built manufacturing bases in Thailand as well.

In this boom, domestic capital formation also played an important part. In order to facilitate raising of capital, a stock exchange was founded. In the early 1990s, restrictions on banking business were eased and the interest rates were left to the market. The financial sector boomed. "At one point it was just a license to print money." Speculating in the stock exchange became a popular pastime. In the mid-1990s, the domestic savings rate amounted to no less than 34% of the GDP (Henderson 1998: 85). Also large amounts of foreign capital streamed in — no longer only in the form of direct investments but also as portfolio investments. As a result of this development, bubbles were formed both in the stock exchange and in the real estate sector. All this led to the emergence of a new economic elite and a new middle class, and both, as in Mexico, wanted to rapidly turn Thailand into a First World country. And everything seemed to indicate they would more or less succeed in this in the foreseeable future. In 1990, the GDP growth rate amounted to 11.2%; until the middle of the decade, it varied between 8.1% and 9.1%. Per capita GDP doubled between 1985 and 1996. The employment rate in the manufacturing industry increased in the same period from 7% to 15%. Exports grew between 1990 and 1995 on average by 18.8% per year: in 1995, the rate of growth was 24.7%. During the same period, the national budget had an average yearly surplus of 3.2% of the GDP (all figures from Henderson 1998: 84, 87, 92). The Thai economy was at the time one of the fastest growing economies of the world.

This rapid development, however, came to an abrupt end. In 1996, the growth rate of exports plummeted to only 0.1% (93). It nose-dived in all branches — both in the traditional ones, such as textiles and shoes, and in the new ones, such as computers and electronics, which the country had built up in recent times with great effort. The main reason for this fall was the Reverse Plaza Agreement of 1995 (see above), which brought about an overvaluation of the baht. But, regardless, a growth rate of exports to the tune of approximately 20% per annum was simply not sustainable for long. Firstly, there are normal business cycles in the world economy (overproduction, etc.). For example, there was at the time a strong downturn in the world market for electronic goods. And secondly, competing industrial locations do not sleep at the wheel. Because of increased labor costs, companies in labor-intensive industries relocated their production to countries with still lower wage costs, such as Southern China, Vietnam, Bangladesh, and Pakistan.

The revaluation of the baht cheapened imports. Although it grew in 1996 by only 4% (Henderson 1998: 93), this growth rate was much higher than that of exports (0.1% for the same year). This would not have become a big problem on its own if the economic outlook had otherwise remained positive. But it did not. In the last quarter of 1996, the budget deficit crept up to 1.1% of GDP (94). In the boom period, in spite of a high growth rate of exports, Thailand (as also some other East Asian countries) regularly had deficits in current account balance. These deficits were financed by budget surpluses and by the inflow of foreign capital. Since now export growth collapsed, the deficit in balance of trade grew and with it grew also the current account deficit. Since the budget too ran a deficit, Thailand's dependence on inflow of foreign capital increased considerably. But, as we know, foreigners do not gladly invest in a country whose economy is in bad shape, which was clearly the case in Thailand towards the end of 1996. The country suffered from loss of confidence among foreign investors.

For reasons stated above, Thailand neither wanted to devalue the baht nor give up its pegging to the US dollar. This was indeed a problem. Thailand wanted to defend the clearly overvalued baht in a free currency market. For this purpose the central bank always had to buy baht as soon as its exchange rate started to fall below the lower limit of the set fluctuation range. That was a kind of situation that always attracted both anxious holders of the concerned currency as well as speculators. For the market players expected that the efforts to defend the currency would fail. The baht was attacked.

Apart from the changed world economic situation, there were also some homemade causes of the problems of the Thai economy: corruption, incompetence, and power struggles, in which the military also participated. There was talk of crony capitalism, because in economic decision-making personal relationships weighed more than objective criteria. The consumption lust of the rich and the middle class, who imported costly luxury goods, contributed to the deterioration of the trade balance. The entrepreneurs' greed for profit led to over-investing. Large sums of money borrowed abroad were invested in unproductive ventures, that is, in projects with less and less yields. Too many houses and apartments were built for which there were no buyers or tenants. The financial sector had been liberalized far too much, and there was too little supervision of the financial institutions. There were too many bad debts. For all these reasons no one could imagine that the central bank would be able to defend the exchange rate of the baht.

But the government and the central bank were determined to do exactly that. The government created a 70-billion-baht rescue fund to save the financial institutions that held bad debts from having lent the construction sector too much money. The central bank drew on its foreign currency reserve, which was very large for normal times, to buy baht. In order to make speculative borrowing harder, it doubled the interest rate for overnight borrowing. Later, it simply ordered Thai banks to not give credit to foreign customers anymore. In this way, it was able to fend off the speculators' attacks for the time being. But it was all in vain. The rescue fund, although an impressive sum in absolute terms, was too little for the outstanding debts of the construction sector, which totaled 600 billion baht.

Credit given by the financial institutions to the private sector as a whole amounted to almost 150% of the GDP, and 14% of that amount — some 155 billion baht — were bad debts (Henderson 1998: 99f.). In January 1997, Finance One, a large bank, was behind with paying interest due on securities it had sold. What happened thereafter was devastating. In February 1997, a large US investment fund stopped recommending Thai securities — as there was a risk that the baht would soon be devalued. In April, Moody's — an important US rating agency — downgraded Thailand. Soon thereafter, the Bangkok stock exchange had to stop trading in stocks of financial institutions, and then stock prices were in free fall.

In short, it was simply an impossible task for Thailand to simultaneously save the baht, the economy, the financial institutions, and the real estate companies. The central bank finally understood that. In the struggle to defend the exchange rate of the baht, its foreign currency reserve had considerably shrunk. Whereas on July 1, 1997, the prime minister still swore the baht would never be devalued, the central bank announced on July 2 that it would no longer defend the pegging of the baht to the US dollar. On that same day, the baht lost 20% of its value in relation to the US dollar (Jakob 1999: 15).

Now we need to say only briefly what happened in the other countries of the region. With the exception of China, their respective currencies and stock exchanges were also caught up in the vortex of events. The economies of some of these countries were in similarly bad situations as Thailand's; others, however, landed in trouble even though their economic situations were not so bad. In the case of the latter group, the main trouble was fear: in technical terms, the fear of "contagion."

The deeper cause of mass selling of a currency — be it, at the superficial level, for speculation purposes or out of panic — is that the basic data of the economy in question are interpreted as miserable, whether or not they are in fact. Malaysia was, like Thailand, running a relatively high current account deficit, had been bearing the burden of some megaprojects, and its real estate market was suffering from oversupply. It was simply a case of overinvestment; the country had borrowed too heavily abroad. Indonesia's current account deficit was not in the danger zone, but its foreign debt was too high. Also its companies, including banks, had too many foreign debts denominated in the US dollar.

South Korea's main problem was the weak balance sheets of its industrial conglomerates: their gearing ratios (the ratio of a company's loan capital to the value of its ordinary shares) were too high, which is why some had made heavy losses or had already gone bankrupt. The banks were too highly involved in these over-indebted conglomerates, also through shareholding. Too large a portion of such conglomerates' loan capital was denominated in foreign currencies. The country's current account deficit was of course not yet in the danger zone, but it showed a rising trend.

The economies of countries with otherwise sound basic data had some weak spots as well. The Philippines was running a large current account deficit, though not as large as Thailand's. Hong Kong's real estate market was overheated. Only Singapore's and Taiwan's basic economic data appeared to be without blemish. Yet, they were all drawn into the maelstrom of the currency crisis.

In the beginning of the crisis, all of them tried — with different degrees of vehemence — to defend the exchange rate of their currency pegged rather rigidly to the US dollar. But, as shown in the table earlier, all except Hong Kong failed; they succumbed to market pressure. Their central banks either officially let their currency float, or practically stopped trying to defend it, or they further broadened the fluctuation range.

Why did all these economies fail? Firstly, revaluation of a currency is, with regard to economic policy, simply irrational when the basic data of the economy have changed for the worse. Foreign investors lose confidence in such an economy. After that there is little the government or the central bank can do in the short run. Secondly, in order to successfully defend its currency in such a situation, a central bank needs a large reserve of hard currencies with which to buy its own currency on a massive scale. This precious reserve, whose purpose is not (or not only) to buy one's own currency, but (or but also) to balance out current account deficits, can quickly run short, as it did in Thailand, Malaysia, Indonesia, and the Philippines. Thirdly, in the final analysis, the other two measures to defend the currency — raising the interest rates in order to make borrowing money costlier for speculators, and raising the legal reserve requirement for banks in order to make lending more difficult for them — harms the country's real economy. As we have seen above, the East Asian economies had great problems with their exports well before the beginning of the crisis. It was therefore a dilemma, a conflict between two contradictory self-interests. Eventually, the costs of defending the currency became too high. The central banks gave up. They did not want to squander their valuable foreign currency reserve any longer; nor did they want to harm the economy.

For two countries with very solid basic economic data — Taiwan and Singapore — there was an additional reason to give way to the market. Their exports were additionally disadvantaged by the fact that the currencies of some other countries of the region, their competitors, had already undergone some devaluation. In order to recover the lost competitiveness of their exports, they also let the exchange rate of their currency fall, although they would probably have been able to successfully defend it. Hong Kong — whose basic economic data were also very solid, with the exception of an overheated real estate sector — refused to follow this logic and managed to successfully defend its currency. For its government, the arguments for an unshakable stability of its currency were more convincing. In their view, the long-term welfare and prosperity of the country and its economy depended on this stability. And for this, they were prepared to pay a high price in the short term.

On this issue, two more points have to be added. Firstly, it was not just foreign speculators who sold the region's targeted currencies on a massive scale. After the panic had broken out, local and regional companies and banks also rushed to sell their national currency and other regional currencies for US dollars before the former fell further. The reason for such actions was that they needed foreign hard currencies, because they had to pay or pay back their import bills or short-term debts denominated in a foreign currency in that same currency. Most of those liabilities were unhedged and, hence, if they had not taken the aforesaid actions, the debtors/importers would have had to pay a much higher sum in Thai baht or Malaysian ringgit on the due date. Secondly, US rating agencies such as Moody's and Standard and Poor's played an important role in this process. They downgraded the affected countries' ratings, during the crisis and even before, on more than one occasion. This too aggravated the crisis. As a result, these countries and their companies had difficulties in getting credit and investments from abroad, and they were forced to offer higher interest rates.

The effects of these turbulences on the region's real economy were catastrophic. Production dropped sharply; many businesses, especially small ones, went bankrupt; unemployment increased by leaps and bounds; and large parts of the population sank into poverty. At the same time, banks had two kinds of problems: many of their debtors — companies as well as individuals — had gone bankrupt, as a result of which bad debts accumulated, while their creditors, the international banks, were demanding repayment of the short-term credit they had given to such banks. Many national and regional banks defaulted. This situation can be depicted with a few figures:

|  | Growth rate of real GDP (in %) | | | Unemployment rate (in %) | | |
| --- | --- | --- | --- | --- | --- | --- |
|  | 1996 | 1997 | 1998 | 1996 | 1997 | 1998 |
| South Korea | 7.0 | 4.7 | −6.9 | 2.0 | 2.6 | 7.0 |
| Thailand | 5.9 | −1.4 | −10.5 | 2.6 |  | 5.0 |
| Malaysia | 10.0 | 7.3 | −7.4 | 2.6 | 2.5 | 5.2 |
| Philippines | 5.8 | 5.2 | −0.6 | 10.9 | 7.9 | 13.3 |
| Indonesia | 8.0 | 4.5 | −13.1 | 7.2 | 2.8 | 22.0 |
| Hong Kong | 4.3 | 5.1 | −5.0 | 2.8 | 2.2 | 4.7 |
| Singapore | 8.1 | 8.6 | −0.9 | 2.0 | 1.8 | 3.2 |
| Taiwan | 6.1 | 6.7 | 4.6 | 2.6 | 2.7 | 2.7 |

(Sources: for South Korea: OECD 2004; for the rest: IMF 2004, *Fischer Weltalmanach* 1998 to 2000, Statistisches Bundesamt Deutschland 1999. Thailand's unemployment rate in 1997 could not be found.)

In view of the dramatic fall in production in the two crisis years, there cannot be any doubt that several million people lost their jobs — at any rate, more people than the unreliable official statistics say. According to reports from 1999, the total number for the first six countries on the chart came to about 20 million. Real wages fell by 8% (in Thailand) to 30% (in Indonesia). Poverty grew enormously in the whole region. According to an IMF study, the percentage of poor people in Indonesia doubled (figures from Jakob 1999: 52; Huffschmid 1999: 165). Indonesian migrant workers in Malaysia were deported on a large scale. In May 1998, following increases in food, petrol, and cooking kerosene prices due to the elimination of (or cuts in) subventions, there were violent riots in Jakarta that left about 1,000 people dead.

We must also mention here that the IMF played an infamous role in aggravating the crisis. Together with other international financial organizations it granted the countries in crisis bridging loans to the tune of US$111.9 billion (Jakob 1999: 51). But it utilized this opportunity to impose upon the receivers, as conditions for the loans, extensive structural adjustments: opening-up of their markets (which had mostly been protected until then), sharp increases in interest rates, drastic cuts in state spending, and a stronger general liberalization of the economy. While the received bridging loans streamed directly into the coffers of the international creditor banks, the high interest rates and the drastic cuts in public expenditure choked the economy and thus aggravated the crisis.

It was to be expected that in globalized neo-liberal capitalism this great crisis would have effects beyond the borders of the East Asia region, even just through the normal channels of trade and capital flow. Suddenly, the world economy was missing a large chunk of demand from East Asia. The Japanese economy especially, as it is very closely intertwined with the aforesaid East Asian economies at many levels, was understandably the worst hit (see further on). But also more distant countries, such as Russia and some Latin American ones, felt, to a greater or lesser extent, the brunt of the East Asian crisis.

### f) *Russia*

The crisis in Russia, which was of a quite different kind because of the system transformation going on at the time, had several aspects to it. One of them was the severe financial crisis of the state, which was highly indebted both at home and abroad. On August 17, 1998, Russia declared a partial default. That is, the government stopped servicing the domestic debts for ninety days. It also imposed a ninety-day moratorium on repaying private foreign debts and discharging foreign liabilities of Russian companies. This crisis had something to do with the East Asian crisis inasmuch as South Korean banks were big buyers of Russian state bonds and other securities. When these banks got into difficulties, they began to withdraw their money, which made it difficult for Russia to roll over its external debts. In the Russian crisis the other known factors also played a part: deregulation of the finance sector, free convertibility of the ruble and its pegging to the US dollar, short maturity time of the credits (bonds), high interest rates, etc. And then came loss of confidence among international investors, flight of capital, currency speculation, devaluation of the ruble after it was left to float freely, and a crash at the stock exchange (in just one week the stock index fell by 40.9%). Nevertheless, the Russian crisis cannot, strictly speaking, be put in the category "crisis of capitalism," since the economy was at the time just making the transition to capitalism (for details on this topic see Garnreiter et al. 1998: 22–28).

### g) *Latin America*

Latin America felt the brunt of the East Asian crisis more strongly. During the crisis and also thereafter it had seemed as if Latin America would actually benefit from it; investment advisors now recommended investments in the "emerging markets" of this region. But Latin America soon got caught up in the maelstrom of the East Asian crisis, which had been additionally aggravated by the Russian crisis.

One of the causes lay in the real economy. Because of the crisis in East Asia and the recession in Japan, where in 1998 the growth rate fell to −2.5% (OECD 2000: 211), the demand for almost all raw materials dropped dramatically, and that at a time when there was general overproduction in the world economy. Compared to the average of 1997, the world market price of oil fell until August 1998 by 39%, from US$19.1 to $11.7 per barrel. The raw materials price index (of the HWWA Institut in Hamburg) fell within a year by 25%. Latin American countries that exported raw materials such as oil (Mexico, Venezuela, Ecuador) or copper (Chile) were hit hard by this slump.

A further cause of the deterioration of the economic situation in Latin America was the increasing general nervousness of international investors following the crisis in East Asia and Russia. They became generally cautious with regard to emerging countries. And an exodus of international capital started. Stock prices and exchange rates showed a negative trend. In Chile, from January to October 1998, stock prices fell by 40%. In the same period, the exchange rate of the Mexican peso fell by 28%, and that of the Venezuelan bolívar by 14%. The terms of trade deteriorated. The interest rates had to be considerably increased in order to again attract capital, which in turn harmed the real economy (see Garnreiter et al. 1998: 29–30). It was a crisis of all emerging countries, all over the world.

### BRAZIL

Brazil, the largest economy in Latin America, was hit the hardest by the new series of crises, even more so by the widespread nervousness of international investors. It was one of the countries with the lowest savings rate and, hence, depended on inflow of international capital.

The anti-inflationary measures taken since 1993, when the inflation rate reached 2,146%, had proven successful. By 1997, the rate had sunk to 7.5%. And otherwise the general economic situation was not bad. But this changed with the Russian crisis. Some large investors (among them also South Korean banks), who had suffered great losses in East Asia and Russia, sold their Brazilian securities. Moreover, many investors (wrongly) believed that there were similarities between the Brazilian and the Russian situation, since Brazil — like Russia — had persistent and large budget deficits: in 1998, 8% of GDP. They were afraid that Brazil was in for a drastic devaluation of its currency. For weeks an average of US$500 million was daily pulled out of the country. As a result the country's foreign currency reserve shrank rapidly, and the rating agency Moody's downgraded Brazil's credit-worthiness. In order to induce foreign capital to stay in the country, interest rates were increased. But this measure, together with the ongoing flight of capital, caused a stock exchange crash. In mid-September 1998, the prime interest rate was raised twofold; it came now to 49.75%. But all that was of no avail. While the real economy groaned under the high costs of credit, capital continued to leave the country. At the end of December, the IMF offered Brazil help amounting to US$41 billion — as usual, tied to several conditions: state spending had to be reduced, taxes had to be raised, the exchange rate of the real (the Brazilian currency) must not be touched, the policy of high interest rates had to be continued, they should even be further increased, etc.

On January 7, 1999, the government of the state Minas Gerais declared its inability to pay back in time its debts to the federal government. This triggered a panic, which intensified the flight of capital. The central bank was every day losing foreign currency reserve amounting to US$1 billion (it is not clear whether, apart from the panic of investors, machinations of currency speculators also played a role in this predicament). On January 13, the central bank devalued the real by 8%. Two days later it stopped intervening and let the real, which was until then flexibly pegged to the US dollar, float freely.

Businesspeople now hoped that the financial authorities — freed from the task of defending the inflated exchange rate of the real — would reduce the interest rates. This expectation pushed the stock exchange index up by 33%. But the government disappointed the business world. On January 18, it announced it would stick to the IMF's conditions, that is, it would not lower the interest rates. But in spite of this resolve, it could not prevent the free fall of the real. Between January 13 and January 28, the real dropped by 72% (see Krugman 2000: 111ff., 146ff.; Filc 2001: 164ff.; Garnreiter et al. 1998: 30f.).

The effects of these turbulences on the real economy were bad: economic growth fell from 3.3% in 1997 to 0.1% in 1998. At the end of 1999, after a modest recovery, it had barely reached 0.8% (IMF 2004). The unemployment rates in these years were 5.71% (1997), 7.7% (1998), and 8% (1999) (*Fischer Weltalmanach* 1998 to 2001).

## h) *Japan and the USA after the East Asian Crisis*

### JAPAN

The manufacturing industry of Japan and some other countries that either traded with the USA or were their competitors benefited from the rising exchange rate of the US dollar in the second half of the 1990s. Japan might have succeeded in 1996–1997 in bringing about a sustained upswing, but the East Asian crisis thwarted this opportunity. In the mid-1990s, 44% of Japan's exports went to East Asia (Schmid 2001: 18). The crisis in this region caused a further deterioration of the whole economic situation in Japan, which had already been stagnating since the beginning of the decade. Its exports fell, and the banks accumulated bad debts. In addition to this, the government — being under the influence of the general neo-liberal climate of the era — had tried since April 1997 to consolidate the budget. This was understandable, for in 1997 the public debt totaled 100.3% of the nominal GDP, a ratio considered to be too high (OECD 2004: 234). The US government's deficit reduction policy and the European Union's strict Maastricht rules for maximum deficit and debt levels served as models for the Japanese in this matter. The government increased the consumption tax (sales tax) by 2% and did not extend a temporary income tax reduction, each of which had a negative impact on consumption demand.

The combination of these two measures caused a contraction of the economy. In 1998, private investments dropped by 11.4% (Schmid 2001: 18), and economic growth fell to -2.5% (OECD 2000: 211). From 1999 to 2004 GDP growth registered, in chronological order, -0.1%, 2.4%, 0.2%, -0.3%, 1.5%, and 2.6% (OECD 2005: 51). These figures show that, throughout the 1990s and up to the middle of the first decade of this century, the Japanese economy had unusually low growth. Occasionally there were growth spurts, as, for example, in the years 2000 and 2004. But they were short-lived.

In the course of the crisis years, the unemployment rate rose from 2.1% in 1991 to 4.7% in 2004 (OECD 2000: 231; OECD 2005: 61). Compared to EU figures, these ones look astonishingly good. This is because in Japan's economy — due to cultural and institutional reasons — it was neither easy nor usual to lay off workers immediately after output fell. In Japan there has been a tradition of having a lifelong job in the same company. But, still, the above unemployment figures meant a 123% increase in 14 years.

It is not as if the efforts to rescue the Japanese economy described above were of no use. Such efforts could at least avert a collapse. The continuous devaluation of the yen since 1995, helped increase exports. However, this benefited mainly the large multinational corporations that preferred to invest their profits abroad. And when they invested in Japan, there was too little employment effect because of the high degree of rationalization in the economy. Moreover, in this respect, exports at that time did not play any big role, because the share of export in GDP was only 10% (Garnreiter et al. 1998: 16). A very special manifestation of the Japanese crisis was deflation, a phenomenon that had not occurred since the Great

Depression of 1929–1933. From 1999 to 2004, the consumer price index dropped continuously on average by 0.5% per annum (OECD 2004: 220). This allowed companies to reduce wages, which in turn caused consumption to fall, which aggravated the stagnation. It was a vicious circle.

### THE USA

The crisis forced the manufacturing industry of every East Asian country to intensify its export offensive in the US market, while at the same time the American industry's export market in this region contracted. The yearly growth rate of total US exports, which in the third quarter of 1997 still amounted to 17.4%, fell in the third quarter of 1998 to –0.5%. Because prices of US export goods had to be reduced to compensate for the high exchange rate of the dollar, and because of increased competition in the domestic market resulting from falling prices of imported goods, the profit rate of American manufacturing industry fell sharply (see Brenner 2003a: 169). Then it became too much. Stock prices started to fall and investors fled corporate bonds. Bank shares too began to fall. The peak of this negative development was reached when the big hedge fund LTCM (Long-Term Capital Management) threatened to go bankrupt.

The boom seemed to be coming to an abrupt end. And since the US boom had pulled the rest of the world economy along, as it had many times before, the latter too now appeared to be on the verge of a depression. At this point the Fed intervened. Not only did it organize the salvation of LTCM, but it also lowered the prime interest rate three times in a row. The purpose of the latter action was to revive the stock exchange boom; the Fed wanted the stock prices to rise again. The successive reductions in the prime rate brought about the desired change. The decisive factor thereby was not the lowered costs of borrowing, but the signal that the Fed wanted a continuation of the stock exchange boom in order to stabilize the domestic as well as the international economy. Thereafter, the gigantic speculation wave started rolling again. The necessary liquidity had already been provided through the reductions in the prime interest rate and by foreign investors, who tried their luck in Wall Street.

Above all, US companies took out enormous loans — firstly, to finance large investments in equipment, which had meanwhile become essential due to technological developments and which were also to increase their productivity and competitiveness. Secondly, they used the cheap loans to buy back large chunks of their own shares. They did this in order to push up the price of the shares, which benefited the shareholders and the executives themselves, whose compensation to a large extent consisted of share options. The rising price of their shares increased the assets of the company (wealth effect), thus making it easier for them to take out more loans.

In this speculation spiral the administration played an important part. It deregulated two key areas of the economy: banking and telecommunications. The hitherto existing separation between commercial and investment banking was done away with. Henceforth, banks were allowed to do both kinds of business. This soon led to big balance-sheet falsification scandals. Commercial bankers, whose duty it is to take care, in their own interest, that their credit-clients do not incur too many debts, often ignored this duty, since at the same time, as investment bankers, they were interested in seeing the same corporate credit-clients expand. For investment banks earn large commissions from conducting on behalf of their clients business like mergers, acquisitions, issuance of new shares, etc. Also, stock analysts of the investment banks and auditing firms fell into corruption and gave the market players false information on companies they favored.

The US telecommunications market was deregulated in 1996. Several new companies entered the market hoping to make big profits soon. This hope was based on technological developments of the previous years in the IT (Information Technology) sector. Investors were convinced that due to the seemingly endless expansion of the Internet and the other new achievements of the sector an endlessly expanding demand would arise. The strategy of the new entrants was to quickly become big through mergers and acquisitions and to impress the market players and banks through their size. Once the company's size and the prospect of large profits in the future made the price of its shares go up, it would also be easy to get large amounts of credit from banks and issue overpriced shares. The telecom companies soon laid several million kilometers of fiber-optic cable in the USA and under the oceans. They could increase their investments on average by 15% per year and they also created 331,000 new jobs. With the expansion of the telecom sector, also those industries expanded that supplied equipment and components to the former.

Thanks to the speculative frenzy all of them were also very "successful." In the spring of 2000, market capitalization of the telecom companies (i.e., the market value of all their shares) made up almost 15% of the total market capitalization of all US public limited companies (not including those of the finance sector), although their contribution to the GDP was less than 3%. In other words, it was a huge stock exchange bubble. The utilization rate of their networks totaled only 2.5% to 3%, while that of the underwater cables came to only 13%. This was clearly a case of overinvestment and oversupply with a gigantic mountain of debts. No wonder that their profits fell sharply, from US$35.2 billion in 1996 to US$–5.5 billion in 2000 (Brenner 2003b: 54f.).

Another big bubble that was formed simultaneously was that of shares of the so-called dot-com sector, a collective name for all kinds of Internet companies. Their contribution to the US GDP was negligible, and the great majority of them made only losses. But their market capitalization during this period made up 8% of the market capitalization of all public limited companies in the USA (56), an absurd ratio.

The speculative frenzy did not stop with the telecom and dot-com spheres. It befell also other sectors, whose expansion had a relatively solid basis. The wealth effect of the stock market boom also caused the savings rate of US households to fall from 8% in 1993 to 0% in 2000 (54). Consumption on credit increased since people thought they were wealthy. What is so astonishing is that still the inflation rate was not particularly high. From 1999 to 2001, it registered 2.2%, 3.4%, and 2.8%, respectively (OECD 2004: 220). In my view, the only explanation for that lies in the massive import of cheap consumer goods from low-wage countries of the Third World, whose currencies, moreover, were very much undervalued at the time.

Considering all sectors together, investment expenditure of US companies grew in the second half of the 1990s on average by 9% per year. The combination of growth in consumption and growth in investment caused an enormous increase in demand, which led to economic growth, a fall in unemployment, and wage increases. Furthermore, this development in the USA helped many other countries come through the lull of the early 1990s and the world financial crises of 1997–1998, for instance, South Korea.

## 3. A Long-Drawn-Out Crash and a Collapse in the New Millennium

In the beginning of the new millennium, it looked like capitalism was again facing a big crisis. On the one hand, in all important industrialized countries the huge stock market bubble of the New Economy had burst, which was followed by a plunge of the growth rate, and on the other hand again an economy considered until then as a model case of neo-liberal economic policy collapsed, that of Argentina.

### a) *A Great Crash in Installments*

The situation of the US dot-com sphere mentioned in the previous section simply could not go on as it was. In the spring of 2000, many dot-com companies ran out of money. Investors who had, during the stock market boom, made totally irrational investments of billions of dollars in companies that had never made a profit and still did not promise any, suddenly remembered that companies, in the final analysis, are supposed to make profits. They now refused to pour more money into a bottomless pit. Then came the crash, and the whole sector collapsed. In the summer of 2000 it was telecom's turn, which also had been making big losses. That was the beginning of the collapse of the so-called New Economy as a whole. The crisis of the dot-com and telecom branches spilled over like a chain reaction to their suppliers. And the crisis of the latter, in turn, caused a crisis among their suppliers. Computer sales fell sharply. This, in turn, adversely affected the semiconductor industry, and so on and so forth. The multiplier effect, as we know, works also downwards.

The NASDAQ, the index of the stock exchange of the US technology sector, in which all these branches are covered, fell between March 2000 and March 2001 by 59.8% (Engel 2003: 441). In the year between July 2000 and July 2001, the 4,200 companies listed in this exchange made losses totaling $148.3 billion — more than the total profit they had made in the five-year boom from 1995 to 2000 (Brenner 2003b: 56).

By mid-2002, telecom shares lost 95% of their value; $2.5 trillion in capital, i.e., market capitalization, disappeared into thin air. Between December 2000 and December 2002, telecom companies with a market capitalization of $230 billion went bankrupt. In the same period, the telecom branch laid off half a million workers — 50% more than it had recruited during the boom between 1996 and 2000 (56).

As the share of the above-mentioned sectors in the total accumulated capital in the USA was disproportionately large, their crisis also had a large negative effect on the whole US economy, which was anyhow burdened by global overcapacity and low profit rates. The Dow Jones, the general stock index of US industry, fell between March 2000 and March 2001 by 9.5% (Engel 2003: 441). In the manufacturing industry, between 1997 and 2002, the profit rate dropped by 42% (Brenner 2003b: 56). Investments too fell. The real GDP growth rate of the US economy dropped from 4.4% and 3.7% in 1999 and 2000, respectively, to 0.8% in 2001. In 2002 it improved somewhat, rising to 1.9%. The unemployment rate rose from 4% in 2000 to 5.8% in 2002 (OECD 2004: 203, 215).

The Fed naturally tried, as it had done before, to stop the plunge. From January 2001 to the beginning of 2003, it lowered the prime interest rate twelve times: from 6.5% to 1.25%, the lowest mark in the post-war era (Brenner 2003b: 56). This, however, had little effect on the companies.

Their investment in equipment — the most important factor in the health of an economy — fell continuously. Private households, however, took advantage of the low interest rates to refinance their mortgages, that is, to replace high-interest loans with low-interest loans, through which they got more purchasing power. The low interest rates also motivated other households to take out more loans in order to increase their consumption. This explains why the real GDP again rose in 2002.

The crisis in the USA could not but have negative effects on the other industrialized countries. It was inevitable. One can see that relatively clearly in the data on Germany. In the years in which the US economy boomed, between 1996 and 2000, the German economy grew steadily — by 0.8%, 1.5%, 1.7%, 1.9%, and 3.1%. Thereafter, however, the growth rate fell abruptly: in 2001 to 1%, in 2002 to 0.1%, and in 2003 to -0.1%. As for the unemployment rate, it fell between 1997 and 2000 from 9.2% to 7.3%. From 2001 onwards it rose — from 7.4% to 9.1% in 2003.

In the Eurozone as a whole the growth rate rose from 1.4% in 1996 to 3.7% in 2000; it then fell to 0.6% in 2003. The unemployment rate, which had fallen during the boom from 10.7% in 1996 to 8% in 2001, rose again to 8.8% in 2003. In Japan, after a long time, the growth rate reached a good figure in 2000 (2.8%), only to drop again to 0.4% and -0.3% in 2001 and 2002 respectively. To be brief, the economies of all the OECD countries were also hit by the crisis. Taken together, their growth rate fell from 3.9% in 2000 to 1.1% in 2001, and then it went up in 2002 to 1.6% and in 2003 to 2.2%. The unemployment rate rose from 5.9% in 2000 to 6.9% in 2003 (all data from OECD 2004: 203, 215).

To make a complicated story more understandable, it was a crisis in installments. Between downswings, now and then, there were also brief periods of recovery — e.g., from April to June 2001 and from October 2001 to March 2002. In the whole crisis period — from March 2000 to the beginning of October 2002 — the NASDAQ fell by 75.5%, the Dow Jones by 33.3%, the DAX (the German stock index) by 66.8%, and the TOPIX (TOkyo stock Price IndeX, the index covering 30 industrial shares in Japan) by 62.7%. The destruction of capital in terms of market value of shares during this period was as follows: at the New York Stock Exchange US$2,184 billion, at the US technology exchange (NASDAQ) US$4,280 billion, at the German Stock Exchange (CDAX) US$771.4 billion, and at the Tokyo Exchange (TOPIX) US$2,401 billion (Engel 2003: 446f.).

Generally speaking, by 2003 the crisis was over. Between 2003 and 2005, the US economy registered growth rates from 3% to 4.4%. In the other industrialized countries and economic zones, economic growth was

weak to moderate. Only Italy registered –0.6% in 2005. The unemployment rate, however, had a different development. It remained in general high to very high, as it does not depend on economic growth alone.
The labor-intensity of the industrial branches prevailing in the country
and their degree of automation play an important part in it. In the OECD
countries as a whole, both the economy and unemployment grew in 2003.
Only in Japan, the United Kingdom, and the USA did unemployment fall
or remain under 6% (OECD 2005: 51, 61).

### b) *The Collapse in Argentina*

On December 19 and 20, 2001, and also on the following days, TV view-
ers heard and saw astonishing, even shocking, news and pictures coming from Argentina: mass demonstrations against the government, the
president fleeing his palace, twenty-eight people killed by the police,
400 others wounded, looting of supermarkets, the parliament building
stormed, declaration of a state of emergency, four presidents in five weeks,
stock exchanges closed because investors had no money, freezing of bank
accounts, servicing of foreign debts stopped, etc., etc. At the end of December 2001, reports on the unemployment rate varied between 16% and
20% (*Fischer Weltalmanach* 2003: 86). It was reported in February 2002
that 100 children died daily of hunger or illness, that 40% of the population lived below the official poverty line, that the middle class was being
destroyed (Saunois 2002), and that Argentina could no longer afford a
middle class (*Financial Times*, 2 January 2002). Argentines of Italian or
Spanish descent stood in line in front of the Italian or Spanish embassy
in order to apply for papers for emigrating to these countries. These were
snapshots of the collapse of a capitalist society. It is not the purpose of this
section to repeat sensational news. I would like to present here only briefly
the economic developments that led to this collapse.

Argentina was not a typical Latin American country. It was relatively
developed. Its abundant arable land is very fertile. In the early decades of
the twentieth century, it became a leading exporter of grain, meat, and flax
yarn. In addition, there was an industry — mostly owned by foreign investors — that exported processed food. Continuous economic growth made
Argentina a rich country. Although World War I and the Great Depression
of 1929–1933 diminished its prosperity because exports dropped, Argentina was in the 1930s the tenth richest country of the world; sometime

earlier it had been even richer than France. In 1945, its population is said to have enjoyed a higher standard of living than that of Canada. It was therefore no wonder that it became a preferred destination of European emigrants.

From 1930 onwards, in response to the problems the country faced during the Great Depression, successive governments pursued a policy of import-substituting industrialization. The aim of this policy was to make Argentina largely self-sufficient in respect of both industrial and agricultural products. For this purpose high customs barriers were put up against imports and domestic industries were protected and promoted. After 1945, the Argentinean economy experienced a further growth boost, which was based on the fact that a starving post-war Europe imported huge quantities of beef from Argentina at very good prices.

By 1960, Argentina was so much industrialized that the manufacturing industry's contribution to GDP was larger than that of agriculture. The country was now largely self-sufficient in consumer goods; for fuel and heavy machinery, however, it still very much depended on imports. In the following years, the state heavily invested in basic industries such as steel, oil, gas, petrochemicals, and transportation. By the mid-1970s, Argentina produced the greater part of its demand for oil, steel, and cars, and it exported a number of industrial products. In fuel, it was self-sufficient.

Argentina was an unusual case in Latin America, inasmuch as not only the middle class but also workers had a share in the growing prosperity. The populist president Juan Domingo Perón (1946–1955), a former army officer, won their support by utilizing the economic prosperity to increase wages and implement social reforms. He nationalized the railways and other utilities, and he also financed public works on a large scale. But towards the end of his second term, inflation, corruption, and repression increased, which caused a group of democratic-minded officers to topple him. But in the following years, in spite of occasional turmoil, the basic directions of economic and social policy remained more or less the same. Perón lived eighteen years in exile; however, both he and Perónism remained popular. In 1972, he returned triumphantly to his country and was again elected president in 1973.

Perón died in 1974, and that was roughly also the beginning of the end of the success story that was Argentina. The following years were marked by revolutionary-terrorist activities and other kinds of political violence. In 1976, the military seized power — not for the first time — and their brutal rule lasted until 1983. We should recall that three years earlier, in 1973, the military of Chile had also set up its bloody regime there.

Like in Chile, in Argentina the military regime started a neo-liberal restructuring process, which was continued and intensified by the following regimes until 2001. The policy of import-substituting industrialization was given up, and the customs barriers that had until then protected domestic industries were lowered. These measures were justified by the assertion that they were needed to fight inflation. It was also argued that the protected inefficient Argentine industries had to be exposed to foreign competition for the sake of increasing their efficiency. These measures led to a certain degree of deindustrialization, because some Argentine companies could not withstand the competition of cheaper imports. Between 1975 and 1981, the share of the manufacturing industry in the GDP dropped from a third to a fourth, and this trend continued in the next decade, though at a slower pace (*Encyclopedia Britannica* 2001). In the period of state-led and protected industrialization, all successive governments had neglected agriculture. But now the government thought of the country's comparative advantage in agriculture and relied again on the export of grain and beef. The government also liberalized taking out credit abroad. In the first section of this chapter, I have given an extensive account of the debt crisis in Latin America in the 1980s. As regards the role of the military rule in that crisis, Argentina's foreign debt grew from US$7.8 billion in 1975 to $43 billion in 1982 (Herzog 2002: 55) — an increase of 551%. The greater part of this amount, $28 billion, was debts incurred by private companies. But towards the end of the military regime, they were taken over by the central bank at an exchange rate very favorable to the companies. The government promoted private companies with state funds as well.

In the whole of Latin America, and also in many other developing countries, the 1980s were labeled "the lost decade" (see section 1 of this chapter). In Argentina this decade was additionally marked by galloping inflation. It was caused by mounting state expenditures and steep wage increases side by side with poor performance in production and, therefore, low tax revenue. Between 1980 and 1991, the average annual growth rate of real GDP came to −0.4%. It could also be said that wage increases had become necessary because of inflation. It was therefore partly a classical wage-price spiral. But it was also partly a case of strong increase in money supply, which had become necessary due to mounting state spending financed through budget deficits. Successive governments indeed tried to control the inflation — through measures such as wage-and-price controls, cuts in state spending, and limiting the growth of money supply.

They also introduced new currencies that replaced the old ones, which had been rendered worthless through inflation. But these measures did not bring any success. Between 1980 and 1991, the annual average inflation rate came to 416.9% (*Fischer Weltalmanach* 1994: 254). In 1989, it amounted to 4,900% (Husson 2002: 28). Foreign debt remained high, because large sums were thoughtlessly borrowed abroad for state and private industrial projects. At the end of the 1980s, *foreign* debt amounted to 75% of the GNP (*Encyclopedia Britannica* 2001). The relatively high exchange rate of the successive currencies — which were kept high despite inflation — impaired exports, and the revenue from the same could not keep up with the costs of servicing the growing foreign debts.

In 1989, a new president was voted in: Carlos Menem. Although he called himself a Perónist, he actually pursued a strict neo-liberal policy. In 1991, in order to put an end to hyperinflation, the peso was pegged to the US dollar, at a rigid exchange rate of 1:1; and its convertibility in US dollars was guaranteed. This way, a substantial restriction on the growth of money supply was also enforced. The government had great success in this undertaking. The inflation rate dropped continuously. Already by 1991, it had fallen to 172%, and in 1992 it fell further to 17.5% (*Fischer Weltalmanach* 1994: 254). This policy was so successful that it eventually became detrimental to the economy. After 0.2%, 0.5%, and 0.9% in 1996, 1997, and 1998, respectively, the inflation moved on to deflation. In 1999, 2000, and 2001, the rate of change in price index was –1.2%, –0.9%, and –1.1%, respectively (IMF 2004: 217), which was connected with a simultaneous recession.

While fighting inflation, Menem simultaneously wanted to pursue an austerity policy aimed at reducing the state's debt burden. But he did not quite succeed in this. Then he privatized several state-owned companies: the telecommunication system, the water works, the bus services in the capital, the national airlines, etc. The pension insurance system based until then on the solidarity principle was also privatized by changing it into a pensions system covered by capital investment, thus opening up a large business area for insurance companies. The costs arising from this transformation were borne by the state. In the wake of this privatization frenzy, large amounts of foreign capital flowed into the country: in 1992 and 1993 alone, US$21 billion. In the six previous years, the sum was only $9 billion (Husson 2002: 29). This helped mitigate the problem of current account deficit.

All these measures and, especially, the end of the decades-long monetary instability, were initially very helpful for the economy. The inflow of foreign capital was often accompanied by the introduction of productivity-increasing technologies. The economy recovered very quickly from the deep recession of the last years of the 1980s and, in 1992, it achieved a growth rate of 8.6% (*Fischer Weltalmanach* 1994: 254). The upswing, though somewhat weakened, continued for two more years. But in 1995, the economy suddenly plunged into a bad recession; the growth rate fell to –2.8% (Mussa 2002: 7), which however was caused by an external shock, namely, the severe financial crisis in Mexico (see section 2 of this chapter). After this shock was overcome, the Argentine economy also returned to the growth path. In 1997, the growth rate came to 8.1% (IMF 2004: 209).

But it dropped sharply in 1998, to 3.8%. This was the beginning of a recession.[15] In 1999, 2000, and 2001 the economy registered consecutively very negative growth rates: –3.4%, –0.8%, and –4.4%, respectively (IMF 2004: 209). During this almost four-year-long recession, the per capita income fell by 14% and unemployment rose to almost 20%. Share prices, which had begun the year 2001 with a bull market (boom), fell by December to a ten-year low (*New York Times* online, Dec. 17, 2001), and Argentina was on the brink of a financial collapse. As mentioned above, unrest and riots followed.

The explanations given by bourgeois as well as leftist economists can be summarized as follows. There were simultaneously three partial crises, which were having their combined effect at a very bad time for the world economy, and that is what brought about the collapse in Argentina. (1) The Argentine peso, pegged to the US dollar at a 1:1 rate, was simply overvalued. That, of course, helped overcome the hyperinflation and initially also had a strongly stimulating effect on the economy. But this effect could not last long, as, generally, an overvalued currency brings disadvantages in international trade: for one, exports become costlier, although imports become cheaper. Then the exchange rate of the US dollar rose, and, along with that, also that of the Argentine peso. That was also the time, 1997–1998, when, in quick succession, financial crises were raging in East Asia, Russia, and Brazil. Moreover, Brazil, Argentina's largest export market, devalued its currency in 1999 by 40%. All that had the effect that international as well as Brazilian buyers of Argentine products could henceforth buy similar competing products at much cheaper prices.

Also foreign financial capital became hesitant to invest in Argentina and found other countries, Brazil for instance, more attractive for financial investments. Every country that is heavily indebted abroad must as a rule accumulate trade surpluses in order to service the debts. But Argentina's trade balance ran a deficit in 1992, 1993, 1994, 1997, 1998, and 1999 (Mayer 2001: 28).

Moreover, even before the recession years 1998 to 2001, the wave of privatizations had made a large number of workers redundant. That had a negative effect on wages. The share of wages in the national income fell from 30% in 1989 to only 18% in 1994 (Saunois 2002). The privatization process had also made many indispensable products and services, such as electricity, telecommunication, and transportation, very expensive. Bus travel, for instance, became 40% to 100% dearer (Husson 2002: 29). These price rises negatively impacted the demand for other goods. All this intensified the downward spiral of demand and production that had begun in 1998.

After having a surplus in 1992 and 1993, thanks to the revenues from the privatizations, the budget ran a deficit even in the years marked by substantial economic growth: 1994, 1996, 1997, and 1998 (Mayer 2001: 27). State spending (including debt services) could not be reined in. On the contrary, it increased. Tax revenues were not high enough to make new debts unnecessary, and in the recession years — 1995 and 1998–2001 — they were naturally lower than otherwise. This predicament made it all the more necessary to incur new and larger and larger debts. The foreign debt grew from US$63 billion in 1989 to $147 billion in 2000 (Herzog 2002: 56). And by mid-2001, the amount spent in one year for servicing the foreign debts rose to $15 billion. This sum was equal to half of the export earnings of that year and almost a fourth of the total tax revenue (29).

The public debt that the Menem administration had inherited was already large; yet they incurred even more debts. The privatization of state-owned companies could not significantly reduce the extent of new debts, for those companies were sold away at bargain prices. As a result, the ratio of public debt to GDP rose from 29.2% in 1993 to 41.4% in 1998. In Menem's second presidential term, which included three of the five recession years, the government had to further incur high debts. As a result, the said ratio rose to 50% in 2000 (Mussa 2002: 8, 9). That caused the domestic interest rates to shoot up, which was detrimental to business and investment. Eventually, the interest rates on the foreign debts rose too, because Argentina's status as debtor had been tarnished through negative economic data.

In 1999 a new president was elected: Fernando de la Rúa, from the opposition party UCR (La Unión Cívica Radical). But his government found no other solution to the country's problems than drastic austerity measures as demanded by the IMF for granting credit. As part of its austerity program, the government in July 2001 cut pensions and remunerations of state employees by 13%. A "zero-deficit law" was passed, which however remained a pious intention on paper. Further cuts were introduced in the social welfare budget. The concerned minister, however, protested against the plan and stepped down. In their desperation the people voted, in the October 2001 parliamentary elections, largely for the candidates of the Perónist party, now in opposition. That now complicated also the political situation and made resolute action on the part of the government more difficult. In November 2001, the government announced its ninth reform package, the central point of which was a debt swap, from which the government hoped for a reduction in debt servicing costs. But it was to actually cost more in the long term.

The long recession, the drop in exports, the heavy burden of debt servicing, and then also the political crisis were harbingers of the coming collapse. The retreat of foreign investors began. By the middle of 2000, several large foreign companies had pulled out of the country: Unilever, Goodyear, General Motors, etc. Then a rapid flight of finance capital began as well. From February to November 2001, US$18 billion was withdrawn from the country (*Fischer Weltalmanach* 2003: 87). In mid-November 2001, it became clear that the IMF, which had until then several times helped the Argentine state with large credit packages, was no longer prepared to help. The IMF management even refused to receive Argentina's finance minister when he wanted to fly to Washington to request more loans. It was a situation in which the state was in danger of becoming insolvent. In this predicament, the population feared that the peso would soon be devalued. In order to avert losing their savings and other monetary assets, people rushed to the banks and withdrew cash in US dollars at the fixed rate of 1:1. The result was a run on the banks. The banking system threatened to collapse, because savings drastically diminished. In the last week of November, the run on the banks escalated with almost US$1 billion being withdrawn daily; on November 30, it was $1.3 billion. The following day, December 1, the government imposed a freezing of all accounts for ninety days. Account holders were not permitted to withdraw more than 1,000 pesos a month, and international transfers could not be made without the authorization of the central bank. On December 5, the IMF refused to disburse a credit of US$1.26 billion, which had already been approved, on the grounds that the government had failed to meet the set deficit reduction target. Also, the World Bank and the Inter-American Development Bank (IADB) had earlier frozen already approved loans to the tune of US$1.1 billion (Mussa 2002 and *Fischer Weltalmanach* 2003: 87).

The freezing of accounts aroused even more fear and anger and gave grounds for unrest and mass protests against the now totally discredited political class.

The second interim president, Adolfo Rodríguez Saá, announced that the country would stop servicing its foreign debts. However, he wanted to continue the financial policy in place, and also the rigid pegging of the peso to the US dollar at the ratio of 1:1. But at the same time, he envisaged the creation of a second currency for the purpose of paying wages and pensions, the argentino, which would not be pegged to the US dollar and whose exchange rate could thus fall freely. Not only did he uphold the freezing of accounts, but he also ordered the closure of banks for several days in order to prevent further cash withdrawals. This policy led to renewed unrest, which culminated in the storming of the parliament building. On the following day, December 30, 2001, Rodríguez Saá stepped down — only a week after taking office.

On January 1, 2002, Parliament elected a new president, Eduardo Duhalde. He was the common candidate of both the large parties, and his mandate was to build a government of national unity. In the framework of an "emergency program to overcome the economic crisis" passed by the parliament, the government partially annulled the pegging of the peso to the US dollar and temporarily stopped servicing the public debts to private creditors. From then on, Argentina serviced only the debts to multilateral institutional creditors such as the IMF. As now there were again signs of political stability (though only in the sphere of the parliament and political parties), these institutions were again willing to help. The IMF granted a period of grace for the repayment of a loan that had fallen due. However, since the freezing of accounts was still in place, people protested and demonstrated again, this time for several days and partly violently. On February 1, the Supreme Court declared the freezing of accounts unconstitutional. The government, however, criticized the ruling. It was not prepared to lift the freeze immediately and decreed two bank holidays in order to delay the expected massive withdrawal of funds. But the peso's pegging to the dollar could no longer be saved. On February 7, the peso was allowed to float, which immediately led to its devaluation. The depositors reacted to the government's resistance to the Supreme Court ruling with a flood of lawsuits against the freezing of accounts. The government on its part, on July 23, extended per emergency decree the freeze for a further period of four months.

A further aspect of the crisis was that the Argentine banking system was in a great confusion and became practically dysfunctional, almost insolvent. One cause of this predicament was that the government had stopped servicing public debts denominated in US dollars. A large part of such debts had been incurred by the state by taking out credit with Argentine banks. Another cause was two government orders issued after the peso was allowed to float (which had led to a devaluation of the currency): the banks had to convert depositors' dollars into pesos at an exchange rate that was much higher than the dictated rate at which they could convert the dollar loans given to customers. This was disastrous for the banks' balance sheets. In May 2002, a large number of banks had to formally declare bankruptcy.

In June, there was a violent protest demonstration of organized unemployed people in which two demonstrators were shot dead by the police. On July 9, the Argentine Independence Day, tens of thousands of demonstrators protested against the cooperation of the government with the IMF and the US government. The economic and social situation, moreover, kept on deteriorating. In 2002, the GDP slumped, the growth rate coming to –10.9% (IMF 2004: 209). The unemployment rate rose to 21%. According to official statistics, 53% of the population lived under the poverty line and a fourth did not have enough to eat (*Fischer Weltalmanach* 2004: 98, 99). However, inflation remained under control despite the steep fall in the exchange rate of the peso after it was allowed to float: 25.9% in 2002 (IMF 2004: 217).

For the purpose of this book, the story of this crisis can now be concluded with a few more pieces of succinct information. In 2003, the economy began to recover. The freezing of accounts was completely lifted on April 9. The GDP recorded a real growth of 8.8% (209). Unemployment fell in the fourth quarter of 2003 to 14.5%. However, at the same time, 16.3% of the workforce was underemployed (*Fischer Weltalmanach* 2005: 53). Also the inflation rate fell to 13.4% (IMF 2004: 217). Real GDP growth in 2004 came to 9% (*Fischer Weltalmanach* 2007). That same year, the unemployment rate fell further to 13.6% and the inflation rate to 4.4% (*Fischer Weltalmanach* 2006: 60). Whereas exports had stagnated in 2001, 2002, and 2003, and trade surpluses of these years had been achieved only by reducing imports, in 2004 exports increased considerably — from US$26.8 billion in 2003 to US$34.5 billion. Moreover, a surplus of US$12.2 billion was achieved despite a parallel increase in imports (*Fischer Weltalmanach* 2003, 2004, 2005, and 2006).

Since the beginning of the Duhalde government, the IMF and other institutional lenders had again become prepared to help and granted new loans as well as grace periods for debt repayments. Also the government of President Néstor Carlos Kirchner, who took office in May 2003, cooperated with these institutional lenders, repaid the credit that had fallen due, and successfully pressured these lenders to grant Argentina new loans and grace periods for repayments. But the government stubbornly demanded of the private creditors that they agree to not insist on 100% repayment and offered to pay back a part of the sum owed.

In early January 2006, Argentina paid off all its debts to the IMF totaling US$9.5 billion before they were due and thus won back autonomy in its economic decisions (*Frankfurter Rundschau*, 5 January 2006).

# VII.

# Can Keynesianism Solve the Problems This Time?

Now that I have presented the stories of the big economic crises of the past and the widely known theories of crisis and business cycle, it is now time to critically review the most important one among these theories and its corresponding economic policy recommendations, namely Keynesianism.

Keynesianism's ambitious objective was to make the capitalist economic system largely crisis-free. As we have seen, to a certain extent it succeeded in doing so until about the mid-seventies, although this success was not in all cases, or not entirely, *its* success. After Keynesianism "failed," it seemed for a long time as if it were dead. However, it was never completely dead. Brave Keynesians, with support from the trade unions, have always criticized the dominant neo-liberal economic policies, and they continued to fight for their political economic positions. They could do so because neo-liberalism also couldn't make the capitalist world crisis-free.

Since the beginning of the new millennium, Keynesians are again on the way up. And they are making themselves heard. For instance, at a UN panel discussion, many of them — e.g., Nobel laureate Joseph Stiglitz, former chief economist of the World Bank and President Clinton's former chief economic advisor — advocated an expansive fiscal and monetary policy to stimulate consumption, investment, and employment (*International Herald Tribune*, 7 November 2001). Stiglitz has long been of the opinion that Keynes's core ideas have repeatedly been tested in reality and they have always proved their worth. Evidence for this assertion he sees, firstly, in the fact that, since the 1930s, there has not been any other big depression. He attributes this to the fact that leading people in the governments of the world learned the Keynesian lesson and stimulated the economy, when necessary, by means of appropriate fiscal and monetary policies. Secondly, he points out that in East Asia (1997–1998) and Latin America (Argentina 2001), the IMF, by pursuing an opposite policy of tax increases and spending cuts — worsened an ordinary downturn first into a recession and then into a depression (see Stiglitz 2006). In the USA, in 2002, the federal government put together an economic stimulus program. In

Europe, Attac — a leading organization in the movement against globalization — is calling for a Keynesian economic policy. In their "Manifesto
2002" Attac-France wrote:

> The thought that full employment is a backward-looking or
> dangerous Utopia, because it fuels inflation, is nothing but the
> fig leaf of a conservative discourse that covers up the real
> interests of the economic elite, who want to prevent any change
> in income distribution. (2002: 10)

In Germany, many Keynesians have organized themselves in the association "Alternative Wirtschaftspolitik" ("alternative economic policy," popu-
larly called "the Memorandum Group"), which has been publishing for the
last thirty years an annual critical-alternative experts' report on the state
of the German economy. In 2005, a leading member of this group claimed
they have been right; that their recommendations had not been accepted
did not prove that they were wrong.

I think the Keynesians are making it too easy for themselves. Even a
leading figure among them, Professor Rudolf Hickel, said on a self-critical
note: "We have reduced the complexity of the matter to simple structures
and have been writing the same things since 1980" (*Frankfurter Rundschau*, 22 October 2005).

## 1. Inflation

One of the complexities in connection with Keynesian economic policies is
the danger of inflation associated with an expansive monetary and/or fiscal policy. Curiously, in his article from which I have quoted above Stiglitz
did not mention the inflation problem at all. But it is a real danger. One
could see that in the 1970s. The only two relevant questions here appear to
be how detrimental inflation can be for the economy, and thus for society,
and if politicians should give up the objective of full employment because
of this danger. I have already dealt with the problem of inflation in chapter V in connection with the question of why Keynesianism failed in the
mid-1970s. It is necessary to take up the issue once more because of its
great importance.

Inflation is detrimental to the economy in two ways. Firstly, it disrupts
the established price relations, because the prices of different goods and
services do not increase at the same rate. The quality of price signals is
then no longer reliable. With unreliable price signals entrepreneurs cannot have reasonably solid expectations in regard to future business, which,

as especially Keynesians know, makes it difficult to make investment decisions. That was one of the neo-liberal explanations for the stagflation of the mid-1970s. Secondly, it also disrupts the established relations in the distribution of income and wealth among different classes and groups, which generates anger among the losers and thus damages the stability of society and, along with that, the stability of the economy. At the other end of the trade-off is the misery of excessive unemployment, which remains or even increases when priority is given to fighting inflation and thereby the possibility of recession or stagnation is accepted. In standard economics, this trade-off is traditionally depicted by the so-called Phillips curve. It is (perhaps) an insolvable quandary, a conflict of objectives that Samuelson and Nordhaus call "the cruelest dilemma, ... the dilemma of needing high unemployment to contain inflation." They quote economist Arthur Okun, who labeled it "the most serious unsolved problem of stabilization policy throughout the Western world" (Samuelson and Nordhaus 1989: 340, 322).

In order to halfway resolve this dilemma, economists have invented a new concept: "non-accelerating inflation rate of unemployment," NAIRU (see Stiglitz 2003: 71f.). The idea behind it is as follows. If the inflation rate does not accelerate, that is, if it is stable or kept stable for several years, say at 2 percent per annum, then participants in the economy can adapt themselves to this stable and expected rate of inflation and act accordingly. Then the disruptions in price and income relations mentioned above cannot take place or cannot be too severe. Such an inflation cannot cause any damage to the economy. NAIRU advocates conceive of an economic policy that accepts a certain unemployment rate at which the inflation rate does not accelerate. They call this rate, oddly enough, the "natural rate of unemployment." Full employment is then considered to have been reached when unemployment does not exceed the "natural rate." If unemployment falls below the "natural rate," the danger of an accelerating inflation can arise, for then workers and their unions would be able to put through higher wage demands, which would trigger a wage-price spiral. There is a consensus among neo-liberal economists — also in the Fed — that this natural rate of unemployment lies currently at 6% to 6.2% (see Stiglitz 2003: 71f.). The European Central Bank, for instance, has set itself the goal of keeping the inflation rate stable just below 2% per annum. It is thus, as Douthwaite suggests (see chapter V), a sort of battlefield of class struggle: on the one side, the banks and the money-aristocracy, who demand an anti-inflationary policy; on the other side, the working class and the *industrial* capitalists. For the past thirty years, the former have been the victors.

This understanding of the matter is, in my view, far too simple. As Douthwaite himself concedes, anti-inflationary policy has not been unpopular. Throughout history, always, inflation has also harmed ordinary people by devaluing their small savings — at least in the developed countries where even ordinary people save some money. Moreover, workers do not suffer only under unemployment. They suffer more under inflation than the rentiers (money-aristocracy) do. For, because of their weaker negotiating position, they can attain neither an immediate nor a full compensation for real wage losses resulting from inflation. Welfare dole recipients are totally helpless.

So it is quite imaginable that workers and employees in general — at least those who are not directly exposed to the danger of losing their job — approve of the policy of giving priority to fighting inflation. This was the case in Argentina at the beginning of the 1990s (see chapter VI, section 3). And in the middle of the same decade, in Germany and some other EU countries, where hyperinflation like in Argentina was ruled out, there was strong opposition to the introduction of the euro because there was fear it would become an inflationary currency. The purely theoretical stance of Keynesians and economists like Douthwaite — that a relaxed attitude regarding inflation is necessary to avert or overcome a recession — is for most people far too abstract.

However, it must be noted here that the attitude of workers and employees towards an anti-inflationary policy differ from country to country. In those countries where, generally, many workers are more or less heavily indebted, e.g., in the USA, they profit on balance from an increasing rate of inflation because their debts become smaller *in real terms*. In addition, they fear unemployment more than anything else, which normally increases with anti-inflationary policies. But for many years now, banks and others who give credit can keep the interest rate flexible, so that it can go up with inflation. Debtors can be totally ruined through flexible — that is, increasing — interest rates.

It is not just conservative and right-wing politicians, but also social democrats — at least those in the rich industrialized countries — who could not and cannot have a relaxed attitude towards high inflation. There is a further reason for this: with increased prosperity, the ability of the state to pay a satisfactory amount of welfare benefits to a larger number of unemployed has also increased. In such states, high unemployment figures do (did) not cause problems for governments that are too big, whereas high inflation rates do (did) — undoubtedly also because of pressure from financial capitalists.

Now the question arises whether, today, politicians have any reason to be concerned about the danger of inflation. Clearly not. For in most of the OECD countries, in the past years, the inflation rate has remained moderate. The only countries where, in 2004, the rate was above 5 percent were Turkey, Slovakia, and Hungary (OECD, May 2005: 59). At present, neither the Eurozone nor the USA is likely to have too high an inflation rate, because no government can force the central bank to start printing money in order to get it out of trouble, or to unnecessarily lower the interest rates. The central banks are, as a rule, independent and conservative. For them the stability of the value of their currency is more important than anything else.

Inflation, however, is not just a matter of the size of demand. An increase in production costs, particularly in wage costs, can also cause inflation. As we have seen, in the 1970s high oil prices caused inflation. That happened again in 2007. Crude oil prices fluctuated around US$95 per barrel. Industrial metals as well as food products became much costlier than before. A new round of moderate inflation appeared to be unavoidable, despite falling real wages. But this time it was due to the geological and geographical limits to growth.

## 2. Had Keynesianism Really Been Buried?

For the last thirty years, Keynesians have been blaming the departure from Keynesianism for the problems that befell the industrialized countries — weak growth, high unemployment, stagnating or falling real wages, downscaling of the welfare state. But that was only half the truth. Keynesianism was never completely dead; it lived on in practice. In the USA, it lived on in the form of "armament Keynesianism" even during the presidency of the archconservative and neo-liberal Ronald Reagan. In most industrialized countries the state continued to incur heavy debts. In Germany, the constitution allows the government to incur new debts for new investments.

In the Japan of the 1990s, the government tried to overcome economic stagnation through several stimulus programs. Until 1998, there have been seven such programs, and the amounts spent totaled — expressed in the German currency of those days — DM 1,200 billion (today it is roughly €600 billion). Even the radically neo-liberal IMF advised the Japanese to stimulate demand and strengthen the domestic market (Garnreiter et al. 1998: 16). All that, of course, did not help much. But this fact shows that Keynesian solutions were not looked down upon in Japan.

The Argentina of the late 1990s is also an example that shows Keynesianism was not really dead. Although the IMF urged the government to maintain strict budgetary discipline, the Argentines ignored it. According to an expert, the basic cause of the Argentine tragedy was that public spending hugely and continuously exceeded public revenue. The large deficits led to an unbearable accumulation of public debts (Mussa 2002: 10). Although these debts were not incurred to finance new Keynesian stimulus programs against the recession, the latter would have been much more severe without them.

And Keynesianism is not dead even in cases where the state runs up very little or no new debts, where budgets are balanced. For in such cases its spirit lives on and continues to be effective. In the neo-liberal era, active stimulus policy to promote growth and employment has been privatized. It is not the state that runs up new debts for this purpose; instead it is companies, speculators, and consumers, spurred on by politicians. The central bank helps them by keeping the interest rates low. In the beginning of the Clinton era, the Fed took measures to ensure that the real interest rates fell to almost zero (Bofinger 2005: 76). And this proved very effective. The 1990s were then called "the roaring nineties" (see chapter VI, section 2).

We have also seen in the previous chapters how the authorities in Japan and in the USA practiced, so to speak, a stock exchange Keynesianism. By reducing the interest rates, they created a stock exchange boom. The resulting wealth effect[16] and the low interest rates encouraged businesspeople and consumers to increase their investments and consumption spending respectively.

Actually it was not mainly stimulus programs of the state financed through public debts that made possible the long boom that lasted until the mid-1970s. It was rather the debts piled up by the private sector. As we have seen in chapter V, the British government in 1972 made it possible that in the same year the sum of loans to the private sector rose by 345%. The situation in the USA was well described by *Business Week* in 1974 in an article called "The Debt Economy":

> The US economy stands atop a mountain of debts $2.5 trillion high — a mountain built of all the cars and houses, all the factories and machines that have made this the biggest, richest economy in the history of the world. ... To fuel nearly three decades of postwar economic boom at home and export it abroad, this nation has borrowed an average of $200 million a day, each and every, since the close of World War II.

Of the $2.5 trillion total debt only $700 billion was public sector debts. The rest, $1.8 trillion, was piled up by the private sector, the share of private consumers in it being $200 billion (Editors, *Monthly Review* 1975: 6).

As for the present, the situation has not changed much. Only the mountain of debt has grown considerably. For example, in the United Kingdom, a much smaller country, the personal debts of its inhabitants alone totaled at the end of 2005 £1.13 trillion. Thousands of such debtors faced bankruptcy. Very high personal debts were reported also from France and Ireland (*The Independent*, 3 January 2006). In Germany in the same year, 3.1 million households were over-indebted — far more than in 1999 (2.7 million) (*Frankfurter Rundschau*, 16 February 2006). The German Statistical Bureau forecast that in 2005 private insolvencies would rise by 40% to 70,000 households (*Frankfurter Rundschau*, 3 December 2005).

Also the savings rate is falling. It fell from 1991 to 2004 — with some fluctuations in between — as follows: in Germany from 13% to 11.1%, in Japan from 15% to 5.1%, in the United Kingdom from 10.2% to 6.4%, and in the USA from 7.3% to 0.8%. Only in France did it rise, from 8.7% to 10.2% (OECD 2004: 225). Hence, when in 2005 in Germany people talked about panic saving as being a cause of the crisis — indeed, in 2004 the savings rate increased in comparison to the previous year — then it must be understood as being so only relative to the high sales expectations of the entrepreneurs. Against the backdrop of the gigantic mountains of debt that somehow keep the highly developed capitalist economies going, a few billion more of new public debts cannot indeed cause a significant increase in the currently low inflation rates, especially in view of under-utilized production capacities. However, these relatively low sums will not be able to bring about a strong recovery either. Their multiplier effect will be a mere flash in the pan — as was the case in Japan in the 1990s. So it must be economic subjects of the private sector who will again have to spend huge sums, for which they will have to run up yet more debts. And savers will almost have to stop saving altogether, as they have done in the USA. Of course, the administration of George W. Bush, as a result of the wars it waged and the tax cuts it passed, again piled up huge debts. But, as before, it was high consumer spending and real estate purchases — stimulated by the low interest rates and the wealth effect of the speculative boom — that were mainly responsible for the good growth rates.

Of course, traditional Keynesian theory says an expansive monetary policy, that is, cheapening of credit through low interest rates, is not very effective. But this wisdom does not seem to be valid for some nations. Referring to the USA, Paul Krugman wrote in 1998:

> [T]he simple Keynesian story is one in which interest rates are independent of the level of employment and output. But in reality the Federal Reserve Board actively manages interest rates, pushing them down when it thinks employment is too low and raising them when it thinks the economy is overheating. . . . you can hardly dispute his [the Fed chairman's] power. Indeed, if you want a simple model for predicting the unemployment rate in the United States over the next few years, here it is: It will be what Greenspan [the Fed chairman at the time] wants it to be, plus or minus a random error reflecting the fact that he is not quite God. . . .
>
> Instead of an invisible hand pushing the economy toward full employment in some unspecified long term, we have the visible hand of the Fed pushing us toward its estimate of the noninflationary unemployment rate over the course of two or three years. . . . And so all the paradoxes of thrift, widow's cruises, and so on become irrelevant. In particular, an increase in the savings rate will translate into higher investment after all, because the Fed will make sure that it does. (1999: 31)

Stiglitz, a Keynesian, does not accept this contention on the near omnipotence of the Fed's monetary policy. He refers to statistical evidence that indicates that investments often did not react significantly to variations in interest rates. He gives two examples from the USA: the recessions of 1991 and 2001, on which the Fed could not have any effect through its monetary policy (Stiglitz 2003: 42).

So history does not definitively prove the victory of the one theory or the other. Stiglitz (2003: 198–200) thinks that Keynesianism has, by and large, worked well, although it failed to eliminate business cycles. Since the end of World War II, the downswings have been shorter and flatter, and the upswings longer. Of course, it has become clear that there are limits to the effects of active interventions, and there are some other difficulties too. Nevertheless, basically, he advocates a Keynesian economic policy because the costs of recessions (losses in national income) are too high. On Clinton's deficit reduction policy he comments: "Today we live in an odd world in which supposedly fiscally conservative Republicans are claiming that deficits do not matter — they have become today's Keynesians — while the Democrats ... are preaching deficit reduction, even in times of recession!" (55). Clinton's Democratic administration presented the proposal to reduce capital gains tax with supply-side arguments: it would promote saving and investing. Republicans were also very much pleased with its deregulation measures and cuts in welfare benefits. Clinton's campaign platforms included "ending welfare as we know it" (172), which Republicans too wanted to do. Republicans wanted to reduce the role of the state, and that fit well into the agenda of the New Democrats. The same can be said about the Social Democratic Schröder government in Germany (1998–2005).

When one considers all these facts from recent economic history, then the bitter controversies between neo-liberals and Keynesians seem a little like shadowboxing. Already in 1994, Res Strehle felt compelled to comment:

> In the future, supply-side economic policies and demand-oriented Keynesianism will alternate in the major economic centers like fashion trends. They may even be synthesized, because, alone, both have only a limited ability to avert capitalist crises: supply-side economic policies increase the degree of exploitation and thus attract investors; demand-oriented Keynesianism prevents a drop in mass purchasing power, but scares off investors. Keynesianism will only then finally come out of fashion when the interest payments on growing public debts cannot be financed any longer. (Strehle 1994: 32f.)

Strehle wrote these words just at the beginning of the Clinton era. The New Democrats were however very successful. They succeeded in doing something that the conservatives had failed to achieve in the previous decades, namely, to bury John Maynard Keynes. But Keynes was only apparently dead.

### 3. Recipes of German Keynesians Against the Stagnation

The recovery of the highly industrialized economies from the great crash and the crisis (or weak growth) of the first years of the new century (see chapter VI, section 3) began in 2003/2004. However, it was very weak. In April 2005, the *Financial Times* reported that the weakness of economic growth had not really been overcome yet, except in the USA. It painted a picture of stagnation. It reported that the manufacturing industry of the Eurozone stood close to a stagnation or even a recession, while the confidence of Japanese manufacturers had fallen sharply. The latest gloomy reports on Japan and Europe, which stressed the negative effects of high crude oil prices and worries about exports, came at a time when the US job figures disappointed expectations. Without doubt, people in the whole world were worried about the strength of the recovery (*Financial Times*, 2 April 2005)

In order to round off and concretize this summary overview, I quote below some figures on the economic situation at the end of 2005 (all figures in %):

|  | Growth rate of real GDP | Unemployment (%) | Inflation rate (consumer prices) |
|---|---|---|---|
| United Kingdom | 1.7 | 5.0 | 2.0 |
| Germany | 0.9* | 11.3 | 2.1 |
| Italy | 0.1 | 7.5 | 2.2 |
| Japan | 2.9 | 4.4 | −0.1 |
| USA | 3.5** | 4.7 | 3.4 |
| Eurozone | 1.6 | 8.4 | 2.4 |

(Source: *Frankfurter Rundschau*, 15 February 2006. **Frankfurter Rundschau*, 1 March 2006. Otherwise, *The Economist*, 11 February 2006.)

Germany, where the situation was worst, is particularly suited as an example for dealing with the theme of this chapter a little more concretely. In February 2005 and February 2006, the official unemployment figure exceeded the alarming point of five million. Unofficially, at least eight million employable people were unemployed.

In chapter VI, section 2, we have seen that in Germany, reunification of the country caused an economic boom in 1990 and 1991. But it also caused a rise in the inflation rate. In the years 1990, 1991, and 1992, the consumer price index rose by 2.7%, 3.6%, and 5.1%, respectively (OECD 2000: 224, 226). The central bank was not prepared to tolerate so much inflation and took measures to cause a massive increase in the interest rates for short-term loans, which was promptly followed by a recession. The inflation rate also fell. This was the beginning of a long period of sluggish growth and high unemployment. No wonder that the controversies on economic policy were the most heated in Germany.

Keynesians put the blame for the misery on weak domestic demand (exports were booming). Between 2000 and 2004 it fell by €27.7 billion. In their opinion, this weakness was "above all the result of an income distribution that hampers development and of a counterproductive economic and social policy" (Arbeitsgruppe 2005: 2). They, of course, did not say anymore that an expansive monetary policy was not effective enough to increase domestic demand. But their focus was on public spending, which had been cut drastically in the previous years. Every year between 2003 to 2005, on average, public investments fell by 5.9% and spending on personnel by 0.3% (Bofinger 2005: 238).

In 2005, the Arbeitsgruppe Alternative Wirtschaftspolitik demanded that the state take up responsibility for creating more and better jobs. It suggested the following instruments for pursuing this policy: public investment programs, increasing the number of jobs in the public sector, a complementary labor market policy, reducing individual working hours in the public sector, and promoting shorter working hours in the private sector. It demanded, in concrete terms, the following: (1) A public investment program to the tune of €75 billion per year for ten years. This would create over a million additional jobs, and the investments would prevent the decay of public infrastructure; (2) Expenditures totaling €30 billion per year to create a million new jobs for improving the quality of public services; (3) A proactive labor market policy that would aim at improving the qualifications of people seeking a job. €20 billion should be spent for the implementation of this policy; (4) A 10 percent reduction of working hours at full pay. This would create or secure almost two million jobs. Fourteen billion euro would be needed for this measure in the public sector and for temporary wage cost subsidies to weak, small, and middle-size companies (Arbeitsgruppe 2005: 10, 11f.).

The Arbeitsgruppe attributed the weakness of domestic demand especially to the implementation of a policy of restrained wage demands. Restrained wage demands were, in its view, "a key element in the vicious circle of growing inequality of income, sluggish growth, and mounting unemployment." Hence it called for putting through higher wage increases, which were also macroeconomically sensible and important, because they would stimulate aggregate demand and thus create more jobs. "That is," in their words, "not only not a policy at the expense of the unemployed, but also a policy to the advantage of the employed *and* the unemployed" (2005: 12).

The Arbeitsgruppe proposed that the recommended increase in state spending should be financed through tax increases. Moreover, for helping the world's poorest countries, the Arbeitsgruppe proposed the introduction of a Tobin tax (foreign exchange transaction tax). It demanded an increase in the welfare payments to the unemployed in order to ensure a reliable provisioning of their material livelihood needs at an "acceptable level." In order to guarantee that, the Arbeitsgruppe demanded, the system should be financed by drawing contributions from all kinds of income — that is, not only from wages and salaries, as is the case today, but also from profits, rents, and all other kinds of income from capital and wealth. This meant that the system should be financed partly through taxes. The Arbeitsgruppe demanded further that contributions of employers to the social security funds should be increased over the current 50 percent, while the employees' contributions should be held constant at the current level (13, 14).

## 4. My Doubts

It all sounds very good. But then why can't the Keynesians convince the majority of the people? Peter Bofinger (2005), himself a Keynesian and a member of the council of economic advisors of the federal government of Germany, thinks that more academically trained economists should take part in the debates. But how will that change anything? He knows very well that he could not also convince the great majority of his economist colleagues. It may well be that for some reason these colleagues — against their better judgment — have decided to fight on the side of the employers. But I do not share the interests of capitalists, yet I had some doubts, while reading on the subject, about the persuasive power or correctness of the arguments of the Keynesians.

Let us first address the argument of weak domestic demand and the advantages of higher wages. "Cars do not buy cars," Keynesians argue (this was a famous saying of Henry Ford's). Bofinger (2005: 258) wrote: "Therefore, German entrepreneurs ... must have a *strong interest* in a dynamic development of the purchasing power of their customers." He wrote further: "[O]r to put it pithily: if the farmer wants his cow to give him a good quantity of milk, he must also see to it that the cow gets enough fodder" (emphasis added).

Bofinger reproaches anti-Keynesians for allegedly not being able to differentiate between the logic of the single firm (microeconomic level) and that of the national economy (macroeconomic level). But he is here making almost the same mistake. The farmer is a single firm. He gives *his* cow enough fodder; and the cow gives him, *only him*, all the milk it produces. The farmer usually gets more from selling the milk than what the hay for the cow costs. As against that, an entrepreneur can, theoretically, decide to pay his workers higher wages than what is strictly necessary. But he knows that his workers will not necessarily buy his products with their wages. At best, they will only spend a part of their wages to buy one or two of the products of their employer. These now better-paid workers produce goods for their employer. But whether these goods, now produced at a higher cost, can be sold at profitable prices is uncertain. This is the reason that *an* entrepreneur has no *interest* in paying *his* workers higher wages. Even if all entrepreneurs of a country paid their workers higher wages, one cannot be sure that the workers would buy with their higher wages only products made by manufacturers of this country and not those of their foreign competitors. But even otherwise, it simply does not make any sense to pay one's workers higher wages without being compelled to do so, especially when the workers cannot be compelled to buy the products of one's own company. That is not the logic of capitalism, which Keynesians, in any case, do not fight against.

In 1914, Henry Ford had to pay his workers wages above the market rate (see Braverman 1979: 145f.) because of a special situation. He had to persuade the versatile workers of the time to accept the new, monotonous, and undemanding work at the assembly line. Mass production for the huge US domestic market brought down the unit costs considerably. And so Ford could pay his workers higher wages. The contradiction between the capitalist drive to produce more and the insufficient purchasing power of potential car buyers was overcome through successful cost reduction, not by paying higher wages to the workers. The few thousand Ford workers made up only a tiny fraction of the buyers of Ford cars. Henry Ford later presented the matter in his memoirs in such a way that it seemed as if it had been one of his objectives "to pay maximum wages in order to hand out maximum purchasing power" (quoted in Kurz 1999: 371; retranslated). But in reality, the ultimate purpose of the exercise was to reduce costs.

The unusually high profits that Ford could make were the profits of a Schumpeterian entrepreneur who has introduced an innovation. Such entrepreneurs cannot make such high profits for a long time, especially not nowadays. For innovations soon become normal practice in all factories of the competitors around the world. That is why, in our times, Daimler-Chrysler had to eliminate in its factories even the toilet break for its workers in order to remain competitive. This brings us to the next point in the discussion: globalization. But before we take up that issue, let us discuss another objection to the above Keynesian argument.

In support of their demand for higher wages to workers and employees of the lower income groups and their opposition to tax concessions for the rich and the affluent in a stagnating economy, Keynesians repeat a thesis of their master, namely: the affluent have a very low propensity to consume (see chapter III, section 1). This thesis might have had its justification in Keynes's times, but it is no longer convincing. If rich people, for instance, spend US$20 million for a short trip to space — something that has indeed taken place a number of times — they help create or maintain thousands of jobs in the industries involved. The same can be said of luxury cruises, golf playing, world tours, and the like. All these pastimes are very popular among averagely rich people. And, generally speaking, the lifestyle of the yuppies and the jet set involves intense consumption and thus stimulates growth. As all economists know, the economy of the United States, with its extremely unequal distribution of income, does not suffer particularly from weak demand.

In the age of globalization, neo-liberals could not but see the most important cause of the long stagnation in the German economy in high labor costs, which they thought were undermining the competitiveness of Germany as a location for industrial investments. Keynesians do not dispute that wage costs per hour of labor are higher in Western Germany than in all other countries except Norway (see Bofinger 2005: 49). Nevertheless, flouting common sense, they make the recommendation that German workers should be paid even higher wages. They justify this with the following argument:

> [A]ll labor is not the same. In high-wage countries, as a rule, much more is produced per hour of labor than in regions with low hourly wages. Therefore, it is unit labor costs ... that are decisive for employment. ... A country with low hourly wages can thus have relatively high unit labor costs if its productivity is very low. (50)

This is the weakest point in the present-day Keynesian argumentation. Firstly, facts refute much of the claim made in the above quote. Why did Western European and US-American companies in the recent past massively relocate much of their production in low-wage countries? It is not that just simple goods like shirts, shoes, and umbrellas are manufactured in low-wage countries and then imported from there. It is well known that this is being done also in respect of very complex products: computers and many other electronic goods, software products, car motors, small aircraft (Brazil), etc. Many US-American patients fly to India to undergo complicated and costly surgery in private clinics. And Western companies are utilizing the services of private Indian research labs for industry-oriented research and development. Obviously, unit labor costs are in such cases much lower because of low wages.

Keynesians, like many other educated people in the West, appear not to have understood the secret of high productivity in the industrialized countries and the secret of low wages in developing countries. (1) In the usual discourse on the subject, productivity always means *labor* productivity. This is primarily a function of the extent to which production facilities are equipped with capital goods, and has only secondarily to do with the ability of the workers. Given the same ability, those workers who work with more machines and a higher degree of automation will have higher labor productivity than other workers. Also, better infrastructure at the production location plays an important role in this matter. (2) Wages in the Third World are not lower because workers there have less ability, but mainly because even in professions that demand a high qualification too many people with the required qualification are willing to work for a very low wage. A further reason for this is that, for various reasons, poor countries and their companies simply cannot afford to pay higher wages. When workers from India, for instance, go to Saudi Arabia, they earn there many times their wages in India. This is so because Saudi Arabia, firstly, does not have enough workers, not to speak of qualified workers, and, secondly, simply can afford to pay more.

When First World companies relocate their production in Third World countries or in Eastern Europe, they generally equip their plants there with the same kind of machines as in their original locations and give the workers the needed training. Then all labor is the same, especially in these days of a very high degree of automation, which renders personal abilities of workers relatively unimportant. Then, with lower wages, the unit labor costs in the new locations are lower. It can be that the workers in the new locations do not get the most modern equipment, but rather one-generation-older ones. Even then, the wages there are low enough to more than offset this disadvantage.

Two fairly strong points in the Keynesian argumentation are the facts that, firstly, Germany is at the moment the biggest exporter-country of the world, and that, secondly, foreign investors continue to invest in Germany. The first fact alone proves sufficiently that Germany as an industrial location is outstandingly competitive, despite its high wages. It should be added here that since 1993, Germany has almost continuously been achieving an increasing trade surplus (OECD 2004: 249). As regards the second fact, in the period 2002–2003, Germany stood on average at the fifth place in the ranking for foreign direct investments. In the same period, foreign direct investment in Germany was higher than German direct investment abroad (Bofinger 2005: 35).

Are not these pieces of information contradictory? On the one hand, German companies are leaving the production location Germany and moving to low-wage countries; on the other hand, foreign capital continues to be invested in Germany. What should be made of this? I think we can understand this if we understand the notions "foreign direct investment" and "production location" properly. According to a dictionary of economics, foreign direct investment "is a form of investment by foreigners, mostly by foreign companies, in order to acquire, or buy a stake in real estate, enterprises or parts of enterprises" (*Großes Wörterbuch Wirtschaft* 2005). Such acquisitions of stakes do not necessarily entail building new production plants, in which hitherto unemployed people can find jobs. They rather mean, at least in most cases, that the (foreign) investors acquire only the relatively healthy parts of an existing company that has run into difficulties, or they rehabilitate only a part of the company. In course of such a process, a part of the workforce is usually retrenched. Sometimes whole companies are bought up at a throwaway price and then closed down in order to eliminate competition for the acquiring company. That often happened in the 1990s in the former German Democratic Republic, when the Treuhandanstalt (the organization that was charged with managing and, if possible, privatizing the property of the former GDR) privatized state-owned companies. Foreign investors can also acquire a company whose headquarters are, to be sure, in Germany, but whose products will soon be manufactured in a low-wage country. In such cases of relocation of production new jobs will no doubt be created in the low-wage country, but only at the cost of redundancy of the workforce in the plants in Germany. Any positive effect for Germany that might result from such direct investments most probably would not compensate for the job losses. Such foreign direct investments are, therefore, no proof of the strength of Germany as a *production* location.

The matter is actually not so difficult to understand. The German economy — despite all neo-liberal talk about too-high wages — is competitive in the world market. But it is only competitive in respect to goods and services that it currently exports. In respect to many goods and services, those that it currently imports, Germany is *probably* not competitive. Hans-Werner Sinn thinks that German consumers are not well informed about German weakness in international competition and he feels called to explain the matter to them, to shake them up. He wrote:

> Consumers think they are buying German products, but, in
> reality, the products are often only assembled in Germany and,
> in many cases, ... the product comes, 100 percent finished,
> from the Far East, with even its German brand name printed on
> it. ... Only ... behind the sales counters are there still German
> jobs. Otherwise, the income generated through production is

> earned abroad. Germany is insidiously turning into a bazaar
> economy. (Sinn 2004: 67)

The question now is: if, despite high labor costs, some German goods and services are competitive, why are other German goods and services not? The explanation that seems to suggest itself lies in the difference between labor-intensive and capital-intensive production. For cost reasons, labor-intensive production is relocated in low-wage countries; capital-intensive production can remain in high-wage countries because in such production labor costs do not matter much. It is just that an entrepreneur wants to produce his goods (or get them produced) where the costs are the lowest. This, however, is only generally true. Naturally, there are also some other factors, such as proximity to the market, good will, image, infrastructure, political climate, etc. They too play a role in business decisions.

Yet, with the exception of counterfeiting, what is so deplorable about this state of affairs? After all, people who buy German export products must also have a way to pay for their imports. Therefore, Germans must import their goods and/or services. In the middle term, as everybody agrees, it is not good for the world economy that a country always has large trade surpluses. Hasn't David Ricardo, the father of the theory of international trade, shown that it is, *generally speaking*, advantageous for every party involved in trade if a country does not produce everything it can, even if it could do that at a lower cost than the others? (See chapter VIII.)


Where does the problem lie then? Germany is the biggest exporter country of the world, the inflation rate is low, and the economy is growing, although at a low rate. Why then did so many people speak of a crisis in 2005/2006? Why did Professor Sinn give his book the title "*Can Germany Be Saved?*"? The crisis was and still is the employment crisis, the official unemployment figure of 5 million. In addition, the state finances were/are in crisis. Tax revenue and citizens' and companies' contributions to social security funds are not sufficient to maintain, for an aging population, the level of educational facilities, pensions, health care, and welfare benefits that the people have in the meantime gotten used to.

In the opinion of all groups of politicians and economists, the ultimate and general solution to all these problems is a strong and continuous economic growth. For only so will it be possible to increase employment, wages and salaries, tax revenue, and contributions to social security funds. An economic growth of about 1 percent per year, for instance, is not enough. It has to be higher. But whereas, for this purpose, Professor Sinn and co. want to see labor costs reduced so that Germany's competitiveness in the world market increases, Keynesians say Germany is already competitive enough; what is lacking is a strong domestic demand, which they want to increase.

Keynesian Bofinger wrote in connection with a ten-point program that he has tabled:

> [O]ur country has a realistic chance ... of again attaining a path of about two percent GDP growth. Compared to the dynamics of the economic miracle of the fifties or the growth rates of some Asian countries, it seems modest. But one should not underestimate the effects of exponential growth. If the economy of a country grows for 35 years at a two percent yearly rate, then at the end of the period, the prosperity of the population has doubled. (2005: 259)

Let us assume Bofinger's hope will come true. Will it be enough to solve the problems mentioned above? The state could perhaps solve the problems of the social security system by increasing taxes and charges. But unemployment is a totally different kind of problem. In the mid-1980s, when unemployment in West Germany stood at about two million, economists of the Green Party had calculated that at the rate at which labor productivity was increasing at the time it would be necessary for the GDP to grow at 6 percent per annum so that enough jobs could be created for all unemployed people. Since the 1980s, labor productivity has received an enormous boost through the rapid progress in automation and electronic technology. How high then must the growth rate of the economy today (2006) be to create jobs for the 5 million people who are officially unemployed? And productivity keeps increasing; in 2004 it rose by 1.4 percent (Institut der Deutschen Wirtschaft 2005: 20). A yearly growth of 2 percent will not be sufficient at all.

To think that this problem can be easily solved by reducing the weekly working hours is very naïve. By referring to a rise in productivity Keynesians and trade unions try to justify two demands at the same time: higher wages and a reduction in weekly working hours. But that is illogical. For capitalists cannot at all be interested in increasing investments in capital equipment of their plants only to reduce the working hours of their workers *and* increase their wages at the same time. And they also *cannot* do that. They must think of *capital productivity* and return to investment. Moreover, they face international competition.

## EFFECTS OF GLOBALIZATION

Actually, Keynesians, who accept globalization as something good, seem not to have understood fully its negative effects. Of course, Bofinger (2005: 241), for instance, makes the critical comment: "[I]f a country, *on the whole*, benefits from globalization, it does not necessarily mean that *all* citizens become equally rich from the process." But he then also affirmatively refers to a finding of economists Heckscher and Ohlin that says that globalization is rather disadvantageous for poorly skilled workers, whereas it is associated with increases in income of highly qualified people. And, as a whole, the gains of the latter are larger than the losses of the former. Bofinger fails to see that, for some years now, in the First World, even highly qualified people like IT specialists, scientists, and engineers, have been losing their jobs or have had to acquiesce in income reduction because their jobs are being (or could be) outsourced to low-wage countries. Moreover, it is wrong to talk only of the *"losses"* of unskilled workers when they are being retrenched by the thousands. Those who have accepted capitalism cannot reject globalization. And they must put up with these consequences of globalization.

The impoverishment of the unskilled and under-skilled can, of course, be alleviated by the state, and this is also something that Keynesians demand. But the great idea of Keynesians, namely, that the state can and should intervene in the economy in order to continuously steer it towards equilibrium at full employment and thus to ensure steady economic growth, has in the meantime become unrealistic. Globalization has thrown a monkey wrench in the works of this idea.

The state has lost its ability to steer the economy. Its hands are even tied by international agreements: by the WTO, the Maastricht Agreement of the EU, etc. And even if it could still somehow do something in order to increase aggregate demand, nobody could be sure that the multiplier effect of the stimulus measures would create new jobs within the country and not in foreign countries.

Actually, even in 1976, that is, at the time of the stagflation, Ernest Mandel had suspected this difficulty of Keynesianism with globalization. At the time there was no globalization as we know it today, but *internationalization* of production, i.e., international division of labor among highly industrialized countries, was already under way. On the difficulties of doing something for overcoming the stagnation, Mandel wrote: "This internationalization of production unavoidably collides with the attempts of national imperialist states [i.e., big industrial nations] to pursue an anti-cyclical policy limited within the national borders" (1977: 12). And the simultaneity of high inflation in several countries necessitated simultaneous anti-inflationary measures, which caused a widespread recession.

A further key element of globalized neo-liberal capitalism that makes a systematic Keynesian policy against sluggish growth well-nigh impossible is the system of floating currencies. Given that calculations related to real investments are made in the global context, they can be unfavorable to a country with an overvalued currency. Of course, governments and central banks sometimes try to intervene in the international currency market in order to prevent overvaluation or undervaluation of their national currency. On this matter there have even been international agreements (e.g., the Plaza and Reverse Plaza Agreements). But, as shown in the previous chapters, since 1973, when the system of fixed exchange rates was dropped, movements of exchange rates have always been chaotic. Attempts to keep a desired exchange rate stable have mostly failed, not the least because of attacks by speculators. An unexpected movement in the exchange rate of a national currency can bring a Keynesian economic policy to naught.

Hutton (1986/2001: 185), a Keynesian, recommended in 1986 that the British government give foreign companies access to the British market subject to the condition that they in return invested in Britain. Perhaps at the time such a condition was still imaginable. But ever since the WTO and its agreements have come into existence, it is almost impossible to impose such a condition, unless a state is not a member of the WTO and is determined to fight neo-liberal globalization.

Referring to the United Kingdom's and New Zealand's dependence on the global capital market and foreign investments, John Gray wrote in 1998 that the changes brought about by neo-liberal globalization in those countries had become irreversible. With respect to New Zealand he wrote:

> [T]he restructuring of New Zealand's economy which opened it
> to unregulated capital flows conferred on transnational capital
> an effective veto power over public policy. Wherever public
> policies might be perceived as impacting upon competitiveness,
> profits and economic stability[,] they could be quashed by the
> threat of capital flight. ... The social democratic objectives of
> earlier periods of public policy in New Zealand were not merely
> dismantled, abandoned or reversed, they were removed as
> options in democratic practice. (Gray 1999: 43)

According to Gray, the social and political arrangements that the victory of neo-liberalism destroyed (the welfare state, the Keynesian consensus on economic policy) cannot be restored anymore. "Those who imagine that there can be a return to the 'normal politics' of post-war economic management are deluding themselves and others" (19). Gray seems to have given up. Nevertheless, his words are valuable, because they make it clear to us that a return to the ideal Keynesian world is no longer possible.

For Keynesians in the First World, globalization has created a particularly dichotomous situation. When they point out that nowadays there is hardly any real danger of inflation, they conceal an important reason thereof: the flood of all kinds of damn-cheap consumer goods imported from low-wage countries, which also forces manufacturers of similar products in the First World (if they are still being produced there at all) to keep their prices low. Globalization, however, is also the reason why many jobs are being moved away from the highly developed industrialized countries. This dilemma can be well observed in the US policy on relations with China. On the one hand, the USA vociferates loudly against China's policy of keeping the exchange rate of its currency abnormally low, which enables Chinese industrialists to flood the US market with cheap consumer goods and compete away local manufacturers of similar products. On the other hand, they shy away from trade sanctions against Chinese goods because that could fuel inflation (see *The Wall Street Journal*, 28 March 2006).

However, despite all that, the Keynesian cause might not be fully lost yet. Earlier on, I have quoted Paul Krugman, who claims that the Fed is nearly almighty and can indeed steer the economy in the United States. This claim has been contested. We have also seen that the administrations of Reagan, Bush Sr., Clinton, and Bush Jr. have, without doubt, attained some desired economic results through their either very expansive or very restrictive fiscal policy. It was perhaps the sheer size of the US economy and the unusually high inclination of US companies and consumers to borrow money that made the (occasional) successes possible that the Fed and the governments could achieve in their efforts to steer the economy. However, it is doubtful that the successes that have been possible in by far the largest economy of the world would also be possible in a smaller economy. Even in the second largest economy of the world, that of Japan, this policy did not work during the long stagnation of the 1990s. Keynesianism in one state — that is probably no longer possible, except perhaps in the United States.

## 5. Global Keynesianism?

Do Keynesians have an idea as to how this difficulty could be overcome? At a meeting of the critics of globalization I once heard a strong plea for a "global Keynesianism." The speaker, a leftist Social Democrat, could not say much more than that all industrialized countries should pursue a Keynesian economic policy, which should however be harmonized with the measures of the others. In Hutton's book, from which I have earlier quoted, I found a rough outline of the same idea. In October 2000 he wrote:

> [I]f Keynes were alive today, ... he would have been ceaselessly worrying about the potential for colossal instability created by the scale and speculative proclivities of the international financial markets. ... His advice would have been unambiguous. The world must develop a financial architecture in which short term financial flows were either more limited, or if they are to continue on their current scale, then there must be much more capacity for international institutions to act as a lender of last resort for those economies at the receiving end of destabilizing capital flight or the shock waves of a US stock exchange crash. He would have urged much more aggressive international financial regulation.
>
> And this implies intelligent action by public authority — in this case *international* public authority. Keynes would have been in the forefront of those arguing for new international agencies and even for forms of global economic governance; globalization requires global governance. But this would not have been to assert the state against the freedom of individuals and capitalists to act as they choose; ... And he would have been searching for clever means of finding the maximum purchase to control financial flows for the minimum effort. He might even, at the extreme, have argued for global demand management if the world faced a chronic demand shortfall or excess of demand — but only if other interim interventions had failed to produce the desired result. He would have made Keynesianism international. (Hutton 2001: xiif.)

That is not much. But one can nevertheless say in general terms that, clearly, Hutton and people like him underestimate the difficulties that would stand in the way of a project of that sort. Willingness to cooperate and appreciation for solidarity among the representatives of states would be indispensable preconditions for the success of a global Keynesianism. But, in general, both are lacking in international economic relations. We have seen that the Plaza and the Reverse Plaza agreements were attempts at cooperation among a few industrialized countries, but we have also seen that the results of these attempts were not good for all the parties involved. The IMF was initially a lender of last resort, and the World Bank was supposed to help Third World countries in their development efforts. Political activists know only too well that these two international financial institutions and the WTO have been turned into instruments of the economic imperialist powers. We have seen that industrialized countries even wage small "trade wars" — over bananas, steel, genetically modified food, etc. A few years ago, disputes over fishing rights at open sea even led to the deployment of naval ships (Canada against Spain). And countries compete with each other as manufacturing locations. It is no longer enough to grant potential investors long-term loans on favorable conditions and/or tax breaks. Even highly industrialized countries have to offer them large subsidies in order to attract them. Joseph Stiglitz wrote in 2003:

> The world has become economically interdependent, and only by creating equitable international arrangements can we bring stability to the global marketplace. This will require a spirit of cooperation that is not built by brute force, by dictating inappropriate conditions in the midst of a crisis, by bullying, by pushing unfair trade treaties, or by pursuing hypocritical trade policies — all of which are part of the hegemonic legacy that the United States established in the 1990s, but seem to have become worse in the next administration. (2003: 28)

All this belongs to the essence of capitalism. And Keynes had accepted this system.

It is striking that the beginning of the newest phase of globalization, which is steamrollering everything, coincided with the turn towards a brutal neo-liberal policy in the United Kingdom, the USA, and New Zealand. Globalization functioned as the catalyst for this turn, and it is still the biggest and the most difficult hurdle for any attempt to revitalize Keynesianism.

As already stated, there is a fundamental contradiction between a globalized world economy and Keynesian economic policy, which presupposes a strong, truly sovereign, and socially committed state. Keynes was a realist. As such, were he alive today, he would without doubt put up with globalization as a given fact and try to improve it. But he would not deny the existence of this contradiction. He presented his true *vision* on economic policy relating to this question in 1933 — that is, after experiencing the devastations of the Great Depression — in the following well-known words:

> I sympathize, therefore, with those who would minimize, rather
> than those who would maximize, economic entanglement
> between nations. Ideas, knowledge, art, hospitality, travel —
> these are the things which should of their nature be interna-
> tional. But let goods be homespun whenever it is reasonably
> and conveniently possible; and, above all, let finance be primar-
> ily national. ... But I am not persuaded that the economic
> advantages of the international division of labor to-day are at all
> comparable with what they were. (Keynes 1933: 755–769)

This position of Keynes compels us to point out two contradictions
in today's world: (1) Economic globalization is an ineluctable and logical
outcome of the growth dynamics of capitalism. Over time, in the successful industrialized countries, the total mass of accumulated capital became
so large that in order to invest it optimally it became absolutely necessary
to go beyond the narrow borders of one's own nation state. And it also
became necessary to bust the power of foreign nation states with the help
of one's own nation state. In the past, this necessarily led to overt imperialism. In our days it has inevitably led to contractually guaranteed globalization, which, in many cases, is a poorly concealed form of imperialism of
large corporations of the highly industrialized countries and of the international institutions they control, such as the IMF, the World Bank, and
the WTO (see quote from Stiglitz above). No national economy in the
First World can alone offer the total capital accumulated within the country optimal investment opportunities. And no capital-poor country can
realize its desire (in fact compulsion) to achieve economic growth without
importing foreign capital. Even rich industrialized countries try to attract
foreign capital. The interwovenness of the economies is already so complex
that one can today hardly speak of national capital. In this world, therefore, there is no room for Keynes's maxim "above all, let finance be primarily national!"

Keynesianism, therefore, had to be, if not eliminated, then at least
pushed into the second row. *True* Keynesians of today in turn should,
therefore, logically, reject globalization *as well as the growth dynamics*
of capital. And this means, in the final analysis, they should reject capitalist market economy. For, as Keynesian Heiner Flassbeck had to admit,
"the whole system of market economy is designed to grow. ... With zero
growth, ... it would collapse at some point" (*Freitag*, 18 July 2003). But
Keynes himself did not reject capitalist market economy — nor do present-
day Keynesians want to do so. As for global economic governance in the
interest of the global community, it remains for the time being a task for

the distant future. If Keynes were to demand some such thing today, then he ought to first cease to be a Keynesian (i.e., an economic nationalist). For the foreseeable future such a governance does not come in question. The peoples of the world haven't yet become one humanity. Strong nations are still exploiting the weaker ones, which they would also do in the name of global economic governance.

(2) There is also a contradiction between the current level of industrialism — the system in which growing needs are satisfied by means of large-scale industrial production — and Keynes's dictum "[L]et goods be homespun!" For *purely material* reasons, it is just not possible to set up a computer, cell phone, or car industry in every country. The thousands of kinds of raw materials and intermediate products needed for those industries cannot be found or produced in every country, and if at all they could, it would not be economically viable. *True* Keynesians, therefore, ought to question the current level of industrialism. They ought to do so at least on ecological grounds, which all people of good will nowadays do. But, as we know, Keynesians do not. These contradictions are so severe that, in my opinion, they cannot be solved through some compromises. Zero-growth and questioning industrialism are taboos for Keynesians.

## 6. Keynesians Do Not Know Any Limits to Growth

"In the long run we are all dead." These are the best-known original words of Keynes. He had said this as a reply to the thesis of orthodox economists that, in the long run, market forces would themselves bring an economy that had lost balance back to equilibrium at full employment. Of course, Joan Robinson criticized Keynes for ignoring the long term, but she meant thereby only the problem of long-term equilibrium in the economy. Today we also think of the long-term *ecological* balance in nature. Today, these words of Keynes could sound to the uninitiated like "After me, the deluge!" Keynes, however, did not mean that. In those years, the ecological question just did not exist.

But, actually, the *spirit* of Keynesianism is very much opposed to the spirit of *ecological* balance (sustainability). For instance, the thesis that in developed industrialized countries thriftiness is something bad because it is one of the causes of unemployment (paradox of thrift) is totally incompatible with the idea of a sustainable economy. In Keynesianism there is no room for a thrifty approach to the use of resources, nor for forgoing superfluous consumption. On the contrary. As we have seen in chapter III, Keynes had nothing against wasting resources if necessary — building cathedrals and pyramids, digging holes, etc., in order to increase aggregate demand. He had however believed that a sensible society would not make itself dependent on such wasteful expenditures and that stimulus spending would be financed by utilizing the savings of society. His confidence in the rationality of modern societies has proved wrong. Although no unnecessary holes are being dug, "pyramids" continue to be built. For instance, in Berlin they will soon rebuild the old royal palace of the Prussian kings. Many wasteful projects are being touted by their supporters and promoted by the state. Industrial societies are nowadays wasteful societies; consumption is mostly throwaway consumption.

We can forgive Keynes for his myopic view of economic problems. But the ecological blindness of present-day Keynesians is unpardonable. They demand increases in state spending for environmental protection, which, they say, will stimulate economic growth. While Keynes would finance these expenditures with the savings of citizens, which the state would borrow, present-day Keynesians would borrow money from all over the world and would even let the central bank arbitrarily increase the money supply. On average, today's American households save almost nothing. The critical point here is not so much that Keynesians are prepared to burden the future generations with unbearable public debts. What is worse, they seem not to have ever heard of the limits to growth. Keynesianism — no matter whether national or global — remains an agenda for the continuation of growth madness in already over-industrialized countries. It merely proposes a different strategy for the same.

Let us look, for example, at the *Memorandum 2005* by the already mentioned Arbeitsgruppe Alternative Wirtschaftspolitik. In reply to neoliberals, who see in public debt an uncovered check at the expense of future generations, the group says: "[B]udget deficits ... do not burden the future generations: along with the debts they also inherit claims to interest and repayments — additionally, they inherit a foundation for economic development which has been strengthened by public investments" (Arbeitsgruppe 2005: 7). These Keynesians seem to have missed the whole discussion on the ecology, energy, and resource problem. At least the energy problem should not have escaped their attention. Energy is after all the basis of every industrial society. Future generations will not inherit a stronger foundation for economic development. They will inherit empty oil wells, unprofitable coal mines, exhausted mineral deposits, eroded agricultural land, roads with potholes, run-down houses, etc. To put it succinctly, they will inherit a devastated biosphere if the growth madness continues. And since still no renewable, environment-friendly, economical, and plentiful energy sources are in sight, a renaissance of nuclear energy is in store for us. Future generations will then also inherit mountains of radioactive waste and ruins of atomic power plants. (I have discussed these issues in detail in my earlier book. See Sarkar 1999: chapter 4.)

Bofinger should actually be praised, for he does not simply ignore these issues. However, he devotes only two pages of his book to them. After presenting his hope of a twofold increase in prosperity in thirty-five years through a continuous 2 percent annual economic growth, he poses in all honesty the following questions: "For many people it is difficult to imagine such a development. Don't we already have a very high living standard? Where will the additional goods come from that would lead to a two-fold increase in our standard of living? What will be the effects of sustained economic growth on the environment?" (Bofinger 2005: 259). Although his questions prove his sincerity, his answers are disappointingly shallow: "People who are skeptical about [the blessings of] growth are often people with a relatively good income. . . . If . . . we want to improve the situation of people with a low income *without having to deprive the 'prosperous,'* then the only way to do that is economic growth" (emphasis added). And therefore, in his opinion, one should "not underestimate the wonderful effects of exponential growth." Obviously, Bofinger has no idea of the problems relating to the resource base of industrial economies, the ecological effects of exponential growth, and of the *problématique* of renewable resources, although the whole world has been discussing these issues since 1972, when the first report to the Club of Rome *The Limits to Growth* was published. And why shouldn't the prosperous be made to pay more for improving the situation of people with a low income? Why must the goal "prosperity for all" have the highest priority and not protection of the biosphere in the interest of the future generations and other species? To the question of whether so much growth is technically possible he replies condescendingly: "Growth-skeptics are sometimes also people with a low degree of imagination." He pins his hopes on research and innovation. As for the effects of economic growth on the environment, he turns the causality around: "The developments of the last decades have shown that in the case of most societies, the more their material prosperity increased, the more environment-conscious they became." So, Bofinger seems to say, more prosperity brings more environmental consciousness. A question remains, though: What is the use of such an environmental consciousness, when material prosperity itself is the main cause of environmental destruction? (All quotes from Bofinger 2005: 259f.)

In this context we should return to an issue we have discussed earlier, namely, the price of crude oil. Towards the end of 2007, we experienced an epochal turning point. A barrel of crude oil cost in New York more than US$90. The era of cheap oil is over. The increasing oil price is causing the inflation rate to rise. The new element in this situation is that now inflation is not being caused by excessively high wage settlements, but mainly by the physical limit of the resource oil (peak oil). New in this kind of inflation is also that it is not workers who get more money, which Keynesians would welcome, but the few oil-exporting countries and large oil companies. How then can prosperity in Germany increase twofold in the next thirty-five years? On the contrary, it is more likely that just this situation (peak oil) will cause a widespread recession or stagnation or even a new stagflation.

## 7. A Half-Socialism Cannot Function

At the end of this chapter one question still remains: Why do Keynesians advocate that in times of recession and stagnation the state should preferably incur debts for increasing state spending? Maybe it does not give rise to any big problem if the state incurs debts at home. Even so, a permanently high interest burden (every politician knows that the accumulated public debt can hardly be reduced!) limits the ability of the state to finance necessary and important tasks for social welfare and for the future. "Reagan had let deficits get out of control, risking the long-term growth of the economy ... " claimed Stiglitz (2003: 18), a Keynesian. After all, growing amounts of interest cannot forever be paid by taking new credit. At some point, taxes have to be increased. Then why not from the very beginning increase taxes on the incomes of the rich, who, according to Keynesian theory, spend too little of their income in a way that stimulates demand?

This is a dilemma, which draws politicians inevitably into class struggle. On the one hand, reducing income tax (especially for the higher income brackets), corporate tax, inheritance tax, wealth tax, and other direct taxes; and on the other hand, at the same time, increasing indirect taxes such as the value-added tax and miscellaneous charges for the lower income groups, which is what has been happening in Germany for some years now: all these are political decisions taken for the benefit of the wealthy and to the detriment of the poorer classes. According to standard economic criteria, Germany is not becoming ever poorer. The real GDP is growing, albeit sluggishly. That is not the problem. The problem is that no one wants to pay taxes.

Another solution, the privatization of deficit-financed economic stimulus, which I mentioned in section 2 of this chapter, also has its limits. The author of the *Business Week* article, from which I quoted there, saw "signs of tension everywhere" and commented: "Never has the Debt Economy seemed more vulnerable, with a distressing number of borrowers and lenders in a precarious shape" (quoted by the editors of *Monthly Review*, 1975: 6f.). This was the situation shortly after the first oil price shock — a strong recession was then under way. But even in normal times, private individuals and companies have to keep an eye on their balances. If their debts are too high, they run the risk of going bankrupt. And if a very large number of them go bankrupt, that may, directly or indirectly, adversely affect others and even the whole economy. Especially banks can get into a crisis due to too many bad debts in their books. This is something we have already seen in the 1990s in Japan and East Asia (see chapter VI, section 2). Private economic activity with borrowed money is, therefore, not a pure blessing for the economy. That is also the reason why banks ought to refuse loans to problematic clients. But that is what they often do not do. Today we have a new, instructive example of what happens when banks fail to exercise this caution: the great worldwide credit crunch and the wave of bankruptcies that resulted from the hundreds of billions of dollars of loans without security, which US banks had granted to poor real estate purchasers (the so-called "subprime credit crisis").

We see therefore that for the purpose of stimulating the economy the state should rather impose higher taxes on the incomes of the wealthy. This alone is solid economic policy. However, politicians then reach the limit of their power in capitalism, where, in the final analysis, it is big money that determines policy.

Keynes had pointed out the shortcomings of capitalism and had clearly said that this system was incapable of guaranteeing full employment and the welfare of the people. For this reason, he had insisted on the responsibility of the state and the primacy of politics. He had called on the state to intervene in the economy, even to steer it. And he had advocated "socialization" of investment activities. All this was too dangerous for capitalists; for them it was almost a socialist manifest. Keynes himself was perceived by some as a socialist and criticized accordingly, although he was not one. "Sometimes it [capitalism] filled him with rage and despair but on the whole he approved of it or at any rate he felt it worthwhile trying to patch it up and make it work tolerably well" (Robinson 1974: 71f.). He only wanted to protect capitalism from itself. If his theory was later made innocuous, then it was his own fault. If the whole thing, namely, the system as such, is the problem, then one cannot want to remove just a few of its faults and succeed thereby. A half-socialism is doomed to failure.

# VIII

# Why Globalization Should Be Criticized

The various crises of the 1980s and 1990s were reason enough for those nations whose economies had been ruined by them for a couple of years to be against neo-liberal globalization. While they suffered much during these crises, the North American and European economies benefited from them. But in 1998, the authors of a book published in Germany wrote:

> How can it be that our economy is growing, Germany is becoming ever wealthier, technological development is incessantly going on, and, despite this, the situation of large sections of the population is becoming ever worse? The media offer us every day a feeble attempt at an explanation, namely, that we are on the way to the era of globalization. (Boxberger and Klimenta 1998: 10)

No wonder then that since 1997 there is a movement in large parts of the world against economic (but also cultural) globalization. Among its activists there is a mild, unclear dispute over whether it is an anti-globalization movement or it is only *critical* of globalization, that is, a movement that does not fundamentally oppose globalization, but would rather like to give it a better form. Some new activists ask in amazement: how can globalization be bad at all? Surely, they say, it has some negative aspects that should be corrected. But isn't it useful and good if the peoples of the world prosper through international trade, cross-border investments, and global communication? And even otherwise, isn't it good if they come closer to each other? Also US economist Joseph Stiglitz, who trenchantly criticized his own powerful country because of its "hypocritical," "unfair," "self-centered," "bullying," and "double-standard" globalization policy (2003: chapter 9, passim), wrote: "The issue is not whether globalization can be a force for good which benefits the poor of the world; of course it can be. But it needs to be managed in the right way and too often it has not been" (203).

There is also a question that goes further: Is it not actually an anti-capitalist movement? The movement's most popular slogan — "the world is not a commodity" — is clearly directed against capitalism, which seeks to turn everything under the sun into a commodity. Also the slogan "another world is possible," though a bit vague, more likely means that a world other than the capitalist one is possible.

I have argued in chapter VII that in the course of technological development and as a consequence of ever greater capital accumulation, capitalism *had to* smash the limitations imposed by nation states. On the other hand, it was not just capitalist propaganda — it also made sense to many progressive thinkers — what David Ricardo had already said in the nineteenth century, namely, that free international trade benefited all countries involved. That is why in the movement one could hear the opinion that the EU should stop subsidizing and protecting its farmers from foreign competition because that was against the spirit of free world trade. For developing countries, the critics said, this amounted to loss of large export incomes. Even before this, similar criticism had been expressed against regulations protecting the textile industries of developed industrialized countries. The basis of such a position is the approval in principle of growth in world trade. For instance, the development aid organization Oxfam (England), which has been participating in the globalization-critical movement from the very beginning, wrote:

> World trade has the potential to become a strong motor for
> reducing poverty and promoting economic growth. But this
> potential remains unused. It is not as if international trade in
> itself conflicts with the needs and interests of the poor. That is
> not the problem. The problem is that the agreements that
> regulate it were made to favor the rich. (Oxfam 2002)

At present there is hardly anyone in the movement who calls for a *totally* free world trade. What one demands are fair rules for the same. Or one wants to shape world trade in such a way that it benefits the whole humanity, especially the underdeveloped countries. At the level of slogans a certain consensus has been reached: we are against neo-liberal, corporate-driven globalization, and we are for globalization from below (which however has remained quite vague). Nevertheless a question remains, namely, whether growth of world trade is to be welcomed or whether it is not better to strive for more national/regional self-sufficiency. All this calls for a lot of explaining.

## 1. The Theory of Comparative Advantage and the Arguments for Globalization

In theory, the arguments for free international trade appear quite convincing. It does not make any difference whether a country (or region) is highly developed or underdeveloped — all participants benefit from international trade so long as it is free or so long as the rules are fair and apply equally to all. This is also the argument of the "liberalizers" in the WTO, the World Bank, and the IMF. To the criticism that the rules are neither fair nor universally applicable they respond by demanding they be made fair and universally applicable in the medium or long term.

Their argumentation can be presented as follows. The country (or region) A imports the commodity X, that it cannot produce, from the country (or region) B, that can produce this commodity. A pays for the import by exporting the commodity Y, which it can produce, but that B cannot. Both A and B benefit from this trade because both need or want to enjoy the commodities they import. This is the simplest and most convincing argument for international trade. (The argument applies also to individuals living in the same country.) But what should one say when both countries can produce both the commodities? Should each produce both commodities for their own consumption? No. This is where the well-known advantages of specialization (division of labor) and economies of scale come in as argument. Each country (or region) should specialize in the commodity that it can produce at a lower cost than the other country (or region). This too is easy to understand.

The argument becomes a little more complex when A can produce both commodities at a lower cost than B. According to the theory of comparative advantage, A should even then specialize in Y, in the manufacture of which it has a higher productivity than in the manufacture of X. A should import X from B, which in turn should import Y from A. In this theory one then says: A has a *comparative* advantage in the Y branch, while B has its comparative advantage in the X branch. For the cases discussed in the previous paragraph, one uses the term *absolute* advantage.

In 1817, David Ricardo illustrated this notion with an example, in which Portugal and England imported from the other cloth and wine respectively, although Portugal was more productive in both branches. I here present the theory with the help of the schema used by Samuelson and Nordhaus (1989: 903), in which they assume that only two countries (regions) are participating in trade and only two commodities are being traded. They also assume that expenditure of labor is the only cost of production.

**American and European labor cost of production (required working time)**

| Product | In the United States | In Europe |
| --- | --- | --- |
| 1 unit of food | 1 hour | 3 hours |
| 1 unit of clothing | 2 hours | 4 hours |

In this hypothetical example, the United States has a lower labor cost of production for both food and clothing. American labor productivity is three and two times, respectively, higher than European labor productivity. Nevertheless, it is profitable for the United States to import clothing from Europe.

For a better understanding of the theory, I would like to add here a few more sentences. The productivity *gap* between the two regions is different for the two branches taken separately. The US *superiority* in productivity is higher in the case of food (1:3) than in the case of clothing (2:4). This means that the US has an advantage in food production *in comparison* with clothing production. It should therefore specialize in producing and exporting food. Europe's inferiority in productivity is lower in the case of clothing than in the case of food. That means, its comparative advantage in trade lies in the production and export of clothing. The question that unavoidably arises here is why Americans should at all import clothing from Europe if they are more productive also in the production of clothing. The answer lies in the assumption that in the process of trade and specialization, Americans have to draw laborers away from the production of clothing in order to employ them in the more profitable production of food. (The theory is premised on the assumption of full employment, that is, on the scarcity of the resource labor.) Europeans do the opposite. Because now Americans do not produce clothes anymore, Europeans can sell their clothing products in the United States. A further point that we should consider is one we already know from the trade relationship between industrialized and developing countries. Because in this schema, generally speaking, productivity in Europe is lower than that in the United States, European incomes (wages, among others) are generally lower than those in America. It is argued that through trade, existing resources (in this case, only labor) are used most efficiently on both sides. This brings advantage to all participating parties.

In theory, at least, this argument appears convincing. This is also confirmed by Herman Daly (1990: 209), a renowned economist who criticizes neo-liberal globalization and the growth of world trade. Naturally, in the real world economy circumstances are much more complicated than in this theoretical schema. But in the real world economy too there are thousands of sensible specializations. Japan, for instance, imports jumbo jets from the United States, although it could also produce such airplanes. And the United States imports cameras from Japan, although they too could produce such apparatus themselves. One cannot therefore deny the advantages of specialization and of liberalized world trade and its growth.

It is also clear that attempts to protect certain national industries by means of customs barriers and the like are detrimental to the process of division of labor (specialization) among the different national economies, and that they consequently reduce the resulting advantages of economies of scale. If, for instance, US industrialists would try to produce cameras in the United States, and if the state would try to protect them through higher import duties, then both the Japanese and the American camera industry would produce a smaller series with large investments, with the consequence that production costs would rise. Moreover, Japan would probably retaliate with protection measures for other products. The world production as a whole would decrease as a result of such economic policies.

The world economy already experienced that in the 1930s. During the Great Depression (1929–1933) most industrialized countries tried to promote or protect their own industries by devaluing their currency or eliminating the gold standard and then allowing their currency to fall at the international foreign exchange market. As is well known, devaluation of the national currency promotes exports and curbs imports. That was a generalized form of protectionism. But there was also open and particular protectionism through imposition or increase of import duties. But since every industrialized country tried to attain the same objective using the same methods, in the end there were no winners, only losers. This policy only deepened the depression. Therefore, when today establishment economists call for a liberalization of world trade so that trade, and along with it production, grows, that has a certain justification. For otherwise, in the absence of specialization, the possibilities of modern technologies, which require large investments and large series, could not be utilized fully. In that case, the world economy would also grow more slowly than otherwise.

A few promises and hopes are associated with this prospect of growth of the world economy: globalization would bring prosperity to all peoples or increase it; the poor Third World countries would finally get a development boost, would overcome widespread poverty and leave the debt trap behind; mass unemployment would be eliminated, both in the First and the Third World; exchange between the cultures of the world would increase. It has even been claimed that with the growth of world trade democracy and human rights would also spread.

So that these promises can come true, protagonists of liberalization of world trade further demand liberalization of foreign investments and free mobility of all kinds of financial capital. Only in this way, they claim, can the most efficient use of capital be achieved. Particularly the capital-poor countries of the Third World could develop economically only if they became attractive for investors of the rich countries.

All these arguments sound very convincing. Stiglitz could even speak of a vision:

> America needed a vision of where the global economy was going and how it might shape it. . . . I would have liked us to try to work toward a vision of how a world without economic borders — a world with true free trade, consonant with our rhetoric — might have looked. It would have meant that we would have had to eliminate our agricultural subsidies. . . . It would have meant that we would have had to open up our markets to labor-intensive services, such as construction and maritime. It would have led, too, to an elimination of a whole variety of other protectionist measures; it would have meant that we would have looked at "unfair" trade practices by foreign firms through the same lens that we use for firms at home. (2003: 236)

This means, according to Stiglitz, Oxfam, and the numerous critics and "designers" of globalization, the world would be a far better place if *true* free trade could be realized, if globalization were better managed. Why then do so many people criticize economic globalization at all, "a world without economic borders"? Why do they criticize it *fundamentally*? In reply, it is not sufficient to point at the bad experiences made until now, at the fact that through this arrangement the rich countries have been able to exploit the poor countries much more strongly than before. We have to ask further: Why in history did so many countries reject the principles of free trade, liberalization of foreign investment, and free mobility of foreign finance capital? Why did so many countries reject them even after the apparently convincing formulation of the theory of comparative advantage, and even after the bad experience with protectionism during the depression of the 1930s? Why did they strive after comprehensive industrialization instead of trying to specialize themselves in a few areas?

## 2. The Assumptions of the Theory and the Reality

The answers to these questions lie partly in the sphere of political reality and partly in the sphere of economic reality.

A theory can only be right if, and to the extent to which, its basic assumptions are correct. This is not, or only to a limited extent, the case here. Of course, a theory must abstract from concrete singular and exceptional cases; otherwise it is not possible to develop a theory. But if it, so to speak, abstracts from the normal case, then its persuasive power is meager.

### a) *The Political Reality*

The theory of international trade assumes that all parties involved enjoy equal rights, that they voluntarily participate in trade, and that they strive to become rich only by trading fairly. An important and very common historical reality and possibility has not been considered at all in this theory, namely, that powerful imperialist countries conquer, or control by military means or through economic/political power, other countries — especially weak and economically underdeveloped ones (or at least their markets) — in order then to quasi *pillage* their natural wealth, occupy their land, and exploit their labor through colonial, semi-colonial, or neo-colonial dominance. This, however, was, still is, or is again becoming a large part of the reality. Referring to negotiations on world trade Stiglitz (2003: 232) wrote about "America's tendency to use muscle to get what it wants," to issue threats to negotiation partners, to force them to comply, etc. Against this background, it was and still is understandable and even rational that weaker economies indulge(d) in nationalistic sentiments and want(ed) to pursue a policy of political and economic independence and autonomous development. Given the importance of food security — and given the fact that the United States has in the past used wheat exports as a political weapon, as a means of coercion — an agricultural policy of "food sovereignty," i.e., maximum possible self-sufficiency, is very important for *all* countries, including the EU (see Shiva 2002, and Bové and Dufour 2001).

Today, the conquest of weak countries, i.e., their markets and resources, is carried out mainly through the transnational corporations (TNCs) of the powerful industrialized countries. The use of armed forces directly for this purpose is, of course, not ruled out, but it is rarely necessary, for the TNCs and their nation states normally have enough means of coercion in the sphere of economy and trade.

The fact that protectionist measures aggravated the depression of the 1930s is a convincing argument against such measures. But when discussing this issue one should bear in mind that in the 1930s (and also for some time in the next decades), the discussion was limited to countries of Europe and North America that were already industrialized and did not have the problem the emerging and underdeveloped countries are suffering from today, namely, economic colonialism. Nevertheless, even in the highly developed industrialized countries one can today observe political conditions that look, in a somewhat different sense, colonial. To be sure, not foreign political powers, but certainly the global cartel of transnational corporations effectively dictate to the people's representatives of these countries the parameters within which their economic and other relevant policies can move. This they can do through their associations such as the International Chamber of Commerce (ICC), their friends in the governments, their lobbyists, etc., and through multilateral organizations and pacts such as the WTO and NAFTA. This de facto nullification of democracy and parts of the sovereignty of states is sufficient reason for many people in the industrialized countries to oppose neo-liberal globalization.

When textbook authors try to demonstrate the logical soundness of the theory, they also assume that politics does not play any role in trade. But politically motivated embargos, boycotts, preferences, and other similar measures regularly play a role in international trade — and these activities are not negligible.

In view of all these realities, one can regard well-intentioned people and NGOs (non-governmental organizations) like Stiglitz and Oxfam as naïve. They expect the powerful countries to share their pretty vision of a capitalist "world in which there was more global social justice, in which our sense of caring also went beyond our borders" (Stiglitz 2003: 236f.). But such sentiments are totally alien to capitalism. And Adam Smith even morally legitimized the selfishness of capitalists. According to him, it also serves, through an "invisible hand," the common good. Thus, during a state visit to some African countries, President Clinton, whose chief economic advisor Stiglitz was, could say with a clear conscience that not development aid but rather trade would be more helpful to the Africans — trade, the real objective of which was, according to Stiglitz, "to take resources out of Africa" (237). Stiglitz provides a second piece of evidence for his naïveté, when he repeatedly calls American globalization policies "mistaken policies" (see 238). In the framework of capitalism, all that was not mistaken, but quite the right policy.

### b) *The Economic Reality*

Textbook authors also write about a great discrepancy between the assumptions of the theory and the economic reality, and they therefore relativize the validity of the elegant theory of comparative advantages. Like the whole orthodox (classical) theory, this theory also assumes that prices, wages, and interest rates adjust quickly to market conditions and that therefore, in the middle term, there cannot be any unutilized production capacities in national economies — neither labor nor capital, and also no uninvested savings. From this point of view, therefore, there is no *involuntary* unemployment in any capitalist market economy. Everyone knows that these assumptions have always been unworldly. Not just short-lived deviations from equilibrium, but also more or less long-lasting ups and downs, recessions, stagnations, and depressions simply belong to capitalism, to its wave-shaped development pattern (see chapter III, section 2). And there simply is involuntary unemployment, both cyclical and structural. The assumption that labor is scarce — so that, for expansion in one branch resulting from specialization, labor has to be drawn away from another branch — is utterly wrong. It was also wrong back then, when Ricardo conceived this theory. Otherwise Thomas Robert Malthus need not have written about an overpopulation problem. Both Portugal and England had in those days more than enough young men to serve in the warships, to conquer foreign countries, and then to colonize and exploit them.

If today the leadership of a country does not want to simply accept mass unemployment, then they must do without some advantages of specialization and free world trade. They must then also try to create or protect jobs in those branches in which their country has a comparative disadvantage. In order to save these branches and their workers from ruin, they just have to build tariff barriers, and other types of barriers too.

One must here differentiate between agricultural and industrial production. Unlike specialty items such as wine, bananas, and coffee, non-specialty items, garments, shoes, and the like, can be easily produced in every country (since raw materials can be imported) — and in the not too distant past they were produced in almost every country. Therefore, Stiglitz was absolutely wrong when he still, in 2003, affirmatively repeated Ricardo's thesis: "Each country has a comparative advantage, goods that it has a relative advantage in producing. It is those goods which it exports; and it imports the goods which it produces at a relative disadvantage" (233). In the production of industrial goods, there are no *natural* comparative advantages, but only fortuitous ones or those that have arisen from historical circumstances, advantages that can quickly disappear. Transportation costs being very low, raw materials can even be imported from distant countries. Japan imports iron ore from India and produces steel. Germany imports coal and oil for all its industries. India imports computers and supplies software. Theoretically, any country can do that. Whatever deficit there may be in technical know-how and/or infrastructure can be overcome in the medium term. Even capital can be imported. Today, the most important (but not the only) factor in deciding the location of production seems to be labor costs, and these are a function of the level of unemployment and of the power of trade unions. The lower the wages, the more attractive is the location. These are the comparative advantages and disadvantages of the present time. Because of these advantages, industrial and services productions are being relocated on a large scale from First World to Third World countries. I once heard the despairing question of a German worker: "Is there any area at all in which the Chinese do not have a comparative advantage?"

However, it is not that any country or any single capitalist can produce any and every industrial good. The market for a product is mostly occupied by the pioneers and early entrants, and these are not necessarily countries, but mostly corporations that can have their goods manufactured in almost any country. It is very difficult for newcomers to win a share of the market, or for a long-standing producer to regain a lost market share. Moreover, a market share that is too small is simply not profitable. Only this explains why, for instance, the Indians do not try to produce computers, and the Germans do not try to again produce ordinary cameras.

Unlike in theory, there is in reality no certainty that the workers who would be retrenched from the branches that would be given up, because of their comparative disadvantage at the world market, would find work in the branches that would flourish because of their comparative advantage. For even in the area of goods, in the case of which one can speak of a natural comparative advantage — wine, bananas, coffee, etc. — there is just too much competition among the countries that enjoy this advantage. This (in reality) nonexistent certainty is, strangely, a fundamental assumption of the orthodox (classical) theory of free world trade.

This assumption is wrong for another reason: workers are not abstract laborers who can be trained at will and moved around to places where they are needed. They are human beings who, generally, want to live with their families in their native country and to work in the trade they have learned. It is not just extremely difficult but also inhuman to try, for instance, to make out of a ruined elderly Bavarian farmer a steelworker in the Ruhr area. Of course, these sorts of things have happened again and again in history (even mass emigration into distant foreign countries), but historians have rarely described their high price in terms of the resulting concrete and, not least of all, emotional distress suffered. Ignoring the human dimension is, however, an integral part of the rationality of the whole capitalist economic system, not just of orthodox economic theory. Only a state that intervened in the economy, which also had to be a welfare state, the trade unions, the parties of the left, and leftist movements: only these have managed throughout history to make the worst consequences of the brutal rationality of capitalism somewhat tolerable.

It is not only that involuntary unemployment exists — nowadays its size has swollen into millions of unemployed in every medium-size country. In many countries there are also factories running below capacity and uninvested savings. Daly and Cobb Jr. point out that when Ricardo formulated his theory of comparative advantage, he assumed the international *immo*bility of capital (and high mobility of goods). Ricardo referred to the "difficulty with which capital moves from one country to another to seek a more profitable employment." This was exactly the basis on which *comparative* advantages could exist and the reason why capital had to be invested in one's native country. On this basis international trade made good sense. With reference to Ricardo's famous example, Daly and Cobb Jr. explain the argument as follows:

> [I]f capital flowed freely across national boundaries, the
> situation internationally would be the same as that within a
> single country. English capital would flow to Portugal to
> supplement Portuguese capital, and both wine and cloth would
> be produced there. If labor also flowed freely across national
> boundaries, English labor would also go to Portugal, since there
> would be no employment in England. (1990: 213ff.)

In today's world, the unimpeded flow of capital across national borders has become possible and usual. But workers are not allowed to enter foreign countries as they please in order to earn money there. The consequence of free flow of capital and goods is that investment decisions are made on the basis of *absolute* profitability, not on the basis of comparative advantages. This, of course, has the effect that the total product of the region that constitutes a unified market, the EU, for instance (or the world), grows. But that does not guarantee that the total product of each of the countries of the unified market also grows. For the work of producing the increased total product of the economically unified region can be very unevenly distributed. This means that job creation and hence the creation of new income can also be unevenly distributed. One can see that, for example, in the current economic boom in China and the underdevelopment in most African countries. It also applies to enjoyment of the total product. The experience so far shows that the highly developed industrialized countries can manage to get hold of the lion's share of the value additionally created through world trade — even without pushing down the prices of products of the developing countries by manipulating the markets, which they can do and in fact do in many cases. As for the profits, here too there is no guarantee that they will be fairly distributed among all countries participating in international trade. Transnational corporations of the First World can easily press down the profits of their suppliers from the Third World.

Free world trade also does not guarantee that the countries/regions A and B won't seek to make profitable deals with each other to the detriment of other participants in the unified market. It can also be that A and B are developed countries/regions (EU, US, Canada, Japan), and that, from a business point of view, they do not need to trade with the underdeveloped countries/regions C and D, or that they find the latter simply uninteresting. In this case, capital and goods could flow past C and D. This, in fact, is the situation today. Many African countries, for instance, appear to have been totally uncoupled from the world economy. They are the poorest and they are becoming even poorer. Under such circumstances, specializing in one or a few products — coffee, cocoa, tea, or a few industrial goods — is bad business policy. More advisable are diversification and a domestic market orientation.

But these criticisms should be leveled at the whole capitalist system. A part of the system, namely, free world trade, cannot be fundamentally different from the whole system. A just distribution of the growing total product or of the total number of jobs among the regions does not even take place in a nation state.

It is also not as if free world trade benefits only the capitalists. It also brings advantages to at least those workers who have not lost their jobs after the opening up of the markets. For it is indisputable that the prices and/or the quality of imported goods (at the same prices) that have pushed away similar local products from the market are lower and/or better than the latter. That is tantamount to increasing the real income of the buyers of such goods. Anyone can find evidence for the validity of this statement in an American or German supermarket.

However, a very well-known claim of the champions of globalization is wrong, namely, the one expressed in the metaphorical saying: "A rising tide lifts all boats." Numerous studies on poverty in different countries have shown that large parts of the population (in many cases the majority), even the whole country, have become poorer through globalization, while the total product of the country or of the world has grown. However, the rich and the middle class profit from such a situation. Furthermore, millions of industrial workers in the First World have lost their jobs on account of globalization. And as far as farmers are concerned, at least in the EU, hundreds of thousands of them, who managed to survive the earlier concentration and mechanization process, will become superfluous when the world agriculture market is totally liberalized. The metaphor is simply wrong; people live on uneven ground at different heights, not on a level water surface. The other metaphor using water, which speaks of a "trickle-down effect," is also not quite right. Water does not trickle down everywhere unless it is channeled to do so. But this criticism too should be leveled at the whole capitalist system.

Because not all boats can be "lifted" by a rising "tide," globalization critics, who do not reject capitalism and globalization in principle, have an ambivalent attitude towards the protests in the First World of workers and farmers who are threatened by unemployment or bankruptcy. As everybody knows, workers in the First World are threatened by relocation of production in low-wage countries, and farmers are threatened by competition from products of countries such as Argentina, where the soil is more fertile and the production costs are altogether lower.

In 1817, Ricardo did not think this possibility through, probably because at the time it was purely hypothetical. But we can think it through today. We cannot say that unbridled mobility of capital is clearly evil. In the above quote, Daly and Cobb Jr. have spoken of incoming foreign capital *supplementing* local capital. For capital-poor developing countries and their unemployed masses such a supplement is welcome. The only negative aspect of the matter is that the profits and interest do not remain in the country. Here we see a conflict of interests between the working classes of developed and underdeveloped countries. But competition for location of industries exists also among industrialized countries. Footloose capital also flows from one industrialized country to another, as well as from one underdeveloped country to another. The existence or lack of strong trade unions and other small advantages or disadvantages are enough motivation for homeless capital to move. That reality, and especially the activities of speculative hot money, increases the anarchy and crisis-proneness of the capitalist system (see chapter VI, section 2).

What also happens because of the unimpeded mobility of capital is that in some branches small local capital is totally or partially pushed out by strong transnational capital instead of being just supplemented—for example, local snack bars pushed out by McDonald's, or local farmers by transnational agribusiness corporations. This happens both in the First World and in the Third World. Today, in the world *as a whole*, in contrast to Ricardo's assumptions, neither capital nor labor is scarce.

Local small capital is also being pushed out through the expansion of international trade in goods. For instance, many cattle breeders in the Sahel zone of Africa were ruined through competition from meat imported from the EU, which could be sold at cheaper prices due to subsidies. Consumers in the region, naturally, bought the cheaper meat.

There is a problem in our criticism of imports of this type. Why shouldn't consumers in the Sahel zone be enabled to buy meat at a lower price — just as European and American consumers can buy cheap clothes or electronic goods produced by cheap-wage laborers in East Asia? For such consumers, globalization is something good. After all, in the Sahel zone too the economy is based on a free market. A few years ago, US steel workers faced the same problem. Thousands lost their jobs, because steel consumers in the US (in the construction branch, for instance) were able to buy duty-free imported steel that was cheaper than steel produced in the US. And then there would be yet another problem if the US government tried to protect the US steel industry and its workers by means of higher import duties. Then other workers, for example in the South Korean steel industry, would lose their jobs.

We see that the conflicting interests of many social groups we sympathize with make our lives difficult. Our dilemma is the worst when companies relocate their production. When, for instance, thousands of Indians, who were previously unemployed, find a job in the Indian subsidiary of IBM or Microsoft, thousands of Americans lose their jobs in these companies. If the world agricultural market were totally liberalized, then many farmers in developing countries (probably only big and midsized farmers) would benefit from this by exporting their products to Europe. This would, however, totally ruin the small farmers of Europe. Therefore, it is not enough for us as critics of globalization to criticize — such is our baseline consensus — the transnational corporations, to demand controls over the international finance market, etc.

### 3. The Sustainability Criterion

Why should we then, in spite of these doubts and dilemmas, criticize globalization? A really convincing criticism *in particular* of globalization and growth of world trade (and not of capitalism in general) comes from a different sphere, namely, from our concern about the sustainability (future viability) of our economies and the state of the environment.

By now, so far as the future perspective is concerned, there is a baseline consensus, a basic principle of our political work, namely, that the economy of every country, of the whole world in fact, ought to be sustainable. As regards the meaning and use of the concept "sustainability," there are major differences in our movement, and they are actually the deeper cause of other differences among us. An exemplary manifestation of these differences was a dispute between Oxfam (England) and Vandana Shiva, both very active in the movement from the outset.

In one of its reports, Oxfam wrote what it means by "sustainability":

> One cannot defend the present world trade system, and it is not sustainable. No civilized society should be prepared to tolerate the extremes of prosperity and poverty that the prevailing trade practices generate. Large parts of the developing countries are becoming enclaves of despair that are increasingly being marginalized and excluded from the growing prosperity that is being generated by trade. Shared prosperity cannot be achieved on such a basis. Just like the economic forces that are driving globalization forward, anger and social tensions, which accompany unequal distribution of wealth and opportunities, will not respect any national boundaries. The instability that they will give rise to is threatening us all. In today's globalized world, more than ever before, our life is inseparably linked with that of others. That applies also to our prosperity. As a global community, we shall swim or sink together. (Oxfam 2002; retranslated)

For Shiva (2002), however, sustainability means something diametrically opposed to Oxfam's understanding. While Oxfam welcomes the growing wealth created by trade and only fears the coming instability and the anger and despair of the poor that threaten the prosperity of the rich, Shiva is concerned about the *ecological* sustainability of the developing countries and about securing the modest livelihood of the poor. Obviously, she has given up the hope that the majority of the people of India, her country, can ever achieve the prosperity that Oxfam is talking about. That is why she sees in the export of beef from India the loss of a valuable source of energy and manure, which the animals would supply if they were not slaughtered. (It is not clear if she would also oppose the slaughtering of cows that provide neither energy as draft animals nor milk.) She also wrote of the enormous amount of foreign currency expenditure that India could spare itself (by importing fewer chemical fertilizers and fossil fuels, I assume) if it let these animals live longer.

Shiva has accepted the limits to growth as a fact — not just with respect to nature's ability to absorb human-made environmental damages, but also with respect to availability of resources. She wrote:

> Since trade in agricultural products depends on the use of land, water, and biodiversity, and since availability of land and water are limited, export-oriented agriculture policy diverts land and

water away from production of basic foodstuff for local consumption. Prioritizing export shifts the use of natural resources of the poor countries to production of luxury items for rich consumers in rich countries, and that at very low costs. This has the effect that control over the resources is removed from the hands of small farmers and fishermen and goes into the hands of agribusiness corporations. This development destroys the natural resource base through its unsustainable use, destroys in the process the livelihood basis of small producers and creates poverty instead of overcoming it. (Shiva 2002; retranslated)

I can imagine that Oxfam also thinks of environmental protection and the resource problem and that it, nevertheless, like many other people and groups, thinks that sustainable economic growth is possible. Then it cannot have any problem with the stance it has taken in the above-mentioned report.

In a different book I have explained in detail why I consider sustainable economic growth to be impossible (Sarkar 1999). Here it is a matter of a conflict between two opposing paradigms: the growth paradigm and the limits-to-growth paradigm. Every well-informed person knows that in most developing countries the natural resources — land, water, and biomass — have already become scarce and that environmental destruction there has already reached a high level. In this situation, a policy of exporting more from these countries to the industrialized countries means that the industrialized countries are importing sustainability from the Third World countries at the price of non-sustainability of these countries (Pearce et al. 1989: 45). Under neocolonial conditions this could also be termed plundering. The big and middle-level farmers who export their produce to the First World will surely become richer. But the poor will become poorer.

The minimum objective of globalization critics — to make world trade a bit fairer — deserves, in general, to be supported. Who can be against that, although in matters of detail, as shown above, in view of opposing interests of different parts of the population, it is often difficult to say what is fair. But will everything be all right when world trade has been made a bit fairer? Even with fair world trade, environmental degradation and depletion of resources will go on. Everyone knows, for instance, that China is the country that benefits the most from globalization; it has become, so to speak, the factory of the world; it floods the whole world with its export products. And still — according to a white paper of the Chinese government itself—300 million people there have no access to potable water. Respiratory diseases are the most frequent cause of death, 90 percent of the grasslands are in danger of drying out or being buried in sand, etc. (*Frankfurter Rundschau*, 7 June 2006).

Shiva, however, is mistaken about one point in her argumentation: a country does not necessarily need an export-oriented economic policy in order to degrade its environment and to make its poor people even poorer. This can also be the result of policies oriented towards the domestic market if, at the threshold of limits to growth, further economic growth is pursued, come hell or high water, and if the ruling politicians want to make the local rich and middle class richer at the expense of the local poor. Then, from the point of view of poor people, the national interest and the national border are no longer important. A protectionist policy could then only be in the interest of the local entrepreneurs (in the interest of the cattle breeders of the Sahel zone, for instance). Seen in this light, the internal economic policy of a regime is at least as important an object of critical scrutiny as its external economic policy and the policies of organizations like the WTO, the IMF, and the World Bank.

A vague passage in the Oxfam report can also be favorably interpreted. Oxfam wrote: "If Africa, East Asia, South Asia and Latin America could each increase its share of total world export by only 1 percent, then the profit resulting from this increase could free 128 million people from poverty. In Africa alone, this would create income to the tune of US$70 billion" (Oxfam 2002; retranslated). Oxfam does not say here that these developing continents must necessarily export foodstuffs or natural resources. As we know, many countries in these continents also export industrial products, even high-tech products like computer software. If they would export more of such products and less foodstuffs and natural resources, then they could create more jobs and income than otherwise. And in this process, they would cause less environmental damage *per dollar* export. But the *absolute* extent of environmental damage would probably increase, since every industrial activity damages the environment, and since, as a rule, more industrial activity causes more environmental damage. From a *global perspective*, in any case, this does not solve the environmental and resource problem. The raw materials have to come from somewhere, and the environmental degradation, alas, has to take place somewhere. These things will then only be redistributed among the participating countries.

If we further interpret the above passage favorably, Oxfam hopes that the profit from the increased exports will be used to eradicate poverty. This presupposes a regime that is determined to eradicate poverty at the expense of the entrepreneurs who are producing the exported goods and the businessmen who are organizing the export. That is too naïve. Such a regime must be a socialistic one, or poverty will only increase in the process, as Vandana Shiva fears.

If world trade grows, and not just domestic production for domestic consumption — if, for instance, Irish butter is sold in Germany, although it tastes no different — environmental degradation and resource depletion will increase more than otherwise. In their contributions to discussions on this subject, champions of globalization never mention transportation costs, as if transporting goods over great distances had no cost whatsoever. Of course, because of low energy prices, such costs were, until recently, not an important factor. But lately, these prices — especially oil prices — have gone up considerably, and they will inevitably continue to rise in the future. Then, to produce as much as possible (especially essential goods) within the country with local resources — instead of importing them from distant countries — will seem to be a rational idea, not just from a political but also from an economic point of view. From an ecological point of view it is sensible in any case. The International Forum on Globalization (IFG), an important organization in the movement, wrote:

> Globalization is inherently destructive to the natural world
> because it requires that products travel thousands of miles
> around the planet, resulting in staggering environmental costs
> such as unprecedented levels of ocean and air pollution from
> transport, increased energy consumption and fossil fuel emis-
> sions (furthering climate change), increased use of packaging
> materials, and devastating new infrastructure developments —
> new roads, ports, airports, pipelines, power grids — often
> constructed in formerly pristine places. (2001: 21)

# IX.

# Aspects of the Crisis *of* Capitalism

In the previous chapters I have described and discussed several economic crises of different kinds in different parts of the capitalist world. None of them actually endangered the capitalist system. One could say they were all crises *in* capitalism. But the question is whether there could be a crisis *of* capitalism in the foreseeable future. According to Schumpeter, in capitalism, economic crises play a positive, that is, a cleansing, role. Will it then go on like this, with some ups and downs, always? And will the economy continue to grow, forever?

In recent times (2006–2007), on the one hand, Western European politicians, Germans for instance, talked of regained consumer confidence, of newly created jobs subject to social security payments, and of a steady, robust growth (+2%). On the other hand (towards the end of 2007), business cycle experts talked of the end of the short upswing in the Eurozone. As for the world economy, Rodrigo Rato, managing director of the IMF, expressed his concern in the autumn of 2006 in the following words: "With the housing market in the US cooling faster than anticipated, there is a risk of an abrupt slowdown in the US which could derail the global expansion" (*International Herald Tribune*, 13 September 2006). In the fall of 2007, a meltdown of the US housing market began.

It is not clear yet whether Rato's fears are proving to be justified. At any rate, between 2004 and 2007 the *world* economy grew strongly, at a yearly average rate of 5.2%. However, at the end of 2007, it appeared as if globalization had split the world in respect of its results. For while the economies of the highly developed industrialized countries were suffering from sluggish growth, those of *some* developing countries were booming — not only those of China, India, Brazil, and other emerging countries, but also, for instance, those of Kenya, Egypt, Turkey, and Chile, which grew in 2007 at 6.4%, 7.1%, 5%, and 5.9%, respectively (see Sheridan and Gross 2007). But *we* have no reason to be euphoric. In India, for instance, only 200 million of its 1.1 billion inhabitants are part of the middle class (measured in Indian standards). Two-thirds of its households have no electricity.

We have seen that both Keynes and Schumpeter raised the question about the future of capitalism and that their answer was not exactly optimistic. They had different reasons for their skepticism. These reasons need to be examined in the light of today's situation, and we should also ask ourselves if today new reasons have come up for a skeptical view.

Keynes's prognosis that in *mature* economies capital would cease to be scarce within two generations has come true. We know that today the majority of the factories in such economies are, in general, not even approximately operating at full capacity. And as for finance capital, investors are at a loss to know where to invest their money. That is why one speaks of "footloose finance capital." Obviously, there are not enough new *profitable* investment opportunities. Enormous sums are being invested in the emerging markets, often in risky bonds (like, in the 1990s, the state bonds of Argentina; Argentina later declared bankruptcy). Billions are being invested as venture capital in risky projects, as was the case in the 1990s with the shady businesses of dot-com companies, which made losses every year and eventually went bust. Hundreds of billions are being wagered at various stock exchanges and commodity markets. One can hardly call such activities investment — they only create huge hot air bubbles. In the case of speculation at the real estate market, there is at least something tangible as basis, a house or a plot of land. In the case of the dot-com bubble, there was nothing but hope.

Among the factors that made rapid economic development in the nineteenth century possible, one, population growth, has definitively ceased to exist in Europe. Without immigration from underdeveloped and less developed countries, which, except in the case of skilled laborers, is generally not desired, population will decrease in most mature industrialized countries. But the other factors still exist: innovations, especially technical inventions, are still being made, in much greater numbers than in the nineteenth century. The number of countries and regions that are waiting to be commercially developed and exploited by foreign capital is still very high. And wars, which increase aggregate demand — small, big, and middle-size wars, asymmetrical wars and civil wars — abound. Why then are so many matured economies stagnating?

## 1. Instability of the International Financial System

One potential cause of the crisis of capitalism is known to us only since the 1980s: the extreme instability of the international financial markets. The first crisis caused by this instability was the debt crisis of the developing countries (see chapter VI, section 1). At the time, many large commercial banks of the First World were hit hard, and with them, the whole international credit system was in danger of breaking down. After that came the financial crisis in Mexico (1994–1995). With great effort on the part of many players, the collapse could be averted in these two cases, but not in the case of the East Asian crisis of 1997–1998 (see chapter VI, section 2). The devastating effects of this crisis were rightly characterized by some commentators as comparable to those of the Great Depression (1929–1933) (with the difference that in 1998 no First World country was hit by this crisis). Nowadays, some critical observers think that today's global capitalism, if it at all collapses, will do so as a result of the next, much greater, financial crisis, which will originate in the USA, the country with the world's leading currency, the biggest mountain of debt, and the largest current account deficit.

George Soros — a notorious and very successful global speculator and a leading expert on the world of international finance — wrote in 1998, that is, against the background of the then still raging East Asian crisis, a book entitled *The Crisis of Global Capitalism*, in which he forecast the "imminent disintegration of the global capitalist system" (1998: 103). He wrote: "I have no hesitation ... in asserting that the global capitalist system will succumb to its defects, if not on this occasion then on the next one — unless we recognize that it is defective and act in time to correct the deficiencies" (134).

After the Russian state declared bankruptcy (see chapter VI, section 2), Soros feared a "catastrophic collapse" (168). He however thought: "The system has a centre [the First World] and a periphery [the Third World and the emerging markets]. This could explain why the process of disintegration should take much longer and occur at different times in different parts of the system" (169). The catastrophic crisis in Argentina in 2001 (see chapter VI, section 3) could be seen as a corroboration of this thesis of Soros's.

At the time (1998), Soros gave three reasons for his foreboding. Firstly, flaws in the international banking system were being ignored. Part of the business of international banks — "swaps, futures, and derivatives" — that they conducted amongst themselves and with their clients, did not appear in their balance sheets. Then, when the Russian banks declared bankruptcy, the international banks got into great trouble. Also hedge funds and speculative accounts made great losses. Reacting to that, panic-stricken banks tried to reduce their lending and risks. This led not just to a sharp fall in the price of their own stocks; it also resulted in a credit crunch that, as always, created problems in the real economy. Secondly, Soros saw at the time how a few individual countries tended to drop out of the global capitalist system because of the extremely high level of their suffering (he could however give only one example, Malaysia) or how a few just fell by the wayside (he mentioned here Indonesia and Russia). Since Malaysia could at the time improve its situation by imposing restrictions on international capital transactions, Soros feared that this would set a precedent for other countries that had run into difficulties. According to him, an ensuing large-scale flight of capital from the periphery would endanger the system. Thirdly, Soros saw how the IMF with its programs failed to help overcome the crisis. The IMF did not have enough money for that, and the G7 countries dropped Russia. Soros found all that frightening. He wrote: "Financial markets are rather peculiar in this respect: They resent any kind of government interference, but they hold a belief deep down that if conditions get really rough the authorities will step in [to help them]. This belief has now been shaken" (171).

At this point it is necessary to have a closer look at the hedge funds (and similar investment funds with different names), which Franz Müntefering, the then president of the German Social Democratic Party (SPD), in an angry outburst compared with locusts. They make highly risky and shady speculative transactions and promise their investors very high returns. Their business has therefore nothing to do with hedging. In 1990, these funds managed approximately US$40 billion. In the following decade, they pampered their investors with returns over 20 percent. Then ordinary people like pensioners and students, were lured by such returns; even pension funds invested in them. In 2005, the total sum managed by these funds increased to $1 trillion (Buchter 2005). One journalist even thought that it was these funds that were actually ruling the world (see Wark 2006). Such high returns and such a rate of growth also motivated many dubious characters to get into this business as fund managers. Consequently, there were a number of bankruptcies and also cases of fraud and embezzlement. In the 1990s, they were partly responsible for more than one big financial crisis in Asia and Latin America. The biggest among them, Long-Term Capital Management (LTCM), was on the verge of bankruptcy in 1998 and threatened to cause a world financial crisis. Politicians have ever since tried to tighten the controls over hedge funds (see Wieczorek-Zeul 2005). However, this is a very difficult proposition, because many of these funds have their formal headquarters in offshore financial centers, where controls do not exist. In any case, as of 2007 there had been no success in this respect. The head of the banking supervision authority in Germany said hedge funds were "a big black hole" of international financial markets; they were "totally unsupervised"; that meant they constituted "a considerable danger for the stability of the financial system"; "no one knows what goes on there" (*Frankfurter Rundschau*, 6 October 2005).

Soros also reflected upon some general shortcomings of the global capitalist system. He identified two basic flaws in the market mechanism: (1) the built-in instabilities of international financial markets, and (2) the failure of politics — at both the national and international level. On the first flaw he wrote:

> [A]fter each bust bank managers become very cautious and resolve never to become so exposed again. But when they are again awash with liquidity and *desperate to put money to work*, a new cycle begins. The same pattern can be observed in international lending.... That is what happened in the great international lending boom of the 1970s. After the crisis of 1982 [the debt crisis] one would have thought that excessive lending would never happen again; yet it did happen again in Mexico in 1994 and yet again ... in the Asian crisis of 1997. (1998: 116; emphasis added)

With regard to the second flaw, he mentions the "inadequacy of international regulations" and "the prevailing antiregulatory mood." He wrote:

> National financial systems are in the charge of central banks and other financial authorities. By and large they do a good job; there has been no breakdown in the financial systems of the major industrial countries for several decades. But who is in charge of the international financial system? The international financial institutions and the national monetary authorities cooperate at times of crisis, but there is no international central bank, no international regulatory authority to compare with the institutions that exist on a national level. Nor is it easy to see how such institutions could be introduced. Both money and credit are intimately connected with issues of national sovereignty and national advantage and nations are disinclined to give up their sovereignty. (120)

With the benefit of hindsight it must be said today that Soros was wrong in his positive opinion on the work of the central banks. The so-called subprime credit crisis in the US real estate market — which unfolded in the summer of 2007 and subsequently dragged many banks, not only in the USA but also in Europe, to the brink of collapse (some, indeed, went bankrupt) — was caused partly by deficient supervision of the Fed. US banks, desperately looking for investment opportunities for huge amounts of liquid cash, had already in the 1990s begun lending large sums to people with no credit-worthiness. The Fed should have prevented this.

In this connection, Soros identified two asymmetries in the system that generate great instability. In highly industrialized countries, in cases of bankruptcy, laws tend to protect the debtors. Banks and other creditors can in such cases lose a lot of money. But in international lending business creditors enjoy great immunity; the risks are not too great. Insolvent debtor states, who cannot simply disband, are compelled by powerful forces in the international financial system — by the IMF, for instance — to repay their debts over a long period of time and to the extreme limit of their ability to pay. This immunity regularly leads to an overexpansion of international credit that in the long run becomes intolerable. Such a situation soon becomes a main cause of instability (Soros 1998: 122).

The other asymmetry is the fact that the economic great powers (the center) with their hard currencies can almost independently determine their own economic policies, but the countries of the periphery cannot. As we have seen, most of these countries officially or unofficially tie their currency to the US dollar. Fluctuations in the exchange rates of the hard currencies and in the interest rates in the center countries inflict exogenous shocks upon the economies of the periphery countries (123).

Already in 1998, Soros could see "anti-American, anti-IMF, anti-foreign resentment" coming up in all of Asia, including Japan. He feared that "elections in Indonesia could well produce a nationalistic, Islamic government inspired by [prime minister of Malaysia] Mahatir's ideas" (133). He believed he could "already discern the makings of the final crisis":

> It will be political in character. Indigenous political movements are likely to arise that will seek to expropriate the multinational corporations and "recapture" the national wealth. Some of them may succeed. ... Their success may then shake the confidence of the financial markets, engendering a self-reinforcing process on the downside. Whether it will happen on this occasion or the next one is an open question. (Soros 1998: 134)

Much of what Soros wrote is convincing, partly also trivial. An anti-American, anti-IMF mood, indeed an anti-globalization movement, is today very much stronger. In the rich countries hostile feelings towards immigrants from the periphery are very widespread. Islamists are fighting against everything Western. Bolivia has nationalized its gas fields. The "herd instinct" of investors and their fund managers, which he speaks of, and which causes capital to flee the periphery at the slightest sign of instability, is a fact. A year later, John Gray wrote in the same vein:

> The regime of laissez-faire [he meant neo-liberal globalization] is bound to trigger counter-movements which reject its constraints. Such movements — whether populist and xenophobic, fundamentalist or neo-communist — can achieve few of their goals; but they can still rattle to pieces the brittle structures that support global laissez-faire. (Gray 1999: 20)

However, Soros overestimates the weight of these undisputable facts. He makes three mistakes. Firstly, if the "flaws" in global capitalism are just flaws, then they can be remedied. They need not necessarily lead to a breakdown or a gradual disintegration of the system. Soros himself has written in his book a chapter on how the breakdown can be averted (1998: chapter 8). Other critics of globalization join Soros in demanding to this end a different architecture of the international financial system. He pillories market fundamentalism. But if this were the main evil, then one needed only to replace it with an internationally controlled world market. I contend that the problems are more than just flaws. Secondly, he does not clearly distinguish between *global* capitalism and capitalism in itself. Even if the former were to break down, the latter could live on — at least in North America and Western and Northern Europe, where fairly orderly conditions are likely to prevail. Thirdly, Soros is too fixated on the international financial system. If this collapsed, then, of course, large amounts of financial capital would be destroyed and lie idle in the center countries. There would also be a credit crunch. But this would not necessarily lead to a collapse of the *real* economy. For, in such a situation, the state would certainly step in to save the system. In the periphery countries business would have to manage without (or with less) foreign capital. While these conditions would definitely cause the growth rate to fall or even cause a severe recession in both parts of the world economy, it would not necessarily result in the end of capitalism, unless other factors undermined its viability. I discuss this possibility in the following sections.

## 2. Mass Unemployment and Workers' Discontent

One could accept low growth rates more easily were they not connected with high unemployment. For the affected people, unemployment is not only a material burden, it also injures their dignity. It weighs heavily on their minds, disturbs their emotional balance and their personal relationships. On top of it all, official unemployment figures usually largely conceal the true dimension of the misery. In February 1998, when the official unemployment figure in Germany rose to almost five million and the unemployment rate to almost 13 percent, Boxberger and Klimenta (1998: 77) wrote:

> If one also considers those people who have given up searching [for a job] but are actually willing to work, those who are undergoing vocational retraining for a short time, those who are reluctantly doing a part-time job or those who have been retired away early [against their will], then Germany has a shortage of over 8 million jobs. This amounts to an unemployment rate of 20%.

Underreporting of the unemployment rate, which serves the interests of the political class, is systematically done by means of a slanted definition of the terms "unemployed" and "employed." This is presumably the case in all industrialized countries, especially in countries where the official unemployment rate is particularly low. In the United States, for instance, a person is considered to be employed if he or she works just one hour a week for payment. And the only persons counted as unemployed are those who are actively looking for a job, not those who have stopped looking out of frustration (Stransfeld 1997; Greenhouse 2006). If one today wants to speak of a crisis of capitalism, then one should first of all highlight its unavoidable, system-determined inability to give all people fit for work the possibility to earn a living through work and in dignity.

A special aspect of this crisis is the widespread despair among the youth. In the United States, even according to the above-mentioned illogical, minimizing official method of tabulation, unemployment in the age group of 20 to 24 amounts to 8.2% — about twice the rate for the whole workforce (Greenhouse 2006) (In 2011, the official unemployment figure for the whole work force reached 9%). In Sweden, unemployment among the youth is particularly high, 25% (*International Herald Tribune*, 26 September 2006). And as of the end of September 2006, in Germany, officially 49,500 young people hadn't received any apprenticeship, the highest figure since the reunification of the country in 1990. Unofficially, that is, according to the German Federation of Trade Unions (DGB), the true figure was about 100,000 (*Frankfurter Rundschau*, 12 October 2006). A journalist commented on this bad situation for young people in an editorial: "It is sanctimonious when everywhere old men bemoan the dying out of the Germans" (Sperber 2006). In France, the underlying cause of the violent youth revolt in the fall of 2005 was unemployment and fear of the future.

As regards wages and quality of jobs, discontent, even outrage, is growing everywhere. In the mid-nineties, there was much talk about an American job miracle in the previous ten to fifteen years. However, at the same time, it was found that the majority of the recently created jobs were characterized by a (partly drastically) reduced social quality:

> There are regions in the United States where two adults gainfully employed with hourly wages of six dollars cannot manage to maintain a family at the lowest standard of living. Child and youth labor is very widespread there. Mind you, they do not work for increasing the pocket money, but just for satisfying the basic needs. For the same reason, more and more people can be found having two jobs working for 70 to 80 hours a week. (Stransfeld 1997)

On the situation in the United States in 2006 it has been reported that real wages of the majority of the workers have fallen despite satisfactory economic growth (see Krugman 2006; Luce and Guha 2006). It comes as no surprise, therefore, that the middle class feels this national economic growth personally as a descent down the social ladder. A union leader explained his dissatisfaction not only in terms of the material situation, namely, the "race to the bottom," more work for less pay, poor health care, etc. What roused his ire even more was the fact that the good jobs were disappearing and that highly qualified technicians were being compelled to take up lowly jobs in Burger King, Walmart, etc. (CNN, 3 September 2006; my personal notes).

Accounts of this kind also abound in Germany. Between 1991 and 2000 the net real wage per worker fell by 2.2% (Müller 2005: 405). With respect to taxes, even since 1970 employees in subordinate positions have been carrying a higher tax burden than people earning other kinds of income and companies taken together (see Afheldt 2003: 38). In 2006, the Federal Statistical Office of Germany confirmed the trade unions' claim that real standard wages in Germany had been falling over the past few years (*Frankfurter Rundschau*, 29 July 2006). And the one-euro jobs that recipients of Unemployment Benefit II (Hartz IV) must accept gnaw at the sense of dignity of highly qualified unemployed people.

According to Krugman (2006), in the United States this "disconnect" — wage stagnation or fall in real wages despite satisfactory economic growth — had already begun in the 1970s. And employers started cutting financial assistance given to their employees in the 1980s. Isn't it logical to think that the explanation for such a long-lasting trend lies in the system itself—to be precise, in an objective turn within the system?

The sluggishness of economic growth alone cannot be the cause of these phenomena or of jobless growth. There are structural causes underlying them. That is why not all workers who are laid off in a recession are again employed in the next upswing. In the United States, during the recession of 2000–2001, 50% of the jobs lost were eliminated for good. And more than half of the jobs created since the end of the recession were part-time jobs. Permanent jobs are being eliminated at record rates. To make matters worse, those who find a permanent job have to accept wages that are on average 57% lower than what they earned before. The number of insecure freelance jobs is continuously rising. And all have to accept a longer working day and lower pay. These phenomena, originally a "Yankee virus," have been spreading for a few years now in Europe. In the Japanese corporate world layoffs have now become socially acceptable. In 2003, a record number of people there committed suicide due to despair over job loss and a high level of debt. It is the picture of a "Darwinian job market" (Foroohar and Emerson 2004). This miserable condition is the unavoidable result of a structural change in the world economy, the result of increasing worldwide competition, a consequence of globalization. "The ripple effects caused by the supply shock of the entry of hundreds of millions of Chinese workers into the global economy has changed the way American workers benefit from trade" (Luce and Guha 2006).

Since globalization, as I have argued in chapter VII, is an inevitable result of the development of capitalism, the inability of this system to solve the problems and remedy the sufferings described above is inherent in the *system itself.* That means, in order to remedy the "Darwinian" character of the job market, we have to do away with the market system of offering labor. This means ultimately that the miserable conditions cannot be overcome without changing the system.

While dealing with this theme we have to discuss two more factors. We must not forget that until the mid-seventies, the highly developed European economies recruited large numbers of foreign workers. The difference between then and today, when job seekers from developing countries are highly unwelcome, is the difference in the productivity of labor. The various developments in technology, but also in company management techniques (for instance, outsourcing of production to low-wage countries) that have eliminated millions of once-respectable jobs are not just products of human inventiveness, but also of the competition principle of capitalism. Apart from the fact that he *wants* to maximize profit, no entrepreneur *can* today forgo the use of labor-saving technologies and rationalization opportunities out of love for his employees if he does not want to go bank-rupt. It is not without good reason that nowadays in business adminis-tration courses one also hears lectures on "retrenchment productivity" (*Frankfurter Rundschau*, 25 January 2006). An entrepreneur cannot pay his employees wages that are higher than what he must pay. But without the competition principle capitalism would not be capitalism. The econ-omy would then be a planned economy — be it a private-monopolistic one or a state-capitalistic one. How inescapable, how objectively compelling this logic is becomes apparent in the failed struggle of the German trade unions for a 35-hour workweek, which was intended to defend or even create jobs. Today, even the already attained 38-hour workweek is being annulled. In France, the 35-hour workweek, which was enforced through a law just a few years ago, is again being called into question.

This trend has recently also reached the finance sector, that is, banks and insurance companies. In spite of sky-high profits, they are cutting thou-sands of jobs in order to stay competitive or to avert hostile takeovers. With the help of information technology, they can *industrialize* many processes in their business. "Millions of money transfers from account to account of customers are now being carried out by a single automatized bank fac-tory. . . . Other services are even being bought in India" (Pauly 2006).

## 3. Unfulfilled Promises of Innovations

In chapter VII I presented my doubts about the Keynesian ideas for solv-ing the problem discussed above. Now we must also examine the ideas of Schumpeter, the father of the dynamic "entrepreneur," according to whom innovations and creative destruction drive economic development forward (see chapter III, section 2).

Schumpeter's concept of "innovation" is particularly relevant in phases of economic stagnation. For this reason, since a few years ago we have been hearing that the government should strongly promote innovation. And politicians in power are doing just that. The objective is to enable ideas to quickly become marketable products.

It was, therefore, probably not purely by chance that the American professor of economics William J. Baumol published his book *The Free-Market Innovation Machine* in 2002. It is a theoretical book, a loud praise of free-market economy and a resistance to ideas of state intervention in the economy. The "growth miracle" and the increase in prosperity in the past 150 years prompt him to see the capitalist economy as "a machine, whose primary product is economic growth." "The point is," he wrote, "once capitalism was in place and fully operational, a flow of innovations and the consequent rise in productivity and per capita gross domestic product were to be expected" (Baumol 2002: 1f.). Up to here, this is Schumpeter pure and simple. But the author revises Schumpeter's thoughts slightly in order to bring it up to date. He wrote: "What differentiates the proto-type capitalist economy most sharply from all other economic systems is free market pressures that force firms into a continuing process of innovation, *because it becomes a matter of life and death for many of them*" (viii; emphasis in the original). It is no longer the dynamic entrepreneur who is innovating, but a firm, a corporation. And while Schumpeter's entrepreneur — unlike a publican — spots a commercially relevant opportunity in autonomously occurring scientific, technological, or geographical developments and tries to make *extra profits* by being the first to introduce an innovation, for Baumol's firm this becomes a "matter of life and death." According to Baumol, for a long time now it has been mainly the few big corporations (oligopolies) active and dominant in the high-tech branch that provide the steady stream of innovations. They do not wait for an innovation opportunity to open up for them; they themselves take care of the matter. And they have routinized innovation activities that are a regular — even normal — part of their overall business.

Baumol also has an explanation for this development: In oligopolistic competition it is no longer the price but innovation that is the main weapon of competition. Every corporation tries to stay one step ahead of its competitors. Dissemination of the successful innovations is guaranteed, because patent holders let others, even their competitors, use their patents against payment of license fees. This accelerates the replacement of obsolete products and production processes with modern and more efficient ones.

According to Schumpeterians like Baumol, this is the main explanation for the growth achievements of capitalism. Now automatically a question arises: Why is it then that for many years now most of the highly developed economies have suffered from weak growth? After all, in the present time far more research and development are being carried out than ever before, and the stream of patent applications has by no means ebbed! On the contrary.

In chapter III, section 2, we have seen that in history a few great innovations stood at the beginning of the first phase of a long wave — i.e., in the phase of accelerated growth. If we see the thirty-seven years since the mid-seventies as the second phase (the phase of slowed-down growth) of the current long wave — as some economists have done by labeling the economic situation since 1974 as a stagnating phase (for instance, Hein

1998) — then the onset of a new long wave with a new phase of accelerated growth is long overdue! One should then be allowed to expect that some groundbreaking innovations give a new strong push to the economies of the highly developed capitalist countries. This, however, has not happened so far. Why? Are such innovations lacking?

Here it is necessary to differentiate between innovations and *epochal* innovations. Baumol speaks of a *continuing flow* of innovations, the production of which has been routinized, whereas the long-wave thesis speaks of technological *revolutions*. Innovations to which the thesis attributes the role of triggering the first phase of a long wave are epoch-making inventions such as the steam engine. There are also great innovations that have, of course, not triggered the first phase of a long wave, but have without doubt made in their day a strong contribution to economic growth: airplanes, photography with small cameras, telephone, radio, TV, etc.

Can we expect in the present day similar successes from innovations of this kind? I see some problems in this regard. (1) Since the nineteenth century, the economies of the highly developed industrialized countries have become so big that one or two innovations — as groundbreaking as they may be — will not be able to help them out of the present stagnating phase. For instance, the mobile phone, a truly epoch-making innovation, has not been able to do so. Mass unemployment persists. (2) The products of routinized innovation activities are for the most part unimportant. They cannot give a big shove to the *economy as a whole*. The continuous flow of new car models can be taken as an example of this kind of innovation. (3) Great technical achievements such as supersonic airplanes (Concorde), space travel, and magnetic-levitation trains (Transrapid) are not innovations in the Schumpeterian sense. They simply are not profitable. Concorde flights (which saved only a few hours' flight time) were discontinued, space flights have to be entirely financed by the state, and only one piece of the highly subsidized Transrapid could be sold so far.

The last three of the innovations mentioned above were desired by the state. So one may say that they would not have been tried if the state had not partly or fully financed them. But there are also examples of innovations that failed on cost grounds, although they had been attempted entirely as private enterprise, e.g., Motorola's venture to offer a mobile telephone service that would enable communication by phone between any two points on the globe (for instance, from the North Pole to the South Pole). The UMTS (Universal Mobile Telecommunication System) project, for which private telecommunication companies paid hundreds of millions of euros, did not prove to be a resounding success. Firstly, many of the companies had to give up the venture due to financial stringency. Secondly, it took a long time before the high-cost handsets with the required functions and qualities could be brought to the market. And thirdly, using them is still fraught with difficulties. That is why inventors are already thinking of a successor technology. Even a much more modest innovation that has already been implemented, the crossing of the English Channel by means of trains plying through a tunnel, is regularly making losses.

I can give an explanation for the commercial failure of some of the greatest technical innovations of the present time. The gain in speed through transition from the horse-drawn carriage to the train was enormous. The gain in freedom resulting from the invention of the automobile was also great. That is why these two inventions were very popular and hence also commercially successful. The same applies to the gain in time and comfort resulting from the transition from propeller-driven airplanes to jet planes. But such great gains could not be had from the Concorde, space travel (one-week travel costs US$20 million), and the Transrapid. This can also be expressed in terms of economic theory: the marginal utility of an additional saved hour attained through a Concorde flight was too little for most customers. I presume something similar can be said of most of the big technical innovations of the present time.

In my view, the days when innovations could give a strong boost to the economy as a whole, to employment and hence to prosperity, are over. The LCD and plasma TV sets, for instance, whose only advantage seems to be more air behind the screen, may, of course, soon entirely replace cathode-ray-tube TV sets. But through such replacements no additional jobs would be created.

Innovations in the area of production processes — be they of the technical kind, such as conveyor belts, or innovations in management, such as just-in-time supply — are mostly of labor-saving nature. They are profitable for the pioneers for as long as the competitors have not imitated them. But the biggest problem today is mass unemployment, which only increases with additional productivity gains. Also, outsourcing of production to low-wage countries should be included in the category of management innovation. No jobs are destroyed thereby, but no new ones are created either. Existing jobs are only redistributed through this process.

There are product innovations that promise something of vital importance, for instance, innovations in the area of medicine. But recent such innovations — e.g., an AIDS therapy or a device for magnetic resonance imaging (MRI) — are also very expensive. For this reason they cannot become such a big sales success as the railway or the automobile was in its day, especially not in the Third World.

As we all know, if the current industrial civilization is to survive, innovations in the area of renewable and at the same time environmentally friendly resources are very important. A number of such innovations already exist: e.g., power generation from sunshine, wind, etc. If these innovations could fulfill the expectations, they would not only solve all our environmental and resource problems, but they would also make unimaginably immense economic growth possible. For we would then get from the sun alone 15,000 times more energy than we consume today. In an earlier book, I examined these expectations in detail and explained why I think they are illusions. And I have explained why these innovations, known for decades now and continuously developed, are feasible but not economically viable (Sarkar 1999: chapter 4). Suffice it to say here that India — rich in sunshine and wind, but poor in oil — in the face of rapidly increasing oil prices, does not put its hopes on solar and wind energy to solve its energy problems, but on the construction of new nuclear and coal-fired power plants. These innovations might perhaps be used in the future in some form or other when the era of fossil and nuclear energy is over. But they will not make an economy possible that will still be growing at a steady rate.

Innovations that can, for whatever reason, successfully push themselves through in the market create in any case at least some additional jobs — even if they do not expand the market but only replace old products and production processes with new ones. For in the process of creative destruction old factories and other installations have to be torn down and new ones built, which generates, among other things, demand for labor. This can also be regarded as a virtually Keynesian method, for it resembles "digging holes in the ground and then filling them up."

## 4. The Crisis of the Welfare State

The process of establishing the welfare state, which had started in the nineteenth century, also had political motives. Otto von Bismarck's social legislation of the 1880s was meant to "let meeting the immediate economic demands of the workers appear as a gift of the state and thus to keep them from engaging in political struggle" (Streisand 1976: 223). After World War II, the establishment and expansion of the welfare state in the rich industrial societies contributed a lot to the acceptance of capitalism.

But for several years now, it is being said that in times of chronic sluggish growth, mass unemployment, globalized competition for location of industries, acute financial crisis of the state, aging of societies, etc., existing social benefits cannot be maintained anymore, at least not at their current level. Spokespersons of the ruling classes everywhere are demanding a downscaling (euphemistically called "reform") of the welfare state. The cutbacks in the welfare state that have so far been undertaken in Germany have been justified with the assertion that this had to be done in order to preserve the welfare state. But as Bishop Wolfgang Huber, chairperson of the Council of the Evangelical Church in Germany, felt compelled to remark in 2004: "The insecurity with regard to the future prospects, which was the starting point of the reform measures, has not been overcome through the now adopted reform package. The insecurity has rather increased." On the low number of children in German society Huber said: "I feel it as scandalous that in our society begetting a child is perceived as risking poverty" (both quotes from an interview with *Frankfurter Rundschau*, 12 January 2004). In a report on the "social plumbers," *Der Spiegel* (29 August 2005) wrote about poor patients: "Then, they look at the doctor as he writes the prescription and say they don't have the money for their own share of the price." On neglected street children the author wrote that the social worker "believes they can be saved. The welfare state has not given up this idea. But it is distancing itself from it. The welfare state is busy trying to save itself."

My German readers know all too well the disputes in their country over "reforms." So let us take another country as example: the United Kingdom and its public health system, the National Health Service (NHS). It is a complex system, very different from the German one. The state finances and guarantees the service. However, in the recent past, privatization and the market system with competition have been introduced in order to reduce costs, all of which has had a negative effect on the service. British newspapers often print complaints about the deplorable state of affairs in the NHS, for instance the extremely long waiting time for operations. Medical centers, all of which get a budget, have increasing deficits. In 2005, the total deficit of the health system as a whole came to £1.27 billion. In reaction to that, 15,000 jobs were cut (figures from *The Times*, 8 June 2006).

As in Germany, there are general accusations of welfare abuse, for instance, against handicapped people, who receive more aid than unemployed people seeking a job. One criticizes, for example, the fact that a large number of people who only suffer from stress or some mental disturbance apply for and are granted disability allowance. The majority of these people are purportedly only unemployed. The disability allowance swallows up about £12 billion a year and is one of the heaviest burdens on the welfare state. According to the reformers, these are unbearable costs for the state, and they must therefore be reduced (data from *The Independent*,

16 January 2006). All this is clearly an aspect of the crisis of capitalism. The pride of being a "social market economy" (the American economy never was one) is gone and so is the broad acceptance of capitalism after World War II. What is being criticized, in political discussions and demonstrations, in newspaper articles and letters to the editor, is not just the current government policy or the recent mass retrenchments of workers in companies that have made huge profits, but also — and increasingly — the capitalist system itself.

Many leftists explain these and other negative developments — for example, the unyielding attitude of employers at collective wage negotiations — by pointing out that since the fall of the Berlin Wall (1989), neither the state nor the capitalists have needed to show much consideration for the interests of the working class as there is no other system as an alternative to capitalism. This, in my view, is too simple an explanation. Bismarck's social legislation also came at a time when there was no alternative system. But there was very much a labor movement, which was gradually growing and gaining strength, and an anti-capitalist social democracy with an alternative, i.e., socialist, vision.

There are therefore two questions to be asked: (1) Why is today's labor movement weak? And (2) Why doesn't social democracy — whichever name it might be using — have an alternative vision anymore? One actually expects the opposite when capitalism is in crisis — in the sense that it has lost its ability to solve the various problems and crises, and in the sense that its acceptance among the people is dwindling. I shall discuss this matter in the following section.

## 5. The Crisis of Social Democracy

When, in the 1890s, Eduard Bernstein started his revisionist criticism of Marxism and the old revolutionary program of the German Social Democratic Party (SPD), he could easily convince most of the contemporary rank-and-file Social Democrats. Anyhow, in their praxis, they were anything but revolutionary. Leszek Kolakowski described the reasons for this as follows: "When Bernstein was writing, the German working class had behind it a long period of increasing real wages and the successful struggle for welfare measures and a shorter working day. It also had a powerful political organization. ... The actual experience of the German working class by no means supported the theory that its position was essentially hopeless and could not be reformed under capitalism" (1978: 445). The idea that socialism could be gradually achieved through parliamentary reform politics seemed plausible.

From the end of World War II to the mid-1970s (but also many years thereafter), the working class could, through much struggle, achieve improvements in their material situation. However, before the SPD could win power, it had to adopt in 1959 a revised basic party manifesto, the so-called Godesberg Program, in which it dropped traditional social democratic positions. "If socialization of the means of production was until now undisputed, at least as an element in the party's program, now public ownership was merely to play a role as a 'legitimate form of public control.' ... In contrast, it was expressly stated that private ownership of means of production has a right to be protected and promoted" (von Freyberg et al. 1977: 359). On this new path, the SPD was, of course, able to come to power in 1969, but it was neither able nor willing to use this power for progressively achieving socialism, but only for a more efficient and more social management of capitalism by means of Keynesian economic policies. Social Democrats did not speak of class struggle anymore. On the contrary, from now on they only spoke of social partnership. The unions, the great majority of whose members and, especially, officials were (and still are) members of the SPD, went along with it.

A social democracy that had undergone such a change was a great help for capitalists, who let the SPD rule in relative peace until 1982. And this social democracy was also very successful in terms of the interests of the employees in subordinate positions (the term "working class" was seldom used, if at all). It was so successful that the free-market liberals (Free Democratic Party, or FDP) as well as the conservatives (Christian Democratic Union, or CDU, and Christian Social Union, or CSU) with their slogan "social market economy" were able to run the country in coalition with the SPD.

This harmony led a theoretician of the FDP, Ralf Dahrendorf, to believe, now that almost everyone had become a Social Democrat, the successful social democracy no longer had a special task, and that, therefore, the Social Democratic century was over, etc. (Dahrendorf 1983). This meant that the SPD could have readily dissolved itself. It was, of course, a sort of "crisis" of the SPD the party, but not of social democracy, which was highly successful.

But the crises of the 1970s — the end of the fixed exchange rates, inflation, stagnation, recession, high unemployment — put an end to this harmony. Not everyone was a Social Democrat anymore. Social democracy slid into a crisis. The Social Democrats could have again seen in the problems, crises, and social brutalities of the following neo-liberal era a special task for themselves, namely, to struggle to defend the interests of employees in subordinate positions and other disadvantaged groups. But when, in the 1990s, after a long period of conservative neo-liberal rule, they were again voted into power in many leading industrialized countries, they had already lost their enthusiasm for social democratic policy. They had adapted to the new Zeitgeist in order to make themselves fit for winning power and staying in power. So they accepted neo-liberal globalization as something that could not be changed. To be in power became now their highest goal. "Being in opposition is garbage," SPD president Franz Müntefering once said.

I have briefly described Clinton's policy in the United States (in chapter VI, section 2). Let us now take the Labour Party of the United Kingdom as another example. In the beginning it wanted to achieve nothing more than to get deputies elected to the parliament, who would be prepared to protect the trade unions from possible disadvantageous changes in law. In 1918, however, the party gave itself a new charter, in Article 4 of which it committed itself to promote "common ownership of the means of production, distribution and exchange." For many party members the article was a declaration of commitment to the goal of socialism. Clement Attlee's Labour government (1945–1951) implemented a far-reaching reform program that aimed at creating a more egalitarian society through state intervention. Party members hoped this would lead to the creation of a society that the manifesto of the party called a "socialist commonwealth." For this purpose, the Labour Party nationalized 20 percent of the economy and created a welfare state that gave the poorest members of society a degree of security unknown until then. These measures necessitated a taxation level that in effect redistributed wealth.

However, Labour could not pursue this policy for long. The conservatives managed to win back the support of the middle class, which they had lost during the war, and Labour lost three consecutive general elections in the 1950s. The hour of the revisionists had come. They, of course, could not annul Article 4, but they succeeded in both making the party less class-conscious and reducing the weight of state control in its program. With such a revision of its policies, the party could again win elections in the 1960s and 1970s.

The loss of power again in 1979 and the long lean period until 1997 led to further revisions of Labour policies. In 1995, at a party congress, Tony Blair finally succeeded in pushing through a revision of Article 4 with the support of 85 percent of the delegates. The new version of Article 4 includes, among other things:

> [W]e work for a dynamic economy, serving the public interest,
> in which the enterprise of the market and the rigor of

> competition are joined with the forces of partnership and
> cooperation to produce the wealth ... and the opportunity for
> all to work and prosper, with a thriving private sector and high
> quality public services, where those undertakings essential to
> the common good are either owned by the public or account-
> able to them; a just society, which ... promotes equality of
> opportunity ... (quoted in Fielding 2003: 77)

Three points stand out in this passage. (1) Private entrepreneurship, free market, and strong competition are essential for a dynamic economy, (2) public services need not necessarily be offered by companies in public ownership, and (3) equality only means equality of opportunities; the final result may well be or remain inequality. All the rest are empty phrases. This is New Labour.

The left wing of the party was enraged. They thought "Labour had now abandoned any pretence of being a socialist party" and "openly embraced capitalism and the free market." A conservative newspaper commented: "Blair buries socialism" (78).

Steven Fielding, however, has little understanding for the left wing's outcry of indignation, for "the new clause changed little of substance. Labor had long before effectively embraced capitalism and accepted the merits of competition." The revision of Article 4 only aimed at making the point clear to the voters (2003: 78, 75).

The policies pursued by New Labour after they came to power in 1997 could not therefore be all too different from those of the previous conservative governments. Friendly observers of all persuasions and many party members thought as early as 1997 that New Labour was merely watered-down Thatcherism. Some called their program "Thatcherism Mark 2."

Dahrendorf's view mentioned above had very soon proved to be a mistake. But now, since almost all Social Democrats have become neo-liberal, the social democratic century seems to have really come to an end — not because it triumphed, as Dahrendorf suggested, but because it can no longer function. One last attempt to save social democracy, that is, to give it a meaningful task, consisted in trying to rein in the world financial market, where many a crisis had its origin, and creating a new international financial architecture. In the months between 1998 and 1999, when he was finance minister in Germany, Oskar Lafontaine tried to do that. He failed because of the opposition of the United States, governed at the time by (Social) Democrat Clinton, and the big players at the world financial market, whose power had increased enormously as a result of globalization (see Richter 2004).

I have already explained why Keynesianism could not function anymore. But why did European Social Democrats have to scale down the welfare state? I have stated above the reasons given by those who are pursuing this policy. Are these only pretexts? The economies of the rich industrialized countries have, after all, not shrunk! Quite on the contrary. Generally speaking, with a few exceptions, they have grown every year, albeit modestly. Have Social Democrats betrayed their voters?

I believe many people in the left make it too easy for themselves when they say: There is enough money around, it must only be distributed fairly; one need only look at the enormous profits of the companies, etc. At the end of chapter V, I explained the social and political factors that led to a decrease in voter support for social democracy, especially among the growing middle class. At the time, traditional social democracy may have become an inadequate political program for getting a majority in parliament, but the social democratic *parties* did not want to dissolve themselves. Nor did they want to give up their by now only and real ambition, namely, to be the governing party. Then happened what seems to be a rule in ordinary politics. Fielding wrote:

> As is well known, the British electoral system promotes emulation between the two main parties; to win a commons majority they usually have to compete for the same small number of electors in the same handful of marginal constituencies. This tends to encourage the promotion of policies designed to appeal to very similar voter types. The success of one party in this regard causes the other to investigate the reasons and then incorporate any lessons into its strategy. (Fielding 2003: 8)

This explains New Labour's program. This also explains why in Germany both big parties want to be the party of the center. And this is the explanation for the policies of the New Democrats under Clinton as well as for the policies of the French Socialist Party. To be the opposition is garbage. Pure opportunism is the dominant characteristic of mass parties.

Those Social Democrats who were not prepared to drastically change (betray) their political stance in order to win power or stay in power left the party feeling let down. The decreasing numbers of new entrants could not compensate for the deceased and resigning members. Between 1990 and 2005, membership in the German SPD fell sharply from over 900,000 to below 600,000 (*Frankfurter Rundschau*, 13 May 2006). The Labour Party's membership peaked (almost 900,000) in 1951 when, under Attlee's presidency, it was still viewed as a socialist party. Under his revisionist successors membership fell almost continuously. In 2001, it barely had 300,000 members (Fielding 2003: 23).

One can now ask why the crisis of traditional social democracy and of social democratic parties should be viewed as an aspect of the crisis of capitalism. As mentioned above, the revisionist concept of social democracy initiated by Bernstein and completed in the Godesberg Program of the German SPD and the social democratic parties that changed themselves accordingly have been, for a long time now, a great support for the capitalist system. Now that these parties have embraced neo-liberal ideology and policies, the previous kind of support does not exist anymore. In other words, they have lost their function to channel anti-capitalist protests and rebellions into forms that do not basically question capitalism. How successfully social democracy fulfilled this function in the past can be ascertained by studying the development of the student movement of 1968, the ecological movement, the Greens, etc. Many activists of these initially rebellious movements landed soon in the various parliaments and became professional politicians, even ministers. Nowadays, this does not function so smoothly. Today's social democracy cannot absorb the anti-globalization movement, not even its lighter version. In Germany, the anger of the losers in the struggle over the distribution of the GDP cake and of workers in general is also directed against the SPD. In the United Kingdom, demonstrations against the Iraq War were at once demonstrations against the Labour government. In 2005, the French Socialist Party was helpless in the face of the violent riots of marginalized youth in the satellite towns. In Germany, even the Left Party (*Die Linke*) — born through a fusion of social-democratized former communists from East Germany and left-leaning former SPD members, who want to return to traditional social democratic policies — cannot fully control and/or absorb the anti-capitalists in and outside their ranks. In France, in the presidential election of 2002, so many left-leaning voters refused to vote for the candidate of the Socialist Party, Lionel Jospin, that he could not even qualify for the second ballot.

## 6. Economic Compulsions, Limitations, and Temptations

In any society, one can distribute only so much as can be produced (and in the case of imperialist societies, additionally, only so much as can be pillaged). So long as there was a rapidly growing mass of affluence-goods and -services to distribute, for instance, in the long boom of the post-war years, capitalism was very successful. But for years now the pie has been growing very slowly. Nevertheless, the question remains why the slowly growing

GDP is not being distributed in such a way that the net real income of all workers and pensioners as well as the real social benefits given to the poor also increase — at least equally slowly. We have seen above that in reality the real wages of even unionized workers are falling. There are reports that say even university graduates in their thirties and forties cannot live off only one job in the profession they trained in and therefore have to moonlight to make ends meet. In addition to this, job insecurity makes it impossible for them to think of starting a family (see, e.g., Bonstein and Theile 2006).

Apart from the already mentioned factors that cause the suffering of employees in subordinate positions — namely, the increasing degree of automation, globalization, limits to demand, etc. — we should also consider some other factors.

We have seen earlier that the policy objective of fighting inflation conflicts with the policy objective of creating jobs. We saw that most economists seem to think that insofar as high inflation is caused by rising costs, it is only increasing wage demands of workers that is to be blamed. But if this were the only cause, then one could think that it is no big problem, because with increasing automation the number of working hours needed for a given amount of output is decreasing.

Rising costs can also come from increasing raw materials prices. Indeed, for some time now world market prices of some key raw materials such as oil, gas, and copper have been steeply rising. There are three kinds of causes of this: (1) Increasing demand from booming emerging industrial countries (China, India, Brazil, etc.); (2) the inability of suppliers to increase supply or to increase it at the same tempo as the tempo of rising demand— the easily accessible reserves of nonrenewable resources are after all limited; and (3) the increasing extraction and production costs. For (2) and (3) there can also be *purely geological and/or geographical* grounds. Insofar as power plants use oil or gas as fuel, electricity prices also rise. Since energy prices partly determine the price of any product — including all services and raw materials — there is today a reason for rising inflation rates, which cannot be eliminated, at least not so long as the world economy continues to grow. In the United Kingdom, for instance, within a year, households have had to accept gas price increases (along with electricity price increases) of up to 47 percent as the result of increasing demand and falling domestic production (*The Guardian*, 23 August 2006). The Germans have to pay mounting sums to Arabs, Russians, Norwegians, Chileans, etc., for the import of oil, gas, copper, etc. But, at the same time, due to strong international competition, they cannot demand rising prices for their export products, such as cars. Therefore net real wages and social benefits have to be reduced and jobs have to be either rationalized away or relocated in cheap-labor countries — especially because, in capitalism, profit margins of companies cannot be allowed to fall excessively. Moreover, it is simply true that in the era of neo-liberal globalization capital is not only very powerful but can also flee very quickly.

Nowadays, another factor is contributing to inflationary pressure. Until recently, the rock-bottom wages in China — "the factory of the world" — were a very important reason for the fact that inflation in the developed industrialized countries was negligible. In the meantime, however, wages are rising also in China. Chinese firms that manufacture finished products for Euro-American companies are now demanding up to 10% more in new contracts. Similar things are happening in India's IT branch, where wages and salaries are increasing at the rate of 8% a year. In Bangladesh in 2006, the world's lowest-paid garment workers went on strike, demonstrated, and set fire to some factories — and obtained wage increases as a result. Ultimately, this leads to price increases for consumers in the First World. In July 2006, the inflation rate in the US and the UK, when annualized, came to 4.8% and 5% respectively (without considering the steeper increases in energy and metal prices). The inflation rate is going up in the Eurozone as well (all data from: Foroohar and Emerson 2004, and *International Herald Tribune*, 24 August 2006).

If now the central banks decide to apply the brakes in order to fight inflation by limiting credit (as is well known, the European Central Bank does not want to tolerate inflation over 2%), then that will negatively impact growth, employment, wages and social benefits, and also profits.

As we have seen above, the Schumpeterian entrepreneur hardly exists anymore. The players who nowadays drive the economy are mainly large investors (including shareholder groups such as investment and pension funds) and top managers. These two groups through their economic philosophy and behavior contributed much to the crisis of capitalism — at least to its acceptance crisis. Unlike traditional family enterprises directed by a patriarch, who, conscious of the future, thinks (or used to think) with a long-term perspective, today's investors, focused on the present, think only in terms of short periods. Their thinking is dominated by shareholder value, current share prices, quarterly reports, and dividend rates. They force top executives of their companies to think alike and act accordingly. The latter, in turn, have only one thought in mind: to become rich quickly, sometimes even at the cost of the company they are working for. They do not flinch from graft and embezzlement. A large part of their compensation is paid as share options, which leads them to try by all means — legal and illegal — to drive up the price of their company's shares (for examples of corruption, embezzlement, and illegal activities in large companies see Stiglitz 2003, Scheuch and Scheuch 2001). A tried and tested way of pushing up the share price is to lay off a large number of employees, which signals to the stock exchange that the company's profit margin will soon increase. No other business practice of the corporations enrages society more. People do not understand how it can be that the more employees a company lays off the higher is the rise in its share prices. But this is easy to understand when one sees it is part of the basic logic of capitalism, as are also the constraints arising from technological developments and possibilities of rationalization.

## 7. Crisis of Capitalism in the Third World

When discussing the crisis of capitalism one should not restrict oneself to the situation in the rich industrialized countries. In the era of globalization all walls are falling. There are no protected islands anymore, and very few effective boundaries. For years now, all rich countries have experienced a surge of economic refugees from the poor countries. Hundreds of them drown while crossing the sea. Didn't its protagonists say globalization would "lift all boats"? The Spaniards can only manage to protect their exclaves in Morocco, Ceuta and Melilla with walls and barbed wire. But it will not be cheap to fully fence off all rich countries with barbed wire. In addition to all their economic crises, people in industrialized countries now also have a moral crisis. The poor people of the world are no longer quietly suffering their fate in the slums of distant countries. They are literally getting too close for the comfort of the prosperous citizens of the world, including those of the Third World. But how can they be kept at a distance without shooting? In Brazil, for years now, hired killers (also police officers) have been murdering street children on behalf of the rich. Should one then live in gated and guarded neighborhoods, like the gated communities one can see in some large cities of the Third World? The United States is already protecting itself by means of a wall along the border with Mexico. What is so surprising in the matter of economic refugees is that they do not only come from destitute countries or from countries devastated by war, but they also come, in the thousands, from so-called emerging industrialized countries — Mexico, India, China, etc. — and Eastern European countries such as Ukraine. Nor do they all come from extremely poor families, but mostly from families that still have some money or property with which they finance the ventures of their sons, sometimes also of their daughters. These streams of unwelcome economic refugees give the lie to the ideologues of global capitalism who talk so much of growing prosperity, of globalization "lifting all boats."

I consider this phenomenon to be a very important aspect of the crisis of capitalism, for in capitalism there is no acceptable solution to it. This proves that capitalist development is failing. At best, it can give a minority some prosperity — in India some 200 million out of 1.1 billion people; in China perhaps 300 million. As the Indian cabinet minister of urban development Kamal Nath said recently, in India two-thirds of the population still has no access to energy (he obviously meant electricity); they burn cow dung and wood (BBC, 2 September 2006; my notes). Very often, when Chinese or Indian companies need land for their factories or for extracting raw materials, they encounter opposition. They must regularly use violence to forcibly evict farmers from their plots. And occasionally they let the police shoot down a few dozen rebels, as happened at the end of 2006 in Nandigram (West Bengal, India). In this particular case, the villagers ultimately succeeded in preventing the building of a big car factory. How much exploitation and how much violence can capitalism perpetrate without jeopardizing its existence? Can capitalism peacefully solve inevitably increasing conflicts over distribution in an overpopulated world?

The crises in the Third World described in the previous chapters did not take place in extremely poor states, but in emerging market countries. Thanks to their good reputation, these emerging regions managed to attract from the First World hundreds of billions of dollars in credit and investments. Each time that precisely was the main cause of crisis. They became too dependent on a continuous inflow of credit and capital from rich countries. Not that the savings rate in these emerging countries was too low. In Thailand, for instance, it was actually very high, 34% (Henderson 1998: 85). But that was not high enough for the ambition of the elite groups in the country. This is an aspect of the crisis of capitalism that lies in the realm of psychology and philosophy of life. Capitalism is premised on greed, and it fuels greed. It was not just the businesspeople of the countries in question who wanted to become multimillionaires as quickly as possible. The average middle-class citizen wanted, in regard to consumption, to catch up with the average middle-class American as soon as possible. The domestic capital accumulation was not sufficient to fulfill these growing wishes; the economic subjects had no patience and they had also no colonies to pillage. A high foreign debt level and high dependence on inflow of foreign capital were preprogrammed.

It is one of the absurdities of globalized neo-liberal capitalism that developing countries, whose companies need foreign capital, have to keep large amounts of money in hard currency as reserves in the First World countries — mostly in the United States and mostly in the form of low-yield government bonds. Without these reserves of their state, the entrepreneurs of the developing countries would not have good credit ratings. But then these large sums are not available for development work, e.g., for necessary investments in education, infrastructure, etc. This is bad for the economy of the countries in question, but good for the state and the economy of the USA getting, in this way, very cheap loans. Kurt Hübner wrote:

> For some years now, the world finds itself in a situation that contradicts all standard macroeconomic theories, namely, that poor countries make net capital exports to rich countries.
> Exactly speaking, it is the United States that let its twin deficits [i.e., the current account deficit and the budget deficit] be financed by the emerging industrial countries of the periphery.

Hübner deems this "an extremely fragile world political situation" (Hübner 2006).

It is correct that an important cause of the never-ending poverty and the increasing number of starving people in the Third World is population growth. However, it is also a truism that in such countries children — especially two or three sons — are considered by poor people as their only old-age and health insurance. It is a problem that cannot be solved within capitalism. The affluent of the Third World and the state controlled by them are not prepared to take up the responsibility for finding a satisfactory solution to this problem. But the hope of the poor that their children will look after them in their old age has in the meantime largely become an illusion. Children who are unemployed or are extremely poor are useless as an old-age insurance, and sons who make a living through small-time crime are a problem, not a help.

Although in the First World the number of children is diminishing, the situation there has a certain similarity to that in the Third World. But, in contrast to the Third World, in the First World countries like Germany, it is the politicians, not the people, who think that more children would solve the problem of old age security. They expect that working young people will pay contributions to the statutory pension fund. But also here more children is not the solution. For many of them will remain unemployed or will work in insecure jobs with low pay, from which they will hardly pay any contributions to the statutory pension fund. One cannot be happy if more children are born. Future pensioners will be compelled to forgo more and more of the pension they are entitled to so that the growing burden of social and unemployment benefit payments to the young generation can be borne.

For some Third World countries that are not emerging industrial econ-omies there is another source of capital: their rich natural resources. But this is not always a boon for them, even when the prices of raw materi-als go up. For some countries their natural resources have become also a curse, as resources are often the cause of separatist movements and civil wars. In the 1960s, in Congo, the province Katanga fought a separatist war; in Nigeria, it was the province Biafra. In the case of Congo today, resources have even caused attacks by neighboring countries. In Nige-ria, local guerillas of the Delta region are fighting for their "fair" share of the income from the country's oil wealth. Bolivia's large gas deposits have divided the people along ethnic lines.

Only when the natural resources are superabundant *in relation to the population* is there prosperity in a country and (maybe) also peace among the various population groups in the country — for instance, in diamond-rich Botswana and in oil-rich Kuwait. But Kuwait was occupied by its neighbor Iraq precisely because of its oil wealth. And the most recent history of Iraq we know all too well. But countries in this category that have not suffered the same bad fate often do not have it easy either. Trin-idad and Tobago, a small oil-rich country trying to develop itself into an industrialized country, is suffering from an official unemployment rate of 11 percent (Dillmann 2006). In spite of its huge oil wealth, Saudi Arabia has several problems: with half its population consisting of young peo-ple under twenty-five, its unemployment rate amounts to over 30 per-cent — while seven million foreigners work there. Before the latest oil price boom, per capita income had been falling for ten years. Surprisingly, Saudi Arabia has even a poverty problem — the underclass is becoming ever poorer. Many children have to beg on the streets (Grobe 2003). It is also not as if foreign workers have found a bonanza in these oil-rich Arab coun-tries. "Low pay, often for months in arrears, shabby accommodation and inhuman treatment: this is how many of the hundreds of thousands of foreign workers ... in Dubai ... fare. Asian workers have already ... drawn attention to their situation by striking." According to reports, some desper-ate foreign workers let themselves be run over by cars so that their family can get cash compensation for their death (Nüsse 2006).

A further symptom of the crisis is the widespread and rapidly increas-ing violence in social life. In Brazil, in the Republic of South Africa, etc., even the everyday life of people is dominated by great fear of crime. In São Paulo in 2006, criminal gangs fought regular battles against the forces of law and order. In Colombia, Mexico, and Afghanistan, the government is powerless against drug dealers. One can go on endlessly listing such things.

This presentation on the crisis of capitalism in the Third World can be concluded with the report that, according to the World Bank's Independent Evaluation Group (IEG), the number of countries in danger of breaking down is rapidly rising. In 2003, they numbered seventeen; in 2006, twenty-six were threatened with collapse. A dozen were considered highly endangered for four consecutive years. New entries to this list were the important oil-exporting country Nigeria, the Democratic Republic of Timor-Leste, Cambodia, and Kosovo (*Frankfurter Allgemeine Zeitung*, 15 September 2006). Two countries were not just endangered, but had already collapsed and are now failed states: Somalia and Iraq. With regard to Iraq, the aggressors still cherish some hope. Fareed Zakaria, the then editor-in-chief of *Newsweek*, wrote on the civil war there: "Civil strife tends not to go on forever. A new nation and a new state might well emerge in Iraq. But its birth will be a slow, gradual process, taking years. The most effective American strategy, at this point, is one that is sustainable for just such a long haul." Zakaria hopes that if the US government accepts his strategy recommendation, "then perhaps time will work for us for a change" (Zakaria 2006).

I am afraid this is a delusion. Time is working against Iraq.

## 8. Growing Defensive and Compensatory Costs

In traditional left circles one often hears apparently sound arguments for their excessive demands, such as: "There is enough money there for the demand," the "GDP is growing after all," and "everyone can see that corporate profits are bursting," etc. Such leftists do not seem to know that the GDP is no reliable indicator of prosperity. But even most economists think, at least in their day-to-day discussions and debates, that GDP growth is the same as growth in national prosperity, although in the meantime even economics textbooks cast some doubt on this belief (see Samuelson and Nordhaus 1998: 490f.). However, a small minority among economists knows that companies externalize many of their costs, particularly environmental costs. That is, they pass them on to a large number of other economic players or to the society as a whole, thus turning them into social costs. K. William Kapp wrote in as early as 1950 that, by externalizing some of their costs, microeconomic units tend to reduce the net income (or benefit) of other economic players (producers and consumers) and increase their own share of the aggregate income (1979: ix, 11). This is a very serious aspect of the distribution question.

Another point in Kapp's criticism is very important for our subject. He and, later, some other economists — for instance, Christian Leipert (1989) and Wouter van Dieren (1995) among many others — consider the usual method of calculating GDP as misleading. They argue: in GDP, all economic activities are included indiscriminately, even those whose purpose is only to prevent damages or to compensate for damages that have already taken place, which, in most cases, have been caused by the economic process itself. An example of this is the cost of repairing a car damaged in an accident.

> This one-dimensional concept is, however, inadmissible when we try to determine the *true net income* [of the nation], that is, after deducting all costs necessary to preserve the capital stock (*including natural capital*) [and including health of the population]. The GNP [nowadays GDP] includes ... transactions to which no positive value can be attributed (Van Dieren 1995: 198; emphasis added)

Such transactions are called defensive and compensatory costs. In this connection, Kapp justifiably warned in 1971 against narrowing down the concept. The growing use of the concepts "environment" and "ecology" in this discussion was, in his opinion, only sensible if they also meant impairment of the social environment (1979: xi). Kapp mentioned as example occupational diseases, cases of death, damage to health, physical and mental stress, etc. caused through exercise of one's profession. Lasting physical and psychical sufferings, just as irreversible ecological damages, cannot be repaired.

Economists like Leipert have tried to identify and quantify such social costs. However, understandably, they could only quantify those costs that had led to spending money — either to avoid or to subsequently compensate for (to repair) damages. *Those damages that were not avoided or compensated for (repaired) could not be recognized.*

Let me here add an insight even more important for our discussion: such defensive and compensatory costs are continuously increasing — both in absolute terms and in relation to GDP growth. Already in 1971 Kapp could generalize in saying: "[I]n spite of the problems that ... render estimating social costs difficult, it is justified to say that the environmental hazards and the social costs arising from [them] show, both in absolute and relative terms, a *rising trend* parallel to growth in production and consumption" (xiii; retranslated).

In 1989, Leipert published the detailed results of his research in Germany, which covered the period 1970–1988. A table with the abridged details follows (Leipert 1989: 126f.).

**Defensive [Including Compensatory] Expenditures in the FRG [West Germany] (1970–1980)**

| | Absolute value in billion DM at constant prices | | | | Share of GDP, in % of GDP | | | |
|---|---|---|---|---|---|---|---|---|
| | 1970 | 1980 | 1985 | 1988 | 1970 | 1980 | 1985 | 1988 |
| I. Environment | 16.8 | 33.15 | 45.25 | 57.7 | 1.5 | 2.23 | 2.87 | 3.4 |
| II. Health | 19.5 | 37.3 | 41.3 | 44.5 | 1.7 | 2.5 | 2.62 | 2.62 |
| III. Transport | 30.8 | 44.8 | 52.2 | 56.3 | 2.7 | 3.0 | 3.31 | 3.31 |
| IV. Housing | 5.45 | 10.14 | 11.87 | 12.75 | 0.48 | 0.67 | 0.75 | 0.75 |
| V. Domestic security | 4.45 | 15.92 | 19.8 | 23.1 | 0.4 | 1.08 | 1.26 | 1.36 |
| VI. Work | 2.2 | 1.9 | 1.8 | 1.9 | 0.2 | 0.13 | 0.11 | 0.11 |
| Total defensive costs | 79.2 | 143.2 | 172.2 | 196.3 | 7.0 | 9.6 | 10.9 | 11.6 |

Like GDP figures, the above figures are also not one hundred percent correct. A special weakness of GDP figures is that they cannot take the quality of goods and services into account, only the monetary expenditures. For instance, expenditures on health care are not increasing only because more and more people are falling sick or having accidents, but also because more and more effective and thus more and more expensive equipment and drugs are being used — innovations that presumably lead to improved quality of health care.

Nevertheless it is indisputable that in order to arrive at a figure for the *true net income*, we ought to subtract from the GDP more and more defensive and compensatory expenditures — for 1970, 7% of the GDP; for 1988, 11.6%. These figures show that in Germany, *prosperity*, understood as *true net income*, has been decreasing for a long time, and in the future, if the GDP growth rate stays at roughly 2%, it will decrease even further.

However, the authorities can keep these figures that are to be subtracted from the GDP low by doing nothing to avoid or compensate for some damages. Then, of course, researchers will get expenditure figures that are low, but the real damages will not be low. And national prosperity will continue to shrink despite lower defensive expenditure figures. The popular leftist claim that "there is enough money there" is not so

convincing after we realize these truths. They should take note of the following prophecy of the Cree Indians:

> Only when the last tree has been felled, the last river has been
> poisoned, and the last fish has been caught will you notice that
> one cannot eat money.

Some damages are not caused by us humans but through natural phenomena or circumstances beyond our control. In the meantime, however, in many cases it has become more difficult to draw a line between
the human and non-human causality. The devastations that took place in
New Orleans in 2005 were caused by Hurricane Katrina. But was it not
the failure to strengthen the dikes and, maybe, also the human-caused
global warming that were the real causes of the devastation? Or is it not
also the massive deforestations that are causing the rising number of flood
catastrophes in the tropical countries? Be that as it may, it is unlikely that
humankind's prosperity (not to be confused with GDP) would continuously rise or remain as it is today. Quite on the contrary.

Criticism of the concept of GDP and of what it comprises has concerned some establishment economists. Therefore, in as early as 1972, two
of them — Nordhaus and Tobin — tried to show that GNP (gross national
product, the term used in those days) was indeed a useful indicator of
prosperity or social welfare. In their inquiry they tried to construct a "measure of economic welfare" (MEW), the purpose of which was to depict the
contribution of the economy to the broader entity "social welfare."

For Nordhaus and Tobin, economic welfare could only be measured in
terms of consumption. So they began with net national product (NNP),
that is, GNP minus depreciations. Then they subtracted a further sum, i.e.,
a sum that must be invested in order to maintain the current consumption
level of a growing population. The rest is consumed. This way they determine the measure "sustainable per capita consumption."

They recognize that not just any kind of consumption contributes to
welfare. Some consumption expenditures are "regrettable necessities"
(that have been termed defensive costs by the critics mentioned above).
In this category they include the costs of commuting to work, police services, health care, road maintenance, and defense. These sums are subtracted from total consumption. Then they add to total consumption the
value for leisure and that for work outside the market (informal economy) — domestic work, for instance. They impute reasonable monetary
values to these items since their real value cannot be statistically determined. After making all these corrections they finally obtain their measure

"per capita sustainable MEW." It is considerably higher than the per capita GNP, as the latter does not include values for leisure and the output of the informal economy included in MEW.

Nordhaus and Tobin concede that their list of regrettable necessities is problematic; it could be longer or shorter depending on the philosophical standpoint. They know that city life also entails some trouble. But they ignore these problems because they are just too deep to be tackled in national income accounts.

Now let us take up the core question of the inquiry: does GNP (GDP) growth mean also growth in welfare? Nordhaus and Tobin answer yes. On the basis of the data they have collected, they show that in the US, in the period 1929–1965, per capita sustainable MEW grew on average by 1.1% per year. Of course, this is lower than the average per capita yearly growth of NNP (1.7%), but per capita sustainable MEW did grow. They conclude: "The progress indicated by conventional national accounts is not just a myth that evaporates when a welfare-oriented measure is substituted" (quoted in Daly and Cobb Jr. 1990: 97). (The presentation of the study by Nordhaus and Tobin is from ibid.: 76–80 and Daly 1996: 151f.)

Daly and Cobb Jr. — two of the many critics of the concept GDP — have subjected the study of Nordhaus and Tobin to a detailed examination. They accept the authors' figures as correct; they also accept the dubious values imputed to leisure and the output of the informal economy. But they find fault with the fact that the authors considered the figures for all the thirty-six years (1929–1965) together in order to reach their conclusion. Daly and Cobb Jr. show that the positive correlation between the per capita GNP growth and the growth in per capita sustainable MEW disappears if the thirty-six years are divided into shorter periods. They (Daly and Cobb Jr.) leave out of the consideration the periods that were very strongly distorted through World War II expenditures and the subsequent drop in expenditures due to demobilization. They focus their attention instead on the period between 1945 and 1965, the long boom period, in which neither war nor depression nor recovery particularly influenced the growth rates. In this period, per capita GNP grew six times as fast as the per capita sustainable MEW — the former grew by 48%, or 2.2% per year, whereas the latter grew only by 7.5%, or 0.4% per year. That means there is no positive correlation between GNP and social welfare.

This conclusion of Daly and Cobb Jr. is surprising, more so because it is based on data (and assumed values) presented by two economists who believe in the usefulness of the concept GNP (GDP) as an indicator of social welfare. It is surprising because people who happened to live in the

USA during the long boom did observe a rapid growth in the standard of living (prosperity) of the average American citizen during this period. This dispute, however, cannot be settled to anybody's full satisfaction because some of the terms used in it — standard of living, regrettable necessities, welfare, (imputed) monetary value of leisure, work in the informal sector, etc. — are by their very nature vague, undeterminable, partly left to individual feelings, and, hence, arbitrary.

Three things should be mentioned whose monetary values Nordhaus and Tobin should also have subtracted from net national product: (1) expenditure on advertising, which cannot be regarded as consumption, nor as a regrettable necessity, (2) a monetary value imputed to emotional/ psychological distress caused by unemployment, and (3) last but not least, the already mentioned costs and losses caused by environmental damages.

A totally different kind of problem that should also be discussed in this connection is the progressive depletion of *nonrenewable resources*. These resources have to be consumed in order to produce goods and services (GDP). In this process their reserves (natural capital) diminish. That means, we are partly living off our assets; we are actually becoming poorer and poorer without noticing it. Samuelson and Nordhaus (1998: 491) reported on a study conducted by the US Ministry of Commerce in 1994 that attempted to include in the relevant calculations the contribution of natural resources and environmental goods to the country's income. But the researchers made thereby a methodological mistake: they added new *discoveries* of sources of nonrenewable resources to their known stock, and claimed that the former compensated for the depletion of the latter. But new discoveries do not amount to new *production*. In fact, nonrenewable resources cannot be *produced* at all. Such resources have existed for millions of years; it is just that they have only recently been discovered. And in our times fewer and fewer easily accessible deposits of such resources are being found. The stock of these resources is relentlessly dwindling.

I would like to conclude this presentation on defensive and compensatory costs with a selection of more recent data: (1) In Latin America, in 1999, the economic costs of crime came to 14.2% of the GDP of the region. Companies were (and are still being) compelled to spend large sums for protecting staff and property (Gould 2006). (2) The US security industry is booming since the terror attacks of September 11, 2001. The yearly budget of the ministry of homeland security amounts to US$30 billion. And that is only about half of the total federal expenditure for security. In Germany, since 2001, the turnover of the security industry has grown by about 11%, and the number of people employed in it has increased by 40,000 to

180,000 (Caspar 2006). (3) In 2005, according to the yearly report of the Stockholm International Peace Research Institute (SIPRI), global spending for military purposes reached the record high of €885 billion, although in the same year the number of armed conflicts in the world (seventeen) was at its lowest since the end of the Cold War. The United States alone spent almost half of this amount (*Direkt*, 13 June 2006).

(4) Unusually strong hurricanes are driving up the cost of insurance against resulting damages. In 2005, US insurance companies had to pay out over $57 billion for compensating storm damages. Since 2005, insurance premiums for houses and apartments located along the entire US east coast have increased by leaps and bounds — in some cases by ten times. At the same time, companies that are particularly at risk of suffering damages due to natural disasters are getting 15% to 20% less coverage from insurance companies (Treaster 2006; Fefer and Hamilton 2006). According to an estimate of the reinsurance company Münchener Rück, in Europe damages to the tune of €310 billion result every year from environmental catastrophes (Brandt, Andrea 2006: 16). (5) According to estimates of the Chinese National Bureau of Statistics, environmental damages in China in 2004 amounted to 3% of the GDP. It would cost the country €106 billion to clean up the polluted environment (what is meant here is surely the accumulated pollution of the previous years) (McGregor 2006). (6) In 2002, Germany spent less for environmental protection than in 1995. The state, manufacturing industries, and privatized public companies spent in 1995 a total of €35.53 billion; but in 2002, they spent only €33.96 billion (Federal Bureau of Statistics of Germany 2005).

# X.

# Where Does the Surplus Come From?

What I have narrated on defensive and compensatory costs in chapter IX gives rise to two fundamental questions: (1) Where does the surplus come from? and (2) why do defensive and compensatory costs arise? Surplus is what one has or produces over and above what is absolutely essential for living. Without a sufficient surplus, there is no investing in defensive and compensatory measures. The production of surplus explains the origin of civilization and our growing *prosperity* in the sense of increasing *desired* consumption, which, *generally speaking*, could be observed throughout the greater part of human history, especially since the Industrial Revolution.

All economists have addressed the question of the origin of surplus (prosperity), as have the protagonists of critique of political economy, namely, Marx, Engels, and the Marxists. We already know the answer of standard economics: surplus comes from continuous scientific and technological progress coupled with increasing accumulation of capital — which makes the continuous growth of labor productivity possible — and from entrepreneurship. Marxists basically share this view; but in the end, they ascribe the whole process to a more basic special quality of *human* labor, its ability to produce more than is necessary to stay alive (labor theory of value).

Until recently, almost all humankind was filled with optimism regarding progress. But different kinds of crises and problems are piling up, and we cannot find acceptable solutions for them. Particularly global warming, which has reached a critical point, and the dire predictions of ecological and economic catastrophes connected with it make many people's belief in progress evaporate. If such catastrophes do occur — some have already occurred — we will be ineluctably burdened with much more defensive and compensatory costs. And we will fail to take many more necessary measures of this kind and, hence, suffer heavy losses. According to the famous *Stern Review*, global warming and its consequences could later cause every year damages and production losses amounting to 20% or more of the global GDP if preventive measures are not started today. This would have apocalyptic effects on the world economy (*International Herald Tribune*, 31 October 2006, and Stern 2006). What is not stated here is that this would also have apocalyptic effects on the social structure of all nations. Some Pentagon scientists wrote in a report submitted to the US government that climate change poses a bigger threat to the security of the United States than terrorists because it would lead to wars over raw materials and food that would devastate continents (*Spiegel* online, 22 February 2004).

## 1. The Secret of Rising Labor Productivity

We need to thoroughly understand this situation. The above-mentioned standard answer of economists to the question as to the source of increasing labor productivity and growing prosperity is clearly not fully satisfactory. For it cannot explain the visible gradual evaporation of the belief in progress. Why couldn't all the scientific and technological progress of the past and the present and all the trillions of dollars of accumulated capital long ago solve the environmental and social problems and crises? Capitalism alone cannot be blamed for this failure. For such problems and crises could not also be solved in the socialist planned economy of the Soviet Union (see Sarkar 1999: chapters 2 and 3). In order to be able to give the right answer to this question, we should delve into the secret of increasing labor productivity, which is still unrevealed to many.

Depending on geographical location, even primitive humans could enjoy some degree of leisure with the labor productivity of the time. They did not have to toil twelve hours a day just to stay alive. In many places there was even abundance (see, e.g., Sahlins 1974: 11). Peoples of as far back as the Upper Paleolithic era also created works of art. In the days of the pharaohs great temples and pyramids were built. In the Middle Ages, Europeans had more holidays than are taken today (see Ulrich 1979). They too created great works of art and architecture and produced luxury goods for a small part of the population. All this surplus was produced before the development of science in the present-day sense. From the very beginning, humans had an urge to understand their surroundings and the spirit of experimentation and invention.

Nevertheless, one cannot say that surplus arises from activities of the human intellect alone, through only scientific discoveries and technological inventions. Marx too recognized this to some extent. He corrected the wrong view held by German Social Democrats, namely, that "labor is the source of all wealth and all culture." He wrote: "Labor is *not the source* of all wealth. *Nature* is just as much the source of use values (and it is surely of such that material wealth consists!) as labor" (Marx 1875/1976: 13).

Nature's contribution to the generation of wealth (of surplus) is here expressly acknowledged. It consists in nature — in its more or less original state — putting at our disposal, free of cost, fertile soil, regular rainfall, pure air, pure water in rivers and lakes, forests as source of fuel and building materials, fruits, fish and game as food, draft animals as providers of kinetic energy, etc. But after we left behind the stage of primitive hunters and gatherers, this contribution of nature became for the most part the resource base for the production of goods by means of labor. Thereafter, according to this understanding of the matter, any *increase* in our wealth only took place through the application of human labor. Nevertheless, it must be said that, with his labor theory of value, Marx himself had led to the above-mentioned mistake of the Social Democrats. For he had expressly banished "use value as use value" — and thus nature's contribution to wealth creation — from the "field of investigation of political economy" (quoted in Immler 1985: 244). According to Marx, political economy should only deal with things that are created by human labor *and* belong to barter/market economy. That means the free contributions of nature — among which also its ability to absorb human-made pollution (its sink function) should be counted — are no part of it. This also applies to useful goods that one produces for oneself (one's family or friends) and not for the market.

Some ecologists — among them some who consider themselves eco-Marxists — criticize Marx for not having considered nature's contribution in his labor theory of value. However, in the complete works of Marx and Engels there are also passages that indicate they were aware of nature's contribution to production, although they did not let this awareness have any clear effect on their theory and vision (see Burkett 1999 and Löwy 2005, among others). But we do not need to delve into this controversy, since it is not our task to defend Marx. Let us leave that to Marxologists.

But is it correct to say, as the labor theory of value says, that the value (i.e., the exchange value) of a good is solely determined by the socially necessary abstract labor needed for its production, and that nature does not play any part in it? I will soon address this specific question. But before I do, we must further deal with the broader question of where the surplus comes from, that is, the question of how humanity could in its history almost continuously increase labor productivity. For this issue is of crucial importance for understanding the crisis *of* capitalism.

So long as humans worked with only their own physical strength, the surplus was very small. Also their experimenting and inventive spirit hit the *energy limit* — the limit set by the physical strength of humans. They could however progress further by making use of the physical strength of beasts of burden and the power of wind and flowing water. And the heat energy provided by burning wood enabled them to achieve the transition from the Stone Age to the Bronze Age. These sources of energy enormously increased humankind's labor productivity. Many inventions — the wheel and the boat, for instance — could only now be widely used. The surplus increased by leaps and bounds. Later on, burning coal became the main source of energy. With the development of the power of steam began the Industrial Revolution. It now became possible or easier to tap sources of raw materials that lay deep underground or far away from production sites. Steam can also be produced by burning wood, but by burning coal one can do it much more effectively. With oil and gas, in the case of many machines (namely, automobiles), it also became possible to bypass the need to produce steam. Industrial civilization, its enormous labor productivity, and its prosperity are mainly based on fossil energy sources. Nuclear power came additionally, but it is not as indispensable as fossil fuels.

There is, however, a downside to this. Fossil energy sources — unlike wood, naturally flowing water, and naturally blowing wind — are a once-only gift of nature. They are exhaustible. Their stock is continuously diminishing. In this respect, Marx made a mistake. He — like Ricardo, from whom he received the labor theory of value which he then developed further — assumed a general constancy of nature. Hans Immler wrote:

> The critique of political economy [of Marx], however, becomes uncritical at the point where it forms the bourgeois conception of nature — eternally existing and hence available at will — into a positive building stone of its theory of value, which then ends in the theory of the general productivity of labor. Marx fails to show that in [his] concept of abstract labor he has implicitly presupposed the non-existence of physical nature *as a value-forming element*. ... However, this assumption of valueless nature is only valid ... as long as physical nature makes itself available, unconditionally and *indestructibly*, to productive appropriation. But the moment the natural conditions, which are assumed to be constant, prove themselves to be variable and susceptible to change through human influence, ... the labor theory of value reflects a distorted reality. (1985: 253; emphasis added)

Natural conditions are variable and susceptible to change in more than one sense. Rainfall, climate, and weather are variable, which may mean that in one year the amount of labor necessary for producing a hundredweight of wheat is more, in the next year less. Consumers mostly notice this when the price of wheat rises or falls. The value (i.e., exchange value) of wheat is, in this case, partly determined by nature. The extraction of nonrenewable, hence exhaustible, natural resources, which are becoming ever harder to access (coal, oil, copper, etc.), requires ever more labor. That drives their value (in most cases also their price) ever higher. This can also happen with renewable natural resources, such as wood and groundwater, if the rate of their extraction exceeds the natural rate at which they grow again or are replenished. The natural environment can be polluted/degraded through human activities or through failure to undertake compensatory repair operations, which in turn can make it necessary to expend more labor on the production of certain goods than before. This increases the value (and the price) of these goods. It is therefore wrong to maintain that the value (exchange value) of a commodity is only determined by the socially necessary abstract labor expended on their production.

Marx and the Marxists made yet another mistake in their theory of value. When they talk of labor, they mean labor performed on the foundation of the scientific and technological progress achieved until the time in question, without however ascribing to it any value-building role. As we know, there is a great difference between labor in the Stone Age and labor in a modern factory. For instance, whereas the hammer of the Stone Age worker is a hand ax, that of the industrial worker of today is a pneumatic hammer. Marx and the Marxists do not realize that the pneumatic hammer was not produced through labor alone, not simply through so many times more labor hours than was necessary for the production of the hand ax. A pneumatic hammer incorporates, apart from materials and labor, a great amount of scientific knowledge and a great number of technological inventions. Therefore, actually, the value of a pneumatic hammer is not made up of only labor and labor congealed in the machines and materials used, but also of the *knowledge and inventions congealed in these machines.* The latter are quantitatively much more and qualitatively of a much higher level than those incorporated in a hand ax. And it is precisely this that makes the difference in productivity between a worker using a hand ax and a worker using a pneumatic hammer. Just as an entrepreneur has to pay for the labor power of his workers, he must also pay for a certain length of time patent fees for using the new inventions congealed in his modern machines.

In chapter I, in the section on the tendency of the rate of profit to fall, we saw that Marx's assumption that the rate of surplus value ($s'$) remains constant, while the organic composition of capital ($q$) increases, is wrong. Normally, an increasing ($q$) (more machines and other means of production per worker) goes hand in hand with increasing labor productivity, which means, ceteris paribus, also an increasing surplus value. This is to say that not only labor, but also means of production — machines such as a pneumatic hammer (to be more precise, the knowledge and inventions congealed in them) — can create surplus value. (This issue was briefly addressed in the preface.) The fact that one can see in history a tendency of the rate of profit to fall can have many reasons other than the increasing ($q$). The matter becomes clearer if we ask ourselves why even a monopolistic entrepreneur, who does not have to worry much about competition, invests more in machines than in labor power. When one realizes that machines too can create surplus value, it becomes clear why entrepreneurs replace workers with machines.

It is not correct to subsume the activities of scientists, inventors, and developers under the general category *labor*. Those who try to develop useful products out of scientific knowledge do not *directly* manufacture such products as workers and engineers do in factories. Quite on the contrary, they devour in their work enormous amounts of value (goods and services) that other people have produced, with very uncertain results. Since the inception of patent laws, those who have succeeded in making a marketable invention must be paid patent fees for the use of their invention. But the activities of those inventors who have not been successful have, in the final analysis, been paid for by the general public. That is not a wage for some productive labor. They are not workers in the Marxian sense. Even when their employer is a corporation that maintains a department of research and development, the payment for their fruitless activities comes from the results of the labor of the rest of the workers of the corporation.

There is not only fruitless technological research. There is some (at least partly) fruitful research that does not increase labor productivity but rather only defensive costs, e.g., the enormous costs incurred for medical research, weapons research, research on criminology, research on climate change, etc. The expenses incurred for all kinds of fruitless and defensive research are normally passed on to the general public — in the form of taxes and in the form of higher prices of goods and services. People then have a smaller surplus for desired consumption. Also such costs, which are known to be continuously increasing, have undoubtedly contributed to the fact that the average real net income of German households fell between 1991 and 2005 by 2 percent (Federal Statistics Bureau of Germany, cited in *Junge Welt*, 28 November 2006).

Let us take another example: In the eighteenth century a shoemaker worked in his workshop. He combined his know-how and his tools (both results of previous discoveries and inventions) with his physical energy, which provided the driving power for his tools. These tools too had been produced with the help of physical energy (*to a great extent*, if not solely; wind and water power may also have made a contribution). He produced shoes, value. Let us now imagine a fully automatic shoe factory with only an overseer (in chapter I, I mentioned Tugan-Baranovsky's hypothetical factory without any worker). In this case, the driving power mainly comes from fossil fuels. In this factory with almost no worker in it shoes (value) are also being produced, but a thousand times more than in the shoemaker's workshop. In this way, the prosperity of society increases enormously. (The question whether the owner of a factory without a worker can get some surplus value has been answered in chapter I with yes. In any case, he can make a profit if he can sell his products at a price that is higher than the production costs.)

The difference in productivity between the two modes of production does not result only from the difference in quantity and quality of scientific knowledge and technological inventions congealed in the tools or in the fully automatic machines, nor only from the quantity and quality of the materials used, but also, perhaps primarily, from the difference between the energy content of the driving powers used. Fossil fuels, especially oil and gas, present each citizen of the highly industrialized countries, so to speak, with hundreds of energy slaves ready to work round the clock. No other energy source can match oil when it comes to energy content, versatility, transportability, and storability. And, until recently, it was very cheap. During the first sixty years of oil extraction, until about 1920, at the cost of one foot of exploratory drilling 240 barrels of oil could be found. In the 1930s, the figure rose to 300 barrels (Heinberg 2003: 109). In the beginning of oil extraction in Texas, energy return on energy invested (EROEI) was approximately 20:1 (Kunstler 2005: 107).

Now we can succinctly answer the question of where the surplus really comes from. It comes from: (1) the existence of all kinds of *easily exploitable* natural resources ("sources"); among them, modern energy sources are the most important, for most modern technological inventions are of little use without energy drawn from sources other than human and animal physical strength; (2) the ability of nature to absorb human-made pollution ("sinks"); and (3) scientific and technological developments that enhance (have enhanced) labor productivity and help develop new useful products. We will not here take into account the exploitation of one nation by another as a source of surplus, because from the point of view of all humanity it is a zero-sum game. It is not relevant to our inquiry.

That we do not take all the necessary defensive and compensatory measures means that we save costs by degrading the natural environment. So we can say that our *unpaid debts* to nature are also a source of our *present* prosperity. But we also cause damage to our environment that is, at least in the short term, irreversible — by not desisting from activities that are already recognized as dangerous for the environment. As for the exhausted deposits of nonrenewable resources, they, in any case, cannot be refilled. Since the future generations will most certainly have to live in an environment degraded by us, we can say that the impoverishment of our descendants, which we accept without the slightest qualm, is also a source of our huge present-day surplus.

What I have said here about the natural environment can also be said about the social environment (Kapp, as we have seen, wants to consider them together). States have been reducing expenditures on social welfare in order to finance tax cuts in favor of the rich, so that the latter can spend more on luxury consumption, or in order to be able to finance senseless projects. We are degrading the social environment by neglecting interpersonal relationships. Violence, crime, and social indifference are on the rise. Homelessness, moral degeneration, drug addiction, alcoholism, and illnesses are increasing. The social fabric is falling apart. In this sense, too, we can say we are enjoying our prosperity at the expense of the future generations.

On the basis of these answers to the question of where the surplus (our prosperity) comes from, we can also answer the question of when and how the surplus can shrink. This will enable us to have a better understanding of the cause of the crises and problems of capitalism. When the natural sources of energy and raw materials are exhausted, or when they do not flow in abundance as they used to do, or when they have become difficult to access, then the surplus begins to decrease. And when the capacity of nature's sinks is no longer sufficient for naturally absorbing the (poisonous) wastes of our economies, then defensive costs increase. In both these situations there is less and less to distribute, and then social as well as international conflicts also increase.

## 2. Sustainable Growth?

But there still remains the third source of surplus: scientific and technological achievements. One hopes for many of these in the future.

Ever since we have become aware that we are massively changing the environment, mostly by degrading it, and that the supply of concentrated natural resources is continuously shrinking, the assumption of the constancy of nature has become very shaky. We now ask ourselves whether nature, which we have ourselves changed/degraded, can continue to serve us with its sources and sinks as before and whether our economy can continue to produce ever more wealth.

Even Marx and Engels had noted in many passages of their writings the destructive side of the industrial mode of production. For instance, Marx wrote in *Capital, Volume 1,* that "capitalist production ... develops technology ... only by sapping the original sources of all wealth — the soil and the labourer [her health]." (Marx 1954: 506f.). Engels wrote that for each of our victories "nature takes its revenge on us." Their implicit assumption of the constancy of nature was, however, not shaken by these insights. Both remained optimistic on the issue of progress. Engels indirectly expressed his confidence in some kind of constancy of nature when he wrote:

> [A]ll our mastery of [nature] consists in the fact that we have the advantage over all other creatures of being able to learn its laws and apply them correctly.
>
> And, in fact, with every day that passes we are acquiring a better understanding of these laws and getting to perceive both the more immediate and the more remote consequences of our interference with the traditional course of nature. In particular, after the mighty advances made by the natural sciences in the present century, we are more than ever in a position to *realize and hence to control* even the more remote natural consequences of at least our day-to-day production activities. (Marx and Engels 1976b, vol. 3: 74f.; emphasis added)

And Marx wrote: "The fixed capital invested in machines, etc., is not improved by use; on the contrary, it depreciates. ... The earth, on the contrary, continuously improves, *as long as it is treated correctly.*" He also wrote of "the advantage of the earth, that successive capital investments can have their benefit *without the earlier ones being lost*" (Marx 1981: 916).

Confronted with this issue, people of our times — most politicians, economists, and publicists, but also all kinds of leftists and eco-activists, who are full of faith in progress — imagine an economy that can, thanks to new scientific and technological breakthroughs, grow in a sustainable way, that is, also in harmony with the environment. Of course, there are some differences between their lines of argumentation, but their conclusions are the same. They express their optimism in one or more of the following five articles of faith, all of which are based on belief in unlimited scientific and technological progress: (1) There is no scarcity of nonrenewable resources; (2) almost everything can be recycled; (3) environmentally harmful wastes and emissions can be technologically intercepted and made harmless; (4) thanks to technological progress, resource consumption can be reduced by up to a factor of ten without curtailing growth (efficiency revolution); and (5) renewable resources, which are known to be environmentally neutral, can fully replace all the nonrenewable and polluting resources without any loss or negative effect.

The best example of the first article of faith is supplied by Wilfred Beckerman (1972), economist and emeritus fellow at Balliol College, Oxford University, who believed that the minerals occurring in the top one mile of the earth's crust would suffice for continuous economic growth for the next 100 million years. And Julian Simon and Herman Kahn (1984: 3) wrote: "Mineral resources are becoming less scarce rather than more scarce, affront to common sense though that may be." The second article of faith is best exemplified by a statement of the famous leftist author André Gorz, who in the 1970s expressed the hope that "entire" amounts of raw materials could be recycled or reused (Gorz 1983: 79). And in the German ecology movement one often says: "garbage in disposal sites is resources at the wrong place." The most absurd recommendation in connection with the third article of faith (but also in connection with the second) was made by Professor Jero Kondo, at the time president of the Science Council of Japan. He said that in order to solve the problem of global warming, we should capture, by using solar energy, the excess atmospheric $CO_2$ as well as the $CO_2$ that flows out of chimneys and transform the gas into useful industrial chemicals (see Schmidt-Bleek 1993: 80). An only marginally less absurd recommendation, the implementation of which, if at all possible, would cost enormous sums of money, has been made by Nicholas Stern (2006) among others. The idea is to separate $CO_2$ from the gas emissions of coal-fired power plants, to liquefy it and store it safely in deep hollow spaces, such as empty oil wells (Carbon Capture and Storage = CCS). The works of Ernst Ulrich von Weizsäcker (e.g., 1997) and Friedrich Schmidt-Bleek (e.g., 1993) are good examples of the fourth article of faith.

The best example of the fifth article of faith is a quote from Hermann Scheer, the high priest of solar energy:

> For an inconceivably long time the sun will donate its energy to humans, animals, and plants. And it will do that so lavishly that it could satisfy even the most sumptuous energy needs of the worlds of humans, animals, and plants experiencing drastic growth: the sun supplies every year 15,000 times more energy than what the world population commercially consumes. (Scheer 1999: 66)

In the meantime, Scheer and his political friends include in the term "solar energy" all forms of renewable energy: wind energy, hydropower, biomass, etc. They maintain that materials for all kinds of goods can be produced out of reed.

Elsewhere, I have thoroughly examined the idea of sustainable growth — on the basis of all its arguments and its proposed concrete problem solutions by means of allegedly promising products and technologies (Sarkar 1999: chapter 4; Sarkar 2001b; Sarkar and Kern 2008). I think the idea has resulted from a wrong philosophy, illusions, and unrealistically high hopes and expectations. In my view, the main explanation for these illusions and false hopes is the inability of the protagonists of the idea to differentiate between feasibility and economic viability of the proposed technologies and products. What is feasible is not always economically viable. It is neither possible nor necessary to repeat here all the details of my arguments. Here I will present only two arguments that I did not put forward in the above-mentioned literature.

If solar energy in the comprehensive sense could solve all energy problems of humankind without degrading the environment, then why, against the background of possible climate catastrophes, are governments all over the world granting permission to build more and more coal-fired power plants and dozens of nuclear power plants, the latter of which are known to be dangerous? Why, in spite of the catastrophe at Fukushima Daiichi, are many other people still demanding more nuclear power plants as part of the solution to the problem of global warming, even the famous James Lovelock, father of the Gaia theory? Lovelock's earlier hopes about wind energy have vanished. And why does India, a country that has to pay very large sums for importing oil and gas and is rich in sunshine and wind, want to build more nuclear power plants?

The two aforementioned technological solutions to the $CO_2$ problem are, it seems, economically not viable, even if they were technically feasible. According to estimates, CCS technology would consume 7 to 14 percent of the electricity produced by the power plant it would serve. This means that in order to maintain power generation at the same level, it would be necessary to burn up to 40 percent more fossil fuels. Together with the necessary additional construction and other associated measures, that would, according to estimates, more than double the costs of power production (Dannheim 2006: 9). As for Professor Jero Kondo's idea, of course, from the industrial chemist's point of view it is feasible. But there is a catch in the matter, namely, that solar energy depends on large subsidies. These subsidies come from the economy at large, which — as is well known — draws most of its energy from $CO_2$-spewing fossil fuels, exactly that which is to be replaced with solar energy. When, in the early 1970s, the idea was mooted for the first time in connection with all pollutants, physicist Klaus Meyer-Abich (1973: 177) pointed out that such chemical retransformations require, among other things, almost the same amount of energy as the original production process had required.

More debate on this point is not possible here. But what I hope to interest my readers in (and convince them of) is a relatively unknown theoretical background of my argumentation. I shall now delve into it a little.

### 3. Entropy, Low Entropy, and the Economic Process

There is a law of nature called the entropy law, which is also known as the second law of thermodynamics. Without some understanding of this law, many things remain incomprehensible to us, for instance, why it is economically nonsensical to try to produce oil from the carbon of the $CO_2$ in the air (Professor Kondo's idea). Below I give, in my own words, a succinct and simplified presentation of what I have learnt from Nicholas Georgescu-Roegen (1981, 1987). It is he who first stated that the entropy law also applies to the whole economic process.

In order to understand the concept "entropy," we must first distinguish between energy that is *available* and energy that is *unavailable* for us humans in general and for our particular purposes. The heat energy contained in ordinary seawater is unavailable (i.e., not sufficient) for the purpose of propelling a ship, but it is available to (i.e., sufficient for) fish for their life processes. Then we should think of the law of conservation, according to which in an *isolated (closed) system* its energy content (its total amount) remains constant. This is the first law of thermodynamics. (The law of conservation also applies to matter.) For human purposes, however, it is the second law of thermodynamics, the entropy law, that is more relevant. It states that in an isolated (closed) system, the energy that is (or has been made) available continuously and *irreversibly* gets transformed into unavailable energy. This can be illustrated as follows. Let us imagine a four-room house that can in winter be perfectly isolated in respect to outside temperature. Let us further imagine that in winter we raise the temperature in one of the rooms. Once the room is heated, we feel comfortable inside it. But it does not remain so for long. After some time, the temperature in this room drops, while that in the other rooms goes up marginally. The heat energy in the heated room was available to us for some time, but now it no longer is. The air in the other rooms is now a little warmer, but not warm enough to make us feel comfortable. The total amount of heat energy in the house remains the same, but the initially higher amount of heat energy in the heated room has dissipated (dispersed). The temperatures in the four rooms finally become equal. The entropy of the system (i.e., of the temperature distribution in the house) has increased. The heat energy in the house has become unavailable to us.

Let us take another example. Imagine a kitchen where wood is used as fuel for cooking. Burning wood makes its energy available to us and produces enough heat to enable us to boil water and cook our food. After the wood has been completely burned, only ash is left, which cannot supply any more energy. But the energy released by the wood has not been totally lost; it has only dissipated in the house and has become unavailable for use in cooking. Entropy, thus, is the measure of unavailability of a given amount of energy. Increasing entropy means increasing unavailability of energy.

For the economic process this means that we can cook only so long as we have a supply of wood. Now wood is a renewable resource. If, while consuming this resource, we do not exceed the rate at which trees grow again, then future generations too can have enough wood at their disposal. But fossil fuels are not renewable. When they are exhausted or have become unaffordable due to exorbitant costs, those parts of the economic process that depend on these fuels will come to a standstill. For the dissipated (formerly concentrated) energy of these fuels cannot be concentrated again at any reasonable cost, even if it were chemically possible (producing oil from $CO_2$).

Georgescu-Roegen asks us to keep the elementary fact in mind that, for our economic process, matter also exists in the two states "available" and "unavailable," and that — just like energy — matter that is (or has been made) available to us also gets continuously and irreversibly transformed into unavailable matter. Examples of this are the rusting of iron and the wearing out of engines and car tires. Georgescu-Roegen calls this fact the fourth law of thermodynamics.

This law explains why 100% recycling is not possible. The rubber particles of worn car tires are so widely dissipated on the streets that they cannot be gathered again. When we have burned coal or oil, the carbon in the form of $CO_2$ is so widely dispersed in the atmosphere that it is difficult to imagine how it could be collected again without an enormous expenditure of energy (and many other things). But some degree of recycling is possible, and this is also done in our economic process. Pieces of iron that have not rusted completely can be collected with some expenditure of energy, etc., and can be smelted again with some more expenditure of energy. In developing countries, where labor power of the poor is very cheap, many useful materials can be recovered even from household garbage dumps, where hundreds of items lie around in a totally chaotic mixture. In high-wage countries this is uneconomical.

Now we can understand why Beckerman's assessment mentioned above is wrong. Since economical recycling is feasible only to a limited extent, it would be necessary to process ores with very low metal content, even ordinary rock, in order to realize Beckerman's vision. Georgescu-Roegen refers to a so-called "energetic dogma": "All we need to do is to add sufficient energy to the system and we can obtain whatever material we desire" (Brown et al. quoted in Georgescu-Roegen 1978: 17). But where will "enough," i.e. — in the case of Beckerman's idea — very large amounts of very cheap energy come from? Energy cannot be recycled at all. And fossil fuels, the main energy source of industrial societies, are becoming more and more scarce and expensive. Fortunately, with respect to energy, the earth is not a wholly closed system, but a relatively open one. We receive a considerable amount of solar energy from space, and that is why life on earth is possible. But, unfortunately, the difficulties of using solar energy for driving *industrial production* are far too great. For at least thirty-five years now, we have been hearing that solar energy, using liquid hydrogen as a storage medium, would replace problematic fossil fuels and dangerous nuclear power. Why hasn't this happened so far? Why is it that not only energy prices are rising, but also the prices of raw materials, such as iron, copper, nickel, zinc, and rare earth minerals? The entropy law gives the explanation for all this.

Our *industrial* civilization lives off irregularly located accumulations of resources in a state of low entropy. That is, they are available for our purposes because they occur in *sufficient concentration*. These resources — be they sources of metals and other materials or energy sources, such as coal, oil, gas, and uranium — are exhaustible. (The dangers related to concentration of $CO_2$ in the atmosphere and to radioactive contamination are a different story.) Sunshine is a practically inexhaustible source of energy. But it reaches us in a very high entropy state. In other words, its energy density is very low. It is therefore *not readily* available for most purposes of industrial production, which require high temperatures or electric power. What makes fossil fuels so indispensable for such purposes is, precisely, their high energy density. However, solar radiation is available, i.e., its energy density is high enough, for agricultural production (except in very high altitudes and in high latitude regions).

Solar energy enthusiasts maintain that solar electricity can also supply the high intensity energy necessary for industrial production. Correct, that is indeed feasible, with sufficient investment in technology. Several technologies have already been developed for this purpose. However, though *feasible*, it is not economically *viable*. Despite research and development for over forty years, large subsidies, and much promotion, it cannot yet be used on a large scale for industrial production. Why? Georgescu-Roegen gave an answer in 1978 that is still convincing to me. To state it briefly, according to him, manufacturing all the equipment, from A to Z, that belongs to a solar power plant — equipment that is necessary for collecting the highly dissipated solar radiation and then converting it into electricity — costs more *energy* than the total *energy* the same solar power plant can supply in its twenty-year life span. In other words, the *energy balance* of solar electricity is negative. For the average person this may be difficult to understand, but many understand the argument that, without subsidies, solar power is too expensive compared to electricity generated by burning fossil fuels. In the case of the other sources of renewable energy in the form of electricity — wind, flowing water, biomass, etc. — the energy balance may be more or less positive (in the case of hydroelectricity it is very positive), but they are not available so regularly (wind) and/or in such a quantity (biomass, wood) that they could approximately replace the currently consumed total of nonrenewable energy. (For a more detailed discussion of this issue see Sarkar 1999: chapter 4.)

Georgescu-Roegen (1981: 296) calls the supplies of nonrenewable energy sources and other minerals in a state of low entropy "the limited dowry of mankind's existence on earth." A dowry is not only a limited but also a one-time gift. Therefore, Georgescu-Roegen comes to the logical conclusion: "Even with a constant population and a constant flow per capita of mined resources, mankind's dowry will ultimately be exhausted if the career of the human species is not brought to an end earlier by other factors." The reason why the dowry is limited is that, in respect to matter (the nonrenewable fuels are also matter), the earth is a closed system. It does not receive any matter from outside (if we ignore meteorites), let alone matter in a state of low entropy. Therefore, all our efforts to increase *resource* productivity by increasing technological efficiency or through a little more rational consumption cannot change the exhaustibility of this dowry. Such efforts can only slow down the process a little.

## 4. Perspectives

In the above quote Georgescu-Roegen has made a mistake. He seems to believe that with the exhaustion of what he calls our dowry the career of the human species will also come to an end. That is wrong. What will come to an end is only our current industrial civilization. The daily solar irradiation, the more or less regular rainfall, and the fertile soils are also part of our dowry. And these are, practically speaking, inexhaustible, although global warming and other kinds of environmental degradation have partly jeopardized the reliability of this inexhaustible dowry. But, as we know, despite natural soil erosion, there is a lot of farmland all over the world that has been cultivated for thousands of years. If managed properly, these soils can remain fertile for several thousand years more. Other gifts of nature — trees and game in forests and fish in bodies of water — are of course not inexhaustible, but they are renewable. A different civilization with a smaller world population will definitely be *possible*, a civilization that will again live *mainly*, though not exclusively, off solar energy in its *original*, renewable forms — off solar radiation, rainfall, biomass, wind power, the power of flowing water, and the physical energy of both beasts of burden and our own bodies. True, at present, this world is unthinkable for most people, but such will undoubtedly be the future civilization, if a civilization at all exists. Jeremy Rifkin wrote about such a civilization, which he referred to as the "Solar Age" (the current one could be called the civilization of the Fossil Fuels Age):

> Those wedded to . . . the industrial age will no doubt regard
> these observations about solar technology as pessimistic. Many
> will consider it inconceivable that urban life, industrial produc-
> tion, and all the creature comforts that make up the so-called
> American Dream are antithetical to the Solar Age. However,
> ecologists and economists like Georgescu-Roegen, Daly, Odum,
> Bookchin, and Ophuls would argue that to ignore the historical

reality in front of us ... is sheer madness and will lead to an even greater fall for humankind, perhaps an irreversible one. Regardless of which course we follow, the coming transition is sure to be accompanied by *suffering and sacrifice*. (Rifkin 1980: 203; emphasis added)

However, even in the Solar Age, people could try to extract out of nature more than is sustainable. If all or even a part of the members of a "solar" society should try to become rich, they could do so only by, so to speak, "mining" their renewable resources and ultimately exhausting them. That would lead to the collapse of their economy. This has happened several times in history (see Ponting 1991, Diamond 1996). As Mahatma Gandhi said: "Earth provides enough to satisfy every man's need, but not for every man's greed" (Gandhi 1997: 306). Many, indeed, fight against this perspective of a "Solar Age." For all their ideas on how to solve the problems ahead there is a catch-all concept: "sustainable growth," which I discussed earlier on. They believe that sustainable growth will enable the people of the First World to maintain the affluence they are used to without any problem, or even to increase it. It will then be just a "new model of affluence." What is more, they even think that such affluence is also possible in the Third World. Elsewhere (Sarkar 1999) I have thoroughly examined such perspectives, which are being propagated with a lot of din. I have demonstrated that they are mere illusions. There is no space here for again describing the old illusions and repeating my old counterarguments. There are, however, new reports on developments that are more important for understanding the current state of the world.

RECENT REPORTS

The technological and economic breakthroughs in the area of renewable resources, which the naïve optimists have been hoping for for a long time, have not yet taken place.

For instance, in 1984, the EROEI of ethanol from sugar cane, which already covers some 20% of the fuel requirement of motor vehicles in Brazil, was estimated to be a mere 0.8 to 1.7, that is, negative or only slightly positive. In 1996, it was estimated to be even lower, i.e., 1.14 (Heinberg 2003: 152f.). Without subsidies, hardly anyone would produce ethanol. But given the concern about the dangers of global warming, the production of renewable energies is being strongly subsidized and favored with tax benefits. As a result, production of such energies has grown considerably (*Wall Street Journal*, 5 December 2006). In addition, the strong growth in production of crops used for producing bioethanol or biodiesel is causing conflicts over the share of arable land in densely populated countries. In Indonesia, for instance, 5.6 million hectares are already being used for oil palm plantations. In Kalimantan, the Indonesian part of Borneo, now more land is to be converted into oil palm plantations. A presidential decree will reportedly allow expropriation of land of all those who refuse to plant oil palm trees. In Indonesia, Malaysia, and Brazil, primeval forests are being clear-cut and burned down for the purpose of producing biofuels. Since nowadays corn produced in the United States is more and more being used to produce ethanol, the price of corn tortillas, staple food of the Mexicans, has increased steeply. European countries that import palm oil from Southeast Asia for producing biodiesel cannot use much of their own arable land for this purpose. In Germany, biodiesel produced from locally grown rapeseed can replace only about 5% of the total diesel consumption of the country. The goal of the EU in this respect is also modest, a mere 5.75% by 2010. (All figures are from Offer 2006.)

Another problem is that in many places such plantations empty the aquifers, e.g., in the United States and India, where corn or sugar cane is grown to produce ethanol — in areas where water is just as scarce as oil. In the case of the new oil palm plantations in Malaysia and Indonesia the water catchment areas are being modified to the detriment of the local population. Also from a solely narrow ecological standpoint, this boom is far from acceptable. A large part of the great smoke haze that veils the skies of Southeast Asia every summer and harms the health of people living there is caused by the burning down of forests for clearing land for oil palm plantations.

A report from the USA questions the whole rationale of such projects:

> David Pimentel, who teaches environmental policy, has long held doubts about the value of bio-fuels. He argues that [in the USA] expanding corn production for bio-fuels would deplete water resources and pollute soils with added fertilizer and chemicals. It would also *require huge volumes of conventional energy for farming equipment and ethanol-conversion facilities — a toll that could nullify gains from the less-polluting fuel produced.* (*Wall Street Journal*, 5 December 2006; emphasis added)

What has not been said in the above quote is that the production of fertilizers and other agrochemicals also require consumption of large quantities of fossil fuels and other nonrenewable raw materials. Pimentel's doubts had already been expressed in EROEI studies conducted in 1984 and 1996. Those studies calculated the EROEI of ethanol extracted from corn at just 1.3 and 1.1 respectively, and the EROEI of palm oil at just 1.06 (Heinberg 2003: 152f.).

The most highly subsidized renewable energy is solar electricity. In Eastern Germany, solar cell manufacturers can get subsidies that cover 45% of the eligible investment costs — for an investment of €250 million this amounts to more than €100 million (*Frankfurter Rundschau*, 14 November 2006). In addition, a law guarantees that producers can sell all their solar electricity to electricity companies at a guaranteed price that is more than six times as high as the production cost of coal-based electricity. In similar ways, there are also subsidies for wind power; offshore wind farms get larger subsidies than inland ones do (see Uken 2007).

With regard to the subsidies, one ought to ask where they come from. In the final analysis, they come from the production of the whole economy, which is powered to the greatest extent by fossil fuel–based energy. When this source of energy is exhausted or becomes unaffordable, then there will also be no more subsidies.

And in Germany, Fritz Vahrenholt, who until now has been a great advocate of renewable energies and who owns shares in a company that produces wind turbines, nowadays advocates extension of the life span of nuclear power plants. He expresses his current opinion on the economic viability of renewable energies as follows:

> Wind and solar energy have a disadvantage: they will not be sufficiently reliable until storage technologies become competitive. … Solar power is still too expensive. … We will not experience in the coming twenty years that the present-day price of 50 cents per kilowatt-hour will fall to 7 or 8 cents. We must therefore spend a lot of money to build gas-based power plants in order to compensate for the loss of nuclear power. Such power stations make us even more dependent. … I am very much optimistic that by 2050 we will be able to meet half of our energy needs from renewable sources. But even then the question remains: what are we going to do for the remaining 50%? (*Die Tageszeitung*, 7 October 2006)

But, in spite of this realization, Vahrenholt remains a naïve optimist. He has not really understood the problems yet. Why are storing technologies not yet competitive? The answer is that, whereas fossil fuels are *already compressed and stored* solar energy, renewable solar and wind electricity must *still* be compressed and stored — in the form of liquid hydrogen, battery power, or in some other form — in order to make them reliable. This work consumes a lot of conventional energy (apart from consumption of scarce and expensive materials). This additionally required effort makes the end product — electricity from hydrogen fuel cells or batteries (which are moreover known to be very inefficient) — not only all the more uncompetitive compared to fossil fuels, but it also makes the energy balance of this end product even more negative than that of electricity, e.g., from photovoltaic modules. The whole undertaking is therefore pointless.

Vahrenholt appears not to have yet understood a further problem: when it comes to replacing nuclear power plants with gas-fired power plants, the problem is neither money nor dependence. The Russians must also sell their gas. The problem is, firstly, the increase in $CO_2$ emissions, which he mentions, and, secondly, the limitedness and hence scarcity of this resource, which he does not mention. An observer wrote: "[A] more uncomfortable truth [is]: Russia may not have enough gas to keep both Europeans and Russians themselves warm in winters to come." She quotes an expert: "The fact is that there is a limit to how much gas Russia can sell to Europe. I don't think Europe realizes it, but we are reaching the limit of Russian exports. Russia needs the gas for themselves" (Dempsey 2006).

The argument against some renewable energy technologies, namely, that their EROEI is negative or not positive enough, and that they are not feasible without a large supporting structure of basic technologies such as metallurgy, etc., which mostly use fossil fuel energies, is not new (Georgescu-Roegen 1978; Sarkar 1999: chapter 4). This is so because we cannot *increase* the total quantity of our dowry of low entropy. If we try to reduce entropy (by means of concentration) at some point of the economic process, then we cannot do that without increasing entropy (in some cases more than proportionately) at other points of the process. For example, if we try to produce metal out of ore, biofuels out of crops, electricity out of sunshine or wind, etc., we have to use up (increase the entropy of) conventional fuels, various metals, and other highly concentrated materials.

It is therefore no wonder that for a long time, all over the world, there has been wrangling about control over the known deposits of nonrenewable resources — which are becoming ever scarcer and ever dearer — especially about control over sources of oil, gas, and uranium, but also over sources of freshwater, a renewable resource. In the recent past, Russia tripled overnight the price of its gas supplies to neighboring countries, and those countries have had to accept it. The wrangling about oil and gas below the seabed has already begun, e.g., in the Arctic Ocean. The

US government now wants to allow oil exploration and extraction in a protected area of that region. In the past, wars have been waged over resources. And there is again talk of the possibility of such wars. Actually, the recent wars in Iraq and Eastern Congo were essentially, at least largely, wars over the oil/mineral resources of those regions. No one talks anymore about increasing resource productivity by a factor of 4, by a factor of 10, etc.

## 5. The Pincer-Grip Crisis

All things considered, the world is caught in a pincer-grip. It is caught between the danger of climatic catastrophes and the danger posed by the exhaustion of fossil fuels, especially of oil. On the one hand, if we succeed in finding new abundant and cheap sources of oil and gas (cheap coal is still very abundant) and if our economies keep functioning as today, the global temperature will continue to rise and we shall for sure suffer even greater climatic catastrophes than what we have suffered so far. And global warming, it so happens, increases the possibility of our tapping new energy sources. Since the ice cap is receding farther to the north, it is becoming ever easier to explore for oil and gas under the seabed of the Arctic Ocean. A huge oil and gas deposit has already been found in the Barents Sea (Traufetter 2006: 114). On the other hand, if we are forced, or decide of our own accord, to drastically reduce the consumption of fossil fuels in order to avert worse climate catastrophes, then the downfall of modern industrial societies, whose lifeblood fossil fuels are, will set in. For example, reducing fossil fuel consumption includes drastically reducing the production of fertilizers; as a result, the already overpopulated under-developed countries — whose population contines to increase (in India, for instance, the population is growing by 18 million per annum) — will be ravaged by famines.

Nuclear energy will also not be able to help us further. For, firstly, supply of uranium ore is limited. According to expert estimates, at the current consumption rate the known deposits would last at the most another sixty years. Secondly, according to the World Nuclear Association, the world production of uranium already peaked in 1981, and its production is gradually falling (Meacher 2006). The price of uranium was in 2006 more than six times what it was five years before (*International Herald Tribune*, 5 September 2006). The reason the falling production of uranium has not yet caused the closure of any nuclear power plants is that large quantities of fissionable material have become available to the nuclear power industry as a result of reductions in the nuclear weapons arsenals of the superpowers. It is however likely that within ten years about 25 percent of the world's nuclear power plants will have to close down (Meacher 2006). And thirdly, for us it is not enough to have electricity, the product of nuclear power plants. The world economy also needs a cheap, storable, and liquid fuel, not the least to be able to build nuclear power plants with. Liquid hydrogen, as already stated, would not only be too costly, it would also be pointless to produce because of its negative energy balance.

Georgescu-Roegen published his pessimistic prediction ("Even with a constant population and a constant flow ... of mined resources, mankind's dowry will ultimately be exhausted if the career of the human species is not brought to an end earlier ... ") in 1981. After that, two oil price shocks and the danger of climate catastrophes ensued. In all the years thereafter, thanks to scientific and technological progress, we have developed many almost magical products, such as the computer and the Internet. One of our space vehicles has traveled three billion miles in space, taken a sample from a comet, and brought it to Earth. But until now, we have not been able to find or create economically viable renewable energies that could in the foreseeable future replace fossil fuels — in today's required quantities. The human intellect cannot overcome the entropy law.

The question now is whether, in the face of the pincer-grip crisis, there is any hope for humankind. Both "yes" and "no" has been said in answer: "yes" by naïve optimists, and "no" by people of the "die out" movement, who believe that industrialism is a deadly disease of humankind (Kunstler 2005: 5). In the middle, there are those who say "yes and no."

Nicholas Stern, from whose review I have quoted, belongs to the optimists. He estimates the yearly costs of stabilizing the global $CO_2$ emissions to be the relatively modest 1% of the global GDP until 2050, which he considers to be considerable, but bearable. With this opinion Stern encounters criticism even from like-minded people. For example, Robert J. Samuelson (2006) (not the Nobel prize winner Paul Samuelson) wrote:

> The notion that there is only a modest tension between suppressing greenhouse gases and sustaining economic growth is highly dubious. Stern arrives at his trivial costs ... by essentially assuming them. His estimates presume that ... technological improvements will automatically reconcile declining emissions with adequate economic growth. ... To check warming, Stern wants annual emissions 25 percent below current levels by 2050. The IEA [International Energy Agency] projects that

economic growth by 2050 would more than double emissions. At present, we can't bridge the gap ...

*We need more candor.* Unless we develop cost-effective technologies that break the link between carbon-dioxide emissions and energy use, we can't do much. Anyone serious about global warming must focus on technology — and not just assume it. Otherwise, *our practical choices are all bad*: costly mandates and controls that harm the economy; or costly mandates and controls that barely affect greenhouse gases. Or, possibly, both. (emphasis added)

As I have shown above and in more detail in my previous book (1999), the technology that Samuelson is demanding is an illusion. We simply cannot protect the current climate (and the rest of the environment) without harming the economy as it is today. We cannot eat our cake and have it too. George W. Bush was at least sincere when he decided to abandon the Kyoto Protocol on the grounds that it would harm the American economy.

Moreover, Stern obviously has not heard anything about the problem of defensive costs (see chapter IX). If we took all the measures that he recommends — building dikes, CCS, etc. — the world GDP would naturally increase. But by how much would thereby the measurable economic welfare (MEW) increase? Will we not have to forgo a great deal of our desired consumption in order to finance those measures?

In his latest book, *The Revenge of Gaia*, James Lovelock (2006b) looks at global warming and gives the bad news that it is too late to stop the accelerating rise of global temperature. He maintains that the same negative feedback mechanisms that in the past kept the earth cooler than it would otherwise have been will now intensify the warming process. Before this century is over, he predicts, billions of humans will die as a result. He wrote in a newspaper article:

> We have given Gaia a fever and soon her condition will worsen to a state like a coma. She has been there [in that state] before and recovered, but it took more than 100,000 years. We are responsible and will suffer the consequences: as the century progresses, the temperature will rise 8 degrees centigrade in temperate regions and 5 degrees in the tropics ...
>
> We [the Britons] could grow enough to feed ourselves on the diet of the Second World War, but the notion that there is land to spare to grow biofuels, or be the site of wind farms, is ludicrous. We will do our best to survive, but sadly I cannot see the

United States or the emerging economies of China and India cutting back in time, and they are the main source of emission. The worst will happen, and survivors will have to adapt to a hell of a climate.

Despite his pessimism, he makes an appeal to humankind:

So let us be brave and cease thinking of human needs and rights alone, and see that we have harmed the living Earth and need to make our peace with Gaia. We must do it while we are still strong enough to negotiate, and not a broken rabble led by brutal warlords. (Lovelock 2006a)

For the American author James Howard Kunstler, the imminent "peak oil" (which may already be behind us) — that is, the point at which the maximum rate of oil extraction has been reached and the decline starts — is even more fateful for modern industrial societies. For

[e]verything characteristic about the condition we call modern life has been a direct result of our access to abundant supplies of cheap fossil fuels. Fossil fuels have permitted us to fly, to go where we want to go rapidly, and move things easily from place to place. Fossil fuels rescued us from the despotic darkness of the night. They have made the pharaonic scale of building commonplace everywhere. They have allowed a fractionally tiny percentage of our swollen populations to produce massive amounts of food. They have allowed us to develop industries of surpassing ingenuity and to push the limits of what it even means to be human to the strange frontier where man imagines himself into a kind of machine immortality. (Kunstler 2005: 23)

In the 1980s, the oil crisis of the 1970s was overcome through new discoveries — e.g., through those in the North Sea and in the north coast of Alaska. This was followed by an oil glut, which caused prices to fall steeply. At present, the new discoveries in the Caspian Sea do not have such an effect. Quite on the contrary, the specter of rising oil and gas prices is haunting modern societies. Kunstler wrote: "We are now headed off the edge of a cliff. Beyond that cliff is an abyss of economic and political disorder on a scale that no one has ever seen before. I call this coming time the Long Emergency" (1). But Kunstler is not as pessimistic as Georgescu-Roegen or the "die out" people. With regard to the United States, his home country, he views the "period ahead as one of generalized and chronic contraction," a process he calls the "downscaling of America" (18).

In chapter I, I dealt with the question of why Marx and the Marxists expected an insurmountable crisis and then either the breakdown of capitalism or its abolition by the proletariat. They expected all that as a consequence of the inner contradictions of the system. Capitalism, however, could withstand such contradictions; it did not break down, it was not abolished (except in a few countries). It could survive because it was able to pacify all its opponents by means of Keynesian economic policies, the welfare state, the social democratic parties, and the unions. But in the final analysis, all that was possible because the gifts of nature, especially the fossil fuels, were flowing in abundance. But the pincer-grip crisis outlined above has little to do with the *inner* contradictions of the system: its cause lies in the laws of nature, which are *beyond* the control of the system. It does not look like capitalism will be able to survive this crisis.

The reader may not now help asking: why are the crises and problems dealt with in this chapter included in a book on the crises of capitalism? They are after all crises and problems of any modern industrial economy, irrespective of the political system! The question is justified. Nevertheless, these issues are important for this book because (and in the sense that) due to the system's inner logic — competition, profit motive, growth compulsion, etc. — these problems and crises cannot be overcome within the framework of capitalism. The imminent, inevitable, worldwide, and long-drawn contraction of the economies can be peacefully[17] coped with only if humanity is prepared to abandon capitalism and, parallel to the contraction process, to build a *newly conceived* socialist society.[18]

# XI.

# The Future of Capitalism

In the previous two chapters I presented the different aspects of the current unmistakable crisis *of* capitalism. Now the question arises whether capitalism can survive this crisis, and, if yes, in which form. In this chapter I want to present my reflections on this question as well as those of some other authors.

In the preface to *A Contribution to the Critique of Political Economy*, Marx wrote a passage very well known among leftists: "No social order ever perishes before all the productive forces for which there is room in it have developed; and new, higher relations of production never appear before the material conditions for their existence have matured in the womb of the old society itself." He continued: "With the change of the economic foundation the entire immense superstructure is more or less rapidly transformed" (Marx 1859/1977: 504). What Marx meant in 1859 by the words "the change of the economic foundation" was something very different from what we today must mean when we say these words. Today, the economic foundation is changing because, firstly, the assumption of constancy of nature is no longer valid (see chapter X), and, secondly, because the existence of limits to growth can no longer be denied.

The question now is whether all the productive forces for which there is room in capitalism have already been developed. Particularly for Marxists this question is very relevant. For should the answer be no—and should that be actually true—then capitalism can still exist for a very long time and possibly also flourish. But I believe the question has today *become irrelevant*. For any development of productive forces in the Marxian or traditional bourgeois sense—further development of automation, for instance—will, if it is also widely used, inevitably result in greater consumption of nonrenewable and scarce resources and with it greater destruction of the environment. That is something humankind can no longer afford.

Today any technical invention or revival of any old and, as a rule, labor-intensive technology that reduces resource consumption should be called a development of productive forces. Many technologies of the pre-industrial age, which are still being used in some parts of the Third World — oxcarts, for instance — should be counted among them. But all Marxists and other leftists I know would refuse to accept as such a redefinition of the concept appropriate to our times. For them, development of the productive forces must lead not only to affluence in terms of goods and services but also to true affluence, namely, as Marx said, to more free time. With labor-intensive technologies (that save resources) this is not possible. Quite on the contrary, they lead — all things being equal — to *less* free time.

For the topic future of capitalism, therefore, the more relevant question *today* is whether capitalism can continue to be the appropriate or sufficient framework for a future economy in which not growth but contraction, not more and more automation but increasing labor-intensity of technology, will be the rule. Naturally, this question does not arise for people who believe sustainable economic growth is possible. They deal with other questions.

## 1. Harry Shutt's Vision of a Regulated, Egalitarian, and Global Capitalism

After a comprehensive review of the new developments in global capitalism published in his two books (1998, 2005), Harry Shutt, a critic of the system, comes to the conclusion that in the rich industrialized countries there will probably be no recovery from the present chronic stagnation (2005: 123), and that capitalism is in decline. He even sees "the palpable signs of unfolding economic disaster" (131), and he thinks it is probable that "social and political tensions will build to an explosive level" (129). He wrote:

> Although the powerful propaganda machine of the ruling
> vested interests has partly succeeded in blurring the public's
> perception of the full extent of the *systemic crisis*, there are
> unmistakable signs not only of breakdown in the functioning of
> global capitalism but of rising discontent with it. (83; emphasis
> added)

Many points in Shutt's line of reasoning are like those I have dealt with in chapter VIII. His most important arguments for the thesis that this time it is a crisis *of* the system can be summarized as follows.

In order that the capitalist growth model remains alive, two conditions must absolutely be met: (1) New investment opportunities must be found in order to give the increasing flow of money wanting to be invested the possibility of making profits. And (2) the profit rate — at least the market value of the investments — has to be maintained. This is, however, becoming increasingly difficult. Even when new profitable investment opportunities can be found, that only aggravates the problem. For then, in the medium term, even more money capital that wants to be profitably invested flows into the market.

This is not much different from the Marxist view of the contradictory dynamics of capital accumulation. In Marxist theory, the causes of crisis are called overinvestment and overproduction. In the present time, however, the contradiction has become acute because through the invention of pension funds, investment funds, etc., in which hundreds of millions of ordinary people are participating, a "wall of money" has been created that is looking for profitable investment opportunities. Fund managers are therefore compelled to buy shares, etc., and speculate. But now the returns are expected from increase in the market value of the investments rather than from the actual profits made by the companies. In past years, income from dividends has almost continuously fallen (2005: 35). Theoretically, of course, one could say that the high share prices of the present time are justified by expected high profits in the future. But, given the chronic low growth rates of the economies, that is not plausible. Shutt considers this to be an extremely dangerous situation, which will unavoidably lead to a "financial holocaust" which will be far more devastating — especially for ordinary people — than any previous one (1998: 230).

On the legitimacy problem of capitalism Shutt wrote that in a modern democracy sustained justification of capitalism does not depend only on its ability to guarantee adequate returns for investors but also on its ability to guarantee "adequate and stable living standards for the vast majority of the population." But it is not possible to achieve both, as "there are limits to expanding the output of goods and services perpetually" (2005: 124).

The explanation for the chronically low growth rates is for Shutt, as it is for Keynesians, insufficient demand. But he does not think much of lowering the interest rates as a means to stimulating demand. He criticizes "governments' increasing tendency to use what has become their only instrument of demand management, changes in interest rates, to induce consumers to take on more and more debt in a desperate effort to boost economic activity, apparently heedless of the fact that such an artificial boost to demand is bound to be matched by a subsequent downturn" (38).

But although Shutt speaks of "manifest breakdown in the functioning of the global economic order based on the capitalist profits system," he thinks that capitalism could still be saved through a change in *form* that would make it "less destructive" (121). He presents his vision of a future sustainable world order both as a forecast and as a recommendation. He expects that the greater part of humanity, especially people in the developed West, will realize that "self-regulated, profit-maximizing capitalism" is no longer a vehicle for progress and "compatible with the priorities of modern democracies" (2005: 123; 1998: 229). Shutt thinks "it might be expected that Western society would have developed the capacity to adjust to inevitable change without the need for violent revolution" (2005: 121).

The main element in Shutt's recommendations is a total rejection of the policy of liberalization, which should be replaced with politically resolved regulation of the economy by the state. He wants to liberate society from the tyranny of market forces.

His transformed capitalism would give up the objective of indiscriminate maximization of GDP because, firstly, that is not possible due to very sluggish growth in demand and, secondly, because it should not also be allowed in the face of the dangers to the environment. In an economy with low or nil growth, unlimited profit maximization cannot be accepted as the main objective of corporations. Allocation of resources should be increasingly and implicitly guaranteed by the state, and that must be done in a transparent and egalitarian manner. Unfair competition must be prevented, and cooperation instead of competition should be stressed more strongly. The state should also influence pricing as well as investment strategy.

In an economic order controlled in this way, the role of private capital will be gradually reduced. If necessary, the state must take over companies or transfer them to collective ownership. In such cases, compensatory payments should be based on a valuation far below their market value. However, in this process, priority should be given to the livelihood of pensioners who are participants in private pension funds, and to small savers. Actually, high-risk pension funds should be dissolved, and state pension for everyone should be introduced.

Companies, be they privately owned or state-owned, will only be allowed to trade within a given market (national or regional). This will be indispensable in order to avoid reemergence of the race to the bottom caused by competition.

Rigorous accountability will apply to all kinds of companies as well as to government departments. Additionally, business policies of companies, whose financial solidity is ultimately guaranteed by the state, will have to be endorsed by public authorities. This will apply especially to financial institutions, as in the meantime it is widely acknowledged that the stability of the financial system is a public asset.

There will no longer be an obligation to pay investors high returns on their overvalued shares. A larger portion of the total value added will be used to (1) reduce the deficits and debts of the public sector, (2) reduce the prices of consumer goods, (3) pay sufficient and fair wages to employees, and (4) increase social benefits, which should include a guaranteed minimum income for non-working people. Generally speaking, Shutt wants to lay greater emphasis on egalitarian distribution of income and wealth.

Although the principle of profit *maximization* is downgraded, companies will have to show a minimum profit rate as evidence of their efficiency. This will in any case reduce the importance of competitiveness. In the labor market too, pure competition will not be the rule. Shutt toys with the idea of some kind of labor rationing. As for income distribution, inequality will be limited, especially because the prospects of economic growth will be limited.

Shutt is no opponent of globalization, but he wants it to be regulated. Capital movement — between countries that implement the reforms proposed by him on the one side and countries that do not on the other — must not be free. Otherwise capital transfers would have negative impacts on the economies of the countries of the first group. For similar reasons, international trade must also be regulated. Limits have to be set to the growth of trade in specific goods and services, whereby underdeveloped countries and regions should be favored.

Shutt advocates an increasingly integrated global economic structure. He thinks economic independence is an illusion, and he especially calls upon the developing countries to integrate themselves in such a global economic structure. He demands of the rich countries more or less permanent and abundant development aid for the poor regions. The poorest countries, as well as the industrialized ones, must then give up their sovereignty. They will then be progressively integrated in a functioning democratic world community. He has in mind a model similar to today's European Union.

Shutt goes even further. Long-term economic aid will be given to only those developing countries prepared to begin to integrate themselves with the developed world. Countries that would like to remain outside this integrated structure will not enjoy the privileges of those willing to integrate. They may, however, receive support for their development and will be allowed to carry on trade with the "core bloc" of the developed countries, but only if they keep to a minimum standard of democracy, human rights, and accountability. Countries that do not do that cannot expect anything more than humanitarian aid in case of catastrophes. Shutt even has no objection to imposing embargos on such countries, and attempts to topple tyrannical leaders are, in his view, not improper. He thinks nothing of the principle of non-interference in the internal affairs of sovereign states. He wrote: "Only through a willingness to experiment with such new forms of international association, transcending the nineteenth century model of the nation-state, can we hope to address the crippling problems of global economic imbalance and the related rise in civil disorder" (1998: 229).

### MY CRITICISM OF SHUTT

Although I sympathize with Schutt's basic attitude, I think his half-concrete vision of a reformed and benevolent capitalism is illogical, contradictory, unrealistic and, therefore, useless.

His vision reminds me of India's mixed economy from the 1950s until the 1970s, an economy that was generally steered through five-year plans and regulations, in which a large part of the heavy industries belonged to the public sector, and in which all large banks (since the late 1960s) were nationalized. The state also did a lot in favor of the poor and the oppressed. Those governing the country at the time called that system socialism. But still, the much greater part of the economy remained capitalistic and feudal, and there was exploitation and oppression as always. Shutt does not use the term "socialism" even once. At one place he speaks of the "dethroning of the profit motive" (2005: 127), but at other places he only rejects the principle of profit *maximization*. He seems to be afraid of stating openly that capitalism has to be abolished after a transition period, although at one place he also calls his conceptions "a new collectivism" (1998: 217). He envisages an egalitarian allocation of resources, but no planned economy. He wants to place greater emphasis on cooperation, yet he only wants to prevent unfair competition (2005: 126). So, competition remains. However, in capitalism, cooperation only means formation of cartels, which results in unfair competition. All these contradictions result from Shutt's lack of courage to fully and openly oppose capitalism.

Nationwide economic cooperation, instead of competition, is only possible in a socialist planned economy.

Among the immediate responses to a global financial catastrophe that he would demand of collectivistically minded Western national governments is also increased financial aid to impoverished Third World countries (2005: 130). But how can this be possible particularly in times in which large numbers of companies go bankrupt, unemployment goes up massively, millions of people including pensioners (who participate in pension funds) become destitute, and states are threatened with insolvency? This might be conceivable if the population and the ruling politicians have a very strong moral sense of duty. Shutt obviously assumes this. But is such an assumption realistic in Shutt's vision of a good society that, despite all reforms, remains capitalistic and is undergoing a severe economic crisis?

A strong indication of the crisis of capitalism is, in Shutt's view, the profitability crisis. His analysis of the cause of the crisis outlined above is too simple. A profitability crisis can also be overcome through cost cutting and tax reduction measures favoring companies. Both measures have been practiced for a long time. Production costs are being reduced primarily at the expense of workers, i.e., by means of mass retrenchment, which is increasingly becoming possible through technological development, reduction in real wages, and relocation of production to low-wage countries. One can have understanding for the limitedness of Shutt's causal analysis of the crisis of capitalism if one bears in mind that his two books I have quoted from were written against the background of the crises of 1997 to 2003. For capital, the situation has improved since then. In 2006, the stock markets all over the world were booming again, and corporate profits were skyrocketing. As I have explained in chapter VII in detail, it is too simple to say that sluggish demand is the main cause of the crisis.

Shutt seems not to be aware of the other aspects of the crisis I discussed in chapter X. He prognosticates that economic growth will cease to be a priority. But why? In his view, because "there are limits to expanding the output of goods and services ... because of short-term limits to demand growth." He mentions cautiously and in passing environmental problems that might limit the growth of demand (2005: 124). He does not state categorically that economic growth *should* stop out of environmental considerations. He does not even mention the fact that, in the middle term, the limitedness of natural resources and the ecological crisis will force an economic *contraction* on humankind. Quite on the contrary, he expects of the future collectivistically minded governments a redistribution of income and *wealth* (123), an increase in social welfare benefits, improvement of

social services, and a guaranteed minimum income for non-working people. All of this, including the generous aid for poor countries that Shutt
demands, presupposes *business as usual* in the industrialized countries.

## 2. A Few Success Stories

In contrast to Shutt's diagnosis that capitalism is in terminal decline, there
have been, since the 1980s, some success stories — phoenix-from-the-ashes
stories. There is much talk about the Dutch polder model and the exemplary reform of the old and famous Nordic model.

In the early 1980s, a general mood of crisis prevailed in the Nether-
lands. The economic growth rate fell between 1980 and 1982 from 0.9%
to –1.5%. The official unemployment rate rose from 4.6% in 1980 to 11.8%
in 1983 (OECD 1994: A4, A23). State expenditures and the public debt
increased rapidly. In this situation, in 1982 the union leader Wim Kok and
the president of the employers' association issued a joint declaration aimed
at rescuing the economy. The unions committed themselves to moderate
wage-rise demands. The employers too made concessions. The purpose
of this statement was to initiate a long-term policy, the objective of which
was to always find a consensus on acceptable compromises. In the following years, the economic situation improved — something that might have
happened also without this polder model.

However, the situation deteriorated again in the early 1990s. Economic
growth fell from 2.1% in 1991 to 0.4% in 1993. And unemployment grew
from 6.7% in 1992 to 9.3% in 1994 (OECD 1994: A4, A23). In 1994, Wim
Kok was elected prime minister and the polder model was fully accepted.
A series of reforms was pushed through in order to create jobs. Shops were
allowed to stay open from 6 AM to 10 PM, even on Sundays. Low-wage jobs
were introduced, which helped reduce unit labor costs and made the country more attractive for entrepreneurs. At the same time, employers pushed
ahead with part-time jobs, and their share in the economy strongly grew
in the following period. Such jobs are socially insured, and they are particularly popular among women who want to overcome the conflict between
family and profession. Also child care was improved. In 1996, a law was
passed that made it possible to oblige unemployed people to accept, in
return for social benefit payments, a job that had previously been voluntary work. All these reforms brought the official unemployment rate down
to 2.5% by 2001 (OECD 2004: 215). (For a detailed account of the polder
model see Fokken 2006: 103ff.)

In the 1990s, the Scandinavian countries — famous until the mid-
1980s for their affluence and generous welfare state — had their economic

problems as well (oil-rich Norway was an exception). Finland suffered much from the collapse of the Soviet Union. Trade with the Eastern neighbor broke down. In the 1980s, rapid liberalization of the economy had fueled consumption and inflation. Between 1986 and 1989, the inflation rate had shot up from 2.9% to 6.6%. The overvalued national currency, the markka, caused a lot of problems to the exporting industries. Bubbles in both the stock exchange and the real estate market ultimately burst. GDP growth recorded negative values from 1991 to 1993: -7.1%, -3.6%, and -2%. In 1993, the unemployment rate reached 17.9%.

In this severe crisis, a social democratic government carried out a radical cure program. The convergence criteria to be met for joining the Eurozone, to which Finland wanted to belong, helped a great deal in the process. Wage increases were stopped for several years, cuts were made in unemployment benefits, child allowances, pensions, and health care — all on the basis of consensus. Also unions agreed to all these measures — the employers too, needless to say. But no cuts were made in education, training, and research. Quite on the contrary, they were generously promoted, also with funds from the industry. The Finns had realized they could only be competitive in products in which knowledge and technology played a greater role than labor costs. That is how Nokia has become the most successful cell phone manufacturer in the world.

The results of this policy — except in the area of unemployment — were excellent. In the period 1990–2002, GDP grew on average by 2.9% per annum. In early 2006, the growth rate was estimated to be 3.6% and the inflation rate 1%. Since 1998, year after year, the budget had shown a surplus. Public debt in terms of percentage of GDP also sank. In early 2006, it was just 45%, an indication of the good health of the economy. The unemployment rate also fell, albeit moderately because of the concentration on high-tech industries: from 9% in 2003 to 7.6% in early 2006. (Figures from OECD 1994, Gamillscheg 2006, and *Fischer Weltalmanach* 2005.)

Within the broad term "Nordic reform model," the Danish model rose to the status of an international role model, because the Danes succeeded in almost completely removing at least the *official* unemployment. In the early 1980s, there was an overall crisis atmosphere in the country. The GDP fell, and unemployment rose in 1983 to 10.4%. The inflation rate stood in 1980 at 12.3% (OECD 1994: A4, A18, A23). The conservative government elected in 1982 gave highest priority to the fight against inflation and eliminated the then existing system of automatic wage raises linked to price trends. That, of course, gave rise to a great deal of unrest in the beginning. But the inflation rate fell thereafter almost continuously — from 6.9% in 1983 to 1.3% in 1993 — and the budget regularly showed a surplus

(A18, A34). The official unemployment rate, however, steadily rose from 1986 onwards: from 7.8% to 12.2% in 1993 (A23).

The Social Democrats, who had come to power in 1993, wanted of course to reduce unemployment, but they were not prepared to abandon the stability policy pursued by their predecessors. And they succeeded. While the inflation rate remained low—the highest rate was 2.9% in 2000—and the budget continued to show a surplus, the official unemployment rate began to fall, and in 2001 it reached the enviable rate of 4.3%. What is surprising is that, all along, economic growth remained between modest and low. In 2001 it came to only 1.6% (OECD 2004: 220, 215, 203). The official unemployment rate remained low also in the following two years — 4.6% in 2002 and 5.6% in 2003 — although the economic growth rates, with 0.5% and 0.7% respectively, were even lower than in the previous year (OECD 2005: 51, 61).

In the process of economic globalization, many jobs were lost, but more new ones were also created. Year for year, a third of all Danish working people changed jobs (Frederiksen 2006). The scarcity of skilled workers was so great that Danish companies had to recruit skilled workers from northern Germany (Moring 2006). Denmark has been considered a job creating machine. Remarkably, the Danes were able to achieve this without introducing low-wage jobs. How did they do it?

In 1994, the government ended the policy of generous and unlimited state-financed unemployment benefits. A new labor market policy, called "flexicurity," was introduced. Less protection against dismissal makes it very easy to lay off workers when they are no longer needed. This also means that when companies receive more orders, new workers can be hired without hesitation. This is the flexibility that employers enjoy. As compensation for this job insecurity, laid off workers have a right to high unemployment benefits for four years—90% of the last wage up to an upper limit of €1,820 a month. During this period, unemployed workers are also entitled to state support for finding a new job. For young people under thirty there is even a guarantee of a job or an apprenticeship.

Such rights are, however, tied to obligations. One who does not cooperate with the labor market authorities and, for instance, turns down an offer of a training or a reasonable job, does not receive unemployment benefits for three weeks. One who turns down such an offer a second time totally forfeits one's right to unemployment benefits. After that one gets only the much lower welfare benefits. Almost anything qualifies as a "reasonable" job offer.

For financing the high unemployment benefits and other benefits pertaining to a welfare state, the government naturally needs high tax revenues. In 2004, the ratio of public spending to GNP was 55.6%, as against 47.8% in Germany and 35.6% in the United States (Institut der Deutschen Wirtschaft 2005: 136). The various tax rates are relatively high. For incomes above €42,000 the tax rate is as high as 63%; the rate of value-added tax is 25%. The majority of the Danes agree to such tax rates. They are prepared to pay this much for their model. (Figures from Gamillscheg 2004, 2005a, 2005b, Walker 2006.)

Within the old Nordic model of the welfare state, the Swedish model was the most famous. I presented it in chapter III. In Sweden, too, there was a crisis atmosphere in the early 1980s, though not as severe as in Denmark. The growth rate ranged from very low to zero. But from 1990 to 1993, the situation was even worse. There were also negative growth rates; the official unemployment rate rose from 1.7% to 8.2%, and it remained high in the following years. No wonder then that, given the generous welfare benefits, the budget balance fell during this period from +4.3% to −12.8% of the GDP. The inflation rate increased; its highest level was 10.5% in 1990 (OECD 1994: A4, A18, A23, A34). The Swedes realized that their generous welfare state in the then existing form was no longer affordable. They now wanted to reform it. Outside Sweden, there was now talk of the end of the famous Swedish model. The ideologues of neo-liberalism saw in this development the proof that there was no alternative to their economic policy.

Between 1991 and 1994, the rightists were in power. They initiated a wave of market-oriented reforms: tax reduction, deregulation, privatization, and outsourcing of some public services. But this policy was disliked by the majority of the Swedes because they loved their welfare state despite its many problems, and additionally because the economic situation deteriorated under the rightist government. In 1994, they elected the Social Democrats back to power.

The Social Democrats, however, could not or did not want to undo all the changes that their predecessors in government had made. And they too wanted to downsize the old welfare state in order to adapt it to the given economic resources. Successive Social Democratic governments have since then made many changes in the *Volksheim*, which is no longer as cozy as it used to be. Because of economizations, there are, for instance, deficiencies in care for the elderly, new youth problems, waiting periods in the health care system, a fee of €16 for every visit to a doctor, etc. Unemployment benefits have been reduced to 80% of the last wage, capped at 3,400 krona ($510) per week for the first 100 days. After that one gets less. The policy of "flexicurity" applies to the labor market in Sweden as in Denmark. The retirement age has been raised to 67. (Data from Toynbee 2005, Perger 2005, Ertel 2006, Clevström 2006.)

These reforms again made Sweden a success story, but they did not change the basic character of Swedish society. Sweden remains a welfare state. Referring to Sweden and the other Scandinavian countries, Peter Auer, a leading figure in the International Labour Organization (ILO), wrote in 2001:

> It is not the countries that have reduced social spending most, have curbed government intervention drastically or minimized social partnership that are the leading successes today. It is rather those that have retained, while adapting, their institutions which now see their economic success spilling over into the labor market. It is not the flexibility of the market but the existence and adaptability of institutions and regulations that explain success. (quoted in Taylor 2005: 30)

This *new* Swedish model too inspires the European left's social democrats.

> While the new Swedish model continues to seek an accommodation with a more individualistic society, ... in its welfare state reforms, it also emphasizes that the management of democratic change is best achieved through a clear focus on ... stability in the widest sense of that word.
> ... But perhaps the most important lesson ... is that the core values of Social Democracy are more relevant than ever. ... Sweden has succeeded in creating a grand narrative for a progressive process of modernization in response to the complex challenges of our times. It is based primarily on an idealistic and attractive focus on the meaning of freedom. ... This is not a selfish, individualistic egoism concerned with the mere satisfaction of material wants and appetites. ... Nor is it based on a stifling conformity of outlook and behavior imposed on a reluctant people by ... [the] state. It is a social freedom that, while it balances rights and responsibilities in the interests of the wider society, also affirms a genuine emancipation ... from the rapacious power of an unregulated market economy. (26, 32)

There are a few more success stories of different kinds that I don't have the space to describe here. But they must at least be mentioned: the success story of the "better Germans" (Austria), the boom in Slovakia, and the economic rise of the "Celtic tiger" (Ireland), that however later proved to have been built on sand.

What I want to convey with these success stories is that they considerably weaken Shutt's conclusion that capitalism is in decline. Also, Shutt's perception that it is very likely that "social and political tensions will build to an explosive level" (2005: 129) appears at the time of writing to be very much exaggerated, at least so far as the rich industrialized countries are concerned (the lone exception is Greece in 2010–2012). All the above reports rather show that the so-called social partners — i.e., management and labor — and the political parties lay great store by cooperation, harmony, and consensus. Taylor wrote on the new Swedish model:

> The trade unions continue to embrace ... technological change and cooperate in the restructuring of companies and promotion of worker empowerment. Organized labor seeks to improve the quality of working life and not to obstruct progress but to welcome it. For their part, employer associations, private companies, public authorities, financial institutions and the like remain important partners in the modernization process. (31)

Why, then, should there be a crisis *of* capitalism? In Scandinavia, social life is so harmonious and well ordered that there, in recent times, even the right-wing opposition parties have been trying to present themselves as the better social democrats in order to be elected to power. It is true that also in the Scandinavian countries the unemployment problem remains unsolved. In Denmark and Sweden too, the true unemployment rate is considerably higher than the low official one. But the crisis phenomena outlined in chapter IX do not seem to threaten the system anywhere. They can *in principle* be coped with within the framework of capitalism. In Scandinavia, the model of high public spending and better social benefits has also been accepted by capitalists and the wealthy. If other countries do not follow the example of the Scandinavians (or the Dutch), they will for sure have great problems. But the Scandinavian path remains open to them.

Even in milieus in which resistance is strong — for instance, in the anti-globalization or globalization-critical movement — it is not capitalism per se that is being attacked, but only its neo-liberal, globalized form. As an alternative, the great majority of activists in this movement have in mind the *old* Nordic model of a welfare state in combination with a Keynesian economic policy.

In the recent past there have been some cases of social and political tension or even an explosion resulting from a severe economic crisis. I am thinking here of the rebellion of the indigenous population in Chiapas (Mexico) in 1994, the frenzied revolt of youth without jobs or hope in the suburbs of large French cities (2005), the events in Argentina including the numerous cases of factories occupied by workers after the collapse of the economy in 2001 (see chapter VI, section 3), and, last but not least, the often violent protests in Greece in 2011–2012 against the austerity measures imposed upon the people. But not even in Argentina was there a serious attempt to eliminate capitalism. I believe the reason for this was not only the various weaknesses of the local leftist forces, but also, and mainly, that there was a quiet hope among the vast majority of Argentines that the crisis could still be overcome without having to fight the *system*. This was in fact the case.

### 3. Can Capitalism Survive in a Contracting Economy?

For some time now, there have been calls in and from Venezuela and Bolivia for a march towards a not clearly defined "socialism of the twenty-first century." On closer look, however, one sees there not much more than a more egalitarian distribution and (partial) nationalization of the oil and gas riches of the country. One could here speak of *petro-socialism*. It is of course better than petro-capitalism, but it can have only a short life in a few countries. It can remain alive only as long as the fossil fuel riches flow.

For the greater part of the world, however, as I have shown in chapter X, what I call the pincer-grip crisis leads to a crisis *of* capitalism. I have also argued that the world economy, whether we want it or not, will begin to contract in the foreseeable future, that even if the world GDP grows, well-being, i.e., the measure of economic welfare (MEW) per capita, will continuously fall (chapter IX). The question that arises now is whether capitalism as a system can survive the long economic contraction.

### a) *Herman Daly's Steady-State Capitalism*

In my previous book (1999) I have discussed this question at length. I will therefore present here only a brief summary of that discussion.

Herman Daly and many other ecological economists do not believe a long contraction can threaten the survival of capitalism. In as early as the 1970s, Daly presented his conception of a "steady state" economy. His main idea for attaining a steady state is to control consumption of raw materials by means of depletion quotas that can be traded in the market.

For the same purpose, he also recommends controlling population growth by means of transferable birth licenses. All ecological economists demand that consumption of raw materials be strongly reduced. Of course, some of them cherish the absurd thought that the economy can grow despite a strong reduction in raw materials consumption. But Daly wants to achieve a steady-state economy at a lower level. Such an economy will have only a moderate, i.e., tolerable, impact on the environment. There will be no capital accumulation. Companies will have to pay out all profits as dividends. In order to make such an economy acceptable to the broad masses, there must also be an upper limit to income and property. Daly thinks that state control of the total, greatly reduced throughput of raw materials will not function without a capitalist market. He wrote:

> Markets allow these quota rights to be allocated efficiently.... [T]o aim for microstability and control is likely to be self-defeating and to result in macroinstability, as the capacities for spontaneous coordination, adjustment, and mutation (which always occur on the micro level) are stifled by central planning.... We should strive for macrocontrol and avoid micromeddling. (Daly 1977: 51)

I think such a perspective contradicts the basic logic of capitalism. (1) A contracting economy amounts to a long-drawn recession, and a steady-state economy at a low level is tantamount to a permanent depression. In such a scenario, thousands of companies would go bankrupt, and millions of people would lose their jobs. According to which criteria should then the state decide which companies or economic sectors should simply be allowed to go bankrupt due to shortage (or exorbitant price) of raw materials in the market? After all, it is the state that would determine the depletion quotas! (2) To the basic logic of capitalism belongs also capital accumulation. Entrepreneurs and other people who have somehow become rich, who earn much more than they consume, want to invest their accumulated profits/savings in order to increase their wealth. As long as they see this possibility, as long as they do not see that the physical limits to growth have been reached, they will have no understanding for the contraction or steady-state policy of the government. As long as capitalism prevails, capitalists will *de facto* be more powerful than politicians. No such radical ecological economic policy can be pushed through against their will, unless politicians are determined to abolish capitalism.

Funnily enough, Daly too knows this. He himself wrote that if the state would put his ideas, which he calls "institutions," into practice, they could also be totally ineffective:

> But ... these institutions could be totally ineffective. Depletion
> quotas could be endlessly raised on the grounds of national
> defense.... People at the maximum income and wealth limit
> may succeed in continually raising that limit by spending a
> great deal of their money on TV ads extolling the Unlimited
> Acquisition of Everything as the very foundation of the Ameri-
> can Way of Life. (Daly 1977: 75)

Daly's last hope is "moral growth." But since when can we expect capitalists to behave morally? Didn't Adam Smith say that everybody should
only pursue his/her own interests, and that by doing so he/she would be
automatically promoting the well-being of society as a whole? In a later
work, Daly wrote of the "corrosive effect of individualistic self-interest
on the containing moral context of the community" (Daly and Cobb Jr.
1990: 50). What Daly is wishing for cannot function for a technical reason as well. Competition is one of capitalism's main institutions, and Daly
finds it good. One of the main rules of conduct in competitive capitalism
is "expand or perish." Therefore, every business must try to grow. In the
long run, this inevitably leads to growth of the whole economy. All entrepreneurs wish this to happen, because otherwise many of them will make
losses and some may even have to close up shop. Only in a growing economy is there a possibility that *all* entrepreneurs will continue to exist and
make profits. Daly wrote: "But competition involves winning and losing,
both of which have a tendency to be cumulative. Last year's winners find
it easier to be this year's winners. Winners tend to grow and losers disappear" (Daly and Cobb Jr. 1990: 49). How can winning and losing, pushing out competitors from the market, etc., be reconciled with the moral
growth that Daly is wishing for? Loske et al. (1995: 372f.) even express the
absurd thought that cooperation could be a guiding principle in their ideal
eco-capitalism. The truth is that such things as moral behavior, cooperation, etc., are neither generally practicable nor logical in capitalism. In a
contracting or steady-state economy, competitive capitalism will become
much more brutal, much more deceitful, and much more criminal than it
already is in the present-day, still growing world economy.

When the physical limits to growth have been reached, that is, when
the economy begins to contract, then a different social system will be
needed — in the framework of which it might be possible to organize the
economic contraction peacefully, with the approval of the majority of the
population, and in a manner that would encourage moral behavior. That
can only be some kind of socialism.

Johannes P. Opschoor, an honest bourgeois economist, thought these problems through in 1991. He admits the dilemma. He explicitly speaks of the necessity of "environmental and economic forecasting and *planning*" (Opschoor 1991: 20; emphasis added). He concedes: "In any case, this would extend the powers of government into areas (e.g., economic planning, pricing policy, etc.) from where it is actually withdrawing" (21). In conclusion, he writes:

> The most profound policy to prevent growth would be that of reducing (world) market insecurity and competition. As this *comes close to the very essence of our economic system* and as faith in the existence of alternatives to that system is dwindling rapidly, one cannot but hope that the environmental crisis can be resolved without having to consider changes as fundamental as these. (21f.; emphasis added)

I do not see any chance for Opschoor's hope to be fulfilled.

A question that was often discussed in the 1980s was whether it was imaginable that in the ecological (sustainable) economies of the future, which would be much smaller than the present-day industrialized economies, firms would also be very much smaller. They would be owned by small farmers and craftspeople, who would produce and sell goods and services with their own labor and, possibly, with the labor of their family members. Such firms would, as the argument goes, neither have the possibility nor the drive to expand. They would, therefore, also not exploit anybody. That would, of course, be a market economy, but not a capitalistic one. Or cooperative firms, whose owners would be the people working in the firm, would do business in a market economy without hiring additional workers.

This exceedingly likeable scenario, which roughly resembles Mahatma Gandhi's conceptions, addresses, however, only the micro level. If we assume that such firms would also need raw materials and intermediate products and would use small machines and tools (all of which cannot be produced in the same region), then there would be need for long-distance trade and some complex industrialized production. And enterprises that do long-distance business and produce industrial goods cannot be the small local firms envisioned above. They would necessarily be large and exert pressure on the authorities in favor of growth. If, however, such large enterprises were owned, organized, and controlled by the state, then, under the regime of depletion quotas for raw materials (also import and export quotas) and with successful prevention of population growth, a steady-state quasi-market economy could function.

Also, the general problem of transition from the present-day capitalist production with huge firms to the non-capitalistic, small farms and crafts firms of a steady-state economy can be tackled only if the state plans and carries it out with determination.

But all that is not Daly's conception of a steady-state economy, which would be a profit-making and competitive capitalist market economy, in which all firms, small and big, would compete with each other for a higher share of the market. There would then be winners and losers, as it happened also in the socialist market economy of Yugoslavia with workers-owned firms. This would amount to negation of moral growth.

### b) *Elmar Altvater's Mutually Supportive Economy*

Although Elmar Altvater says in *Das Ende des Kapitalismus wie wir ihn kennen* (2005) that it is probable capitalism will come to an end, he immediately attenuates this statement by speaking of "capitalism, as we know it." He obviously means that a reformed capitalism, capitalism in a different form, could perhaps survive the crises.

Altvater also sees what I called the pincer-grip crisis. He interprets the imminent end of the oil age — following Fernand Braudel and using his terminology — as "an external jolt of extreme severity" (13) that would destabilize capitalism. However, contrary to my thought, he is firmly convinced that "alternative [renewable] sources of energy are available to us: wind energy, photovoltaic, hydropower, geothermal energy, tidal energy, biomass." According to him, capitalism's energy problem is merely that none of these renewable sources of energy can "fulfill the condition of congruence between energy system and capitalism," which fossil fuels do outstandingly (213f.). He means here the big advantages fossil fuels such as oil and gas provide for *large-scale industrial* capitalism: they can be used almost anywhere and at any time because they are easily transportable and storable, and they facilitate concentration and centralization of economic processes. Electricity that is produced from coal and lignite also allows production to be decentralized (86f.).

Altvater concedes that renewable energies can also provide these advantages as soon as they are converted into electricity. However, in his view, there is another problem that lies elsewhere. He writes:

> [I]t is doubtful whether large-scale power stations can be
> operated on the basis of renewable energy sources. Most

> probably not. That means the power grids would have to be
> designed, regionalized, and decentralized in a different way if
> they were to be predominantly used for renewable ... energies.
> But it is not just a technical difference. It would rather be an
> affront to the operators of large power stations, who ... fight
> against the renewables at all levels. (87f.)

That is why Altvater does not think the necessary transition to a renewable energy regime can be achieved in the framework of capitalism as we know it today: "A new congruence between energy and production can never be achieved if the old production and consumption structures, which are totally tailored to a fossil energy regime, remain in place" (214). So a society based on a renewable energy regime, which he calls "the solar society," can, in his view, "only be realized with and in a mutually supportive economy," not with and in a capitalistic economy.

This line of reasoning is extremely weak. Since when do abstract "affronts" and other similar sentimentalities play an important part in the investment decisions of corporate bosses? For them, the only thing that counts is the profitability of an investment. If solar energy, wind energy, etc., cannot be made profitable through large power stations but only through small, regional, and decentralized ones, then they will simply build power stations of the latter type. We all know that large capitalist corporations do regionalized and decentralizedized business as well, such as local branches of large banks or the Starbucks bars inside large grocery stores.

Moreover, it is not as if large power stations are only built where large coal or oil deposits exist. The coal to fuel some large coal-fired power stations in Germany comes from South Africa or Colombia. So why shouldn't a large electricity company be able to build a large power station in, say, Munich that uses as fuel solar hydrogen produced in the Sahara?

The reason why large electricity companies do not want to spearhead the transition to renewable energies is something that Altvater and other advocates of the latter refuse to accept as the truth, namely, that the renewables are not profitable without subsidies and other favors. And why? Because the energy balance of these technologies is negative or not positive enough, and therefore they are not *viable*, although they are *feasible*. The subsidies come from the economy at large, by far the greatest part of which is driven by fossil and nuclear energy. That means that renewable energies are parasites living off the conventional energies; they cannot replace their hosts. They are not available to us for our needs (see Georgescu-Roegen 1978, Sarkar 1999: chapter 4).

Altvater does not go into these issues at all. To those who reject renewable energies on the grounds that they are too costly, he replies taciturnly that their arguments are "shallow and false" (2005: 155), as if this were a sufficient answer. Even when he writes about the (liquid) hydrogen technology, he does not mention the fact that the hydrogen that is being used at present is produced from natural gas, not from water with the aid of solar electricity.

Fernand Braudel, whom Altvater quotes in agreement, had written that "an external jolt of extreme severity" alone would not bring about the breakdown of capitalism. For this to happen, "a convincing alternative" must also exist at the same time (13). I agree. Altvater sees this convincing alternative in the *idea* of a "mutually supportive economy." What he means by a "mutually supportive economy" is not clear; the outlines of such an economy are lacking in his book. He seems not to want to outline it himself, for "a mutually supportive economy is [after all] the work of social movements" (197).

He counts among the activists and constituents of his "social movements" almost everybody and everything that make out the leftist and alternative scene in the rich industrialized countries (see 203–209). For characterizing his mutually supportive economy, Altvater quotes/paraphrases Paul Singer: "Cooperation and solidarity ... will be preferred to competition." It is a "radical critique of capitalism, because it is also a practical critique." It is not just a response "to necessities that arise in the course of the crisis," but also "a choice of perspective." "With its combination of individual freedom, socio-economic and human security, equality, and fairness" it can *"point beyond capitalism."* It "spreads hope, simply because in it [this kind of economy] work will again get a social meaning" (209). In regard to globalization, Altvater quotes Walden Bello, who proposes "deconstruction of existing globalized institutions, above all of the WTO, the IMF, and the World Bank," and "reconstruction of a deglobalized economy based on regional and local cyclical flows" (207).

Altvater calls the organizations, firms, groups, etc., of the social movements the "non-profit sector." What does that mean? Some of them cannot make any profit at all. But cooperatives — firms without bosses, microcredit enterprises, etc. — do make profit. The profit, however, is distributed among the shareholders, who either work in the enterprise themselves or are small entrepreneurs in the sector (farmer-members of an agricultural cooperative, for instance). Trade unions, too, own (owned) in some countries (e.g., in Germany) firms that operate(d) following the profit principle. In a market economy, such firms are subject to competition; they are not monopolies. Cooperatives and union-owned companies do have bosses and workers. There is also corruption in such firms. They often have to fight for survival. Solidarity and cooperation exists there at the most only among the members/workers of the individual enterprises. At best, if a firm without a boss is running to capacity, it can tell a customer to go to another firm without a boss. The microcredit that the famous Grameen Bank (of Bangladesh) gives to poor people is not interest-free. Its interest rates are higher than those of commercial banks, though much lower than those of private usurers. And it employs well-paid loan distributors and interest collectors from the middle class. When such is the situation on the ground, it is very much overstated to claim that a mutually supportive, let alone "moral," economy is emerging (2005: 205).

The other components of Altvater's mutually supportive economy — NGOs, foundations, aid organizations, research and counseling institutions, trade unions, left-wing parties, etc. — are not enterprises that make money. Their employees and activities are dependent on donations and/or membership fees. But such money comes from people who are more or less well-remunerated employees in the formal profit sector or in state services. Some NGOs even receive money from the state and the EU, both of which are main pillars of capitalism. In Germany, many union leaders earn a lot of money by being members of the supervisory boards of large corporations. That some parts of Altvater's mutually supportive economy depend on donations from the formal profit sector — which lacks solidarity, where competitors are squeezed out of the market, where the exploitation of workers and destruction of nature goes on without scruples — is a cause of serious concern and unease that is usually not discussed in the social movements. But this problem needs to be discussed seriously. Can such a "mutually supportive economy" and such social movements at all have a vision that goes beyond capitalism? Maybe they can want to only improve capitalism a little, to try to give it a more social form. We have seen that trade unions have long ago accepted capitalism. In the Attac movement, too, the dominant forces are those that want only to go back to a Keynesian capitalism and to the welfare state of the late 1960s.

If in the future such movements continue to gain strength, then we can indeed experience the end of capitalism *as we know it today*. But capitalists need not fear that prospect too much. For then only a shift in accent would happen; everything known from before would remain in place, albeit in a somewhat changed form. For:

> In principle it is [just] about a *new form of articulation* of local,
> regional and national economies and the institutions of the

world market. The articulation between informal and formal economy, between small and big enterprises, between local and global economy can be organized in a way different from the subaltern subjugation under the material constraints of the world market. (2005: 208; emphasis added)

The next sentence in the text reads: "Not competition dominates here, but the principle of solidarity." That means competition remains. The only ones who point beyond capitalism (without attributes) are those who are *openly* anti-capitalistic and who speak out with *clear and unambiguous* words for a planned and socialist economy and society.

In what Altvater writes, but also in the social movements he refers to, concepts like equality, justness, and solidarity are used vaguely. So it is not precisely clear what they are supposed to mean. For quite a few years now the ruling class and their friends in the social movements have been more careful when using the term "equality." In order to not provoke any dangerous misunderstandings they speak, very clearly, only of "equality of opportunities." Justness for them means minimum wages. Solidarity means social welfare benefits or, in some proposals, a guaranteed minimum income. They reject the idea of material equality by pejoratively calling it "egalitarianism." But the vaguest of them all are the terms "mutually supportive" and "solidarity." These can mean only a small donation for the poor or other suffering people, or just a verbose, cost-free declaration of solidarity with the striking workers of a firm who are fighting against layoffs. Altvater himself gives an example: a voluntarily paid slightly higher price for fair-trade coffee for the benefit of plantation workers in Central America (208). Solidarity here means the rich person's charity for the poor. Is this supposed to be a vision of a different, a better world? A "mutually supportive economy" of this kind is nothing but a different form of capitalism, a capitalism with a slightly friendly face.

## 4. Conclusion — Perspective on the Future

It is perhaps symptomatic of our times full of confusions that even many honest thinkers express contradictory and even bewildering perspectives on the future. Although he is fully convinced that renewable energies are available to us, and although the sun, as we know, offers us 15,000 times the energy we today consume commercially, Altvater writes: "Resource consumption ... must be restricted" (2005: 210). But why? His political friend Hermann Scheer, with whom Altvater appears to agree, writes that solar energy "could satisfy even the most sumptuous energy needs of the worlds of humans, animals and plants experiencing drastic growth" (Scheer 1999: 66). Why, then, must we restrict our resource consumption? With energy available to us in such abundance, we should even be able to make almost 100% recycling of any waste possible, we could then extract valuable minerals from every piece of stone and produce as much freshwater from seawater as we would like. Then we could also end the over-exploitation of natural resources. Nevertheless, Altvater's call for restricting resource consumption is to be welcomed.

It is also to be welcomed that he does not think much of the strategy of the so-called efficiency revolution. However, in his critique of this strategy he misses the main point. He writes: "Experience shows that as a rule, lower consumption of energy and natural resources per production unit is overcompensated through increasing quantities. For the fall in costs and, hence, in prices ... of products brings about a rise in demand, which leads to higher output" (Altvater 2005: 211), which, I may add, causes higher environmental degradation. This sentence shows that he accepts the claim of the protagonists of "efficiency revolution" that further reductions in the consumption of energy and natural resources per production unit (by a factor of four or even ten) *and*, hence, further reductions in the price of products are technologically feasible. This, however, is wrong. Whatever may have been achieved in earlier centuries and decades in this respect, in present times, generally speaking, it is no longer possible to reduce prices by using less energy and natural resources per production unit. Quite on the contrary: in order to be able to reduce prices, entrepreneurs have to replace workers with machines that devour energy and materials, or they have to relocate production to a low-wage country. In the case of Volkswagen's Lupo 3L (for three liter), for instance, fuel consumption could be reduced only by making the car lighter through the use of aluminum and magnesium instead of steel. But production of aluminum requires more energy consumption than that of steel (Schmidt-Bleek 1999, quoted in Wille 1999). Moreover, the car could not be sold because of its exorbitant price. Generally speaking, if one wants to increase *resource* productivity (and not labor productivity), then one should use more labor-intensive technologies and methods.

What remains as possible is the path of sufficiency revolution. In the 1980s we called it voluntarily forgoing consumption or refusal to submit to the pressure to consume. These practices were expected to become a movement. But because of its unpopularity, and thanks to the despondency of the majority of the ecology movement activists and of the Greens, voluntary forgoing of consumption became a taboo topic. And all kinds of leftists were, in any case, for theoretical and ideological reasons, opposed to such a path. Altvater thinks that the strategy of sufficiency revolution is a "dead end" because the logic and the material compulsions of capitalism will prevail, especially given the pervasive advertising encouraging consumption (Altvater 2005: 212f.). He banks on "broad promotion of renewable energies" as the "means" to our "end of freeing the earth from the straitjacket ... of the fossil energy system." In his view, "nothing else remains for mankind to do" (213). But what actually is the objective of our social movements? Would we be highly satisfied if, for instance, the rain forests were destroyed with chainsaws powered by biodiesel or liquid solar-hydrogen instead of diesel?

I have argued above (and in detail in my 1999 book) that this path does not exist. The renewable sources of energy that are *really* — that is, without much difficulty — available to us (biomass, wind, and flowing water) do not exist in sufficient quantities and in necessary qualities so as to keep the current industrial civilization alive for long. That is why the world economy will begin to contract well before the end of the oil age. So will the world population. Humankind as a whole *will have to* content itself with far fewer goods and services. And for work, we humans *will have to* use far more physical strength than we do now.

The future is in principle uncertain (apart from the fact that all living beings will die sooner or later). That is why hope is the last to die. A few years ago, the British magazine *The Economist* quoted a former oil minister of Saudi Arabia as saying: "The Stone Age did not come to an end because of lack of stones; and the Oil Age will come to an end well before the oil wells are exhausted." This is an expression of hope for alternative/renewable energy technologies! In this context, another quote from Saudi Arabia is also interesting: "My father rode a camel, I drive a Rolls Royce, my son flies a jet airplane, and his son will ride a camel" (Kunstler 2005: 82).

I believe it is this inevitable process of contraction of the world economy, as well as that of the individual national economies, that will be the "external jolt of extreme severity" that Braudel spoke of. However, this jolt cannot be of extreme severity, like an earthquake; it will be a process. But it will be a fast process, and it has already begun. It will cause acute hardship and many more conflicts than we are already experiencing. However, the fact that the contraction is (will be) a process also gives us time and motivation to reflect on and debate over alternative systems, to fight against capitalism and to build up concrete alternatives. Capitalism will not disappear by itself. The majority of humankind must first want it to disappear.

Which of the alternatives that are today going around will be convincing? Can it be a different form of capitalism, a reformed one? And if so, what should it look like? Is it possible that, after the collapse of "socialism" in the former Soviet Union and Eastern European states, a new kind of socialism, a socialism of the twenty-first century, will come up? Can that be an ecological socialism?

I have outlined above why the alternative visions of a — in some way or other — better capitalism, the ones advocated by Shutt, Daly, and Altvater, do not convince me. I believe an ecological socialism is the only convincing alternative (see Sarkar 1999: chapters 6 and 7). Only with such a socialism will we be able to overcome both the ecological and the social crises of the present. Summarized, my line of reasoning is as follows. (1) The contraction of the economies of the world must occur in an orderly way. Otherwise there will be unbearable breakdowns of whole societies. An orderly contraction can only take place in a planned economy, not in a capitalist market economy. (2) Only a socialist political order can achieve, by means of egalitarian distribution of the costs and benefits, a broad acceptance of the necessary economic contraction. (3) Only in a planned socialist economy can the problem of unemployment be solved, which otherwise would become more and more acute in a contracting economy. To this end, a planned socialist economy can consciously use labor-intensive technologies and methods, which, in addition, result in less use of resources.

Ideas, alternatives, proposed solutions may be convincing for thinking people, but they are not necessarily popular. Any alternative that considers economic contraction and reduction in consumption to be imperative, as ecological socialism does, cannot be popular, especially not among the spoiled citizens of the First World and the middle classes of the Third World. But nonetheless these approaches are compelling necessities for survival. After the end of the Oil Age, when a "long emergency" (Kunstler) will prevail, and wars over resources will rage, when all illusions of a new model of prosperity will have evaporated, then people will be more receptive to the conception of an ecological socialism. Until then it remains the task of all selfless and honest political activists to try to convince people of the need for and the advantages of this alternative. Moral growth, which Daly considers to be an essential prerequisite of his steady-state economy, is, in any case, represented in the socialist values of equality, cooperation, and freedom from dominance.

## XII.

# The Global Economic Crisis of 2008–2010

The manuscript of this book was completed towards the end of 2007. At the time I thought it would need only some small changes before going to press. But the world economic crisis that broke out in 2008 and is still going on in some form or another in many parts of the world compels me to write a full chapter on this topic. Many full-length books have already been published on this crisis. That is why, but also for reasons of space, I shall provide only a short summary of the developments of the crisis so far — before offering my own explanation of its causes. That means, I shall rather focus on a deeper causal analysis of the crisis and on the perspective on the future that must logically result therefrom.

Seen superficially, similar, though not equally severe, crises have also taken place in the past decades. But the scale, depth, and spread of the current crisis has been so great that it has brought on panic. Many observers fear for the survival of capitalism. The question is: is this only *another* crisis *in* capitalism, or is this *the* crisis *of* capitalism that Marxists, communists, socialists, and other critics of capitalism have been waiting for all along? At least on one point all agree: capitalism will never be again what it was before the crisis. In other words, unbridled, globalized, neoliberal capitalism will henceforth be bridled, more or less. That work has already begun. On November 15, 2008, the heads of state of the twenty most important industrialized countries met in Washington to initiate a reform process.

In one respect, however, this crisis is essentially different from the previous ones: it is taking place against a very different background. Whereas the previous crises were dealt with by the rulers of the world with a consciousness in which knowledge about the limits to growth had no place at all, the current crisis has broken out in an intellectual atmosphere in which even the rulers display great concern about the ecological balance of our planet and the dwindling resource base of industrialized societies. Thus, Al Gore, former vice president of the United States, has made it his life's mission to motivate humanity to seriously try to stop global warming. And the current president of the United States, Barack Obama, on being

elected on November 4, 2008, spoke about our "planet in peril" in his very
first public address.

## 1. The Course of the Crisis to Date

In the course of the crisis, which started in the summer of 2007 as a vague
uneasiness, five aspects emerged one after the other: the real estate (housing) crisis, the banking crisis, the credit crunch, the recession, which had
already been under way in the USA since December 2007, and the crisis of state indebtedness, particularly in Europe. In 2008, the situation
became more serious. Nineteen million American homeowners, who had
acquired their homes in 2001 or thereafter through a mortgage loan, had
gone bankrupt and were on the streets (Drewermann 2008). It was estimated that in 2008 and 2009, over three million more houses would
be foreclosed. Several European countries also suffered a real estate crisis — especially the United Kingdom, Ireland, and Spain. In the recent
past, thousands of homes and apartments had been built in Spain, and
now there were no buyers for them.

This real estate crisis caused inordinate problems (up to bankruptcies)
not only for homeowners and developers but also for many of the banks,
which had helped create the real estate boom and bubble of the previous
years through imprudently given mortgage loans, and whose debtors could
not ultimately service their debts. But many other banks that had not
given such bad loans themselves were also in great difficulty (the causal
chain is explained below). Some of them even went bankrupt (by the middle of 2010, 103 US banks). Others had to be bailed out by the state or
taken over by other large banks because they were regarded as system-rel-
evant — too large to fail without bad consequences for the whole economy.
Examples abound — in the United States, Bear Stearns, Indy Mac, Fannie Mae (Federal National Mortgage Association), Freddie Mac (Federal
Home Loan Mortgage Corporation), Merrill Lynch, Washington Mutual,
Citigroup; in the United Kingdom, Northern Rock, Bradford & Bingley;
in Germany, Landesbank Sachsen, West LB, IKB Deutsche Industriebank,
and Hypo Real Estate.

Two cases need to be mentioned specially. Firstly, Lehman Brothers, a
huge investment bank of Wall Street, New York, could not be saved. No
large bank wanted to take it over, and the US government refused to bail it
out. It was allowed to go bankrupt in September 2008. Maybe the government thought enough was enough; maybe it wanted to use this bankruptcy
as a warning to other banks. This decision had serious consequences for

the world economy. The second case: BayernLB, a public sector bank in Bavaria, Germany, that had to be bailed out, landed in trouble because it had earlier taken over an ailing Austrian mortgage bank for an unjustifiably high price. It has been alleged this takeover resulted from corruption on the part of the then ruling politicians and leading figures of the bank.

Soon, the great banking crisis turned into a worldwide credit crunch. Fearing that the credit they gave could turn into bad debt, banks in general and particularly the banks in trouble became overcautious in their lending policies, becoming very reluctant to give new credit for fear of taking on risks. And if they did give credit, they demanded high collateral. What made the situation in the credit market still worse was that banks also became very cautious in short-term inter-bank lending. They either did not give any such credit at all, or they demanded a much higher interest rate than before, for they did not trust the balance sheets of even other banks, and they had no way to assess the credit-worthiness of the banks seeking short-term loans. Who knew which bank would go bankrupt next? In truth, the banks did not always have a clear picture of their own financial situations. For through the development of highly complicated innovative financial instruments, the world financial market as a whole had become extremely murky, almost opaque, even for its adepts. It was no secret that every bank and every financial institution of other kinds had liabilities that did not appear in their balance sheets. This crisis of the financial market — the combination of the banking crisis and the credit crunch — could be vividly described by being compared to a tsunami bringing on a core meltdown in a nuclear power station. Altogether, there was widespread panic for a long period.

But credit is as indispensable to the real economy as blood is to the human body. When banks restrict lending it becomes difficult for companies to produce and to invest. Consumers, too, need credit for making larger purchases. Generally speaking, the economy needs people to consume on credit, otherwise it cannot grow. Therefore, a few months after the financial crisis broke out a recession in the real economy set in. In mid-November 2008, statistical offices confirmed that Japan and the whole Eurozone were in a recession, meaning the GDP had consecutively dropped in the last two quarters. The USA had already been in this predicament since December 2007. From January to the end of October 2008, 1.2 million Americans lost their jobs. The unemployment rate stood in October at 6.5% (*Süddeutsche Zeitung*, 8 November 2008). The whole American car industry was almost bust.

In the beginning, many experts believed this was only a crisis in the

Western industrialized economies. Some called it a "North Atlantic crisis." They believed in a "theory of decoupling," which meant that the emerging economies of the developing world were no longer so closely tied to the economies of the highly developed industrialized countries as before. So they also believed these emerging economies were islands of stability that would not be affected by this crisis. These experts even thought that this time around the emerging economies could save the world economy from something worse. Real developments, however, destroyed this hope. In booming China, the engines of growth were reported to have come to a standstill. Official statistics reported that in the first half of the year, 67,000 factories had been closed down (see Wong 2008). The recession became severe and widespread.

The next year, in 2009, a large number of economies recorded a negative growth rate. The few that could show a positive figure experienced a sharp fall in the growth rate. On the next page, I provide the figures for a selection of countries: those that have recently played a role in world economic affairs or on whom I have written in the previous chapters.

It must be noted here that the data on unemployment is not very reliable. Firstly, in countries where the unemployed get no or little help from the state, they are also not really registered. The figures are then mostly more or less intelligent guesses. In some cases, for example in India, figures are not available at all. Bear in mind that where stark poverty prevails, there is hardly anybody who is unemployed. In such countries, even children and old people work in order to eke out a living. Secondly, official figures on unemployment are politically influenced. Underemployed people are generally counted as employed. Those who are receiving some kind of state-sponsored retraining and those who have become unemployable for any reason (e.g., those who can and want to work but are over 55 or partially disabled) are excluded from the figure. And those who have given up the search for a job and are somehow not eligible for state help do not register themselves at all. As of October 2010, in Germany, whereas officially unemployment had fallen below 3 million, critics said that the true figure was over 9 million (*Die Linkszeitung* online, 28 October 2010). In the USA, where the official unemployment rate was 9.6%, the true figure was, according to critics, about 20% (*Der Spiegel*, 30 October 2010: 79). With regard to Germany, one may wonder how the steep fall in GDP in 2009 could not have any noticeable negative effect on the official unemployment figure. One explanation has been mentioned above. Another explanation is that the state gave wage subsidies to companies that did not retrench redundant workers but, instead, let them work for fewer hours per week than normal.

|  | GDP Growth Rate in % | | | Unemployment Rate in % | | |
|---|---|---|---|---|---|---|
|  | 2007 | 2008 | 2009 | 2007 | 2008 | 2009 |
| USA | 2.1 | 0.4 | −2.4 | 4.6 | 5.8 | 9.3 |
| Japan | 2.4 | −1.2 | −5.2 | 3.9 | 4.0 | 5.1 |
| Germany | 2.5 | 1.2 | −5.0 | 8.4 | 7.5 | 7.5 |
| France | 2.3 | 0.3 | −2.2 | 8.3 | 7.4 | 9.5 |
| Italy | 1.5 | −1.3 | −5.0 | 6.1 | 6.7 | 7.8 |
| UK | 2.6 | 0.5 | −4.9 | 5.3 | 5.6 | 7.6 |
| Canada | 2.5 | 0.4 | −2.6 | 6.0 | 6.1 | 8.3 |
| Russia | 8.1 | 5.6 | −7.9 | 6.1 | 6.3 | 8.2 |
| Greece | 4.5 | 2.0 | −2.0 | 8.3 | 7.7 | 9.5 |
| Ireland | 6.0 | −3.0 | −7.1 | 4.6 | 6.0 | 11.9 |
| Iceland | 6.0 | 1.0 | −6.5 | 2.3 | 3.0 | 8.6 |
| Sweden | 2.6 | −0.2 | −4.4 | 6.1 | 6.2 | 8.3 |
| Spain | 3.6 | 0.9 | −3.6 | 8.3 | 11.3 | 18.0 |
| Portugal | 1.9 | 0.0 | −2.7 | 8.0 | 7.6 | 9.6 |
| Turkey | 4.7 | 0.7 | −4.7 | 8.5 | 9.4 | 12.5 |
| South Africa | 5.5 | 3.7 | −1.8 | 23.0 | 22.9 | 25.0 |
| Mexico | 3.3 | 1.5 | −6.5 | 3.4 | 3.5 | 5.5 |
| Brazil | 6.1 | 5.1 | −0.2 | 8.2 | 7.9 | 8.1 |
| Chile | 4.6 | 3.7 | −1.5 | 7.0 | 7.7 | 9.7 |
| Argentina | 8.7 | 6.8 | 0.9 | 7.5 | 7.9 | 8.7 |
| China | 13.0 | 9.6 | 8.7 | 3.9 | 4.2 | 4.3 |
| India | 9.4 | 7.3 | 5.7 | 3.1 | — | — |
| Indonesia | 6.3 | 6.0 | 4.5 | 9.1 | 8.4 | 7.4 |
| South Korea | 5.1 | 2.3 | 0.2 | 3.2 | 3.2 | 3.6 |
| Philippines | 7.1 | 3.8 | 0.9 | 6.3 | 7.4 | 7.5 |
| Thailand | 4.9 | 2.5 | −2.3 | 1.2 | 1.2 | 1.5 |
| Malaysia | 6.2 | 4.6 | −1.7 | 3.2 | 3.3 | 3.7 |
| Singapore | 8.2 | 1.4 | −2.0 | 2.3 | 2.3 | 3.0 |
| Saudi Arabia | 2.0 | 4.3 | 0.1 | 5.6 | 5.0 | 5.4 |
| Venezuela | 8.2 | 4.8 | −3.3 | 7.5 | 6.9 | 7.8 |

(Sources: Statistisches Bundesamt 2010 and *Fischer Weltalmanach* 2008, 2009, 2010)

In addition to this standard picture of a crisis, in several countries — Pakistan, Ukraine, Iceland, Hungary, etc. — the national currency was imploding and capital flow from highly industrialized countries was drying up. In December 2008, large sums of foreign capital were pulled out. Many of these countries had to ask the IMF for help. Additionally, Argentina feared experiencing a crisis like the one that took place seven years before (*International Herald Tribune*, 14 November 2008).

Because of the bad economic situation and already existing extremely high public debt, there was the risk of a few EU states going bankrupt as well. In May 2010, Greece stood on the verge of bankruptcy. Its budget deficit amounted to 8.9% of the GDP, the total public debt to 124.1%, 99% of which was owed to foreigners (*Süddeutsche Zeitung*, 19 May 2010). Only a concerted effort of the bigger Eurozone countries like Germany, who guaranteed an enormous amount of financial help, could rescue Greece. The problem was that the rating agencies had downgraded the credit-worthiness of Greece to junk status. The credit-worthiness of fellow Eurozone countries Portugal, Spain, and Ireland had recently been downgraded as well. They all had difficulty selling their new state bonds and rolling over old bonds falling due for repayment. They therefore had to offer high effective interest rates, which would further increase the already heavy burden of debt servicing.

The stock exchanges all over the world also reflected these different aspects of the crisis. Share prices plummeted everywhere. In one year, from October 10, 2007, to October 9, 2008, the American S&P 500 fell by 38%, the German DAX by 39%, London's FTSE 100 by 33%, Tokyo's Nikkei 225 by 40%, the Parisian CAC 40 by 39%, the Canadian TSE 300 by 31%, and the Italian Mibtel by 44% (*Wall Street Journal*, 10 October 2008). Also the indexes of the emerging countries experienced steep falls. All these indexes continued to fall for some more time. In mid-November, the MSCI World Index and the Dow Jones fell to their lowest level since 2003 (*International Herald Tribune*, 21 November 2008).

The way the governments of the major industrialized countries reacted to the crisis was typically Keynesian. It was not only that the central banks poured money into the finance sector to provide urgently needed liquidity to the banks and other financial institutions, which had also been the case after the stock exchange crash of 1987. This time the state too became directly involved. It put hundreds of billions of dollars and euros at the disposal of companies, which were in danger of going bankrupt, and also allocated billions for spending in order to stimulate the economy and thus avert a catastrophic recession. In some cases the state, in effect, also temporarily took over some large corporations that stood on the brink of bankruptcy: e.g., Fannie Mae, Freddie Mac, AIG, and General Motors in the USA, the Royal Bank of Scotland in the UK, Hypo Real Estate in Germany, etc. The combined rescue and economic stimulus funds of the US federal government amounted to $1.5 trillion. The German federal government provided €500 billion for stimulus spending, the Chinese government €460 billion. In the world as a whole, the sums provided for these purposes amounted to $3 trillion.

This has been usual practice even in earlier decades, albeit at a much smaller scale. This time, however, there were two new and big problems. Firstly, the immensity of the amounts of money thus provided raised fears of unacceptably high inflation once the recession ended, because much of the money was newly created by the central banks (in old jargon, "printed"; in new jargon it was "quantitative easing"). And secondly, this came on top of mountains of already existing public debt, like in Greece, as mentioned above. To give a few more examples: in May 2010 the ratio of total public debt to GDP stood: in Germany at 76.7%, in the USA at 92.6%, in the UK at 78.2%, and in Japan at 227.3% (*Süddeutsche Zeitung*, 19 May 2010). The EU considers a ratio of 60% to be just tolerable.

After a total breakdown of the world economy was averted, in 2010 some major states, e.g., the United Kingdom and Germany (both under conservative-liberal rule), pursued a course of, as the Brits describe it, stepping one step back from the brink of disaster — a stringent austerity policy. The new British government did this with great vehemence. They reduced the budget of almost all ministries and government departments. Roughly half a million public sector jobs were eliminated.

When Greece was rescued from bankruptcy, it had to promise to mercilessly cut government spending. This the "socialist" government did. It cut salaries of government employees, reduced pensions, dismissed surplus staff in government offices, etc. But this course provoked violent resistance: not only protest demonstrations and strikes, but also bombing of the objects of hate. In France, a seemingly unending series of strikes and demonstrations took place in order to protest against the decision of the government to raise the minimum age of eligibility for pension from 60 to 62. Protest demonstrations, however at a smaller scale, also took place in Spain. In Britain, where in the beginning the protests were modest, some 50,000 students demonstrated in November 2010 against drastic increases in tuition fees and cuts in the budgets of universities. At the end of the demonstration violent protesters vandalized the headquarters of the ruling Conservative Party. But, on the whole, the majority of the people in these countries seemed to understand that their governments had no alternative, that they must tighten their belt. They were only demanding that the necessary sacrifices be distributed fairly, that also the rich bear their share of the burden of the austerity policy, and that the guilty be punished.

This intractable dilemma has led to a controversy between the policy makers of the USA, who want to pursue the Keynesian policy of increasing public spending for an additional period, i.e., until a *convincing* recovery has started, and those of the EU, led by Germany, who are afraid of the other, long-term consequences of growing public debt in the member countries. They are especially worried about loss of investors' confidence. Keynesian economists are, so to speak, campaigning against this conservative austerity policy of the EU. Paul Krugman, for instance, wrote recently: "We are now, I fear, in the early stages of a third depression. It will probably look more like the Long Depression [of 1873–1896] than the much more severe Great Depression [of the 1930s]. But the cost — to the world economy and, above all, to the millions of lives blighted by the absence of jobs — will nonetheless be immense" (Krugman 2010). David Leonhardt wrote: "The world's rich countries are now conducting a dangerous experiment. They are repeating an economic policy out of the 1930s — starting to cut spending and raise taxes before a recovery is assured ... " (Leonhardt 2010). Another critic commented: If now many states simultaneously dig holes in their budget, they will dig themselves together into a deeper hole.

The American policy makers are, of course, hoping that the worst will soon be over, that a strong recovery and then an upswing will set in. But this hope of the Americans is unfounded. In the middle of 2009, the US economy indeed started to grow again. But after growing in the first quarter of 2010 at the annualized rate of 3.7%, it could grow only at the annualized rate of 1.6% in the second quarter (CNN, 28 August 2010). This rate is very much below the minimum growth rate of 2.5% that, according to US economists, is necessary to just hold the unemployment rate constant (*Süddeutsche Zeitung*, 5 August 2010). How high must the rate be to reduce the unemployment rate, say, by half? What is worse, the job crisis is threatening to become also a bad social crisis. In the beginning of August 2010, 6.6 million Americans have been looking for a job, without success, for more than 27 weeks. Such people are called "long-term unemployed" in the US. About one million of them had been unemployed for more than 99 weeks, the limit after which the state stops giving aid. The reality for such people is destitution; many land on the streets (*Süddeutsche Zeitung*, 5 and 7 August 2010). Also the finance industry has not been repaired. After the rescue operation big banks became bigger. This shows that the government has failed to attain its declared goal of not allowing any bank to become too big to fail. This being the situation today, there is little probability that Obama's big talk of 2009 about the USA coming out of the crisis stronger than before will come true. It is proving more and more to be empty talk.

The depth and breadth of this crisis exceed those of any other crisis of the past decades. Some experts call it "the great recession," others "the crisis of the century." Some compare it with the Great Depression of 1929–1933. Optimists forecasted that the recession would be over by the end of 2009. In some cases, that came true. At the time of writing (autumn 2010), the German economy seems to have fully recovered from the crisis. In October 2010, it registered a growth rate of over 2%. But all the state interventions in the economy, the rescue and stimulus measures, and the enormous sums of money printed/used/spent for such measures have not yet managed to fully restore the lost confidence of economic subjects in the future. All in all, today, the specter of a second financial crisis, resulting this time from the huge debt burden of many states, and a double-dip (i.e., a second) recession, is haunting both America and Europe.

## 2. The *Immediate* Causes of the Crisis

In the summer of 2007, the American media noticed the so-called subprime crisis. It was a real estate crisis. Earlier, over many years, US regional commercial banks had granted mortgage loans for building or buying houses even to people who actually could not afford to own a house. (In this context, *subprime* means below the normal level of insecurity. Subprime loans are, therefore, very insecure loans.) The interest rates for such loans were fixed for the first two or three years; thereafter, they were variable. They could rise (or fall), depending on the market situation for such loans. In the middle of 2007, the creditor banks noticed that an above-average number of subprime debtors, hundreds of thousands, could no longer service their debts. The reason for this was that, firstly, the interest rates for such loans had increased; and, secondly, the debtors in question had a low income, precarious jobs, or other pressing debts (e.g., car loans or credit card debts). Insolvent homeowners had to sell or leave their homes, and the creditor banks subsequently foreclosed and auctioned the property. Normally, this alone would not have caused a serious economic crisis. But the high number of houses that were now affected by distress selling or compulsory auctioning pushed the prices down. In addition to this, after several years of a building boom, the real estate market was saturated. The more steeply the property prices fell, the more difficult it became for the debtors in trouble to repay their debts.

At this point one might ask in amazement why the banks had lent such large sums to financially weak people in the first place (in the USA, a single-family house can cost from one hundred thousand up to a few million dollars). Normally, lenders are supposed to be cautious, to carefully examine the credit-worthiness of the applicant and demand sufficient collateral. But the banks' credit agents — whose main income does not come from a fixed monthly salary, but consists of commissions on the amounts of business they bring to the employer — tried to produce as many credit deals as possible. They threw all caution to the winds, and vis-à-vis their potential debtors they consciously minimized the risks involved in these loans. For the regional banks that gave the mortgage loans, this practice entailed no risk, since they sold the loans immediately to the large mortgage banks that operate nationwide, for example, to the now infamous Fannie Mae and Freddie Mac.

The real estate crisis described above soon developed into a banking and financial crisis. The large mortgage banks suddenly found themselves sitting on a mountain of bad debts and losses, as they could not recover the sums originally lent from the proceeds of the compulsory auctioning of foreclosed houses.

In order to understand how this predicament of the large US mortgage banks developed into a worldwide banking and financial crisis, we need to understand a rather new aspect of modern banking and finance business. For quite some time now, money jugglers of the world have been using several newly created financial instruments for maximizing returns on a given amount of capital as well as for finding profitable investment opportunities for excessively accumulated money capital. The purchase, sale, and resale of enforceable credit documents is one such instrument. Very much simplified, it can be described as follows. Suppose a mortgage bank is entitled to receive from, say, five borrowers every month a certain amount of money towards interest on and repayment of mortgage loans. The bank bundles these entitlements to back the issuance of a security that it sells to another bank, in most cases an investment bank, that has liquid money capital that wants to be invested but is lying *idle*. This is called securitization. Why does the mortgage bank do this? Because it does not want to wait for years to receive full repayment of the loans. The proceeds from the sale of such mortgage-backed securities (which includes a certain profit margin) can be used by the bank for buying new such entitlements from regional banks. Investment banks (or investment banking units of commercial banks) participate in this business because they cannot themselves deal with innumerable small borrowers. The sale and purchase prices are calculated in such a way that every bank involved can make a profit. The source of their profits is naturally the interests paid by the borrowers.

American mortgage banks carried out this business on a huge scale and sold such securities not only in the United States but all over the world. So long as American borrowers could service their debts, or so long as defaults were limited, business was good. But, in the autumn of 2007, as the American subprime crisis assumed ever larger proportions, banks in the United States and Europe that had invested in such mortgage-backed securities started making great losses. This category of securities in their possession decreased in value, so consequently their capital base shrank, and their balance sheets showed negative figures. Their ability to take risks and give loans dwindled considerably.

### 3. Superficial Explanations

Economists belonging to the various present-day schools of economic thought did not differ much in explaining this development. The main elements of their explanation, which I consider to be superficial, are presented below. They contrast very much with my explanation of the crisis, which will follow.

(1) They blame the faulty structure of the US and international financial markets for the subprime mortgage crisis. Bankers who gave the bad mortgage loans did not have to bear the consequences of their irresponsibility. They could pass over the risks to other banks and institutional investors. Also the rating agencies, who are not really free in their judgment, gave good ratings to bad securities.

(2) There was too little regulation of the banking and finance industry, and also the globalization of the same had happened in an uncontrolled way. As a result of these two facts, a huge amount of highly risky, highly complicated, and barely understandable securities were sold all over the world.

(3) The Fed kept the prime interest rate very low over too long a period and thus made it easy for banks to borrow from it huge amounts of money to lend further to both unqualified borrowers and speculators attracted by the low interest rates. There was simply too much liquid money in the economy that wanted to be profitably invested. This is how the real estate boom and then the bubble came up.

(4) The bankers and managers of other financial institutions were greedy. Since the major part of their remuneration consisted of bonus

payments, which depended on results, they were extra keen to take risks, both in lending business and in speculative transactions.

These points do not only refer to the situation in the USA but also to the situation in most leading industrialized countries.

I find these explanations superficial and unconvincing. No doubt, these were *facts* when the crisis broke out, but they do not give a satisfactory answer to the questions of why the crisis became so severe, so widespread, and so long-drawn-out, and why it could not be overcome as easily as the previous similar crises: the stock market crash of 1987, the East Asian crisis of 1997–1998, and the crisis of 2001–2003. They do not explain why the crisis is still persisting, and why the outlook is still so gloomy.

Moreover, two of the facts are really banal. That bankers were greedy does not explain anything, because greed is an essential pillar of the capitalist economic system. All participants in this system are expected to be greedy, and they are indeed so, more or less. And deregulation of the banking and finance industry is only an essential element of globalized neo-liberal capitalism, which has been in place since the 1980s.

The other two elements were indeed somewhat unusual. Bankers have always given some credit that was a little risky, and some of such credit has always had to be routinely written off. But this time, the *extent* of the subprime credit was so huge that business could not go on as usual when the housing boom ended in the US.

The Fed's policy during the period in question was also unusual. Generally, the Fed (and, in the neo-liberal capitalist regime, almost all central banks) starts tightening money supply as soon as the economy starts heating up, which can be manifested as an above-average inflation or the emergence of a bubble in the stock exchange or the housing market. The usual instrument for this purpose is to cause the market interest rates to rise, which it generally achieves by raising the prime interest rate. In the period in question, however, the Fed let the bubbles continue to grow by keeping its prime interest rate low.

Both the banks and the Fed have been criticized for pursuing these unusual policies. But to blame the crisis on only them is unjustified, and is an obstacle to finding the true causes and understanding the true nature of the current crisis.

It has been reported that the ruling politicians, in fact, wanted a real estate boom. Greed is not a character trait of only bankers and speculators. Ordinary people, especially ordinary Americans, also want to become wealthy. This is a major tenet of the so-called "American dream." And owning a house, as big and showy as possible, is an ordinary working person's way of becoming wealthy — especially because it was said that house prices, unlike stock prices, could only go up. It has also to be noted here that in America, unlike in Western Europe, all people must themselves take care of their old-age security, for which ownership of a house has until recently been a very practical instrument. Politicians, naturally, wanted to promote the fulfillment of this "American dream," especially because the average *real* income of Americans had been stagnating, even falling, since 1978 (*Der Spiegel*, 30 October 2010: 78). Particularly the Democrats had a special interest in promoting widespread home ownership, because they considered the middle and working classes as their (potential) constituents — after all, poor and middle-class citizens make up the majority of the voters. In 1997, the administration of the Democratic president Bill Clinton got a law passed that made capital gains on the sale of property exempt from taxation. This encouraged speculation. But the Republicans wanted a real estate boom as well. President George W. Bush (2001–2009) said he wanted *every* American to become a homeowner. Politicians in general, therefore, applied pressure on the banks, directly or indirectly, to give housing credit to the poor. The banks were only too eager to comply.

It would however be wrong if one concluded from these facts that only narrow electoral considerations of self-interested politicians led to the massive expansion of subprime mortgage loans. For this policy also made macroeconomic sense. We have to remember that, both in the early nineties and in the early years of the new century, the USA suffered a recession. The GDP growth rate fell from 3.5% in 1989 to –0.5% in 1991. In 2000 and 2001 the so-called New Economy broke down. Along with a long-drawn-out stock exchange crash, the real economy suffered a recession as well. The GDP growth rate fell from 4.4% in 1999 to just 0.8% in 2001. Between 2000 and 2002 the telecom companies retrenched half a million workers. The official unemployment rate increased from 4% in 2000 to 5.8% in 2002 (figures from OECD 2000, OECD 2004, and Brenner 2003a). Confronted with this recession even the Republican president George W. Bush had to take typically Keynesian measures to stimulate the economy, which also started to recover in 2003–2004 (the wars in Afghanistan and Iraq also helped). A housing boom promoted through subprime credit perfectly suited such Keynesian efforts. It promoted growth and employment at a time when more and more American companies in the manufacturing industry were relocating their production to cheap-labor countries or even closing up shop. Building houses for Americans cannot be relocated to cheap-labor countries, nor can homes — unlike, for example, cars — be imported wholesale from abroad. They had to be built in America. Moreover, a house is an essential commodity.

A boom promoted through massive subprime credit would not have been possible if that had caused the inflation rate to rise. The Fed would have intervened to stop it. But inflation remained under control, because almost all other commodities that ordinary people needed for living could be had at very low prices — thanks to massive imports from cheap-labor countries.

Yet, in 2006, observers started warning about a housing bubble, and soon thereafter the market began to cool down.

### 4. Why Did the Housing Bubble Burst?

It is too simplistic to say any bubble will burst sooner or later. It is necessary to differentiate between a housing bubble and a stock market bubble, the latter of which also burst in America in October 2008, after the former had burst.

It was said that in the first seven days after the stock exchange crash, wealth amounting to $2.5 trillion was lost, and, since the stock exchange peak of one year earlier, stock owners lost $8.4 trillion (*Wall Street Journal*, 10 October 2008). But what does that actually mean? One says in such cases that the wealth vanished into thin air. But in reality, nothing *concrete* vanished — no house, no car. What vanished into thin air were only some numbers on paper, some zeros after a digit. The $8.4 trillion was only *fictitious wealth*. A year earlier, the same stocks were valued much lower. Only speculation had driven the *market value* of the stocks upwards. After the crash, what was in any case fictitious wealth ceased to exist.

The *real* value of a stock *ultimately* depends on how much demand in the market there is for the product(s) of the company in question. In case the company has to be wound up for lack of sufficient demand for its product(s), the price of its stocks can fall to zero. Houses are however very concrete things with eminent use value. Generally, there is no dearth of demand for them because almost all over the world (including in America) population is growing and people desire better housing. Usually it is only particular houses that may not find any taker.

In our concrete case, the subprime mortgage crisis in the USA, it is not as if the mortgagors lost the desire to live in the houses they had bought on credit. They, at least the great majority of them, were not speculators. It so happened that *under changed circumstances beyond their control* hundreds of thousands of them could not service their debts anymore. The crucial question for understanding the present crisis is, therefore, why the ordinary people who had bought houses on credit lost their ability to service their debts.

When the crisis in the housing market caused a contagion in the stock market, and the tumbling stock prices in turn reduced — through the negative wealth effect — the borrowing capacity and purchasing power of millions of stock holders, the total effect of this downward development worsened the recession in the real economy — which, according to American economists, had already begun in December 2007.

Like houses, cars, among other things, are concrete things with eminent use value. It is not as if Americans suddenly lost the desire to own and drive big cars produced by General Motors, etc. It was simply the case that many people lost the ability to pay the high price of such cars, and rising gasoline prices increased the cost of driving them. They simply could not afford such cars anymore.

### 5. The *Real, Deeper* Cause of the Crisis — Limits to Growth

We then have to understand the *changed circumstances* under which the ordinary people who had bought houses on credit could no longer service their debts and no longer buy the big, gas-guzzling cars made by General Motors et al.

In the beginning of this chapter I referred to the importance of knowing that a paradigm shift in economic thinking is taking place: a shift from the old growth paradigm — the notion that limitless growth is possible — to what I call the *limits to growth paradigm.*

The planet is in peril not only because of global warming. The ecological balance of the earth has been undermined for a long time, e.g., through progressive deforestation, especially of the rain forests, through progressive decline of biodiversity, through increasing environmental pollution of various kinds.

The contraction of the resource base of industrial societies is most clearly manifested in the fact that oil extraction has, according to most experts, peaked or even crossed the peak. That is why the price of crude oil, by far the most important resource of modern industrial societies, had been rising continuously in the few years before the present crisis broke out. In July 2008, it reached $147 per barrel. Also the prices of other important resources — the energy resources coal, gas, and uranium as well as industrial metals like copper, zinc, iron, steel, and tantalum — rose sharply. As of October 2010 there was almost a hysteria over the scarcity and high price of rare-earth metals that are essential for many high-tech products. Even the prices of basic foodstuffs, for hundreds of millions of people all over the world the main source of energy for replenishing their labor power, rose exorbitantly. After the recession began and deepened, the prices of these resources fell again, but they never again reached the low level at which they were, say, in 2000. As of autumn 2010, despite slow recovery from the recession, crude oil price was still hovering at over $80 a barrel.

It is not only a question of too-high prices. Even if one is prepared to pay the high price, one may not get the desired fuel or metal. For example, the supply of gas from Russia to Western Europe is no longer assured. China recently stopped or reduced the supply of rare earth elements, on which it has a near-monopoly, to Japan and other industrial states. The competition for control over essential resources has intensified. China has been making great efforts for several years now to build up in Africa and Australia a solid source of all kinds of minerals. To use the title of a book that appeared in 1975 in German, the planet is being plundered. The search for oil and gas is being extended to deeper and deeper seabeds. The littoral states of the Arctic Ocean are quarreling over control of its seabed because large oil and gas deposits are presumed to exist under the North Pole. China and some oil-rich Arab countries are buying up fertile land in Africa in order to make sure they get enough foodstuffs.

The gifts of nature our earth provides, such as clean air and water, are important resources for any kind of society, as are the environmental services it provides, such as earth's ability to absorb a certain amount of human-made pollution and to regenerate the fertility of arable land. The costs of maintaining such resources in an industrial society have also increased along with the costs of extracting important resources like the ones mentioned above.

The rising costs of extracting or conserving these resources mean that fewer and fewer resources are available to most people. Only those fortunate few, whose real incomes are rising or are not falling despite these circumstances, can consume the same amount of these resources as before. Nobody can know exactly how much of these resources are being consumed by particular people. But if one says that a person has lost his/her job or is working only part-time, if one says that a person's *real* income is going down, then it is tantamount to saying that this person is getting fewer and fewer resources, which include the labor power and services of other people (e.g., that of a doctor, railway workers, or a car mechanic). Particularly in the USA, where several million such people do not have any health insurance, they hesitate to go to a doctor, because they have to *pay cash* for each visit and each purchase of medication. And in Europe, where railway travel is more common, such people can afford fewer railway travels because they have to *pay cash* for each journey.

This exactly happened (is happening) in most parts of the world. Even in Germany, one of the richest and economically most successful countries of the world, the *real* income of the average working person has been falling for several years now. In 2006, just a year before the present crisis began in the USA, German official statistics confirmed that real standard wages in Germany had already been falling for a few years (*Frankfurter Rundschau*, 29 July 2006). Moreover, a large and growing number of workers are finding only temporary and part-time jobs. As to the US, as I have shown in chapter IX, in the same year the real wages of the majority of workers had fallen despite satisfactory economic growth. *Der Spiegel*, a big German newsmagazine, quoted concrete figures: in 1978, the average annual real income of Americans amounted to $45,879; in 2007, it was $45,113 (30 October 2010: 78). This downward slide affected not only workers, but also the middle class.

It should not, therefore, surprise anybody that, in 2007, the US housing boom came to an end and homeowners began defaulting. It began with the subprime mortgagors, but soon also the established working class and then the middle class started losing their homes. It should also be easy to understand now that the big gas-guzzling cars of General Motors et al. became almost unsalable at about the same time that gasoline prices steeply increased (in the USA, $4 per gallon). It is therefore easy to see the causal connection between the beginning of the recession (between December 2007 and mid-2008) and the sharp rise of the crude oil price and the prices of important industrial metals and foodstuffs.

Trade-unionists and all kinds of leftists may blame the current misery of the working people on brutal capitalist exploitation, on the weakness of the working class, on speculators without any conscience, on greedy bankers, on globalization that has caused the relocation of many production units to cheap-labor countries, etc. Of course, at first sight, all these explanations are at least partly correct. But on closer look one cannot but realize that when, *on the whole*, there are fewer and fewer resources to distribute because it is getting more and more difficult to extract them from nature (consider oil exploration at the icy west coast of Greenland!), then, even in a better capitalist world with a strong working class, at best only a fairer distribution could be achieved, not more prosperity for all. It is now necessary that leftists think in totally new terms, in terms of the limits to growth paradigm.

We can further explain the matter in the following way. Workers in the broadest sense produce goods and services by using resources (including energy resources), tools, and machines, which are also produced by using resources. If due to diminishing availability of *affordable* resources a growing number of workers lose their jobs or are forced to work only part-time, then they are producing no goods and services or fewer of them than before. Now, since most goods and services are, *in the ultimate analysis*, paid for by (exchanged with) goods and services, it is unavoidable that these workers can get fewer goods and services from other people.

There is another factor that plays a role in this development. Because of a higher level of automation and rationalization, fewer (or fewer full-time) workers are necessary to produce a given quantity of goods and services from a given quantity of resources than were necessary, say, fifteen years ago. It is, of course, possible to employ more part-time workers (or introduce reduced working hours for all) for the same amount of production. That would ensure a fairer distribution of the required quantity of paid labor among those who can and want to work. But it would not be possible that such workers earn, in total, the same amount that full-time workers earned before. Full pay with reduced working hours — this favorite demand of leftists and trade-unionists has today become absurd.

In this connection, it is useful to recapitulate what I wrote in chapter IX, section 8, on the deceptive quality of the concept of GDP and on the notion of defensive and compensatory costs. If we do that we would not make the mistake that Paul Krugman has made. In his 2006 article referred to in chapter 9, Paul Krugman speaks of a "disconnect" between wage stagnation, or even a fall in real wages, on the one hand, and satisfactory national economic growth on the other. The term "disconnect" suggests that the lacking parallel between wages and economic growth is inexplicable, as if the trade unions were too weak to take advantage of the national economic growth. I, in contrast, have said that the growth figures are deceptive. They do not necessarily mean that national *income* is growing.

In the present-day context, damages caused by ecological degradation are more relevant, because they mostly happen as a *consequence* of the same process that is supposed to be generating prosperity, i.e., industrial production. The $32 billion that is estimated to be the cost of repairing the pollution damages caused by BP's oil spill in the Gulf of Mexico will be added to Britain's and America's GDP in 2010. The GDP thus loses some of its value as an indicator of prosperity. The point I want to make here is that not all of the glorious growth percentages of China, India, etc., are really growth in *real income*. The huge damages caused in China in 2010 by the extreme weather events — prolonged drought, incessant heavy rain causing devastating floods and landslides — are most probably results of global warming. How much it has cost China will be estimated by statisticians only later. But it is safe to say now that these and other similar costs would reduce China's *real* national *income* substantially.

I also wrote in chapter IX, section 8, that K. William Kapp already came to the conclusion in 1971 that the dangers to the environment and the costs arising to society therefrom show, both in absolute and relative terms, a *rising trend* parallel to growth in production and consumption. Paul Krugman (2006) wrote in his article that in the USA, wage stagnation and falling real wages in spite of satisfactory GDP growth began in the 1970s. That was roughly also the time when Kapp came to his above-quoted conclusion. Costs arising to society at large must be borne by members of society. Since in capitalism the rich are powerful and the workers are weak, it is unavoidable that the workers and the poor, so long as they remain weak, are condemned to bear the greater part of such costs. Krugman wrote further that reductions in the allowances paid by employers to their workers had already begun in the 1980s. The correlation between growing social costs and stagnating or falling real wages is obvious.

In Germany as well, the much vaunted welfare state is on the decline. For example, health care costs are rising continuously (a growing part of such costs arise from mental and psychical sufferings). While employers are refusing to increase their contribution to the statutory health insurance fund, pharmaceutical companies are refusing to reduce the prices of medication, doctors are regularly demanding and getting higher remunerations, and workers' contributions to the fund are being increased by law. As for the unemployed, the poor, and people with small pensions, several benefit payments to them have been cut or are being proposed to be cut. For example, it has been proposed by politicians that unemployed people who get their accommodation paid for by the welfare office must now accept a smaller (up to 25 square meters only) apartment than the 48 square meters they are entitled to at present. This development can be easily explained in macroeconomic terms. The gross profit expectation of business in Germany (e.g., that of Deutsche Bank) is at present 25%. If real GDP grows at the rate of only 2% and *real* national *income* — after deducting the continuously rising defensive and compensatory costs — grows not at all or at a still lower rate, then the aspirations of business can be fulfilled only by depriving the poor and the weak.

The situation of the welfare state is equally bad, if not worse, in the other countries of Western Europe. Steven Erlanger wrote: "Europeans have boasted about their social model, with its generous vacations and early retirement, its national health care systems and extensive welfare benefits, contrasting it with the comparative harshness of American capitalism." But now, he continued: For Western Europe, "the lifestyle superpower, the assumptions and gains of a lifetime are suddenly in doubt. The deficit crisis ... has also undermined the sustainability of the European standard of social welfare, built by left-leaning governments since the end of World War II." This is not an ephemeral phenomenon. As to the future, Erlanger concludes: "The deficit crisis in Europe spells doom for the welfare state" (Erlanger 2010). I agree. To take a concrete country as an example, Spain, reporter Sebastian Schoepp wrote: "The crisis has spoilt their wish to beget children. Compared to the previous year, the birth rate fell in 2009 by five percent. Three out of ten Spaniards look without hope into the future" (Schoepp 2010).

Another case in point: in a recent statement, the UK government presented a perspective on the future and gave an example of defensive costs. It says that Britain must reduce its emission of greenhouse gases by 80% in the coming 40 years and that it must therefore use more nuclear, solar, and wind power. But then citizens must be prepared to pay £300 more per capita per year so that the lights remain on (*The Daily Telegraph*, 28 July 2010). Whether nuclear, solar, and wind power will solve the problem of global warming is uncertain, but it is certain that the higher costs will come.

We can now also understand the banking crisis, the credit crunch, and the financial crisis of some states better in the light of the analysis presented above. Before the crisis broke out, banks used to lend as much money as they could, because they earned interest on that. That is, after all, their main business. There are risks in this business. Even in normal times, part of the loans turn out to be bad debts. Banks also lend large amounts for very unproductive purposes, for instance, for speculation at the stock exchange, or for company takeovers. *As long as the real economy grows more or less satisfactorily*, the risk that too many debtors will not be able to service their debts is low. And banks can easily write off some bad debts. But after the subprime crisis broke out, the confidence that the economy would again grow normally after a short recession — the most fundamental condition of banking business — evaporated. And this confidence did not return fully. As of October 2010, in most industrialized countries, recovery was weak, uncertain, and faltering. In the USA it was being debated whether there had been any recovery at all. In Germany, it was being discussed how long the present strong growth would last. Also so far as lending to states was concerned — in the form of buying their bonds — investors were no longer sure that a member state of the EU would not become insolvent. That was why Greece, Ireland, Spain, Portugal, etc., had difficulty in selling their bonds. This skepticism was justified. As of October 2010, there was little hope that the economies of said countries would return to strong growth in the near future.

## 6. Short-Term Perspective

In chapters X and XI, I presented my thoughts on the long-term perspective on the shape of things to come. At the end of this chapter, I think it is necessary to add a few words on the short-term perspective.

As I have argued above, in the ultimate analysis it is the limits to growth that are today preventing the world economy from fully recovering from the present crisis. Since the limits to growth are a fact, it is most likely that the already highly developed, rich industrial states would suffer from a long period of stagnation (anemic growth or no growth) like Japan in the 1990s. I am not saying here anything very new. Even many establishment economists are nowadays saying this. For the immediate future, some economists are even seeing the danger of deflation (*International Herald Tribune*, 7 August 2010), which is worse news for the economy than inflation. In Japan it is already the case, and policy makers there don't see any option for them to utilize (*Süddeutsche Zeitung*, 3 July 2010; *International Herald Tribune*, 24 August 2010). Of late, among economic experts the number of "doomsayers" is increasing, and they are being seriously listened to (Thomas Jr. 2010). The difference is that while these experts are mostly speaking of a decade or so of stagnation, I think it will be a continuous contraction until at some point a steady state will have been reached, all of which will not be a peaceful process. That is simply the logic of limits to growth. Those who do not explain the present crisis with this logic, i.e., those who think that a clever mix of various policies could ultimately overcome it, are naturally looking forward to a new long period of growth and prosperity.

Many among them, the optimists, are hoping that soon a new "green industrial revolution" will/can begin that will generate a strong economic growth, which will create hundreds of thousands of new jobs and will, moreover, be sustainable — both ecologically and in respect of resources. If that hope materializes, then not only would the present crisis be over, but capitalism would also get a very sound basis for eternal growth because solar and wind energy would be available in unlimited quantities. They demand of the governments that "green" enterprises be promoted through investment subsidies, tax cuts, price favors, and other stimuli. They are speaking of the necessity of a "green New Deal." This idea can also be called green Keynesianism.

I have shown above that the way the major industrialized states reacted to the current crisis was typically Keynesian. So why shouldn't they pursue a green Keynesian policy? In fact, this idea has had prominent and powerful supporters. Thus, UN Secretary-General Ban Ki-moon proclaimed: "We stand at the threshold of a global transformation — of the era of green economy." Leading politicians such as Nicolas Sarkozy, Gordon Brown, and Barack Obama held out hope as well. They announced plans to give massive support to key industries for climate protection and renewable energies. The fact that a lot of money would be needed for realizing these plans, and that money was very scarce, especially now, did not bother the leaders. Thus, Gordon Brown said: "I know that some people may be saying that the difficult financial circumstances that the world now faces mean that climate change should move to the back burner of international concern. I believe the opposite is the case" (Dickey and McNicoll 2008).

But how solid is this idea? In chapter X (and in my previous book, 1999, chapter 4) I have shown in detail that simply for material-scientific reasons the idea of green growth, of a green industrial revolution, is an illusion. But also for financial-technical reasons, it is, at least in the present circumstances, impossible. It has now become clear that a people cannot indefinitely go on living well by spending money they have not earned. There is a limit to borrowing. A state too cannot go on stimulating the economy by borrowing money. Above a certain level of indebtedness there is the danger of going bankrupt. And then nobody would buy bonds of such a state, especially when its economy is stagnating. And if there is only modest and uncertain growth, which was, in August 2010, the case in several countries (there are a few exceptions, e.g., China, India, Brazil, etc.), the state cannot increase taxes out of fear of stifling the growth. That indiscriminately printing money does not help when the economy has exhausted its potential for growth need not be explained further.

The hope of a green industrial revolution also fits into Schumpeterian thinking. When, in November 2008, the US government planned a rescue package for the three large US car companies in trouble, some leading American politicians and media people expressed the view that they should be allowed to go bankrupt, as they were terminally ill. Any financial help would only extend their life by six months, but then they would inevitably die. They had not restructured at the right time, and so their production costs were far higher than those of their competitors. In the capitalist world they no longer had a right to live on. They could have added that, instead, innovations in the area of green technologies could be promoted.

However, the current crisis is not merely a cleansing process in the context of economic development (Schumpeter); it is not simply one of those crises through which the economy regularly gets rid of uneconomic, uncompetitive companies. This crisis did not just hit the three large US car companies, but the whole automobile industry. Highly praised, very modern, and efficient European and Japanese car manufacturers like BMW, Mercedes-Benz, Nissan, Opel, and Toyota were hit by the crisis as well.

In the context of the request of Opel (a German subsidiary of General Motors) for state help, journalist Thomas Steinfeld referred directly to Schumpeter:

> The realization that crisis is an integral part of capitalism just as a wheel is an integral part of a car goes to the credit of Schumpeter with his thesis of "creative destruction." ... Hundreds of large companies have perished, often with bad consequences for their workers. And yet, until now, again and again new companies have taken their place. Why then should some companies — and why just these ones and why now — get an existence guarantee? Why should there be a state guarantee for a prolonged life?

Steinfeld also presented his perspective. Referring to the greatest concern of the whole car industry, availability and the price of oil, he wrote:

> Whole branches of the economy will now have to reinvent themselves. Politicians should not stand in their way. If one believes Schumpeter, capitalism does not need particular resources. It only needs resources. It perhaps does not even need oil. It might instead be willing without any problem to switch over to alternative energies — using the money made on the basis of oil — if the profit were satisfactory. In this total indifference that capitalism shows in regard to the material the economy uses lies considerable hope. (Steinfeld 2008)

If the renewable energy technologies were economically viable, then they would indeed constitute a great Schumpeterian basic "innovation," that could start off, together with many other innovations around this basic one, a new expansive phase of a new long wave. But they do not appear to be so, at least not until now.

In the first phase of the crisis, it seemed that now all decision-makers were again Keynesians. Peter Bofinger, whom I have quoted in chapter VII, said that finance capitalism of the Anglo-Saxon type had now died "with a big bang," that the world community now stood at the threshold of an epochal change. He demanded, as a lesson from the crisis, that from now onwards the state should continuously and strongly intervene in the economy (*Süddeutsche Zeitung*, 30 September 2008). I have already expressed my doubts about and criticism of Keynesian policies in chapter VII. The current crisis has, of course, devalued the articles of faith of globalized neo-liberal capitalism. But it has not strengthened Keynesian capitalism. The limits to deficit financing have been reached. In the second phase of the crisis, quite a few states of Europe are pursuing rigorous austerity policies. The severest cuts are being put through in the UK, the conservative-liberal government of which is expecting the private sector to bring about the necessary growth and create new jobs.

However, as we have seen, Keynes also had a nationalistic orientation. This aspect of his teachings has been taken up by several leading states. When the debate over state aid to the three sick US car manufacturers was going on, supporters of the rescue package did not merely argue with jobs in danger, but they also argued in nationalistic terms. They said that the United States could not live off only the income from the finance industry. The country should also produce some goods. In the past, it had lost many industries; it could not afford to lose the car industry too. Gordon Brown, the then prime minister of the United Kingdom, thought that this attempt to rescue the US car industry was a protectionist move, that this could destroy the world economy. He protested, but to no avail. The Europeans followed the US example. They (particularly the Germans) aided their car industry by granting a premium for every destroyed nine-year-old car followed by purchase of a new one. As of November 2010, in connection with the G20 summit meeting in Seoul, South Korea, everybody was talking of the rise of a new protectionism and of competitive devaluation (a new "currency war") aimed at favoring the nation's export industries. This is reminiscent of the Great Depression of the 1930s.

The new nationalistic orientation has also infected the EU, which is supposed to be functioning as one unified economic zone. Thus Christine Lagarde, then the French minister for the economy, industry, and employment, said that Germany's strong export-driven recovery was taking place at the cost of its EU partners. She reproached Germany for letting this happen. Subsequent data corroborated her criticism. In contrast to Germany's strong recovery—the GDP grew there in the second quarter of 2010 by 2.2%—the economy of the whole Eurozone grew in the same period by only 1%, and that of France by only 0.6% (*Süddeutsche Zeitung*, 14 August 2010).

Up to now I have concentrated my attention mainly on the rich industrialized countries. The picture is the opposite in some newly industrialized countries: China, India, Brazil, etc. The growth rate in these countries is very high. But we should not forget that much of it has been possible because, for a long time now, labor-intensive industries have been transferred from the rich industrialized countries to these low-wage countries. China has been (and still largely is) the "factory" of the world, India the back office. Part of the new prosperity of these countries is only the result of a zero-sum game. Moreover, the reason why the Chinese economy is booming despite the stagnation in Europe and America, its main export market, is the great real estate bubble, which has been created by the state through its €450 billion stimulus package at the height of the crisis and which is now threatening to burst (see Wagner 2010). Moreover, nobody thinks here of the horrendous social and ecological costs of growth, although they cannot be hidden. Only the recent prosperity of Brazil is not much dependent on these factors. Brazil is a vast country with a relatively small population, about 190 million, an enormous area of fertile land, and enormous natural resources. That is an exception.

The social costs of the prosperity of the middle class of China and India are escalating and manifesting themselves in one or another kind of class struggle. In China, for several years now, this has taken the form of local revolts, sometimes violent, against the authorities and the entrepreneur class. Recently, it has also taken the form of some successful strikes for higher wages. But it also took the form of physical violence against doctors in hospitals where poor patients were neglected (*International Herald Tribune*, 10 August 2010), and even deadly attacks on schoolchildren of the urban middle class, presumably perpetrated by losers in the struggle for existence. Some recent cases of suicide of frustrated factory workers may also be interpreted as a form of protest against the prevailing situation.

In India, in a large underdeveloped swath of the country, called by the media "the red corridor," "Maoists," i.e., the ignored or exploited local people, who are moreover being threatened with eviction from their land, have taken to arms and are fighting against the state. In the more peaceful regions of the country, in the last ten years or so, about 200,000 bankrupt small farmers have committed suicide. In Bangladesh, the country with the cheapest labor, workers who produce garments for the rich of Europe and America have had to resort to violent strikes to get only a slightly better deal.

Finally, I would like to come back to the question of whether this is just *another* crisis *in* capitalism or *the* crisis *of* capitalism. In as early as October 2008, in San Francisco, an international conference of select leftist and liberal intellectuals discussed the question: Will capitalism be over soon? In the last quarter of 2008 and a few months thereafter, because of the severity of the international financial crisis then, it seemed to many that capitalism might break down; others thought it would not be able to recover from this crisis. I was not convinced. Its financial system is only one of the more important *mechanisms* through which capitalism functions, it is not the system's *foundation*. A defective mechanism can be both patched up and repaired (which process has already been started), but an ineluctably eroding foundation cannot. As long as the foundation can remain strong, the system can remain alive. The foundation of today's capitalism is its material resource base. And this base is eroding fast and irreparably.

The manifestations of class conflict mentioned above in conjunction with the present financial-economic crisis hearten traditional Marxists and communists. But they do not yet understand that this crisis is not simply the crisis of capitalism. It is the crisis of industrialism altogether, in whichever political-economic frame it might be packed. Those who want to work for building a better world must therefore not only fight against capitalism, but also against industrialism. Unfortunately, most ecological activists who are more or less critical of industrialism, at least those I know, hesitate to clearly answer the question of what sort of a political-economic system should or could, in their opinion, replace capitalism and industrialism. It looks as if the old king who is lying in his deathbed continues to rule, simply because no pretender to the throne comes forward and tells him: Your majesty, abdicate; I want to take over.

In this situation, in which everything in the world has become uncertain, in which an economic downward slide is interspersed with political and social unrest, ordinary people are suffering from fear, fear of the future, because they cannot trust the prevailing system anymore. Nobody knows what is in store for us about a decade from now. In my view, humanity must change course toward eco-socialism, or it will sink into barbarianism.

But in no country will this change of course be initiated until a majority supports it. This is not the case yet, in any country. It is still capitalism that enjoys cultural-intellectual hegemony in Antonio Gramsci's sense. That is why capitalism is not going to be over soon. The present crisis can, however, lead to its end if eco-socialists of the world succeed in wresting this hegemony.

# Notes

1. MAI is the acronym for "Multilateral Agreement on Investments." In the mid-1990s the Organisation for Economic Co-operation and Development (OECD) tried to hammer together an agreement amongst its member states that would have by and large deprived nation states of all power in matters of investment by foreign corporations. In 1997 a strong campaign against this attempt emerged that proved successful. In 1998 the OECD dropped the idea.

2. Sweezy uses "breakdown" for the German word "*Zusammenbruch*." Here, the translators of *Das Kapital* used "collapse."

3. Translation by Graciela Calderón.

4. The multiplier effect refers to the fact that an initial change in investment and consumption spending results in further analogous changes. If, for instance, an entrepreneur spends €1 million to buy machines, he creates income and jobs for companies and workers who produce these machines. In turn, these companies and workers buy machines and consumer goods with the additional income, which also creates income and jobs for other companies. This means that the initial €1 million investment creates more income than just €1 million. The same happens in the opposite situation. When an entrepreneur goes bankrupt, not only he and his workers lose income and jobs but also other entrepreneurs and workers.

5. This claim seems somewhat odd to me. I have read so far that in history technical development has tended towards increasing capital intensity and simultaneously decreasing labor intensity. However, here I restrict myself to what Keynesians have said.

6. What is funny in this regard is that Keynes himself was a successful speculator.

7. Potential production (potential GDP): this concept means the highest *possible* aggregate production at stable prices. It can also be called the production level at full employment. Potential production (potential GDP) can change in the course of time.

8. Velocity of circulation of money ($V$): When money received is generally spent fast, then $V$ is high. That generates more economic activity—therefore more employment and income—than when it is spent slowly (low $V$).

9. Current account: "the part of a nation's balance of payments that deals with merchandise (or visible) imports or exports" is called balance of trade. "When 'invisibles,' or services, are included, the total accounting for imports and exports of goods and services is called the balance on current account" (Samuelson and Nordhaus 1989: 966).

10. This quotation has been retranslated from the German translation; the English original is no longer accessible.

11. Open market operations are an important instrument of central banks for regulating the money supply in an economy. By buying and selling government securities central banks can cause the cash reserves of commercial banks to increase or decrease. When commercial banks have higher cash reserve levels, they can grant more loans, and vice versa.

12. Current account: comparison of a country's total exports and imports of goods and services. Formerly, the concept "balance of trade" was used to designate the balance of exports and imports of merchandise (visible goods); it did not take services into account. See also note 9.

13. "New Economy": This was the term used to denote the Internet hype, i.e., the founding and rise of numerous companies in the area of Internet application and the speculation with their stocks at the share markets.

14. Increase in wealth can also come about when the value of existing assets—securities or real estate—increases at the stock exchange or in the real estate market (also through speculation). The assets do not necessarily have to be sold in order to allow the owner to increase her consumption. She can take out a higher consumption loan on the basis of the increased value of her assets.

15. Data on real GDP growth are usually given on a year-on-year basis, that is, the current GDP figure is compared with the GDP figure twelve months before. But one speaks of a recession when the GDP has fallen in two consecutive quarters compared to the previous quarter. Hence, it can happen that in a text one speaks of economic growth and recession simultaneously, which, of course, is confusing for the reader.

16. See note 14.

17. In a contracting capitalist world economy there will be no peace. There will be wars between nations and ethnic groups over resources. Everywhere there will be class struggles and other conflicts. And in every society there will be violence, crime, and societal degeneration. All that together will lead to a process of disintegration of human society.

18. I have substantiated these theses in detail in my previous book (1999: chapters 5 and 6).

# References

Afheldt, Horst (2003). *Wirtschaft, die arm macht: Vom Sozialstaat zur gespaltenen Gesellschaft.* Munich: Antje Kunstmann.

Altvater, Elmar (1992). *Die Zukunft des Marktes: Ein Essay über die Regulation von Geld und Natur nach dem Scheitern des "real existierenden Sozialismus."* Münster: Westfälisches Dampfboot.

——— (2005). *Das Ende des Kapitalismus wie wir ihn kennen.* Münster: Westfälisches Dampfboot.

Altvater, Elmar, and Kurt Hübner (1987). "Ursachen und Verlauf der internationalen Schuldenkrise," in Altvater et al. (1987).

Altvater, Elmar, Kurt Hübner, Jochen Lorentzen, and Raul Rojas (1987). *Die Armut der Nationen: Handbuch zur Schuldenkrise von Argentinien bis Zaire.* Frankfurt am Main: Büchergilde Gutenberg.

Alvey, J.E. (1994). "John Maynard Keynes: A Centennial Assessment," in Wood (1994), vol. 8.

Anonymous (1972). *Lehrbuch Politische Ökonomie: Vorsozialistische Produktionsweisen.* Frankfurt am Main: Verlag Marxistische Blätter.

Arbeitsgruppe Alternative Wirtschaftspolitik (Memorandum-Gruppe) (2005). *Memorandum 2005: Sozialstaat statt Konzern-Gesellschaft* (short version). Bremen.

Arbeitskreis Post-Autistische Ökonomie (2004). *Positionsbestimmung* (leaflet). Heidelberg.

Attac-France (2002). *Manifest 2002.* www.praxisphilosophie.de/mani2002.pdf/.

Barker, Debi, and Jerry Mander (1999). *Invisible Government: The World Trade Organization: Global Government for the New Millennium?* San Francisco: International Forum on Globalization (IFG).

Bass, Hans H. (1998). *J.A. Schumpeter: Eine Einführung.* Bremen: University of Bremen.

Batra, Ravi (1987). *The Great Depression of 1990.* New York: Simon & Schuster.

Baumol, William J. (2002). *The Free-Market Innovation Machine: Analyzing the Growth Miracle of Capitalism.* Princeton, NJ: Princeton University Press.

Beckerman, Wilfred (1972). "Economists, Scientists, and Environmental Catastrophes." *Oxford Economic Papers* 24, no. 3 (November).

Bello, Walden (2003). "Capitalist Crisis and Corporate Crime in America." *Global Outlook* 3:45–46.

Bennholdt-Thomsen, Veronika, Nicholas Faraclas, and Claudia von Werlhof, eds. (2001). *There Is an Alternative: Subsistence and Worldwide Resistance to Corporate Globalization.* London: Zed Books.

Bettelheim, Charles (1978). *Class Struggles in the USSR: Second Period, 1923–1930.* New York: Monthly Review Press.

Bofinger, Peter (2005). *Wir sind besser als wir glauben: Wohlstand für alle.* Munich: Pearson Studium.

Bonstein, Julia, and Merlind Theile (2006). "Auf Nummer unsicher." *Der Spiegel* 31 (July 2006).

Bortz, Jeffrey et. al. (1987). *Schuldenkrise: In der Dritten Welt tickt eine Zeitbombe.* Frankfurt am Main: ISP-Verlag.

Bös, Dieter, and Hans-Dieter Stolper, eds. (1984). *Schumpeter oder Keynes? Zur Wirtschaftspolitik der neunziger Jahre.* Berlin: Springer Verlag.

Bové, José, and François Dufour (2001). *Die Welt ist keine Ware: Bauern gegen Agromultis.* Zurich: Rotpunktverlag.

Boxberger, Gerald, and Harald Klimenta (1998). *Die 10 Globalisierungslügen: Alternativen zur Allmacht des Marktes.* Munich: Deutscher Taschenbuch Verlag.

Brandt, Andrea (2006). "Strahlen über den Köpfen." *Der Spiegel* 38.

Brandt, Götz (2006). "Können Biokraftstoffe die fossilen Kraftstoffe ablösen?" *Tarantel* 34 (September 2006).

Braverman, Harry (1974). *Labor and Monopoly Capital: The Degeneration of Work in the Twentieth Century.* New York: Monthly Review Press.

Brenner, Robert (2003a). *The Boom and the Bubble: The US in the World Economy.* London: Verso.

——— (2003b). "Schwungvoll auf Talfahrt: Ursachen und Mechanismen der US-amerikanischen Wirtschaftskrise." *Lettre International* (spring 2003).

Brusatti, Alois (1967). *Wirtschafts- und Sozialgeschichte des industriellen Zeitalters.* Graz: Verlag Styria.

Buchter, Heike (2005). "Teufelskerle der Wall Street: Hedge Fonds haben sich zur treibenden Kraft entwickelt. Doch die Skandale häufen sich." *Die Zeit* 49 (1 December 2005).

Burkett, Paul (1999). *Marx and Nature: A Red and Green Perspective.* London: Palgrave Macmillan.

Caffentzis, C. George (1997). "Why Machines Cannot Create Value; or, Marx's Theory of Machines," in Davis et al. (1997).

Caspar, Lucian (2006). "Furcht fördert Umsatz: Die Sicherheitsbranche erlebt in den USA einen Boom." *Frankfurter Rundschau* (8 September 2006).

Clevström, Jenny (2006). "Sweden's Labour Overhauls May Pave Way in Europe." *Wall Street Journal* (10 November 2006).

Colm, Gerhard (1947/1965). "Fiscal Policy," in Harris (1965).

Dahrendorf, Ralf (1983). *Chancen der Krise.* Stuttgart: Deutschen Verlags-Anstalt.

Daly, Herman E. (1977). *Steady-State Economics: The Economics of Biophysical Equilibrium and Moral Growth.* San Francisco: W.H. Freeman.

——— (1996). *Beyond Growth: The Economics of Sustainable Development.* Boston: Beacon Press.

Daly, Herman E., and John B. Cobb Jr. (1990). *For the Common Good.* London: Green Print.

Dannheim, Bettina (2006). "Clean Coal?" *Robin Wood Magazine* 90 (March 2006).

Davis, Jim, Thomas A. Hirschl, and Michael Stack (1997). *Cutting Edge: Technology, Information Capitalism and Social Revolution.* London: Verso.

Dempsey, Judy (2006). "Problem for Europe: Russia Also Needs Gas." *International Herald Tribune* (22 November 2006).

Deutschmann, Christoph (1973). *Der linke Keynesianismus*. Frankfurt am Main: Athenäum.

Diamond, Jared (2006). *Collapse: How Societies Choose to Fall or Survive*. London: Penguin.

Dickey, Christopher, and Tracy McNicoll (2008). "A Green New Deal." *Newsweek* (3 November 2008).

Dillard, D. (1983/1993). "The Pragmatic Basis of Keynes's Political Economy," in Wood (1993), vol. 1.

Dillard, D. (1983/1993). "The Influence of Keynesian Economics on Contemporary Thought," in Wood (1993), vol. 3.

Dillard, Dudley (1948/1972). *The Economics of John Maynard Keynes: The Theory of a Monetary Economy*. Delhi: Vikas.

Dillmann, Hans-Ulrich (2006). "Aufstrebende Inseln: Die Karibikrepublik Trinidad und Tobago wünscht sich eine Wohlstandsgesellschaft." *Frankfurter Rundschau* (5 May 2006).

Diwan, Ramesh, and Mark Lutz, eds. (1985). *Essays in Gandhian Economics*. New Delhi: Gandhi Peace Foundation.

Douthwaite, Richard (1992). *The Growth Illusion: How Economic Growth Has Enriched the Few, Impoverished the Many, and Endangered the Planet*. Bideford (UK): Green Books.

Drewermann, Eugen (2008). "Wie im Schlaraffenland." *Freitag* (11 June 2008).

*Economist* (2004). "Back to the 1970s?" (19 June 2004).

Editors, *Monthly Review* (1975). "The Economic Crisis in Historical Perspective." Vol. 26, no. 10 (March 1975).

*Encyclopaedia Britannica* (CD-ROM) (2001). Chicago: Encyclopaedia Britannica, Inc.

Engels, Frederick (1892/1976b). Preface to *The Condition of the Working Class in England*, in Marx and Engels (1976b).

Engels, Friedrich (1973). *Dialektik der Natur*. Berlin: Dietz Verlag.

Erlanger, Steven (2010). "Pushed Out of the Comfort Zone." *New York Times* (30 May 2010).

Ertel, Manfred (2006). "Gefährlicher Wohlfühlfaktor." *Der Spiegel* 37 (11 September 2006).

Fefer, Mark, and Josh P. Hamilton (2006). "Insurance Grows Costly after Ruinous Hurricanes." *International Herald Tribune* (1 September 2006).

Felderer, Bernhard, and Stefan Homburg (1991). *Makroökonomik und neue Makroökonomik*. Berlin: Springer Verlag.

Fielding, Steven (2003). *The Labour Party: Continuity and Change in the Making of "New" Labour*. Basingstoke (UK): Palgrave Macmillan.

Filc, Wolfgang (2001). *Gefahr für unseren Wohlstand: Wie Finanzmarktkrisen die Weltwirtschaft bedrohen*. Frankfurt am Main: Eichborn.

*Der Fischer Weltalmanach: Zahlen, Daten, Fakten* (for the years 1994, 2003, 2009, 2010, 2011). Frankfurt am Main: Fischer Taschenbuchverlag.

Foroohar, Rana, and Tony Emerson (2004). "A Heavier Burden." *Newsweek* (23 August 2004).

Frederiksen, Claus Hjort (2006). "Dänen setzen auf Flexicurity." *Frankfurter Rundschau* (18 May 2006).

Friedman, Milton (1970). *The Counter-Revolution in Monetary Theory.* London: Institute of Economic Affairs.

Galbraith, John Kenneth (1955). *The Great Crash 1929.* Boston: Houghton Mifflin.

––– (1994). *A Journey Through Economic Time: A Firsthand View.* Boston: Houghton Mifflin Company.

––– (1995). *Die Geschichte der Wirtschaft im 20. Jahrhundert.* Hamburg: Hoffmann und Campe.

Gamillscheg, Hannes (2004). "Grund für Entlassung ist in Dänemark leicht zu finden." *Frankfurter Rundschau* (7 January 2004).

––– (2005a). "Dänen schaffen rasch neue Jobs." *Frankfurter Rundschau* (13 September 2005).

––– (2005b). "Steuern bei Dänen hoch." *Frankfurter Rundschau* (8 September 2005).

––– (2006). "Die lachenden Finnen." *Frankfurter Rundschau* (3 February 2006).

Gandhi, Mahatma (1997). "The Quest for Simplicity: My Idea of Swaraj," in Rahnema and Bawtree (1997).

Garnreiter, Franz, Leo Mayer, and Fred Schmid (1998). *Weltwirtschaftskrise?* Munich: ISW (Institut für sozial-ökologische Wirtschaftsforschung).

Garnreiter, Franz, Leo Mayer, Fred Schmid, and Conrad Schuhler (2001). *Abschwung oder Absturz? Krisenpotentiale und Krisenkosten in der Weltwirtschaft.* Munich: ISW.

Garvey, G. (1983/1993). "Keynes and the Economic Activists of Pre-Hitler Germany," in Wood (1993), vol. 2.

Gassner, Marcus (1999). "Japans Weg zur Wirtschaftsmacht Nr. 2." *Marxismus* 16 (September 1999).

George, Susan (1992). *The Debt Boomerang: How Third World Debt Harms Us All.* London: Pluto Press.

––– (1999). "Eine kurze Geschichte des Neo-liberalismus." *Infobrief* (Netzwerk gegen Konzernherrschaft und neo-liberale Politik), No. 1.

Georgescu-Roegen, Nicholas (1978). "Technology Assessment: The Case of the Direct Use of Solar Energy." *Atlantic Economic Journal* (December 1978).

––– (1981). *The Entropy Law and the Economic Process.* Cambridge, MA: Harvard University Press.

––– (1987). *The Entropy Law and the Economic Process in Retrospect.* Berlin: Institut für Ökologische Wirtschaftsforschung.

Goldstein, Morris (1998). *The Asian Financial Crisis: Causes, Cures, and Systemic Implications.* Washington, DC: Institute for International Economics.

Gorz, André (1977). *Ökologie und Politik.* Reinbek: Rowohlt Verlag.

––– (1983). *Ecology as Politics.* London: Pluto Press.

Gould, Jens Erik (2006). "Latin American Crime Is Crimping Growth: Investment Slows amid Insecurity." *International Herald Tribune* (17 October 2006).

Gray, John (1999). *False Dawn: The Delusions of Global Capitalism*. London: Granta.

Greenhouse, Steven (2006). "For Young U.S. Wages Trail Costs." *International Herald Tribune* (5 September 2006).

Grobe, Karl (2003). "Arabien in der Krise." *Frankfurter Rundschau* (13 November 2003).

*Großes Wörterbuch Wirtschaft* (2005). Munich: Compact Verlag.

Guha, Krishna (2007). "Fed Learns Lesson from Past." *Financial Times* (19 October 2007).

Haberler, Gottfried (1947/1965). "The General Theory," in Harris (1965).

Hallwirth, Volker (1998). *Und Keynes hatte doch recht: Eine neue Politik für Vollbeschäftigung*. Frankfurt am Main: Campus Verlag.

Hansen, A.H. (1966/1993). "Keynes After 30 Years (with Special Reference to the United States)," in Wood (1993), vol. 3.

Hardach, Karl (1976). *Wirtschaftsgeschichte Deutschlands im 20. Jahrhundert*. Göttingen: Vandenhoeck & Ruprecht.

Harris, Seymour E., ed. (1947/1965). *The New Economics: Keynes' Influence on Theory and Public Policy*. New York: Augustus M. Kelly.

Hein, Eckhard (1998). "Keynesianismus—ein wirtschaftstheoretisches und—politisches Auslaufsmodell?" *WSI Mitteilungen* 12.

Heinberg, Richard (2003). *The Party's Over: Oil, War and the Fate of Industrial Societies*. Forest Row, UK: Clairview Books.

Henderson, Callum (1998). *Asia Falling: Making Sense of the Asian Crisis and Its Aftermath*. New York: McGraw-Hill.

Herzog, Roman (2002). "Termitenbau zerstoben: Argentinien existiert nicht (mehr)," in Komitee für Grundrechte und Demokratie (2002).

Heuser, Uwe Jean (1993). "Geld, Freiheit, Ideologie," in Sommer (1993).

Higgins, Benjamin (1947/1965). "Keynesian Economics and Public Investment Policy," in Harris (1965).

Hübner, Kurt (2006). "Freundschaftsdienst für Bush." *Frankfurter Rundschau* (9 August 2006).

Huffschmid, Jörg (1999). *Politische Ökonomie der Finanzmärkte*. Hamburg: VSA-Verlag.

Husson, Michel (2002). "Hinter der Globalisierung finden wir den Klassenkampf." *ILA* 252 (February 2002).

Hutton, Will (1986/2001). *The Revolution That Never Was: An Assessment of Keynesian Economics*. London: Random House.

IMF (International Monetary Fund) (2004). *World Economic Outlook*. Washington, DC: IMF (September 2004).

Immler, Hans (1985). *Natur in der ökonomischen Theorie*. Opladen: Westdeutscher Verlag.

Impoco, Jim (2008). "Life after the Bubble: How Japan Lost a Decade." *New York Times* (19 October 2001), reprinted in *Süddeutsche Zeitung* (27 October 2008).

Institut der Deutschen Wirtschaft Köln (2005). *Deutschland in Zahlen 2005*. Cologne: Deutscher Institutsverlag.

International Forum on Globalization (IFG) (2001). *Die Welthandelsorganisation (WTO)*. Cologne: Netzwerk gegen Konzernherrschaft und neo-liberale Politik.

Jakob, Martin (1999). "Hintergründe und Ursachen der Asienkrise." *Marxismus* 16 (September 1999).

Johnson, Harry G. (1971). "The Keynesian Revolution and the Monetarist Counter-Revolution." *American Economic Review* (May 1971).

——— (1973). "Die Keynesianische Revolution und die monetaristische Konterrevolution," in Kalmbach (1973).

Kalmbach, Peter, ed. (1973). *Der neue Monetarismus*. Munich: Nymphenburger Verlagshandlung.

Kapp, K. William (1979). *Soziale Kosten der Marktwirtschaft*. Frankfurt am Main: Fischer Taschenbuch.

Keynes, John Maynard (1931). *Essays in Persuasion*. London: Macmillan.

——— (1933). "National Self-Sufficiency." *Yale Review* 22, no. 4 (June 1933).

——— (1936/1952). *Allgemeine Theorie der Beschäftigung, des Zinses und des Geldes*. Berlin: Duncker & Humboldt.

——— (1936/1973). *The General Theory of Employment, Interest, and Money*. London: Macmillan.

Kindleberger, Charles P. (1973). *The World in Depression 1929–1939*. London: Allen Lane (Penguin).

Klein, Lawrence R. (1947/1949). *The Keynesian Revolution*. New York: Macmillan.

Koesters, Paul-Heinz (1985). *Ökonomen verändern die Welt*. Munich: Stern Buch.

Kolakowski, Leszek (2005). *Main Currents of Marxism*. New York: W.W. Norton.

Komitee für Grundrechte und Demokratie, ed. (2002). *Jahrbuch '01/02*. Cologne.

Krugman, Paul (1999). *The Accidental Theorist*. London: Penguin.

——— (2000). *The Return of Depression Economics*. London: Penguin.

——— (2006). "The Big Disconnect." *International Herald Tribune* (2 September 2006).

——— (2010). "The Third Depression." *New York Times* (27 June 2010).

Kuczynski, Jürgen (1977). *The World Economic Crisis of Capitalism*. New Delhi: People's Publishing House.

Kuhn, Thomas S. (1962/1996). *The Structure of Scientific Revolutions*. Chicago: University of Chicago Press.

Kunstler, James Howard (2005). *The Long Emergency: Surviving the Converging Catastrophes of the Twenty-First Century*. London: Atlantic Books.

Kurz, Robert (1999). *Schwarzbuch Kapitalismus: Ein Abgesang auf die Marktwirtschaft*. Frankfurt am Main: Eichborn AG.

———, ed. (2001). *Marx Lesen: Die wichtigsten Texte von Karl Marx für das 21. Jahrhundert*. Frankfurt am Main: Eichborn AG.

Leipert, Christian (1989). *Die heimlichen Kosten des Fortschritts: Wie Umweltzerstörung das Wirtschaftswachstum fördert*. Frankfurt am Main: S. Fischer Verlag.

Leonhardt, David (2010). "Nations Cut Back, and Shadow of the 1930s Looms." *New York Times* (reprinted in *Süddeutsche Zeitung*, 12 July 2010).

Lerner, Abba P. (1947/1965). "Saving Equals Investment," in Harris (1965).

Loske, Rainer, and Raimund Bleischwitz (1996). *Zukunftsfähiges Deutschland*. Basel: Birkhäuser.

Lotter, Konrad, Reinhard Meiners, and Elmar Treptow (1984). *Marx-Engels Begriffslexikon*. Munich: C.H. Beck.

Lovelock, James (2006a). "The Earth Is About to Catch a Morbid Fever That May Last As Long As 100,000 Years." *The Independent* (16 January 2006).

——— (2006b). *The Revenge of Gaia*. London: Penguin.

——— (2007). *Gaias Rache*. Berlin: List Verlag.

Löwy, Michael (2005). "Destruktiver Fortschritt. Marx, Engels und die Ökologie." *Utopie Kreativ*, no. 174 (April 2005).

Luce, Edward, and Krishna Guha (2006). "Summers and Rubin to Highlight Lagging Wages." *Financial Times* (25 July 2006).

MacEwan, Arthur (2002). "Der IWF schlägt wieder zu: Wirtschaftsdebakel in Argentinien." *ILA* (February 2002).

Mandel, Ernest (1962/1971). *Marxist Economic Theory*. Calcutta: Rupa & Co.

——— (1973). *Der Spätkapitalismus: Versuch einer Marxistischen Erklärung*. Frankfurt am Main: Suhrkamp Verlag.

——— (1977). "Krise und Aufschwung der kapitalistischen Weltwirtschaft 1974–1977," in Mandel and Wolf (1977).

——— (1988). "Der Börsenkrach. Dreizehn Fragen: Dreizehn Antworten," in Mandel and Wolf (1988).

Mandel, Ernest, and Winfried Wolf (1977). *Ende der Krise oder Krise ohne Ende?* Berlin: Klaus Wagenbach.

——— (1988). *Börsenkrach & Wirtschaftskrise*. Frankfurt am Main: ISP-Verlag.

Marx, Karl (1875/1976). *Marginal Notes to the Programme of the German Workers' Party* (better known as the "Critique of the Gotha Programme"), in Marx and Engels (1976).

——— (1954). *Capital, Volume 1*. Moscow: Foreign Language Publishing House.

——— (1976). *Capital, Volume 1*. Translated by Ben Fowkes. Harmondsworth, UK: Pelican Books.

——— (1977a). *Das Kapital, Band 1*. (Marx-Engels Werke [MEW] Band 23.) Berlin: Dietz Verlag.

——— (1977b). *Das Kapital, Band 2*. (MEW Bd. 24.) Berlin: Dietz Verlag.

——— (1977c). *Das Kapital, Band 3*. (MEW Bd. 25.) Berlin: Dietz Verlag.

——— (1982). *Capital, Volume 1*. Translated by David Fernbach. Harmondsworth, UK: Pelican Books.

——— (1981). *Capital, Volume 3*. Translated by David Fernbach. Harmondsworth, UK: Pelican Books.

Marx, Karl, and Friedrich Engels (1963). *Werke, Bd. 22*. Berlin: Dietz Verlag.

——— (1976a). *Ausgewählte Schriften in zwei Bänden: Band 2*. Berlin: Dietz Verlag.

——— (1976b). *Selected Works in Three Volumes: Volume Three*. Moscow: Progress Publishers.

——— (1977). *Selected Works in Three Volumes: Volume One.* Moscow: Progress Publishers.

Mattick, Paul (1971). *Marx and Keynes: The Limits of the Mixed Economy.* London: Merlin Press.

Mayer, Leo (2001). "Lateinamerika: mit dem Latein am Ende," in Garnreiter et al. (2001).

McGregor, Richard (2006). "China 'Faces 136bn Pollution Clean-Up,'" *Financial Times* (8 September 2006).

Meacher, Michael (2006). "On the Road to Ruin." *The Guardian* (7 June 2006).

Meadows, Donella, Jorgen Randers, and Dennis Meadows (1972). *The Limits to Growth.* New York: Signet.

Metzler, Lloyd A. (1947/1965). "Keynes and the Theory of Business Cycles," in Harris (1965).

Meyer-Abich, Klaus (1973). "Die ökologische Grenze des herkömmlichen Wirtschaftswachstums," in von Nussbaum (1963).

Moring, Andreas (2006). "Dänemark meldet Vollbeschäftigung—Arbeitskräfte in Hamburg gesucht." *Hamburger Abendblatt* (13 May 2006).

Morris, Jacob (1974). "Stagflation." *Monthly Review* (December 1974).

Müller, Albrecht (2005). *Die Reformlüge: 40 Denkfehler, Mythen und Legenden, mit denen Politik und Wirtschaft Deutschland ruinieren.* Munich: Knaur Taschenbuch.

Müller, Klaus O.W. (1990). *Joseph A. Schumpeter: Ökonom der neunziger Jahre.* Berlin: Erich Schmidt.

Mumford, Lewis (1980). *Mythos der Maschine.* Frankfurt am Main: S. Fischer Verlag.

Mussa, Michael (2002). *Argentina and the Fund: From Triumph to Tragedy.* Washington, DC: Institute for International Economics.

Neumark, Fritz (1984). "Chancen einer Schumpeter-Renaissance. Bemerkungen zu Schumpeters Ordnungs-, Konjunktur-, Finanz- und geldtheoretischen Ansichten," in Bös and Stolper (1984).

*New Encyclopaedia Britannica: The Micropaedia,* (1991). Chicago: Encyclopaedia Britannica, Inc.

Nohlen, Dieter, ed. (2002). *Lexikon Dritte Welt: Länder, Organisationen, Theorien, Begriffe, Personen.* Reinbek: Rowohlt.

Nüsse, Andrea (2006). "Blutgeld soll Angehörige ernähren." *Frankfurter Rundschau* (13 April 2006).

OECD (Organisation for Economic Cooperation and Development) (1994). *Economic Outlook* 56 (December 1994).

——— (2000). *Economic Outlook* 68 (December 2000).

——— (2004). *Economic Outlook* 76 (December 2004).

——— (2005). *Economic Outlook* 77 (June 2005).

Offer, Christian (2006). "Kein Palmöl in den Tank." *Robin Wood Magazine* 90 (March 2006).

Opschoor, Johannes B. (1991). *Environmental Taxes and Incentives.* New Delhi: Centre for Science and Environment.

Oxfam GB (2002). *Rigged Rules and Double Standards: Trade, Globalisation, and the Fight Against Poverty* (Introduction). Oxford: Oxfam International.

Pauli, Charles (1992). *G-7—der Gipfel, diese Weltwirtschaft?* Munich: ISW.

Pauly, Christoph (2006). "Schmerzhafter Prozess." *Der Spiegel* 26 (June 2006).

Pearce, David, Anil Markandya, and Edward B. Barbier (1989). *Blueprint for a Green Economy*. London: Earthscan Publications.

Perger, Werner A. (2005). "Die bedrängte Idylle—Die Sweden gelten als Vorbild für Reformfreudigkeit." *Die Zeit* 48 (24 November 2005).

Ponting, Clive (1991). *A Green History of the World*. London: Penguin.

Predöhl, Andreas (1962). *Das Ende der Weltwirtschaftskrise: Eine Einführung in die Probleme der Weltwirtschaft*. Reinbek: Rowohlt.

Rahnema, Majid, and Victoria Bawtree (1997). *The Post-Development Reader*. London: Zed Books.

Richter, Edelbert (2004). "Von der Arbeitslosigkeit zum Selbstmord—Über das Ende der Sozialdemokratie." *Neues Deutschland* (25 September 2004).

Rifkin, Jeremy (1980). *Entropy: A New World View*. New York: Viking Press.

Robinson, Joan (1974). *Economic Philosophy*. Harmondsworth, UK: Penguin.

——— (1979/1983). "Has Keynes Failed?" in Wood (1983/1993), vol. 4.

Rosenbach, Marcel (2006). "Es lebe die Röhre!" *Der Spiegel* 24 (June 2006).

Rürup, Bert, Margit Enke, and Werner Sesselmeier (2003). *Fischer Wirtschaftslexikon*. Frankfurt am Main: Fischer Taschenbuch.

Sahlins, Marshall (1974). *Stone Age Economics*. London: Tavistock Publications.

Samuelson, Paul A. (1947/1965). "The General Theory," in Harris (1965).

Samuelson, Paul A., and William D. Nordhaus (1989). *Economics*. New York: McGraw-Hill.

——— (1998). *Volkswirtschaftslehre*. Frankfurt am Main: Ueberreuter.

Samuelson, Robert J. (2006). "The Worst of Both Worlds?" *Newsweek* (13 November 2006).

Sarkar, Saral (1999). *Eco-Socialism or Eco-Capitalism? A Critical Analysis of Humanity's Fundamental Choices*. London: Zed Books.

——— (2001a). *Die nachhaltige Gesellschaft—eine kritische Analyse der Systemalternativen*, Zurich: Rotpunkt.

——— (2001b). "Sustainable Development: Rescue Operation for a Dying Illusion," in Bennholdt-Thomsen et al. (2001).

Sarkar, Saral, and Bruno Kern (2008). *Eco-Socialism or Barbarism: An Up-to-Date Critique of Capitalism*. Cologne and Mainz: Initiative Eco-Socialism. www .oekosozialismus.net/.

Saunois, Tony (2002). "Argentina—Workers Rise, Presidents Fall." *Socialism Today* 62 (February 2002).

Scheer, Hermann (1999). *Solare Weltwirtschaft: Strategie für die ökologische Moderne*. Munich: Antje Kunstmann.

Scheuch, Erwin K., and Ute Scheuch (2001). *Deutsche Pleiten: Manager im Größen-Wahn oder der irrationale Faktor*. Berlin: Rowohlt-Berlin.

Schmid, Fred (2001). "Japan: Kein Ausweg aus der Krise?" in Garnreiter et al. (2001).

Schmidt-Bleek, Friedrich (1993). *Wieviel Umwelt braucht der Mensch?* Berlin: Birkhäuser.

Schmölders, Günter (1955). *Konjunkturen und Krisen.* Hamburg: Rowohlt.

Schoepp, Sebastian (2010). "Spaniens heißester Sommer." *Süddeutsche Zeitung* (1 July 2010).

Schumpeter, Joseph Alois (1934). *The Theory of Economic Development.* Cambridge, MA: Harvard University Press.

——— (1943). *Capitalism, Socialism, and Democracy.* London: George Allen and Unwin.

——— (1947/1965). "Keynes, the Economist," in Harris (1965).

Senf, Bernd (2001). *Die blinden Flecken der Ökonomie: Wirtschaftstheorien in der Krise.* Munich: Deutscher Taschenbuch Verlag.

Sethi, J.D. (1985). "Foreword," in Diwan and Lutz (1985).

Sheridan, Barrett, and Daniel Gross (2007). "Here's the Good News." *Newsweek* (24 December 2007).

Shiva, Vandana (2002). *Export at Any Cost: Oxfam's Free Trade Recipe for the Third World.* Published by Deb Foskey via WTO Watch email list (debf@webone.com.au), no. 59 (18 May 2002).

Shutt, Harry (1998). *The Trouble With Capitalism: An Enquiry into the Causes of Global Economic Failure.* London: Zed Books.

——— (2005). *The Decline of Capitalism: Can a Self-Regulated Profits System Survive?* London: Zed Books.

Sievers, Markus (2006). "Aus der Dose." *Frankfurter Rundschau* (21 April 2006).

Simon, Julian L., and Herman Kahn, eds. (1984). *The Resourceful Earth.* Oxford: Basil Blackwell.

Sinn, Hans-Werner (2004). *Ist Deutschland noch zu retten?* Munich: Econ-Verlag.

Sommer, Theo, ed. (1993). *Zeit der Ökonomen: eine kritische Bilanz volkswirtschaftlichen Denkens (Zeit-Punkte 3).* Hamburg: Die Zeit (Zeit Magazine).

Soros, George (1998). *The Crisis of Global Capitalism.* London: Little, Brown.

Sperber, Katharina (2006). "Betrogene Jugend." *Frankfurter Rundschau* (12 October 2006).

Statistisches Bundesamt Deutschland, eds. (1999). *Statistisches Jahrbuch fürs Ausland 1999.* Stuttgart: Metzler-Poeschel.

——— (2005). *Ausgaben für Umweltschutz.*

——— (2010). *Statistisches Jahrbuch 2010.* Wiesbaden.

Steinfeld, Thomas (2008). "Die Krise als Normalität." *Süddeutsch Zeitung* (18 November 2008).

Steingart, Gabor (2006). "Weltkrieg um Wohlstand." *Der Spiegel* 37 (11 September 2006).

Stern, Nicholas (2006). *Stern Review on the Economics of Climate Change.* http://webarchive.nationalarchives.gov.uk/+/http://www.hm-treasury.gov.uk/sternreview_index.htm/.

Stiglitz, Joseph E. (2003). *The Roaring Nineties: Seeds of Destruction.* London: Allen Lane (Penguin).

——— (2006). "Keynes hätte die Steuern lieber gesenkt." *Financial Times Deutschland* (21 April 2006).

Stolper, Wolfgang F. (1984). "Schumpeter: Der politische Ökonom für die neunziger Jahre? Schumpeter versus Keynes oder Schumpeter und Keynes?" in Bös and Stolper (1984).

Strachey, John (1935). *The Nature of Capitalist Crisis.* London: Victor Gollancz.

Strahm, Rudolf H. (1981). *Überentwicklung: Unterentwicklung.* Gelnhausen: Burckhardthaus-Laetare Verlag.

Stransfeld, Reinhard (1997). "Des Kaisers neue Kleider sind kaum mehr als ein Lendenschurz." *Frankfurter Rundschau* (9 April 1997).

Strehle, Res (1994). *Wenn die Netze Reissen: Marktwirtschaft auf freier Wildbahn.* Zurich: Rotpunkt.

Streisand, Joachim (1976). *Deutsche Geschichte von den Anfängen bis zur Gegenwart.* Cologne: Pahl-Rugenstein.

Stretton, Hugh (1999). *Economics: A New Introduction.* London: Pluto Press.

Sweezy, Alan (1947/1965). "Declining Investment Opportunity," in Harris (1965).

Sweezy, Paul M. (1942). *The Theory of Capitalist Development: Principles of Marxian Political Economy.* New York: Oxford University Press.

Taylor, Robert (2005). *Sweden's New Social Democratic Model: Proof That a Better World Is Possible.* London: Compass.

Tett, Gillian (2007). "Unlucky Sevens Prove That You Can Never Eliminate Risk." *Financial Times* (19 October 2007).

Thielbeer, Siegfried (2006). "Arbeiterpartei gegen neue Arbeiterpartei." *Frankfurter Allgemeine Zeitung* (15 September 2006).

Thomas Jr., Landon (2010). "Economic Pessimists Gain Cachet." *New York Times* (9 August 2010).

Tigges, Claus (2004). "Licht und Schatten der Reaganomics." *Frankfurter Allgemeine Zeitung* (11 September 2004).

Tobin, James (1977/1983). "How Dead Is Keynes?" in Wood (1983/1993), vol. 4.

Toynbee, Polly (2005). "The Most Successful Society the World Has Ever Known." *The Guardian* (25 October 2005).

Traufetter, Gerald (2006). "Urkraft aus der Tiefe." *Der Spiegel* 29 (July 2006).

Treaster, Joseph B. (2006). "Higher Insurance Costs Hit U.S. Coastal Living." *International Herald Tribune* (26 September 2006).

Uken, Marlies (2007). "Abenteuer auf hoher See." *Greenpeace Magazine* 5.

Ulrich, Otto (1979). *Weltniveau: In der Sackgasse des Industriesystems.* Berlin: Rotbuch.

Varga, Eugen ([1962]). *Twentieth Century Capitalism.* Moscow: Foreign Languages Publishing House.

van Dieren, Wouter (1995). *Mit der Natur Rechnen.* Basel: Birkhäuser.

von Freyberg, Jutta, Georg Fülberth, Jürgen Harrer, Bärbel Hebel-Kunze, Heinz-Gerd Hofschen, Erich Ott, and Gerhard Stuby (1977). *Geschichte der deutschen Sozialdemokratie 1863–1975*. Cologne: Pahl Rugenstein.

von Nussbaum, Heinrich, ed. (1973). *Die Zukunft des Wachstums*. Düsseldorf: Bertelsmann Universitätsverlag.

von Weizsäcker, Ernst Ulrich, Amory B. Lovins, and L. Hunter Lovins (1995). *Faktor Vier*. Munich: Droemer Knaur.

——— (1997). *Factor Four: Doubling Wealth, Halving Resource Use*. London: Earthscan Publications.

von Werlhof, Claudia, Veronika Bennholdt-Thomsen, and Nicholas Faraclas, eds. (2003). *Subsistenz und Widerstand*. Vienna: Promedia Verlag.

Vranicki, Predrag (1961/1972). *Geschichte des Marxismus*, vol. 1. Frankfurt am Main: Suhrkamp Verlag.

Wagner, Wieland (2010). "Brüchige Basis." *Der Spiegel* 31 (August 2010).

Walker, Marcus (2006). "Training—an Antidote for Layoffs?" *Wall Street Journal* (22 March 2006).

Wark, Penny (2006). "Selling Themselves Short." *Financial Times* (9 June 2006).

Wehler, Hans-Ulrich (1976). *Bismarck und der Imperialismus*. Munich: Deutscher Taschenbuch Verlag.

Welzk, Stefan (1988). *Vom Börsencrash zur Wirtschaftskrise: Hintergründe, Gefahren, Auswege*. Cologne: Kiepenheuer and Witsch.

Wermter, Margit, ed. (1993). *Wirtschaft vor dem Abgrund? Wege aus der Rezession*. Zurich: Orell Füssli.

Western, David L. (2004). *Booms, Bubbles and Busts in US Stock Markets*. London: Routledge.

Wieczorek-Zeul, Heidemarie (2005). "Schutz gegen Spekulation—Hedge-Fonds müssen national und international kontrolliert werden." *Frankfurter Rundschau* (21 May 2005).

Wille, Joachim (1999). "Die Maschinisten des Wachstums." *Frankfurter Rundschau* (5 October 1999).

Willke, Gerhard (2002). *John Maynard Keynes*. Frankfurt, NY: Campus Fachbuch.

Wolf, Winfried (1987). "Schuld, Zins, Profit: Sieben Thesen zum Verhältnis zwischen Dritter, Erster und westdeutscher Welt," in Bortz et al. (1987).

——— (1988). "Casino-Kapitalismus oder die Dialektik von Boom, Crash und Krise," in Mandel and Wolf (1988).

——— (1997). *Casino Capital: Der Crash beginnt auf dem Golfplatz*. Cologne: ISP-Verlag.

Wong, Edward (2008). "Engines of Growth in China at a Standstill." *New York Times*, reprinted in *Süddeutsche Zeitung* 24 November 2008).

Wood, John Cunningham, ed. (1983/1993). *John Maynard Keynes: Critical Assessments*, vols. 1–4. London: Routledge.

——— (1994). *John Maynard Keynes: Critical Assessments*, vols. 5–8. London: Routledge.

Zakaria, Fareed (2006). "Rethinking Iraq: The Way Forward." *Newsweek* (6 November 2006).

Printed in the United States
by Baker & Taylor Publisher Services